FROM READING TO WRITING

A RHETORIC AND READER
SECOND EDITION

JUDITH OSTER

CASE WESTERN RESERVE UNIVERSITY

HH Heinle & Heinle Publishers
Boston, Massachusetts 02116, U.S.A.

Library of Congress Cataloging-in-Publication Data

Oster, Judith.
   From reading to writing.

   Includes bibliographical references and indexes.
   1. English language—Text-books for foreign speakers.
I. Title.
PE1128.O84   1987   808'.0427   86–21079

Library of Congress Catalog Card No. 86–21079

ISBN 0-8384-2916-5

9 8 7 6 5 4 3

MV

Printed in the United States of America

Acknowledgments

   Anne Frank. Excerpt from *Anne Frank: The Diary of a Young Girl* by Anne Frank. Copyright 1952 by Otto H. Frank. Reprinted by permission of Doubleday & Company, Inc. and Vallentine, Mitchell & Co. Ltd.
   S. I. Hayakawa. "The Value of Unoriginal Remarks" and "The Story of A-town and B-ville" from *Language in Thought and Action,* Fourth Edition, by S. I. Hayakawa, copyright © 1978 by Harcourt Brace Jovanovich, Inc. Reprinted by permission of the publisher.
   Richard Selzer. "Surgery as Love" and "You Are Wine" from *Mortal Lessons* by Richard Selzer. Copyright © 1974, 1975, 1976 by Richard Selzer. Reprinted by permission of Simon & Schuster, Inc.
   Enrique Hank Lopez. "Why Couldn't My Father Read," *The Cleveland Plain Dealer,* September 1, 1979. Reprinted by permission.
   Marsha Rabe. "Passages," *The New York Times,* July 26, 1979. Copyright © 1979 by The New York Times Company. Reprinted by permission.
   Robert Frost. "Storm Fear" from *The Poetry of Robert Frost* edited by Edward Connery Lathem. Copyright 1934, © 1969 by Holt, Rinehart and Winston. Copyright © 1962 by Robert Frost. Reprinted by permission of Henry Holt and Company, Inc., the Estate of Robert Frost, and Jonathan Cape Ltd.

(Acknowledgments continue on page 399)

To Joe—my husband

PREFACE

*"Much have I learned from my
masters, but more from my fellows,
and most of all from my students."*
*"The good student is the one . . .
who makes his teacher wiser."*

Ethics of the Fathers

I suppose most textbooks begin long before the first word is written, or before anything so ambitious as writing a text has been considered. There is a teacher and a class, and a need for something to put into the hands of those students to help that teacher teach what he wants to teach, the way he wants to teach it.* The task begins in searching and thinking, and ends in offering to others the results of that work, knowing full well that the searching and thinking will go on, that there will always be changes and additions to make, and that others would have done it all quite differently.

When teaching writing, one looks for ways to help students learn how to express themselves clearly, to organize their ideas logically, to make their writing vivid and interesting. The student must learn to *think,* to analyze, to reason, and to write compositions that reflect these academic habits. This is a tall order for teacher and student in any circumstances, but the challenge for them both is far greater when the student is not working in his native language, or when he has come from an educational system that may have provided excellent training in mathematics or taught him how to absorb a great deal of information, but may never have asked him to do any

---

* On the troublesome question of third person singular pronoun gender, I could never put it better than Mina Shaughnessey, whom I quote: "After having tried various ways of circumventing the use of the masculine pronouns in situations where women teachers and students might easily outnumber men, I have settled for the convention, but I regret that the language resists my meaning in this important respect. When the reader sees *he,* I can only hope *she* will also be there." This is my policy as well.

thinking and writing of this kind, even in his own language. He may not have been given much good writing to read in his own language either, nor has he necessarily been shown the value of genuine communication between readers and a writer.

My own search began when I first faced a class of university students whose native language was not English. Most of them were international students, a few were immigrants to the United States, and all of them were still having difficulty writing English correctly and even reading English correctly. Some were having trouble understanding why they had to be in the class at all—after all, they had demonstrated their English was adequate for admission to the university and they were not planning to be writers or English professors.

Their first piece of writing showed that they did indeed need more facility in English: more help with sentence structure, more vocabulary, more grammar. But it showed me more. These students needed to understand that by composition, by an essay, we mean something much broader and more important than correct words and sentences, more than a properly structured paragraph, even more than a perfectly correct page of writing. Good writing should have content and substance. It presumes that the writer has something to express; it presumes that the reader will be able to understand him. The academic world in particular expects writing that is intelligent, that is logical and well organized by Western standards.

My first task, it seemed, was to convince my students that what we mean by writing must also be a thinking process that requires intelligence and organization—not just an exercise in covering a page with correct squiggles, or choosing the right words, or applying the proper grammar rules. Certainly, these important tasks must be performed, but not as the final or only goal. A technically perfect composition on a perfectly simple theme—the kind of thinking and writing that a seven-year-old child could do, coming from an intelligent university student—would not impress us in the least!

Of course, one could argue that a more complex idea requires more complex sentence structure, a larger, more precise vocabulary. Yes, of course, it does. And more complex themes would produce papers with more errors, more traps in a language not yet fully mastered. That is a problem—at first. And, finally, many students have never been asked to write such essays even in their native languages!

Yes, but isn't it time, at last, that someone asks them to do it?

What this means, of course, is that students and instructor alike will be facing a greater challenge. Together they will work through the process of thinking and re-thinking, writing and rewriting. But the compositions, the conferences, and the discussions among classmates will be much more exciting. The student will feel he is working on something worthwhile, and consequently will be more willing to correct and rewrite his composition. If he can respect the worth of what he thinks and writes, he will want it to be understood by his reader, and he will not want his reader to have to wade through errors and puzzle over distorted sentences.

There is a limit, however, to how many ideas we can generate when left only to our own resources. We also want to introduce students to new ideas, and to good writing about those ideas. Good reading is an important step toward good writing, and it has been my experience that students feel this too.

The readings in this text are meant to serve several functions: to stimulate, to show by good example, and also to give pleasure. Not only compositions, but class discussion should grow out of these readings and the questions that follow them, many of which can be used for either oral discussion or writing assignment.

Much of this is common to any composition course and not peculiar to the needs of the international student; so is the stimulus of real ideas, of intellectual challenge, of reasoned argument. Too often, though, international students and their instructors are afraid to attempt such assignments until the language is mastered. Some never do attempt them. Such hesitation should not be necessary. The international student needs, indeed welcomes, this challenge; he enjoys discussing ideas. He responds well to writing that moves him to think or to feel. The intention of this text is to offer the international student what we offer his native-speaking counterpart. Our experience over the years has shown that this is indeed possible, that it does work. This book provides a review of basic sentence structure; words that fall outside the most frequently used 6,000 words* are explained as they arise. Thus, we help the student in his reading and writing, and help him enrich his vocabulary. It is *not* intended that he wait for perfection in language before beginning the kind of course that American students have. The international student may not be as well prepared in English, or in our Western ways of thinking and organizing, but he is certainly *ready* to do these things.

The readings have been selected with the international student in mind. While on a university level, they are not inordinately difficult nor do they presume a previous understanding of American culture. Topics covered in the readings are either those to which the student can relate his or her own experience or those that know no cultural, geographic, or political boundaries. Many reading and discussion suggestions are aimed at increasing awareness of what unites us as human beings rather than what divides us as nationals.

While the text is arranged in rhetorical modes, the tables of contents—rhetorical and thematic—are self-evident in suggesting various possible arrangements of materials and assignments. If the order of the text is followed, students can move from experiential modes following spatial or chronological organization toward modes that require more focus and disciplined organization and development. This sequence need not be followed, of course. It can be varied or abandoned altogether. Within each chapter and after each reading there are questions and assignments arising from both rhetorical and thematic considerations, thus allowing for either a rhetorical or thematic approach.

Since writing is never done exclusively in one rhetorical mode, readings are listed in the instructor's manual under different modes in a table of contents entitled Alternate Uses of Readings as Rhetorical Models.

To allow maximum flexibility, nothing really depends upon following the se-

---

* The basis for selecting which words fall into this category has been Henry Kučera and W. Nelson Francis, *Computational Analysis of Present Day American English* (Providence, R.I.: Brown University Press, 1967). Of course experience and common sense have entered into the selection process, especially with regard to idiomatic usage of words.

quence of the text. *Words which require glossing are glossed even if they have been glossed in a previous essay,* thus allowing the freedom of using the readings in any order. A word will not be glossed twice within a single reading, however.

The number of readings and types of lessons should allow each instructor much freedom of choice. There is ample material for two semesters, which allows even *more* choice should the course be needed for only one semester. Variety of length and difficulty can easily accommodate both a course at the developmental level and one paralleling the standard freshman course.

A review of sentence structure has been placed in an appendix. It has been our experience that students at this level still need to review, or at least refer to, basic English sentence structure, whether to understand the nature of sentence boundary problems, or to refine and improve ways of combining and varying sentences. This material has therefore been included in an appendix so that it can serve in any appropriate and convenient way, without intruding itself upon—or delaying—the process of composition or the composition course.

Finally, a word about the student sample compositions at the end of each chapter. My main motive in presenting them is to show the student whose native language is not English what others like him have done. These compositions are not professional essays or stories, but they are sometimes beautiful, interesting, moving, above all, *worthwhile*. They *all* had errors in them. This is important for students to know because it illustrates once again that a student not yet capable of writing correct English can nevertheless write a good, even beautiful paper in English. Errors were corrected so as to avoid distracting the reader or reinforcing incorrect English. However, unless actually incorrect, the words and sentence structures are exactly as the students wrote them. The compositions are there for the use of any class to discuss, to criticize, to improve, or simply to enjoy. Such an essay can put one student, the reader, in touch with another, the writer.

All of the student compositions have been used with the permission of the students who wrote them. I thank them for their generosity in letting me use their work. Above all, I thank my many students for being willing over the years to try the readings and assignments I was organizing and to comment on them. Their honesty, enthusiasm, and encouragement have been inspiration and stimulus to me. Indeed, they have taught me more than they realize: I have learned much from what they have said and written, even more from what they asked and seemed to need. Unwittingly, they gave me as much "homework" as I ever gave them, and I am grateful to them.

FURTHER ACKNOWLEDGMENTS

Ideally, besides a single teacher and his class, there are other teachers of other classes and communications among them. Thus, an embryo textbook can be a collection of materials and ideas for lessons that are tested by more than one instructor and class.

I am grateful to the Cleveland Foundation for affording me an opportunity by means of a grant to refine and expand the ESL composition program at Case Western

Reserve University. It made possible the addition of more sections and instructors, and the time to gather and test the material on which this text was based; it also made possible the opportunity to test, in classes and in carefully monitored before-and-after composition tests, the efficacy of our program to develop academic habits along with language skills. In addition, the precedent was set for continuing cooperation and exchange among those of us who taught the ESL sections. Thank you Mary Annable, Thomas Hemmeter, Mary Kirtz, Margaret Lally, Gary LaPointe, Zita McShane, Clare McCord, Anne Wyatt-Brown—excellent teachers all! In one way or another, your suggestions, your shared teaching experiences, your help and enthusiasm are part of this book.

Special thanks go to Professor William Siebenschuh for his constant encouragement to "turn it all into a book," and for his advice as I did so. Professor P. K. Saha remains my valued linguistics teacher. Always willing to share his expertise and act as consultant, he was especially helpful on Appendix A.

For invaluable aid on the use of the library for the "Research Paper" chapter, I wish to thank Yadwiga Kuncaitis and Arthur Biagianti, reference librarians of Frieberger Library and Sears Library, respectively, at CWRU. For efficient and expert preparation of the manuscript, I cannot say enough to thank Ann Carter, Joyce Martin, and Patricia Dussaux.

I wish to express my appreciation to Betty Azar; William Biddle, Harvard University; Barbara W. Buchanan, Utah State University; Robert Grindell, Kansas State University; James M. Hendrickson, Lansing Community College; Robert N. Kantor, Ohio State University; Kathleen List, University of Michigan; Pamela McCurdy, University of Texas at El Paso; Twila Yates Papay, Hofstra University; C. Ruth Sabol, The University of Georgia; Dennis E. Schneider, University of Kentucky; Pamela J. Sharpe; Maria Stiebel, Housatonic Community College; and June Weber, University of Portland, for reviewing my manuscript at various stages and making valuable suggestions, many of which I have gratefully incorporated. I also continue to appreciate the assistance of Beverly Kolz on the first edition of this book.

Working with Joseph Opiela, editor at Little, Brown, has been, for me, the ideal editor-writer relationship. Freedom, guidance, understanding, pressure, and encouragement came in exactly the right proportions, and at exactly the right times. I also wish to thank associate book editor Barbara Breese for being so helpful in seeing the book through its production.

Finally, to my family for all their understanding, their caring, and their help, I do not say thank you. They know how I feel.

TO THE STUDENT

If you are anything like the students I see at the beginning of each semester, you are in this class because it's required, and you probably wish you were someplace else. You've had English, English, and more English; furthermore, it's not your major. You've been through years of English classes in your native country, or you've spent months in an intensive language school, or both. Perhaps you graduated from an

American high school. Obviously, you've fulfilled the college entrance requirement in English, or you are very close to that point, so why are you here?

For one thing, most colleges and universities require English composition of *all* students, native speakers included. Still, you have a right to ask why. To put it most simply, you are working toward a degree that will label you as educated, and one of the signs of an educated person is the ability to read and write fluently in the language of his education. It may surprise you to learn that in a survey conducted among practicing engineers, communication skills ranked above all other academic skills they felt they needed on the job. Clarity and organization in oral or written presentations are particularly important, especially as the audience is usually the nontechnician who needs clear explanations in nontechnical language. This language is very often English, even where English is not the national language. Frequently, such communication takes place in general conversations at lunch tables, in corridors, and in offices, and requires general English communication skills.

The educated person understands what he reads even if the reading matter is difficult and not in his major field. He is able to read between the lines, to see inferences, to read critically, and he is able to communicate his ideas on any subject clearly, logically, and correctly. It is so much the better if he can do so without being dull, repetitious, and, in general, boring.

If English is not your native language, you face the additional problem of having a smaller vocabulary than your native-speaking classmates. You are probably still making errors in sentence structure and grammar, and using words and phrases that just don't say it the way we do in English. No doubt much of your time and energy have been spent learning these important language skills, and correcting sentences that were incorrect and awkward.

Perhaps so much time and energy had to be spent on these problems that you have not yet experienced what *can* be meant by composition. While correctness is important, what we mean by an essay is much more important than simply being correct. Writing is a form of communication. It should have something to say. It should be genuine. The reader must be able to understand the message, to follow its train of thought or its feeling. Academic communication in the United States requires organization whose logic, order, and directness may be different from the ways in which discussions are structured in other parts of the world.

What we are calling writing, then, must also be a thinking process, an organized, intelligent activity, not just a way of covering a page with correct lines and curves. Grammar and spelling are important, but they are no longer the final goal. If you are an intelligent university student, surely you have more complex, more deeply felt ideas to express. You must feel frustrated at times that having to use English limits your ability to express yourself, that as soon as you begin to speak or write in English rather than in your native language, you feel less mature in your vocabulary or sophistication of style. On the other hand, you may not ever have been required to develop complex ideas in compositions even in your native language. What you will be doing in this course may be a new kind of educational experience altogether, not just a new, more difficult experience in English.

True, as you are asked to write more meaningful and complex papers, you will be worried that the more complicated your thinking and writing, the more errors you will be making. After all, keeping things short and simple is safer; it reduces the possibility for error. But it also reduces the possibility for writing that is exciting and worthwhile. You will be expected to take the risks of error; perhaps you will need to consult your bilingual dictionary for the way to say that more sophisticated, abstract word in English, and may find that it is not precisely the right word in English. Yes, all this will add to the risk, the error, the effort, and the frustration of writing in English. But it is time, at last, to make that leap, for isn't it more exciting to write about real feelings, opinions, experiences? Isn't it more exciting to say something you really feel is *worth* saying, worth arguing about, worth conveying your feelings about? *And such a composition is also more exciting for the teacher to read.*

Now let us make sure you are making sense, organizing your ideas logically. Let us make sure you have control over your sentence structure, that you have chosen the words that really say what you want to say and not something you didn't mean. And, yes, we must clear up those distracting errors.

But now the job seems worth doing. The product will be something a university student can be proud of having written.

It is hard work, there's no doubt about that. All of us, instructors and students alike, need inspiration; we need ideas, we need to see what others have done when they want to communicate with us.

That's why we read.

Reading puts us in touch with other minds and feelings and experiences. We also experience the ways in which the writers have organized information, chosen words, structured arguments. We can see how well a good writer expresses himself; what makes that writing so effective, what we can learn from it. Reading gives us ideas we may not have imagined, information we may not have had. It may show us that our thoughts and feelings are not so "far out." It may stimulate us to think, to feel, to read, or even to argue against the writer's views. We may want to discuss these ideas or, more important, we may be stimulated to formulate our own ideas on that subject or a related one. After each reading in this text there are questions for discussion and suggested topics for compositions. I hope that such reading and thinking will stimulate discussion on those topics you find interesting or relevant to your own experiences. Because people usually write better about what they have actually felt or experienced, many of the suggested topics for composition invite you to use your own experiences in your compositions.

You will see that as you write more and more, your confidence will increase. In fact, students have been surprised to find that, in this course, they were developing greater self-confidence, and confidence not only in their English skills, but in expressing their opinions. We do not expect perfection as you begin, but in writing and rewriting you will be moving ahead on several fronts: you will develop your reasoning and organizational skills, you will increase your ability and willingness to express yourself, and you will make those revisions and corrections, rewrite those awkward, unclear sections, and consequently improve your mechanics and structure as well.

Reading the student compositions at the end of each chapter should give you some encouragement. These were all written by students like you, who are not native speakers of English. They *all* had errors in them (which have been corrected), but otherwise they are as the students wrote them. I hope you will see, as I did, that even the inexperienced writer, the ESL student who is still making errors, is nevertheless capable of writing a good, sometimes even beautiful, moving, and above all *worthwhile* paper in English. You may find ways you could improve on these essays, and that's fine. I hope you will also feel as you read them that a student much like you is communicating with you, the reader of his essay, just as you are learning to communicate with others in your English writing.

Now, on to reading, thinking, and writing: I hope you too will come to feel the way this student did:

> I think writing—no matter what—is good because it . . . makes you think, which is the most important thing. It's very easy to think but it's very hard to write it down . . . try to push students to write as much as they can because when one starts to write, one thinks you have no idea, but when it goes, it comes faster, and after a little while it is *beautiful;* you see how well you can write and how much you can get out of your mind. . . .

Judith Oster

CONTENTS

THEMATIC CONTENTS

Education

Communication

Between Two Worlds

Emotional Needs

"I live with bread like you, feel want, taste grief, need friends ..."*

Matters of Life and Death

* William Shakespeare, *Richard II,* Act III, scene ii.

1

THE WRITING PROCESS

We all want and need to express ourselves. We have feelings that need to be shared or released, ideas we wish to communicate, and knowledge we want to share or prove. We may want to argue a point of view or touch another person with words. We may enjoy writing our feelings and ideas on paper—to send in a letter to a friend or to have for ourselves some tangible proof that an idea or a beautiful expression really existed and was our own.

But then there is that blank piece of paper, often terrifying to professional writers as well as to students who have never before had to write a composition.* What shall I say? How can I fill this emptiness—meaningfully? Even beautifully? Correctly? What do I have to say that is worth putting down? How will readers react to me—will they laugh at me, will they want to correct me? Even worse, will they misunderstand me? We worry about these things when we write letters to friends, but we worry even more when the reader is a stranger—perhaps an English teacher with the power to redden the paper with corrections and comments or, still worse, with the power to fail us in a course.

Another less obvious fear is that of expressing oneself *at all* in writing, as if the written word has the power to betray us or has a kind of permanence that we fear. The spoken word usually is not as inhibiting as the written word, for it evaporates whereas the written word remains. But that, of course, is why we have wastebaskets and erasers. In a way, because we *can* erase or throw away what we have written, writing frees us to say what we like—to try out words, thoughts, and ideas as speech does not—for once someone has heard what we have said it can never be erased. When we write in private, we need never be afraid of feeling foolish or regretting our words. Before anyone else sees what we have written, we can think about it further, add, delete, or explain more clearly. We can even decide no one will ever see those words, or that we will show them only to someone we have learned to trust. If we learn to

---

* Students would be amused and perhaps comforted to see the number of crossed-out false starts I made before writing this page.

think of our writing as changeable and tentative rather than as engraved permanently in stone, and if we see writing as an evolving, sometimes messy process rather than as a one-time commitment by which we will be judged, then we can feel more at ease in experimenting and exploring with our pens.

That is, of course, more easily said than done. It was hard for me, I must admit, to begin writing what you are reading now. All of us can feel reassured when we read what others have written about writing. In literature, in letters, or in compositions by students, we read that others also have feelings, fears, and inhibitions like ours. We learn that the written word is not always perfect, professional, and cold. We learn, too, that even professional writers have had to work through their inhibitions, their poorly expressed phrases, and their unclear ideas.

Why write? We do so for the reasons stated in the first paragraph and for another important reason. We write to clarify our own ideas, not only for others but also for ourselves. Francis Bacon, the sixteenth-century British scientist, said, "Writing maketh an exact man." The very problems that you have in putting something down on paper will generate the thinking, attention, and expression that will turn a vague thought into something clear. The writer C. Day Lewis has said:

> I do not sit down at my desk to put into words something that is already clear in my mind. If it were clear in my mind, I should have no incentive or need to write about it, for I am an explorer. . . . We do not write in order to be understood, we write in order to understand.

Writing, then, can be *exploration,* not just a finished product; it can be creation. We have the power to surprise ourselves by the time we reach the end of a page—especially when we are writing creatively, expressing a feeling, or thoughtfully exploring a question. Yet there is writing and writing and writing. There is the finished product, and there is the often messy start—plus a lot that can come in between.

Perhaps there will be times when you know what you want to say or are sufficiently inspired by a topic to write in an easy flow. This happy state of affairs will most likely occur if you are expressing your own feelings and experiences, especially if the paper is fairly short and does not require you to organize data or structure an argument. *But don't count on it.* More usual is the need to go through a process that includes thinking, playing with those thoughts, deciding which you want to develop, planning how to arrange them, and choosing the best ways to express them. One is tempted to see these elements of writing as steps or stages in the writing process, occurring in a neat sequence: generating ideas, arranging them, writing them, and, finally, checking the paper to correct errors. But it is seldom this neat and clearly divided, for writing is a complex process, especially when we are *thinking* as well as writing and when we are expressing opinions or feelings. Sometimes we have trouble thinking of anything at all. At other times our thoughts and feelings come in undisciplined bunches—emotions, memories from several times and places at once, ideas that may contradict one another all mixed together in a confusing jumble. How do we sort it all out? How do we shape what we have to say? How do we take what feels right when mixed in this imaginary mass and express it so that one word follows another and sentences follow each other in well-ordered, sequential lines of writing?

How do we make what we know, feel, and understand clear to another person, the reader?

Just as these elements in our thinking are not easily divided into neat categories and lines, neither are the steps in writing always neatly divisible. The very act of writing can help us generate ideas, but then these new ideas will force us to change what we have already written. Sometimes we need to write to discover what we are trying to say, but then we need to read what we are writing to see if we are indeed saying it clearly. This inevitably leads to some rewriting—and actually helps us to keep writing. We need to choose what we will focus on and then organize our material accordingly, but often, as we write, we find that our plans must be changed to suit what we are actually saying. Sometimes, what we thought would work just isn't working, and we have to try another way. Other times, a new and better idea seems to fly from our pens, and that one is more worth following.

When we talk about steps in the writing process, it is important to understand that while the writing may roughly follow these steps, there will always be a crossing from one step to another and back—there is no set order. Above all, no one method works for every writer; no one method, even for the same writer, will work for every writing task. With that in mind, let us look at useful ways of moving through the writing process.

HOW SHALL I BEGIN?

Whether you are writing voluntarily or to fulfill an assignment, whether you have a topic you must write about or total freedom to choose your subject, you begin by thinking. Maybe you stare at the ceiling, chew your nails, pace the floor, or go to the refrigerator; but somewhere in the confusion, vague ideas and phrases pass through your head—even if they are expressions of anger at the person who is putting you through it.

Begin by writing your thoughts, or at least by talking to yourself and then putting down ideas. At this stage you are not yet writing a composition. You are recording thoughts, some of which will lead to other, more usable ideas and words, some of which will connect with one another. At the end of this stage you may have a composition, but you are more likely to have a "laundry list" of ideas, words, and images. This is your raw material. (Figure 1 shows a page of my own thinking-with-a-pen as I was planning this chapter.)

Generating and Gathering Ideas

This is often the most difficult stage of all—the stage *before* you are ready to write, before you even know what you will choose to write about. The following suggestions may help you.

Writing Freely.   Perhaps ideas are just not coming to you, or perhaps they seem to come to a dead end. Try writing—just writing—anything at all. Do this for ten minutes.

Don't stop. Don't think too much. Don't worry about correctness. Let your thoughts come onto the paper in a random, undisciplined manner. Don't judge them or yourself. You may find this very difficult at first. You may never have done this kind of writing before. Remember that this is not the composition itself, just a way of generating raw material. Allow yourself to be surprised by some idea or use of language you didn't expect of yourself. It's worth trying. Now look at what you've written. Is there anything of value? Is there anything worth developing? You could choose one of those ideas and write randomly about that one, you could try the exercise again, or you could take an idea and begin to focus your attention on it, making a list of whatever is related to it.

Listing. If you already have a topic, or a more specific assignment, write down whatever it suggests to you, letting what you write generate still more on your list. You may want to ask yourself what you associate with this topic: Feelings? Experiences? Anything you've read? Any people, places, or mental pictures? Let images come to your mind, and capture the picture or situation in a few words.

In any case, *start as soon as possible to put words on paper.* Then you will not have to worry about remembering them, and your mind will be free to play with these

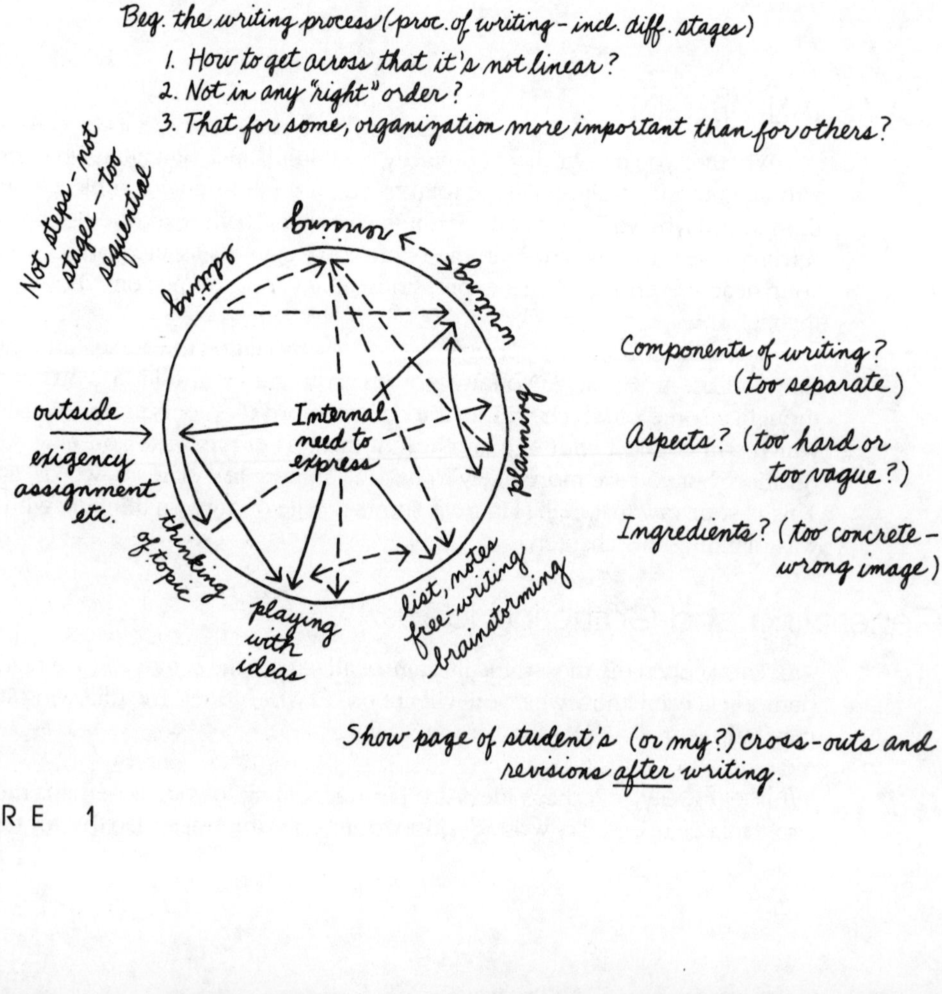

Beg. the writing process (proc. of writing – incl. diff. stages)
1. How to get across that it's not linear?
2. Not in any "right" order?
3. That for some, organization more important than for others?

Not steps – not stages – too sequential

outside exigency assignment etc.

Internal need to express

thinking of topic

playing with ideas

list, notes free-writing brainstorming

planning

Components of writing?
(too separate)

Aspects? (too hard or too vague?)

Ingredients? (too concrete – wrong image)

Show page of student's (or my?) cross-outs and revisions after writing.

FIGURE 1

words and ideas. Besides, the very act of writing will generate more writing, out of which ideas and plans will come.

Purpose and Planning

Now assume that you have such a list, or collection of sentences or paragraphs on a topic you have chosen. *What do you want to say? And to whom?* Is the anticipated reader, or audience, on your side or against you? Is he or she your equal or someone you must address with respect? Does that person know something about your subject, or will you have to provide explanation and background material? Do the topic and the audience call for a tone of conversational informality or a more objective formality? Deciding who your audience is, and determining what it is you want to say and why, may take the greatest thought. Once you can answer these questions, however, your writing will have a purpose, and that purpose will help you shape your material and select the essential details. It will help you decide how to develop your ideas. This is the **planning** stage. Because planning can be a difficult and complex process, Chapter 6 is entirely devoted to organization. As you go through this course, you will continually learn and practice strategies for planning and developing your compositions.

Writing the Composition

You may have written pieces of your composition as you were generating ideas, or you may have waited until you had a plan before writing sentences and paragraphs. Either way, you are ready to begin writing your first draft. If you are extremely fortunate it will come out just right, but because that usually is not the case, do not treat the draft as if it must be perfect the first time. Remember that at this stage the composition is tentative; it need not be seen until you are ready to show it. Therefore, don't worry about errors or small grammatical points or spelling. Don't stop to look up rules or even words you need. Leave a blank space or mark a spot to remind you that you are not satisfied, and *keep going* so that you don't lose a thought before you've put it down. Write the word in your native language if that will allow you to get on with your ideas. You can always fill in the English later. Remember that what you are saying, how you are developing it, and what you are telling or showing the reader is far more important than accuracy at this stage.

Keep in mind that everything cannot go quickly and smoothly in this draft. Unlike the stage of just generating ideas, now you are expressing yourself on a topic you have chosen, and you want to do justice to your thoughts. It is important to see the difference between difficulties caused by mechanical, surface problems in the language (which you can resolve later) and the problems of putting your ideas into language—any language, even your own. This struggle to make or clarify meaning is worthwhile. Winning the battle means getting the concepts clear in your mind. If you can solve these problems in the first draft, do so; if not, go back to them later, when you see the concept more clearly. Then you probably will find that this will not be so much the finding of words for your idea, but the shaping of the idea by means of words. *Complex thoughts do not depend on language simply for their expression, but for their existence.* You may know what you want to express and strongly believe in an idea, but no matter how you put it the words or sentences may seem wrong, incomplete, or misleading. After you rework them repeatedly, they suddenly will seem to "click" into place and say what you want them to say.

READING AND REVISING

Whether you have turned out a composition in one inspired flash or had to go through numerous stages of development, *you must at some point become the reader of your composition,* preferably some hours after you have written it. When you do so, you must listen to the voice of the composition as if you were a stranger to it. Is it believable? Is the point, the feeling, or the experience clear? Does it proceed logically from one part to the next? Can better words be used? It is the rare, exceptional paper that does not require at least some changing and correcting. At times your instructor may ask you to rewrite your entire paper. At other times you may only have to make minor corrections. At still other times, no doubt, *you* may feel dissatisfied with something you wrote and change or rewrite it.

To *revise* means to make changes, but the original Latin meant to *see again, to look back on.* When you reread your composition, you are looking at it once more, perhaps seeing it in a different way, and therefore making improvements or corrections. When your instructor asks you to *revise* your paper, he or she really asks you to look at it again, or in a new way, and *then* make the recommended changes.

Before it ever reaches anyone else's eyes, however, it is a good idea for you to become that "new eye." Learn to read your paper, sentence, or paragraph as if you were someone else. Then ask yourself: Have I really said (or shown) something? Do the ideas follow logically? Have I made myself clear? Have I chosen the most appropriate words? (Figure 2 shows how I revised a page of this chapter even after I had typed it; the finished version is on pages 1–2 of this book.)

Notice that *error* has not yet been *mentioned.* Revising is much more than correcting. There is a difference between dealing with the preceding questions and proofreading, which also is important and will have to be done. Proofreading is what you do when you ask yourself: Can I find any errors in sentence structure or mechanics? You may not be able to find all the errors because you may not be as critical a reader as your instructor is, but you certainly will find some problems; by making corrections, you will improve your paper and your writing. The following composition (Figure 3), which was written by a student, needs minor reorganization and shows some mechanical problems. You may want to try to improve it, following the handwritten suggestions. *Not all errors have been marked.* Can you find and correct any?

There are basically three kinds of revision: major restructuring and reorganization; words and sentence structure that need correction and improvement; and mechanical errors in grammar and spelling that need correction. Theoretically, the first category of major restructuring should not be necessary if you have worked according

We can decide

out?

[what we want to keep to ourselves--what we do not want to make known or we can show our writing only to one whom we have learned to trust.] In a way, because we can erase or throw away what we have written, writing frees us to say what we like--to try out words, thoughts, and ideas as speech does not--for once someone has heard what we have said it can never be erased. When we write in private, we need never be afraid of feeling foolish or regretting our words. Before anyone else sees what we have written, we can think about it further, add, delete, or explain more clearly. We can even decide no one will ever see those words. If we ~~can only~~ learn to *think of* ~~see~~ our writing as changeable and tentative rather than as engraved perma- nently in stone, if we *and* see writing as an evolving, some- ~~can~~ times messy process rather than as a one-time commitment ~~permanent~~ *by which we will be* *then* ~~we feel bound to and~~ judged ~~by~~, we can feel more at ease *in* ~~to~~ experiment*ing* and explor*ing* with our pens.

or that we will show them only to someone we have learned to trust.

(Of course,) That is, more easily said than done. It was *leave in place* hard for me, I must admit, to begin writing what you are reading now. *All of us* ~~We~~ can ~~all~~ feel reassured when we read what others have written about writing. In literature, in let- ters, or in compositions by ~~fellow~~ students, we ~~find~~ *read* that others *also* ~~too~~ have ~~these~~ feelings, fears, and inhibitions *like ours.* We learn that the written word is not always perfect, professional, and cold. We learn, too, that even professional writers have had to work through their inhi- bitions, their poorly expressed phrases, and their unclear ideas. ← *(fn. Eliot here? — "a raid on the inarticulate... the general mess of imprecision of feeling...")*

FIGURE 2

I like your title!

Going Home: After the Fall

one sentence

Today I am going home like a soldier returning from the battlefield. And now is the moment of reflection. As a soldier I fought many battles; I lost a few, but more important was to win the final war. However, this is *How does this fit in?* (never ends) a very peculiar kind of war, *c/s* there are no enemies but myself. And although I was fighting against me, I was not alone.

How does this tie in with your paper? Seems unnecessary.

The first day I came here many others were leaving. And even now they still leaving. I'm always moving forward and never st*sp*epping back. I got all the *redundant* weapons I must need (I got them from the bookstore). So, the armies were ready to fight.

Try to find ways to make analogies without all these ( ). How about "poster-hung bunkers"?

The night after the invasion (1st day of classes) we were all in our bunkers (dorms) waiting for the dawn to begin our attack. In the meantime the tensions were growing, and the intrige was increasing. We must be ready *Good!!* for everything: a surprise quiz, a demolishing test, or a destructive paper to be written. I was ready with my notebooks, pencils and textbooks.

Time is a bit confusing here: Is the invasion the first day of classes, or is it the arrival, with the *attack* *corresponding to first day of classes?*

Word choice fits your war metaphor well.

In the morning we went to the field. They were there, Prof. Oster with her troops, so, *also?* Prof. Ocasio, Prof. Roth and Prof. Satiadi, ready and alert. They were there not as our enemies, but as our allies (believe it or not). They were there to help us to won the first battle, and although it may seem ridiculous, we were about to begin. The rest is history. Make that war history.

After many months of continous fighting we were about

FIGURE 3

to cease fire. But before ceasing the fire, the most

important battle of the year must be completed: The Final

War. No one could be sure how he /or she/ will do in the

"Final," (code name for Final Week) but no matter how we

will do, we will be going home.

switch to keep in chronological order

During these months I have seen many soldiers fall

/myself among them/. Nevertheless ~~they~~ *we* all ~~(me too!)~~

stood up and fought againg annd again, battle after

battle. Just keeping the faith.

Do you need this?

Is cause the logical connection here?
How about: After all, what is...

Now I look ahead to the F.W. (Final Week) Nothing can

stop me now. Hopefully I will get thru, all of us

will. Because what is life but a war game? A continous

fighting for survival and stabilization. ~~So continuity is~~

~~what we all found. Indeed,~~ A continuous voyage to the

confusing – adds nothing – cut this out

fragments

unknown, fighting (winning and loosing) [and love. Let

your own feelings guide you always.]

Love is not really your subject – seems stuck in, and is out of place.

After the finals, I will be gong home. And there I

will be received as a war hero. My mom and dad will be

there. My systers will be there too. There will be a big

parade in my house. And I will be treated as a General,

even though I'm just a corporal.

very well put!

After my vacation/ and like a good soldier . . *?* . .

I will return again. To fight for freedom. A freedom

that only comes with knowledge. It's like having a key to

thousands of doors that could lead to many places() — *review rules for ;*

different places indeed. So, if after four years I

finished the first big battle, then and only then I could

say V*e*ni, vidi, v*i*nci.*

fragments

good!

consistency – battle or war?

* Julius Caesar's words: "I came, I saw, I conquered."

*This is **very good!** I like your school/war analogy, especially as you have expressed it. This is really worth revising: Make your analogies consistent. Reorder some of your material to improve organization, cutting out the unrelated points that detract from the unity of the essay — and correct errors.*

F I G U R E   3   (Continued)

to a well-organized plan. In rereading the paper, however, you may find that the parts are not in the best order or that you have discussed the same subject in two places, and therefore you need to put the like subjects together. You may find that you are repeating yourself and cross out the repetition. Such changes usually are not too difficult to make.

If, however, you are someone who prefers to write entire compositions or at least paragraphs as you are thinking (thus postponing organization until after you have written), your revision process will probably be *more* time consuming. By rereading and rethinking your words, you are really doing much of your planning and organizing at this revising stage. Be prepared to rewrite, but have scissors and tape handy to minimize rewriting. Try cutting up the parts and restructuring the order of paragraphs and sentences by taping them down in a new order. Even if you organize a paper in advance, you may later decide to change the order of some ideas. Even the best writers have new ideas to add that came to mind after the first writing. Mark the places for additional thoughts and write the new ideas to be inserted at each spot. Then reread the composition. How does it sound? Does it move smoothly and logically? Is there more to change? More to add or take out? Keep reworking your paper until *you* are satisfied.

When you are satisfied with the overall structure of your paper, reread it carefully, analyzing your clarity and sentence structure. Are there any fragments or run-on sentences? Could you combine more sentences through appropriate subordination? Should some of the longer sentences be simplified? Have you used the correct words to express your ideas? Have you used the *best* words, the most precise or appropriate words in each case? Have you avoided general, overused words?

Finally, proofread your paper for mechanical errors in spelling, punctuation, subject/verb agreement, appropriate tense, correct verb forms, and *rewrite* your paper as revised. Reread your writing; decide if further improvements and corrections are needed and make them. (You may even have to repeat this process.) When you are satisfied that your paper is the best you can make it, then you are ready to show it to someone else.

The following chapters offer a variety of writing experiences—from the journal, which gives you complete writing freedom, to the term paper, which requires the most structure. Even in the more structured modes of writing, you will have many opportunities to use your own opinions and experiences within the content of your compositions. Most people write best about what is closest to them. Not only are their ideas more credible and their voices more genuine, but also their style is better. Words somehow emerge more smoothly and correctly.

The academic world requires clarity and organization. Universities in the United States will want you to be able to use Western modes of making a point and getting to the point that may differ from the ways you have learned to organize your writing. This type of writing may require you to use a style with which you are unaccustomed, or one that differs from styles more appropriate to expressive writing. Expository writing, that which serves to clarify or explain in detail, requires you to make points clearly and convincingly. It also requires objective evidence and proof. Furthermore, the reader does not want to be distracted by errors or confused by poorly structured sentences or nonsentences. But these disciplines can be learned even as you are finding your voice, expressing what is closest to you, taking pleasure in expressing yourself, and taking pride in the finished product. What you write will not necessarily be perfect, but it can be beautiful, intelligent, and moving. As you keep rewriting and correcting, you will keep improving. *Learning to write takes a lot of time:* time to do the best job you can when writing a single composition, time over the semester or several semesters, and, of course, time over many compositions.

It may help or inspire you to read not only essays written by professional, literary writers, but also the students' essays in this book. Notice the different voices you hear, and remember that *all* these compositions had many errors in them at first. You, too, have much to express, and you can learn to put yourself on paper. You, too, can learn to organize, clarify, and correct. Work hard at it, but *have fun* while you do so.

2

JOURNAL KEEPING

A journal is a completely informal record of yourself. What begins as a notebook of blank pages becomes your voice in writing, speaking about whatever you wish, to any audience you wish to imagine: perhaps yourself, perhaps the friend you wish you had. The word is derived from the French *jour,* which means day. It has, therefore, assumed the related meaning of newspaper (the day's events) or periodical. However, we are not using the word in this journalistic sense. Some people relate the word *journal* to *diary* (from the Latin word *diarum* meaning day); but because a diary is also thought of as a daily record of appointments and events and sometimes as romantic writing, let us be careful not to be limited by these associations either.

You will not necessarily be expected to write in your journal every day. (Your instructor will tell you how often you must write in it.) Nor will events, appointments, where you went, or what you did necessarily be the subjects. Observations, thoughts, and feelings are excellent subjects for journal entries. If you wish to write about what you did today at ten o'clock, or where you went for lunch yesterday, do so by all means. But do not limit yourself to a mere reporting of events. Do not even feel an obligation to mention it if you do not want to.

Students always ask, "What shall we write about?" The freedom to write about anything at all seems to frighten them into silence at first. Perhaps discussing the *purposes* of a journal will help to "unfreeze" you, as well as give you some direction. It may be some comfort to know that students usually enjoy keeping journals once they get started. For some, it becomes a habit they continue far beyond the course.

Freedom and Privacy

Your instructor will explain his or her policy on this delicate issue. To make students feel completely free about writing in their journals, some instructors do not read students' journals unless the students wish them to. In other courses, the journal is part of what is graded or at least read and corrected. Your instructor will, of course, tell you his or her way of using journals. You can then decide how much of yourself and your feelings you are willing to put into it. You may develop enough trust in your instructor that you will want to share your private thoughts with him or her. You may begin to take pride in what you are writing and want to show it to someone who can help you improve, someone who can appreciate your sensitivity or creativity. The following student samples are proof that students can write beautifully and sensitively and that they are sometimes willing to share their innermost feelings.

WHAT WILL KEEPING A JOURNAL DO FOR YOU?

You will become more observant of everything around you. You will become more aware of people, situations, nature, and society. For example, one student, who knew he had to produce a journal entry for class that day, wrote in desperation while he waited in one of those endless bookstore lines that characterize the first week of school. His subject was what he saw at the time: people waiting in line at the bookstore. It was a wonderful essay with a lot of psychological insight about how different types of people react to standing in line for an hour. Had this student not needed a quick journal page, this entry would never have been written, more important, these observations would never have been made.

You will be writing without tension. Let's face it, writing makes everybody tense. A journal is an opportunity for you to "let your hair down," that is, to be yourself, comfortably. To experience this *and* to write at the same time is very important, especially for the person who is *really* frightened by a blank piece of paper. Journal writing is encouraging because it lets you loosen up and enjoy the writing experience.

You will write well because you will be expressing what is close to you and important to you. You may find that journal writing goes more smoothly than does writing on an assigned topic. Sometimes, students who write rather awkwardly are surprised when it is pointed out to them that they do not have this problem with their journal writing. They learn that to express something simply, as one really feels it, leads to far better writing.

You will find that a byproduct of this "relaxation" while writing is a greater expression of your creativity and imagination. Students who have never written imaginatively or just for fun are often surprised to find that they *can* be creative, that they *can* write and think with feeling and imagination.

You will increase your fluency in English if it is not your native language. To you, even more than to native speakers, writing is a strain. There is so much to watch for and think about because the language is not yet completely natural to you. As you write to improve your skills, you worry about errors and about how your writing will be judged. It is especially important for you, then, to have the opportunity to write freely as it comes to your mind—in English. You need an opportunity to let English flow, an opportunity to express yourself without worry and restraint. The journal provides this opportunity.

You will be creating an "idea bank." This idea bank is not only a record of your ideas at a given time; it is also a source of ideas for future compositions. The journal gives you the opportunity to jot down ideas you may wish to develop later. You may also want to record a striking line, paragraph, or verse you have read and jot down your own comments about these quotations.

You will realize that what you think, feel, and experience has value. Just writing something down and then reading it will give you this feeling. Perhaps this will encourage you to think, and to put those thoughts into words. Good! Write reactions to what you read as well. Your opinions have value, too.

You will feel better if you can get feelings "off your chest"; your own journal is sometimes a good place to do that. Writing about your feelings helps you express them and makes them clearer in your own mind. This process can help you better cope and come to terms with your feelings. If you are feeling lonely, or if you have no one with whom you can share your thoughts and feelings, journal writing can help.

In a world-famous journal, Anne Frank, a thirteen-year-old Dutch girl, expressed her feelings about writing in a diary. She began her diary before she, her family, and another family—all of whom were Jewish—went into hiding from the Nazis during World War II, when Jews were being killed systematically. Her diary became a "friend," which she continued to keep until the Nazis found her family and took them to a concentration camp. Only her father survived. He returned to his home and found Anne's diary, which has since been translated into more than twenty languages. It has become a classic not only for its story of living in hiding during such terrifying times but also for its insight into adolescence. Anne discusses problems of growing up, her impatience with her parents, her frustrations about being misunderstood, her search for identity, and her attempts at understanding her increasing physical and mental maturity.

ANNE FRANK

FROM *The Diary of a Young Girl*

Saturday, 20 June 1942

1   I haven't written for a few days, because I wanted first of all to think about my diary. It's an odd idea for someone like me to keep a diary; not only because I have never done so before, but because it seems to me that neither I—nor for that matter anyone else—will be interested in the unbosomings of a thirteen-year-old schoolgirl. Still, what does that matter? I want to write, but more than that, I want to bring out all kinds of things that lie buried deep in my heart.

2   There is a saying that "paper is more patient than man"; it came back to me on one of my slightly melancholy days, while I sat chin in hand, feeling too bored and limp even to make up my mind whether to go out or stay at home. Yes, there is no doubt that paper is patient and as I don't intend to show this cardboard-covered notebook, bearing the proud name of "diary," to anyone, unless I find a real friend, boy or girl, probably nobody cares. And now I come to the root of the matter, the reason for my starting a diary; it is that I have no such real friend.

3   Let me put it more clearly, since no one will believe that a girl of thirteen feels herself quite alone in the world, nor is it so. I have darling parents and a sister of sixteen. I know about thirty people whom one might call friends— I have strings of boy friends, anxious to catch a glimpse of me and who, failing that, peep at me through mirrors in class. I have relations, aunts and uncles, who are darlings too, a good home, no—I don't seem to lack anything. But it's the same with all my friends, just fun and joking, nothing more. I can never bring myself to talk of anything outside the common round. Perhaps I lack confidence, but anyway, there it is, a stubborn fact and I don't seem to be able to do anything about it.

4   Hence, this diary. In order to enhance in my mind's eye the picture of the friend for whom I have waited so long, I don't want to set down a series of bald facts in a diary like more people do, but I want this diary itself to be my friend. . . .

5   "For in its innermost depths youth is lonelier than old age." I read this saying in some book and I've always remembered it, and found it to be true. Is it true then that grownups have a more difficult time here than we do? No. I know it isn't. Older people have formed their opinions about everything, and don't waver before they act. It's twice as hard for us young ones to hold our ground, and maintain our opinions, in a time when all ideals are being shattered and destroyed, when people are showing their worst side, and do not know whether to believe in truth and right and God.

6   Anyone who claims that the older ones have a more difficult time here certainly doesn't realize to what extent our problems weigh down on us, problems for which we are probably much too young, but which thrust themselves upon us continually. . . . That's the difficulty in these times: ideals, dreams, and cherished hopes rise within us, only to meet the horrible truth and be shattered.

7   It's really a wonder that I haven't dropped all my ideals, because they seem so absurd and impossible to carry out. Yet I keep them, because in spite of everything I still believe that people are really good at heart. I simply can't build up my hopes on a foundation consisting of confusion, misery, and death. I see the world gradually being turned into a wilderness, I hear the ever approaching thunder, which will destroy us too, I can feel the sufferings of millions and yet, if I look up into the heavens, I think that it will all come right, that this cruelty too will end, and that peace and tranquillity will return again.

8   In the meantime, I must uphold my ideals, for perhaps the time will come when I shall be able to cárry them out. . . .

9   I know that I can write . . . but—whether I have talent remains to be seen. . . .

10   I want to go on living even after my death! And therefore I am grateful to God for giving me this gift, this possibility of developing myself and of "writing," of expressing all that is in me.

11   I can shake off everything if I write; my sorrows disappear, my courage is reborn.

STUDENT JOURNALS

Only a small percentage of students will become famous writers, but many will write things that are worth reading and remembering. The page that was written because a page *had* to be written can still be interesting; it may contain a thought or feeling that otherwise may never have been written down. What one student writes of his or her feelings may be of value to another student whom the writer will never meet, if only to reassure that student that he is not alone in the way he feels. The following excerpts from student journals may strike familiar chords in your own feelings, but even more important, they may show you the kinds of things one may write about, the sensitivity students like you are able to express. Because the writers of these journal entries openly discuss their thoughts and feelings, the reader develops a close relationship with them. Reading these journal entries will, it is hoped, spark your interest and ability in writing about anything at all, outside or within you. **Buy a notebook today and start keeping your own journal!**

All of these journal entries were written by foreign students in private journals. The students had been told they would not be required to show them to anyone, not even the instructor. In all cases, the students voluntarily showed me what they had written and gave their permission to use it in this book.*

S T U D E N T   C O M P O S I T I O N S

This is really what I need and what I was seeking for a long time. Finally I found it; I found the cure for my worries and my problems. I found the treasure, I mean the Journal. For me, this discovery comes just at the right time, when I need someone who can share my thoughts and feelings, someone I can complain to and tell him my problems sincerely, someone whose chest I can lay my head on and bring out everything that lies buried deep in my heart, someone who can hold my secret. For me it is a tremendous solution for my problems, especially at this time, when I am feeling alone

* In these journal entries, as in all student writings in this book, mechanical errors have been corrected; otherwise, the writing is exactly as the student wrote it.

away from my country, from my mother and father whom I was accustomed to tell my problems and whom I trust most. Even my mother or my father sometimes would not understand me and sometimes I cannot reveal many problems to them, maybe because I don't feel encouraged to, or because I'm ashamed to speak about them. Maybe I would know in advance they won't be able to help me cope with the matter. Now it appears that as soon as I arrived to the States, I found myself having additional problems and my troubles have increased. First I have this big feeling, homesickness. I have been here since August in the States and I'm still longing for my parents, my friends, my relatives, my neighbors; also the places I used to go where I spent a wonderful time with my fiancée, whom I miss most.

The only one I can rely on is the Journal. There is not another such guest that may either make a short sojourn or stay with you as your own shadow, or even as a very limb of your body. It is silent so long as you need silence, eloquent whenever you want discourse. It never interrupts you if you are busy, but if you feel lonely it is a good companion. He is a friend who never deceives you or flatters you and a comrade who does not grow weary of you.*

Before I read the introduction in the book *From Reading to Writing,* writing was just like a ghost that kept haunting me day and night every time I got a writing assignment. So when I read the chapter on writing (Chapter 1) and some of Chapter 2 (on Journals), I felt very comfortable and had some thoughts that actually writing was easy and enjoyable. But when I took my chair, put it in front of the desk, and faced the empty paper, everything in my head disappeared, just like that, and I was just like a living statue staring at an empty paper lying on the desk waiting to be written on. So it is very obvious that writing is still a difficult subject to me and is like a destiny that I cannot avoid at all. I came to the conclusion that . . . the book is right; I should write as much as possible so that I can improve my writing.

Up until now I cannot understand why it is very difficult to write something although your mind is full of thoughts that are ready to explode any time. I feel that I just do not have the power to move my hands and choose the ideal words to write down. . . . The problem became more obvious as I got here and found out that there are English classes where writing is the main subject. My old enemy showed up again, but now is stronger because I have to write in English, which I am not used to yet.

Now, I am in school thinking about something and nothing, because I am sad about my situation here. I am far away from home and I miss my family, my friends, my dog, and my people—especially my parents who have been taking care of me whenever I have needed it. They send me money and keep in contact with me; but it is now that I really know them. I think nobody

* This last paragraph is an adaptation the student has made and translated from Kahlil Gibran.

knows what he has until he is far away or loses it. In my case I have the best parents in the world. And I did not know that until now. Precisely now is when I miss them more than ever, because I know all the sacrifices they have to make to get the money for me, and knowing this I wonder, is it worth it? My father is 66 years old and maybe he won't live too long (I hope this won't be so), but he said to me once: "By life's law, I'll have to die first." He knows it and I would not like to spend maybe his last years of life far away, without enjoying him and the wonderful things that have happened between us. That is why I ask myself if my effort to learn and be here is worth it? Maybe my father will live more but the question will still be there. I think any foreign student with a father and mother like mine would feel the same in my situation. Certainly the most beautiful treasure of a son is to have a couple of parents like mine!

I want to talk about how a student can feel about the pressure . . . [in] school. . . . If I were free, I should quit the school and I should buy my own island to live like Robinson Crusoe or somebody like him because there are no schools, no teachers, no problems. My hard work starts at 7:00 A.M. when I awake and feel not so good. After I take a shower, I remember that I had to do some homework but that I couldn't because I had had two rehearsals and a concert last night. Therefore I run to school and start to do it but, because I am a lucky man—I remember that today is Thursday, and I have a piano lesson! Oh Boy! So, I put my books in my bag and go downstairs to practice a little bit—some Czerny studies—not easy ones. The time goes very fast and the time of class is here. . . . The teacher is a little mad; tells me that I have to practice more and more. After this embarrassing situation, I run to music theory—a class that needs 100 percent of concentration—and eurhythmics. When all is over I have to go to eat something and go back to school for rehearsals and maybe, some concert at night. When I go home after it all, I feel as if I had been in a rodeo or something like that, but we are not free and that is life.

Tonight, I tried and tried to bring your attention to me, but every time your mind was on somebody else and your eyes were looking at somebody else, too. I tried to please, to talk, to catch your attention, but I failed. I tried then to please myself, not to be so sad. But it was such conflict, I smiled and laughed while my heart ached and bled. Maybe after all, you are just fooling around with my feelings. Maybe you are just pitying me? I don't know! . . .

I am a very sensible man and I usually hide my feelings very well. You can't tell that I was really feeling bad, right? . . . You hurt me just like crushing a nut: Can I forgive you? You just carelessly drop me down. I don't know what to say.

Her eyes are razors
cutting my soul
my ego, self-esteem.
I didn't mean to just take
leaving her empty.

The writer of the following poem is Moslem.

The Glass

Have you ever seen a glass wall?
So delicate and not visible at all?
That wall separates our hearts,
our feelings, best of all arts.
You can see me, I can see you;
We can smile and love each other, too,
but that wall is still there
thick and rigid refuses to hear
the sound of our loves.

I wish I could break that wall
smashing it to pieces so small.
To free the love and let it fly
leaving the earth and see the sky
where it can live and not fear
for its color and being far or near.

That wall is our belief, our culture.
Prejudice? You name it human nature—

You are a Christian, I'm a Jew,
Are you a Moslem? I kind of knew.

I'm proud of my history of the past
You, of a glorious age that doesn't last.

I want to show that the Lord loves us all—
I wish I could break the wall.

The following journal entry was written by a student whose major is engineering.

Drawing . . . is my favorite entertainment. Drawing makes me relax even though the activity requires little, but hard work with my emotions. Drawing is also my other language; it enables me to show my views to other people. If my picture can give other people a little interest, I am content. I want to move others with my drawing; it doesn't matter whether the feeling is nice or bad. Even if someone feels terrible, anyway I am satisfied about stimulating him. But if possible, I try to purify the emotion, and to be peaceful, calm.

I think technique is not so important as to concentrate all my attention on it. Anyone can get the technique of drawing by much practice. But if I only have good technique without emotion, I am nothing but a color painter or a photographer. . . . A good picture is not drawn by dexterity of hand, but is drawn by emotion, imagination. My hand is nothing but a servant commanded by my brain. Next, how can I develop my emotion, imagination, as well as technique? Deliberately watch, think about that—to find the proper way to express it, show it according to my views . . . as it is possible, observe famous artists' ways of drawing and their pictures. . . . Reading can't be separated—is related strongly with drawing because it stimulates me to think, and gives me emotion, imagination.

Above all, I have to think about my whole life. . . . whenever I am drawing, I remind myself that drawing a good picture of my life is more important than the picture I am drawing.

This journal entry was stimulated by the following quotation from Franz Kafka, whose conflict with his father the student had been studying.

If the book we are reading does not wake us, as with a fist hammering on our skulls, why then do we read it? . . . what we must have are those books which come upon us like ill fortune, and distress us deeply. . . . A book must be an ice-axe to break the sea frozen inside us.

There are instants that you would like to break your frozen inside, but that is not a general case. I should admit that I saw my inside again, the one that I had almost forgotten. Unfortunately, I cannot claim that I enjoyed it . . . I once had a very similar feeling towards my father that was changed when I came to the United States, but now I am in a dilemma. This means that if you try to break the sea inside you, the sea which is partly frozen and partly clear water, you may lose your axe in the water and fall in the sea; then you don't know whether you should swim or grab a piece of ice.

Blue sky and the bright sun are overhead. Cars passing and people strolling make this afternoon more crowded than ever, although the street is slick from the melting ice. An old black man standing with his stick—the third foot of his—is waiting for the "walk" sign. After I swallow the juice of my gum the light has changed; the man crosses the street. Coming in the same direction of the street towards him, two youngsters are chasing each other in their German-made Audi and domestic Firebird. "My God," the old man will become the proof of my physics of kinetics. Since the cars do not reduce their constant speed of 80 Kmph, he will be hit by a power of 135 hp. Can you imagine how an old man is hit by 135 horses. A scream yelling out caused my heart beat to pause. The old man blew out his life without any message to his family. And, where are the two cars? Damn! A thick smoke has been left by their accelerations. A flock of crows is flying over and shouting the sound of the fall of a man, victim of the modern age.

Besides the kitchen, where can women be? This question is always in my mind these days.

A long time ago, when I heard that women only belong in the kitchen, I was laughing, and did nothing at all. But now, I have, as I never had before, such strong feelings about this that if one day I hear such words, I'll fight back hard.

There are many women in my country who got masters degrees or PhD's, and then stay home as housewives. I am wondering: What does education mean to them?

Education is so expensive in the United States that it makes me think: If one day I finish school, and stay at home, doing nothing besides play piano for my kids, why should my father pay so much money for me to go to college to study the piano? It is not fair.

Two long journal sequences follow. In each case, pages were selected from the journal and kept in chronological order. You should be able, in each case, to hear a voice, become acquainted with a personality, and share with each one a variety of moods. Again, notice that the journal is more than a record of activities; it is a recording of reactions, feelings, and thoughts.

1/27

My mother called. It was nice to hear her voice. Sometimes I think I've forgotten how to speak Bengali and one day I'll pick up the phone unable to speak to her. I think she misses me although she didn't say, but then she never knows what to say when she's on the phone. My father seemed as nervous as usual. He's afraid I won't do well in school; not that he doesn't think I am capable of it but he thinks I might be too immature to realize the importance of an education. I know it's important, especially if I intend to be independent of them as soon as possible. They do so much for me and I feel guilty. I know I'm not spoiled but I have nothing to give them in return except my gratefulness. I wish I could love them as much as they love me. I appreciate them. My father wants to be a part of my education. He wants to feel like he's helping me out. But he doesn't realize it's really all up to me and how much *I* want it. I try to make him feel more involved now. Before I used to be so inconsiderate of his feelings and hopes. I hope I won't disappoint him. I think all he wants me to do is care for myself as a person, independent of anyone and try my best at whatever I am doing.

There seems to be no end to the work I have to do but can't see myself anywhere except here. I feel like I am doing something important here.

When I am home on vacation I feel like I am wasting time waiting for the next semester to start. I do love college, both the work and the independence. You feel for the first time you've been given complete control of your life to do whatever you please with it. It's a big responsibility but it's also a challenge that you'll have faced. And you know some day four or five years from now you can look back on all this and think of all the silly mistakes you've made. I am going to hate leaving.

2/10

I was just thinking how I always call people but never have anything really to say so now I'll just not call at all even when I know I really should because I hate the "tension" on the phone when after two minutes you run out of things to say and you wonder why you called in the first place. But you realize that it's just to check up on the person whether they are all right or lonely. So what if I call my mother up to tell her I have a huge corn on my left foot. Besides, those kinds of things make her happy. Or I'll ask her what she did that day and maybe she'll say some gossip or make fun of my father's eccentricity or how obnoxious he was this morning. I know practically everything she's going to talk about, but that's probably why I call her—so I can make sure that something in my life is a constant and familiar almost to the point of boredom because it makes me feel secure and gets my mind off my problems. I think of her little problems and the triviality of them in comparison to mine.

2/20

It's so hard to wake up to rain and there's no sun in sight. It's so cold and empty. When the sun does come up by midday it's like someone just turned on a light. Nothing seems comfortable here—not the weather, the people, the teachers or any of my classes. I don't know, maybe I don't belong here. Everybody seems to be moving along fine but without me. I like to be alone but it's almost impossible to do that here.

3/5

I hate it when it snows here. It's pathetic ... I shouldn't complain so much or I'll become a grouchy old lady. How can one city be so dingy. It is like an arm pit. It stinks of industry. ... It's dying a slow death. The streets are ashen and smoked. It's crumbling from its corners. I feel guilty going to school here ... I feel like we've cut a private little school in the middle of people's homes and raised a fence around us from which the students can always look over to see how the other half lives. It's gray and tired. The city is falling around us but we don't have to bother with it because we live in our own world, while the other half weeps in silence, probably resenting us. But there is nothing I can do but give it a thought and pass on.

3/8

I really feel bad for the people in this city. They must live here because they have to, because their job requires them to. I would rather live in the country. But the land is so flat. Funny how I never thought about whether flat land would bother me or not. I guess that's because I've always lived on hilly places. It never occurred to me that there are places that are flat. A mountain is more my style. I've always dreamt of living on a mountain.

4/8

This math is killing me. I wake up at 6:00 and do math. I skip meals and stay up till 2:00; that leaves me four hours of sleep. That's not sleeping, it's taking naps! They should put sleep as a part of your syllabus. I can't believe that I daydream in the library about sleeping. Now that's pathetic. I hope this is worth it. *I know it is.* It will be so nice when I become a polymer scientist and live in the country. I'll read everything about polymers. I hope I am a good scientist. I'll teach some too.

1/20

When I was in Los Angeles, I used to write letters every day because there was so much spare time that I didn't know what to do. Now that I'm in this university, I hardly send a letter to my family or friends. Sometimes I'm becoming a very optimistic person. At other times I'm becoming so anxious about my future. Yeah, you're right, I'm not a stable person. At this time I'm still struggling to build my character. I'm used to being influenced by other people. If I do something or if I act some way, I always wonder about what people think about me. It makes my action become so awkward. In fact, there is no guy paying attention to me. In these days, I'm forcing myself to ignore what people think about me because that is only my imagination. I'm trying to think in every situation, making up my mind about what I have to do and doing it without any doubts and then being ready to receive the results even if they might be worse than I've thought before. The die is cast; think about something—the best and the worst results that might happen—do that without doubt if we're ready to face the worst to happen. Now it's half past five. At 6:45 I'll have computer class. Now I'm gonna read the book of computer so I think it's better for me to stop this journal here and I'll continue this journal a few days from now. See you.

1/25

I've just finished my physics homework. During these days I am so busy that I can't think about anything except studying and studying. It's fortunate enough that I've bought a guitar, so if I get so tense after studying too hard, or if I get burned out by an unsolved problem, I can take my guitar and start playing a song. I don't play guitar well but it's very good, I think, to calm down my nerves. Time now is going to be 1:00 in the morning. My eyes are becoming heavier and heavier but maybe this is the consequence of being a student. I have to do all things at once; or maybe I'm so proud of myself that I dared myself to take eighteen credits in this first semester. I know it's hard. One, because I have to adjust to a new situation and the other is that I have some difficulty in English, especially in communicating with people. Thus, if I don't understand something that our teacher teaches us, I daren't ask about it because I realize that I will make myself a center of attention. After almost four months here in the United States, I feel my English is still very weak. You know when first I came to the United States I lived in Los Angeles with two friends from Indonesia, lived in the same apartment, and of course day by day we used to talk Indonesian; therefore my English is still a critical point now.

I feel very glad that now I've moved here and live in a dormitory. My suite-mates are all American. It's good for me because I'm forced to use my English and I am forcing myself to improve my English. I hope in a few months I will be able to keep up with the speaking of my suite.

I'm also very thankful that they're patient enough to listen to my unorganized English and explain things or words that I do not understand. This evening on the way to my dorm "Kusch Building," I came across a campus bus. I joined the bus and asked the driver if he would take me to "Kusch House." He didn't seem to understand me and asked me to repeat which building I wanted to go to. In fact I pronounced the word "Kusch" very strangely. There were two passengers in the bus and they laughed at me because of my pronunciation. What can I do but just try to smile—

1/27

Today I feel so tired because yesterday I couldn't sleep well. I just dozed. At last when I still hadn't slept I saw my watch and it was nearly 5:00 o'clock. Terrible. You know today, I've "stacks" of classes that I had to do. So, what happened in class was that I couldn't pay attention to what the teachers taught. I hope tonight it won't happen again. Till now, I've been studying in this university about two weeks, but I feel that there are so many assignments that I have to do from day to day, I will now change my schedule of studying and will try to discipline myself. I'll get up at 7:00 o'clock in the morning to review the lessons for one hour. In the afternoon I'll also spend about one hour studying in the library, and study again about three hours at night. I believe this way of studying will bring me to success.

3/3

Today I feel so free that I've done all my exams except computer. The time now is approaching 2:00 o'clock in the morning. Tomorrow I can concentrate on English and computer. By the way, I want to write about my belief in God. In these days, I feel that I don't have a strong faith in God but I'm trying to be in touch with Him. I usually pray once a day. That's the time before I go to bed. Although I'm still not sure about God, I still have a belief that someday I'll be able to accept everything about faith. I know that what I write here is very unclear. I think it's better to sleep now.

3/4

The trees outside are bald. They don't have any leaves on their branches. I just heard someone walk behind me. Up to now my English is still weak, my vocabulary particularly for I can't understand a novel very well. I shall read one or two novels to increase my vocabulary. Next Summer or Fall I am planning to have a German course. I'm really interested in languages. In Indonesia, I speak Indonesian and Javanese (that is one dialect of Indonesian). My parents are Chinese; therefore I can speak Chinese, although only a little. Now that I'm here in America, I want to have two more languages in my knowledge, that's English and German. Someday later I'll go to Taiwan to improve my Chinese language. Now I feel that I have a method of how to study a language: I have to get into the language. I mean the language has to be one part of my mind. Usually if I analyzed something, I used to use my Indonesian. Now that I know this method, I try to analyze or think in English so I hope gradually English will be one part of my mind like my native language. Okay, that's all for today. Adios.

4/15

I am now in the library. I've just registered for my fall semester. I am taking six courses which are 21 credits. This summer I am going to take English 150, Physics III, and Economics 101. The weather now is really very good, between 60–70°F. In my home town this kind of weather is very cold. We are used to temperatures between 80–90°F and we never have snow. We have only two seasons, dry and rainy seasons. When I first came to the United States, I was very eager to see snow. Now that I'm here I sometimes feel that snow is boring to me. Anyway, the weather is really good now. The worst thing was that I caught cold due to my lack of sleep. I have an attitude that I sometimes feel is of no good. Whenever I am thinking about a problem I will always think about it until I can figure it out, otherwise I can't sleep very well for I keep thinking about it even in my sleep. That's the way I caught cold last week.

After analyzing my own character for the last few months I feel I can enjoy myself now. Usually I couldn't control my mind and it wandered everywhere it wanted. Then I realized that sometimes I paid attention too much to unimportant things, such as what people think about me, and that kind of stuff. Now that I know, I make a compromise with my mind that I don't have to think about that. Instead, I start to think about people—what kind of people are in front of me? What kind of person is talking to me? How is the way of thinking of this person? And I start understanding people. I start searching: What is the best thing I must do in this condition? At last I feel that I can concentrate more quickly than before. Sometime later, after I changed my way of thinking, I found out that most people are looking for attention. If I give them attention, so they will give back attention to me. If I keep silent and don't care about them, so they also don't care about me. From that experience I can conclude that we have to take initiative to approach people, otherwise most of them will not make any reaction. I think this is related to the law of love. We have to like people first before people can like us. Conversely, if we start by having bias to people, they will also be biased to us. It is really very simple.

☐ QUESTION

What evidence can you find of the progress this young man has made since the beginning of the term? Does he seem to have greater maturity? What about his self-confidence?

Now it's *your* turn! Buy a notebook (perhaps a smaller one, about 6″ × 9″, will be less intimidating) and begin writing today. Once the first page is covered, you will really be on your way.

CHAPTER 3

NARRATION

Narrative writing answers the question "what happened?" Whether we tell a child a story, write a letter about the first day at school, report on an event, or create an imaginary story, we are narrating. People never outgrow their love of stories, or at least the desire to satisfy their curiosity about what happened—and what happened *then*. How did it all end? We enjoy hearing about people we know; we want our curiosity satisfied. Whether the characters and events of stories are real or fictional, people enjoy becoming deeply involved in the lives of others.

Even though you may enjoy telling or writing stories, in this course you are not expected to become a fiction writer. Even if you never write a story, you narrate all the time—in your conversation, in your letters, every time you tell what happened.

Because people are interested in a good story, a narrated event is often used to attract or hold the interest of an audience or a reader. A story, incident, or experience that illustrates the point a writer or speaker is making not only creates interest, but also makes the point more convincing and more memorable. As writers, we all have a treasury of experiences and "stories" that we can draw upon to help illustrate a point. When we reach back into our memories to do this, when we use the past, we may find that we view that past and those memories with new understanding; we see it from a new point of view.

The following story appears in a book on language by a linguist who has been a professor of semantics (that branch of language study that focuses on meaning), a university president, and a United States senator. He uses the incident to illustrate the value, on occasion, of "talk for talk's sake." We can all understand the awkwardness a stranger can feel. We have all begun conversations with reference to the weather. Some of you may also have had the experience of feeling "looked over" with suspicion. Notice the way Dr. Hayakawa (whose family origin is Japanese) uses narration to illustrate and explain his point.

S. I. HAYAKAWA

The Value of Unoriginal Remarks

1   An incident in my own experience illustrates how necessary it sometimes is to give people the opportunity to agree. Early in 1942, a few weeks after the beginning of the war and a time when rumors of Japanese spies were still widely current,* I had to wait two or three hours in a railroad station in Oshkosh, Wisconsin, a city in which I was a stranger. I became aware as time went on that the other people waiting in the station were staring at me suspiciously and feeling uneasy about my presence. One couple with a small child were staring with special uneasiness and whispering to each other. I therefore took occasion to remark to the husband that it was too bad that the train should be late on so cold a night. The man agreed. I went on to remark that it must be especially difficult to travel with a small child in winter when train schedules were so uncertain. Again the husband agreed. I then asked the child's age and remarked that the child looked very big and strong for his age. Again agreement—this time with a slight smile. The tension was relaxing.

2   After two or three more exchanges, the man asked, "I hope you don't mind my bringing it up, but you're Japanese, aren't you? Do you think the Japs have any chance of winning this war?"

3   "Well," I replied, "your guess is as good as mine. I don't know any more than I read in the papers. (This was true.) But the way I figure it, I don't see how the Japanese, with their lack of coal and steel and oil and their limited industrial capacity, can ever beat a powerfully industrialized nation like the United States."

4   My remark was admittedly neither original nor well informed. Hundreds of radio commentators and editorial writers were saying exactly the same thing during those weeks. But just because they were, the remark *sounded familiar* and was *on the right side,* so that it was easy to agree with. The man agreed at once, with what seemed like genuine relief. How much the wall of suspicion had broken down was indicated in his next question, "Say, I hope your folks aren't over there while the war is going on."

5   "Yes, they are. My father and mother and two young sisters are over there."

6   "Do you ever hear from them?"

7   "How can I?"

8   "Do you mean you won't be able to see them or hear from them till after the war is over?" Both he and his wife looked troubled and sympathetic.

9   There was more to the conversation, but the result was that within ten minutes after it had begun they had invited me to visit them in their city and

---

* On December 7, 1941, in a surprise attack, the Japanese bombed Pearl Harbor, an American naval base in Hawaii. Up until that time, the United States had not yet entered World War II. That the United States was taken so completely by surprise caused much suspicion and fear of Japanese spies.

have dinner with them in their home. And the other people in the station, seeing me in conversation with people who *didn't* look suspicious, ceased to pay any attention to me and went back to reading their papers and staring at the ceiling.*

☐ FOCUS ON NARRATION

Let us now look back at the incident and examine the way it has been presented.

1. How has the narrative been organized? In what order?
2. Underline the words that provide a transition from one event or thought to the next. Notice the indicators of time sequence (example: *as time went on, then*), but notice too, the way other kinds of words relate a sentence to what has gone before or to what will follow (example. *again*).
3. Notice Hayakawa's use of summary in some parts, detail in others, exact conversation in still others. Do you think he has used good judgment in deciding how much detail and exactness to use? Explain why. For example, why is it effective that the last exchange is given purely in uninterrupted dialogue? Why was it best to quote that portion of the conversation rather than to summarize it or leave it out?

DIALOGUE

Dialogue, used wisely, can be a very effective aspect of narrative writing. It should not be used simply as "filler," however. Dialogue should be used when the exact words give a better feel of the experience, the characters, or the conflict than narration could. Good dialogue, carefully chosen, can make a piece of writing more dramatic and more real. Notice how natural Hayakawa's dialogue is; it sounds as if real people are talking. Where it is clear who is talking, there is no awkward "he or she said." Where such indicators are needed, they are kept very simple. Attention needs to be focused directly on the quoted words, not on indications of who is speaking.

Punctuating Dialogue

1. Notice that all punctuation marks are INSIDE the quotation marks.
2. Quotations begin with a capital letter. If a quote is interrupted by a phrase like *he said,* it may resume with a small letter, provided that it continues the same sentence.

---

* Perhaps it should be added that I was by no means *consciously* applying the principles of this chapter during the incident. This account is the result of later reflection. I was simply groping, as anyone else might do, for a way to relieve my own loneliness and discomfort in the situation. [Hayakawa's footnote]

Example:

"I will go home tomorrow."

"I will go home tomorrow," she said, "if the weather is all right."

3. *He said* (replied, asked, etc.) is separated from the quoted words by means of a comma, unless the quote is an exclamation or question followed by *he said.*

Examples:

"Don't blame me!" he exclaimed.

He said, "Let's go."

"Shall we wait for a ride?" she asked.

Notice that the period is used at the end of the complete sentence, including the *he said* clause.

4. Each new speaker in a dialogue begins a new paragraph.

□ SUGGESTIONS FOR COMPOSITION

Write a brief dialogue. (1) It can be based on a real conversation you have had or heard. Don't worry about remembering the conversation word for word. Simply reconstruct the dialogue as accurately as you can. (2) The dialogue can, also, represent two sides of an argument. Present the two sides by means of a dialogue between two people, each representing one of the sides. Whichever writing assignment you choose, be sure to use correct punctuation.

ORGANIZATION AND SELECTION

The organization of a narrative is basically chronological; that is, events are arranged in a *time sequence,* and they are usually told in the past time.

If you are using narrative to make a point, that point will give meaning to the narrative. It is not necessary to state your point; it can be implicit in the narrative, in the writer's mind as he or she writes and in the reader's mind as he or she reads. If you don't become sidetracked by irrelevant information, the point you are illustrating will provide unity to your story. If you are telling a story for its own sake, it should still have unity. It should build toward a climax, or high point, and conclude with the resolution of a problem, or with a specific impression or understanding that you wish to leave in the mind of the reader.

To keep the reader interested and the narrative unified, you will need to select details carefully. Not every detail is important. In the incident at the railroad station, for example, we do not need to know what Dr. Hayakawa was wearing, or where he worked, or where he had gone to school. When you write a narrative composition, you will need to decide which facts are unimportant, which can be summarized briefly, and which should be presented in greater detail. The most important or most dramatic part of your narrative should show action and detail more fully so that the reader can participate in the experience.

□ SUGGESTIONS FOR COMPOSITION

---

1. Narrate a personal experience in which you felt awkward or strange and found yourself making small talk to ease the tension of the situation. Use dialogue.
2. Use narration to illustrate the principle that it is unfair to be suspicious of an individual simply because he or she looks different or belongs to a group of people whose government is unfriendly or hostile to one's own.
3. Narrate a dangerous experience in your life, reserving the greatest detail for the most dramatic part.
4. Narrate an experience that was very important to you, one that possibly changed your life. Show how and why it was so significant.
5. Use an incident to prove a point. Be sure you state the point you wish to make and relate the incident to it clearly.

In the Hayakawa incident, since communication was the subject of the narrative, it was more appropriate to use dialogue than description. In the selection that follows, however, conversation is not important, but the physical descriptions and actions are. The author, Richard Selzer, is a surgeon who also writes novels and poetic essays, such as this one, on the "mortal lessons" and the "love" he finds in "the art of surgery."

RICHARD SELZER

Surgery as Love

1   I invited a young diabetic* woman to the operating room to amputate* her leg. She could not see the great shaggy* black ulcer* upon her foot and ankle that threatened to encroach upon* the rest of her body, for she was blind as well. There upon her foot was a Mississippi Delta* brimming* with corruption, sending its raw tributaries* down between her toes. Gone were all the little web* spaces that when fresh and whole are such a delight to loving men. She could not see her wound, but she could feel it. There is no pain like that of the bloodless limb turned rotten and festering.* There is

(1) **diabetic:** referring to diabetes, a disease characterized by excess sugar in the blood and urine, also called **sugar diabetes;** it can result in blindness or **gangrene** (decay of tissue where blood supply is obstructed)
(1) **amputate:** to cut off, usually said of removing a limb or other part of the body surgically
(1) **shaggy:** rough, straggly, sloppy looking
(1) **ulcer:** an open sore, not caused by a wound, characterized by disintegration of the tissues and possible discharge of pus
(1) **encroach upon:** advance beyond the proper limits; to invade; to go where one has no right to be
(1) **delta:** the mouth of the river (shaped like the Greek letter Δ), where the river flows into the sea
(1) **brimming:** full to the top or brim
(1) **tributaries:** streams or smaller rivers that flow into a larger stream or river
(1) **web:** the membrane partly or completely joining the toes
(1) **festering:** getting more ulcerated, producing pus

neither unguent* nor anodyne* to kill such a pain and yet leave intact* the body.

2   For over a year I trimmed away the putrid* flesh, cleansed, anointed,* and dressed the foot, staving off,* delaying. Three times each week, in her darkness, she sat upon my table, rocking back and forth, holding her extended leg by the thigh, gripping it as though it were a rocket that must be steadied lest it explode and scatter her toes about the room. And I would cut away a bit here, and bit there, of the swollen blue leather that was her tissue.

3   At last we gave up, she and I. We could no longer run ahead of the gangrene. We had not the legs for it. There must be an amputation in order that she might live—and I as well. It was to heal us both that I must take up knife and saw, and cut the leg off. And when I could feel it drop from her body to the table, see the blessed *space* appear between her and that leg, I too would be well.

4   Now it is the day of the operation. I stand by* while the anesthetist* administers the drugs, watch as the tense familiar body relaxes into narcosis.* I turn then to uncover the leg. There, upon her kneecap, she has drawn, blindly, upside down for me to see, a face; just a circle with two ears, two eyes, a nose, and a smiling upturned mouth. Under it she has printed SMILE, DOCTOR. Minutes later I listen to the sound of the saw, until a little crack at the end tells me it is done.

5   So, I have learned that man is not ugly, but that he is Beauty itself. There is no other his equal.

☐ FOCUS ON EFFECTIVE NARRATIVE TECHNIQUE

---

1. Is the narrative in strict chronological order? Put the paragraph numbers in strict chronological order. Why is it effective as it is?
2. Underline the transition words of time that help us easily move backward and forward with the writer (example: *for over a year, no longer*).
3. Notice the change to the present, an unusual tense for narrative. Why is it effective? Notice, too, the use of the present perfect. Why is it being used? (You may need to review the uses of the present perfect.)
4. Why is the background of the "trimming" so important? What does it do for the effectiveness of the narrative?

(1) **unguent:** salve or ointment
(1) **anodyne:** a medicine that relieves pain
(1) **intact:** whole, undamaged
(2) **putrid:** rotten, decomposed, and foul-smelling
(2) **anointed:** put oil on, especially in ceremonies that marked the making of a priest or king
(2) **staving off:** evading, postponing, pushing off
(4) **stand by:** wait in readiness
(4) **anesthetist:** the doctor who gives the anesthetic, which is the drug or gas that puts the patient to sleep, or deadens the area for surgery
(4) **narcosis:** a drug-induced stupor or unconsciousness

5. The drama is increased because we are given painful details but also because we have some insight into the characters, the doctor and the young woman. What kind of people are they? How do you know this?

☐ FOCUS ON LANGUAGE

1. Examine the first sentence. What is the effect of the verb *invited?*
2. Discuss the effectiveness of the following words, phrases, and pictures:
   Paragraph 1: the Mississippi River analogy
   Paragraph 2: "anointed"
              "in her darkness"
              the rocket analogy
   Paragraph 3: "We could no longer run ahead of the gangrene."
3. How does Selzer use the words *Beauty* and *ugly* (paragraph 5)?

☐ FOCUS ON SENTENCE STRUCTURE

Examine the following pairs of sentences. For each pair, try to determine why the original structure (a) is more effective than the equally correct structure (b).

1. (a) "She could not see the great shaggy black ulcer upon her foot and ankle that threatened to encroach upon the rest of her body, for she was blind as well." (paragraph 1)
   (b) She was blind; therefore she could not see the great shaggy black ulcer upon her foot and ankle that threatened to encroach upon the rest of her body.
2. (a) "There must be an amputation in order that she might live—and I as well." (paragraph 3)
   (b) If we were both going to live, there had to be an amputation.
3. (a) "So, I have learned that man is not ugly, but that he is Beauty itself. There is no other his equal." (paragraph 5)
   (b) I have learned that there is no other who is the equal of man, who is not ugly, but is Beauty itself.

☐ SUGGESTIONS FOR COMPOSITION

1. Use narration to illustrate the point that "man is not ugly, but . . . he is Beauty itself. There is no other his equal."
2. Do the same for the opposite view: "Man is ugly and terrible. There is no other his equal."
3. Write about someone you know or have heard about who showed remarkable bravery and good humor during a terrible illness or other ordeal. If you personally have had such an experience, you may write about your own.

POINT OF VIEW IN NARRATIVE WRITING

Another way to achieve unity in narrative writing is to tell your story through the eyes and mind of only one person, which will probably, but not necessarily, be yourself. Whether an incident is narrated in the first person (I) or the third person (he or she), it is better if the narration is told consistently from the point of view of that person than if it jumps from one mind to another. Of course, some writers involve us in the minds of several characters, but such movement requires a longer piece of writing and a lot of writing skill. You may want to show different points of view of the same incident, but you will need to develop each one carefully and show how they are related—and why you are giving them to us. One must feel purpose in a piece of writing, even if the purpose is simply to share an experience. This, too, requires a consistent narrating viewpoint so that we can relate to that "voice" sharing the experience with us.

Keep in mind the question of point of view as you read the following experience. In addition to being an author, the writer of this selection is a lawyer who has taught at Harvard.

ENRIQUE HANK LOPEZ

Why Couldn't My Father Read

1   Recent articles on immigration and education remind me of my father, who was an articulate,* fascinating storyteller but totally illiterate.

2   By the time I entered fourth grade in Denver, I was a proud, proficient* reader—and painfully aware of my father's inability to read a single word in either Spanish or English. Although I'd been told there were no schools in his native village of Bachimba, Chihuahua, I found it hard to accept the fact that he didn't even know the alphabet.

3   Consequently, every night as I watched my mother read to him I would feel a surge of resentment and shame. Together they bent over *La Prensa* from San Antonio—the only available Spanish-language newspaper. "How can he be so dumb?" I would ask myself. "Even a little kid can read a damned newspaper."

4   Of course, many adults in our barrio* couldn't read or write, but that was no comfort to me. Nor did it console* me that my hero Pancho Villa was also illiterate. After all, this was my own father, the man I considered to be smarter than anyone else, who could answer questions not even my mother could answer, who would take me around the ice factory where he worked and show me how all the machinery ran, who could make huge cakes of ice

(1) **articulate:** able to speak and express oneself clearly
(2) **proficient:** very competent, skilled
(4) **barrio:** (Spanish) a subdivision of a city or suburb, a neighborhood
(4) **console:** comfort, cheer, especially one who is feeling the distress of loss or disappointment

without any air bubbles, who could fix any machine or electrical appliance, who could tell me all those wonderful stories about Pancho Villa.

5   But he couldn't read. Not one damned word!

6   Whenever I saw my mother reading to him—his head thrust forward like a dog waiting for a bone—I would walk out of the kitchen and sit on the back porch, my stomach churning* with a swelling anger that could easily have turned to hatred. So bitter was my disappointment, so deep was my embarrassment, that I never invited my friends into the house during that after-dinner hour when my mother habitually read to him. And if one of my friends had supped* with us, I would hastily herd them out of the kitchen when my mother reached for *La Prensa*.

7   Once, during a period of deepening frustration, I told my mother that we ought to teach him how to read and write. And when she said it was probably too late to teach him—that it might hurt his pride—I stomped* out of the house and ran furiously down the back alley, finally staggering behind a trash can to vomit everything I'd eaten for supper.

8   Standing there in the dark, my hand still clutching the rim of the can, I simply couldn't believe that anyone as smart as my dad couldn't learn to read, couldn't learn to write "cat" or "dog" or even "it." Even I, who could barely understand the big words he used when he talked about Pancho Villa (revolucion, cacique*, libertad, sabotaje, terreno), even I, at the mere age of ten, could write big words in both English and Spanish. So why couldn't he?

9   Eventually, he did learn to write two words—his name and surname. Believing that he would feel less humble if he could sign his full name rather than a mere "X" on his weekly paycheck, my mother wrote "Jose Lopez" on his Social Security card and taught him to copy it letter by letter. It was a slow, painstaking process that usually required two or three minutes as he drew each separate letter with solemn tight-lipped determination, pausing now and then as if to make sure they were in the proper sequence. Then he would carefully connect the letters with short hyphenlike lines, sometimes failing to close the gaps or overlapping letters.

10   I was with him one Friday evening when he tried to cash his paycheck at a furniture store owned by Frank Fenner, a red-faced German with a bulbous nose and squinty* eyes. My father usually cashed his check at Alfredo Pacheco's corner grocery store, but that night Pacheco had closed the store to attend a cousin's funeral, so we had crossed the street to Fenner's place.

11   "You cambiar this?" asked my father, showing him the check.

---

(6) **churning:** stirring or shaking violently; the verb used for stirring cream until it is made into butter

(6) **supped:** eaten supper

(7) **stomped:** stamped; i.e., brought the feet down forcefully, walking that way in anger or to show authority

(8) **cacique:** (Spanish) one who owns a great deal of land, working the laborers on it cruelly

(10) **squinty:** looking with eyes partly closed or turned to the side

12   "He wants you to cash it," I added, annoyed by my father's use of the word cambiar.

13   "Sure, Joe," said Fenner. "Just sign your monicker* on the back of it."

14   "Firme su nombre atras," I told my father, indicating that Fenner wanted him to sign it.

15   "Okay, I put my name," said my father, placing his Social Security card on the counter so he could copy the "Jose Lopez" my mother had written for him.

16   With Fenner looking on, a smirk building on his face, my father began the ever-so-slow copying of each letter as I literally squirmed* with shame and hot resentment. Halfway through "Lopez," my father paused, nervously licked his lips, and glanced sheepishly at Fenner's leering* face. "No write too good," he said. "My wife teach me."

17   Then, concentrating harder than before, he wrote the final e and z and slowly connected the nine letters with his jabby little scribbles. But Fenner was not satisfied. Glancing from the Social Security card to the check, he said, "I'm sorry, Joe, that ain't the same signature. I can't cash it."

18   "You bastard!" I yelled. "You know who he is! And you just saw him signing it."

19   Then suddenly grabbing a can of furniture polish, I threw it at Fenner's head but missed by at least six inches. As my father tried to restrain me, I twisted away and screamed at him, "Why don't you learn to write, goddamn it! Learn to write!"

20   He was trying to say something, his face blurred* by my angry tears, but I couldn't hear him, for I was now backing and stumbling out of the store, my temples throbbing with the most awful humiliation I had ever felt. My throat dry and sour, I kept running and running down Larimer Street and then north on 30th Street toward Curtis Park, where I finally flung myself on the recently watered lawn and wept myself into a state of complete exhaustion.

21   Hours later, now guilt-ridden by what I had yelled at my dad, I came home and found him and my mother sitting at the kitchen table, writing tablet between them, with the alphabet neatly penciled at the top of the page.

22   "Your mother's teaching me how to write," he said in Spanish, his voice so wistful* that I could hardly bear to listen to him. "Then maybe you won't be so ashamed of me."

23   But for reasons too complex for me to understand at that time, he never learned to read or write. Somehow, the multisyllabic words he had always

---

(13) **monicker** (slang): signature, name

(16) **squirmed:** to twist and turn the body in a snakelike movement; to show or feel the distress of painful embarrassment or humiliation

(16) **leering:** looking with sidelong glance showing bad feeling, sometimes combined with triumph

(20) **blurred:** made indistinct, hazy, smeary

(22) **wistful:** showing longing, wishing

known and accurately used seemed confusing and totally beyond his grasp when they appeared in print or in my mother's handwriting. So after a while, he quit trying.

□ FOCUS ON POINT OF VIEW

1. From whose point of view is the story told? Are there two *different* points of view on the part of the same person, almost as if two different people have had the experience? What is that difference?

2. If you have noticed that the experience is shown to us mainly through the eyes of the young boy, you are correct. You would also have been correct in finding the view of the grown man looking back on a painful childhood memory. There is, however, a difference between the feelings of the boy and those of the man. What are the boy's conflicting feelings? What are those of the grown man? How are they related?

3. When the point of view is limited, knowledge and understanding are limited to what that person knows and is capable of understanding. We are given insight into the feelings and attitudes of the mother and the father, but we are told only what the boy hears, sees, and is capable of understanding. The writer as a grown man seems to understand more than the boy, but he does not provide us with any explanation. Do you feel he himself fully understands? What could he substitute for understanding? Is he proud of his father? How does he feel about the boy he was? Can you see and understand anything that the boy or the adult writer cannot?

□ QUESTIONS FOR DISCUSSION

1. This article raises the question of the relationship between literacy (the ability to read and write) and verbal or literary skills that do not depend on reading and writing (see, especially, paragraphs 1, 4, 8). To what extent is one dependent upon the other? To what extent can they function independently? How educated can one be without knowing how to read and write? Do you also feel Mr. Lopez was "dumb"?

2. How do you explain the violence of the boy's reaction (paragraphs 18 and 19)? Explain the sources and targets of his anger.

3. Do you have any theories regarding the father's inability to learn reading and writing? It is true that it is very difficult for an adult to become literate. For example, there is a great difference between teaching literate adults to read and write a *new* language and teaching them to read and write when they have never learned reading and writing in *any* language. Yet there are literacy programs in which adults *are* learning with some degree of success. There are literacy campaigns that bring university students into villages to teach. Why, then, do you suppose Mr. Lopez gave up?

☐   SUGGESTIONS FOR COMPOSITION

---

1. Retell the story from another character's perspective. Select one of the following four choices, being sure that the thoughts, attitude, knowledge, feelings, and language are consistent with the character from whose point of view you are telling the story. You may use either first or third person.
   a. Retell this story from the point of view of the father. After summarizing the situation regarding the father's illiteracy and his son's shame, focus on the incident at the furniture store.
   b. Retell the story from the point of view of the mother. Remember that she was not at the furniture store. Keep your focus on scenes at home.
   c. Use dialogue to write a narrative in which the father tells the mother what happened at the furniture store.
   d. Tell the same incident from the point of view of Fenner, the owner of the furniture store.

2. Tell of an incident in your childhood, using the viewpoint of the child you were. Choose something that puzzled, frightened, or upset you then, but which you now understand. Or, if you wish, choose an incident that did *not* frighten or upset you then because you did not understand it, but which you now understand to have been potentially dangerous or upsetting. Allow the reader to realize that you, as the grown writer, and the reader, as a grown reader, both understand what that child could not have understood.

WRITING A STORY

Perhaps you would like to try telling a story, writing a narrative other than the types already presented or assigned. You may want to create a fictional story out of your imagination, or, as writers usually do, out of some combination of imagination and fact.

The following story was written by a student. It happens to have been true, but such a story could have been imagined, at least in part, by a person who is familiar with the time and place of the story. The feelings of the story, however, go beyond the specific time and place; they could be expressed in many different settings and stories. You may wish to use an experience of your own, or you may wish to convey a feeling by means of fictional characters and events. Unless you are writing fantasy, however, it is usually best, even when writing fiction, to choose the kind of people and places you know best. The result will be a convincing piece of writing, as is the story you are about to read.

S T U D E N T   C O M P O S I T I O N S

My Place Is Empty

I am lying on my bed. It is in the middle of April and my windows are open. The fresh and cool air touches my face and brings me old memories, old memories of my country, Iran. It reminds me of the time I spent back home, lying on my bed and thinking about the confusion I was in.

It all started last summer when my father asked me to come home. I was so happy that I immediately sent my passport to the Iranian embassy and bought a ticket for May 15th, one day after school ended. I exactly remember May 15th was a rainy day both here and in Tehran, and though rainy days usually make me feel down, I remember this time I was day-dreaming about home. All those good things and beautiful places were passing in front of me like a movie—all those good times I spent with my friends. Oh yes, my friends: They had a big effect on my willingness to go home. My three friends and I were almost always together from the time we started high school. The memories of my friends prompted the memory of the previous summer. That summer had been the best summer of my life. We all had just finished high school and we were waiting to get accepted by universities. All the seventeen hours between New York and Tehran passed so quickly that I was amazed when I heard the stewardess announcing our arrival in Tehran.

My parents were waiting for me, as usual. The feeling was great: My mother could not help crying and my father and I could hardly talk. "You looked so different, so tall, I couldn't recognize you. You looked and dressed just like an American," my mother told me later. The first week passed quickly because I was spending all the days visiting my relatives; when I finished visiting my youngest uncle, I was really happy because now I could spend all my time with my friends.

It was a Saturday morning when I called my friends. I found out that one of them had gone to the United States three weeks before my arrival; the other two were really happy when I called them. We planned to meet each other that afternoon. I suggested going to the Hilton Hotel where we used to go and drink (and probably to meet girls), but one of my friends told me that they had burned that place a long time ago. Finally we all agreed to go to the "Royal Park" whose name had been changed to "People's Park" (I found later that they changed so many of the names that I never learned them all). Everybody knew the place where we were supposed to meet each other. There used to be a little lake in the park with a small restaurant next to it and we used to meet in front of that restaurant. I was there fifteen minutes ahead of my friends and I was not quite sure if I was in the right place. The lake was empty and the windows of the restaurant were all covered with metal. Its door was locked and nailed with big crossed wood. I was staring at the restaurant when a guy with a thick beard and moustache called my name. It was my friend; he looked skinnier and the beard and moustache gave him an unfamiliar look. The other friend of mine came after him; he was just a little skinnier. I was surprised when my friends told me that they had not met each other for a long time. I asked them about the lake and the restaurant and all those beautiful "chicks" who used to walk around the lake; they simply answered "who cares anymore."

It was a boring afternoon; my friends were just discussing politics, which was interesting to me, but I really wished they would change the subject. We walked for a couple of hours. From what they said I found out that most of the theaters that we used to go to were all burned down. "They were the center of dismoralities," one of my friends quoted. The park itself had a different atmosphere; people were gathering in groups, discussing politics. There used to be the statues of some of the old kings of Iran on one side of the park, but now they were mostly broken. I could easily see that nobody had cleaned the park for a long time and the garbage cans were all filled. There was even some garbage around the cans. That night I was in complete confusion—as if I was not sure I was in the real world.

Soon I found that the TV programs were all cut off, so our brand new color TV with a remote control device that we bought for a lot of money was just sitting in a corner of our living room. Soon my parents found out that I was getting bored, so they decided to arrange a trip. I suggested driving the same path as last year, but my mother told me that most of those routes were not safe anymore; then we discovered that most of the good hotels were closed too, and that at the Caspian Sea, where we used to go every other week, it was forbidden to swim. After a couple of weeks we decided the safest thing was to stay home.

One morning my father asked me to go to The Big Bazaar of Tehran with him. This bazaar, the biggest in Iran, is a very large place where you can buy your needs for the cheapest price because they do not have nice stores and therefore they do not charge you extra money. Since I knew it was going to be a long walk, I put on a pair of jeans and tennis shoes. (I should mention that, in Iran, the group of market labor people who work in The Big Bazaar have the greatest religious and therefore political power.) We drove there and when we reached downtown where the bazaar is, the traffic was so bad that we decided to walk the rest of the way. From the time we stepped out of the car until about 3 o'clock, when we went home, I could swear that people found me more interesting than the goods because everywhere we went, I could feel that people were staring at me as if I had come from outer space. From then on I scratched going to the bazaar from my list of possible activities.

By the middle of the summer, I was just meeting my friends once a week, and if my parents had not tried to keep me busy, by asking me, for example, to repair all the radios and service all the electronic things they could find in the house, I would have gone crazy. One day my father suggested that I should go back to the United States earlier because they might not let me in. That was a very poor excuse, but even my mother, who really wished that I could stay all summer, accepted. So we changed my ticket from August 20 to July 20. I remember when I was leaving my mother had wet eyes and my father and I could hardly talk. I remember I was day-dreaming the whole seventeen hours in the airplane about the good time I had here in the United States, and the last sentence of my father who said "My son, your place will be empty."* I was thinking my place is empty.

☐ QUESTION

Point out the specific details that help you as a reader experience the desolation the writer sees. How has he used details to communicate the loss and disappointment he feels?

In the following student composition, narration is used to make an important point.

A New Life Began after Last Wednesday

I don't want to sound snobbish, but I have always considered myself an independent person. I hardly ever ask or expect a favor from anybody. I had truly talked myself into believing that I was an independent person until last Wednesday. Last Wednesday, I found out how much of a jerk I have been. I found out that I had lied to myself for a long time.

I was lying in my bed thinking how boring this school is and how I can't wait till I get out of this place when some guys asked me to play soccer with them. So I said "Why not?" and followed them to the field. I didn't have anything to do anyway. It was a nice summer evening; the sun was getting cool and the grass had been nicely dried. It didn't take long for us to divide up the team and begin playing. I was playing the center field, a very important offense position I was proud of. We must have been playing for about ten minutes when I fell down, hurting my right ankle. I had accidentally stepped into a small hole. I felt tremendous pain in my ankle, as if someone was hopping on it as hard as he could with porcupine shoes. Trying to forget the pain, I bit my tongue so hard that I bled. All the guys gathered around to see what was happening. "Hey, Joe, are you all right?" Jim asked.

"Yeah, I'm all right," I answered with a little smile, trying not to show the pain. As I was saying that I was OK, I was hoping somebody would stick around and help me. Nobody did. They kept on playing the game as if nothing had happened.

Meanwhile my right ankle was swelling up and started to hurt pretty badly. I was quite sure I had a torn muscle because this wasn't the only time I had hurt my ankle. I had to get back to my room. I had to do something to

---

* In Persian this sentence has the meaning: We miss you or we will always remember you.

my ankle to reduce the swelling. There was nobody around me now; I had to make it all by myself. It felt like a nail was being pounded into my ankle every time I took a step. There were lots of people who offered their help as they walked by, even a girl! But I, being a dumb person, just refused. I was still mad at the guys for not helping me. How selfish I was!

The next day I was on crutches that I borrowed from the clinic. The doctor had told me not to put any weight on my right foot. The ankle didn't hurt as much as the day before, but carrying a book with crutches was a very hard thing to do. I was still mad at the guys: I couldn't believe they acted so cold. Of course we weren't that friendly, but I was hurt. They could at least have helped me back to my room. As I was cursing every guy who had played soccer with me, two people passed me by. One of them was sitting in a wheel chair and the other was pushing. They looked back to see who I was and talked by themselves. It was a very friendly sight. Suddenly I felt very lonely; I wished I had a friend who could help me like that. I truly realized how I needed someone to rely upon when I need help.

I don't consider myself such an independent person anymore. Since last Wednesday, I've made a few friends, very good friends. We help each other with our homework and talk about how we all hate this boring school. The world is a big and dangerous place, and now I have a few friends who can help me make it through.

☐ QUESTIONS

---

1. Did you notice the student's informal tone? Underline the words and phrases that convey his casualness, observing the slang, the contractions, and the informal connectors.
2. In the second paragraph, the student thinks of "how boring this school is," and at the end there is a reference to "this boring school." Why is the repetition effective? What differences does it dramatize?

The following composition was written in response to a writing assignment (composition suggestion number 2 following "Why Couldn't My Father Read") to narrate an incident from a child's limited point of view. The style and vocabulary are very simple, but the student has managed to convey the child's lack of understanding, while at the same time providing details to give us a full understanding of the events. The story refers to the Algerian struggle for independence against France, the former colonial ruler.

A Child's Point of View

It was a moonlit night in the summer of 1961. At that time Algeria had not yet gotten her independence. My parents were awake. We had some visitors who used to visit us just at night. My parents called them "the strugglers."

Every time they came, my mother made a very good dinner for them even if they were late. When they came our neighbors always came too until our living room became crowded. Those strugglers were always carrying something like sticks which were wide and brown colored at the bottom, and narrow and black colored at the top. Besides that, they were carrying many staffs. But the most wonderful thing which caught my attention was a very beautiful small radio. It was not like our radio. This radio you can speak with and it will answer you as if you are talking to a human being.

The crowd was in the living room. I did not know what they were doing. I was playing with our neighbor's boy of my age. I went to bed when I felt tired.

After midnight, I was in a deep lethargy. My mother came in a hurry and she picked me up by my arms, and put me on her back. Everybody was running out of his house. I did not know what was going on. The crowd went forth as one man. I was just looking. My mother put a coat on me because it was chilly. I went back to sleep. I did not get up until the sun rose. I saw a huge number of people sitting on the ground outside of our hometown. They were surrounded by some people wearing green clothes. They were carrying the same sticks which I saw the night before. They started picking men. They put them in one line. My father was among them. I heard some women lamenting; then some children crying because their parents were beaten. The people with green clothes gave all the children a piece of chocolate. When I got mine, my mother asked me to throw it away as all the children did. I loved chocolate, so I did not want to throw it away. She took it away from my hand; then I started crying as all the children did.

In the afternoon we went back home, but my father did not. I asked my mother where my father was. She answered me that he went to the market. I had not seen him for one month when he came back. He said he had been arrested by the French army because he was supporting the strugglers. Then I started realizing what was going on, that there were some despotic strangers taking our country by violence, and they were taking the rights of our people.

Leaving

The sun had finally disappeared behind the horizon. Lonely in the dusky sky, the control tower of the airport stood quietly. I turned to my father, a once respectful police officer of the South Vietnamese Republic government. He sat there motionless, thinking of something. I knew his patriotic conscience was hurting him, for he had to desert his position in the police headquarters to satisfy his family's desire to emigrate to the United States.

My family of sixteen people as well as other families had been waiting in these temporary shelters of the D.A.O. Organization since morning. We were all anxious, and scared and disappointed. The American officials kept informing us that the airplanes had not arrived yet.

Suddenly, roaring through the sky, three jet bombers in tremendous speed soared over our heads, and headed toward the Presidential Palace about a mile from the airport. I could see three black bombs from the jets diving rapidly down . . . down . . . and "Bung . . . Bung . . . ," explosions were everywhere surrounding me. The machine guns from land started to fire at the jets. "Tach . . . Tach . . ."; lines of flares and unconnected lightning dots were spraying all over the sky. Such intensified and frightening sound was drilling through my ears.

My younger sisters were crying hysterically; I had to do something. I quickly grabbed my youngest sister while my older brothers and sisters each carried one of my younger ones. We followed our father toward the sandbag roof of the guardhouse. People ran in all directions, looking for a safe shelter as bees from a broken hive. It was a typical chaotic scene which most of us had experienced during the course of our lives, especially during the invasion of the North Army in 1968.

About three minutes later, just as they had come, the three jets suddenly became three tiny dots far away. The quiet and suspended atmosphere returned to the area. Still, across from our guardhouse, a very young American soldier with an M16 machine gun on his arm was running zigzag as if he was in serious combat or probably in an exciting catch and hide game. We all had to laugh at his acting.

Time went by slowly. It was very dark; the stars were the only source of light for the whole area. I was still hungry from the little food I had had during my quick supper. Surrounding me were faces of anxiety and disappointment. We were all praying and hoping.

The happy news finally came at 1:00 A.M. when half of the people were dozing. About ten buses parked quietly outside the gate of the shelter place. With great relief family after family, carrying heavy luggage, slowly got on board.

As if it were performing a secret mission, the caravan of buses started moving quietly and sluggishly in the dark. Our fear wouldn't have ended until we were on the planes. Surprisingly the caravan safely passed all the security stations of the airport without any delay. (It was supposed to be illegal to emigrate to the United States without the authorized visas of the South Vietnamese government!)

As we approached the runways, the three gigantic army air freighter C130s appeared closer and closer. Like little fishes people were rushed to be swallowed into the huge open mouth of the sharklike air freighter. Inside the plane, there was no more empty space; still the crowd was getting bigger and bigger to a degree that I had to stand up for more room.

The shark mouth finally closed; the plane began its motion. Through a round window, I took a last look at the airport, at the sandbag cabins, and at the tiny soldiers. In just a short moment all I could see were the darkness of the sky and little light dots from sparkling stars. I had no idea where the plane would bring us. I knew, however, I could always reach out for a star, whether or not it was a bright one.

The preceding essay has no purpose other than to tell a story—no purpose except perhaps to communicate and share an experience. The result, however, is our increased understanding as well as our satisfaction at hearing a good story end happily. Notice this student's selection of details, images, and sound effects, his small human and dramatic touches, and his way of building toward the climax. Notice, too, that the author does not ask for our sympathy; the facts themselves draw it from us better than would any sentimental appeal.

CHAPTER

4

DESCRIPTION

When we read about people's experiences or listen to them, we are not only interested in finding out what happened; we want to know what the experience felt like, what a room looked like, how the food tasted, what was extraordinary about the view, or exactly how a person behaved. When it is our own experience we want to share, we often feel frustrated that others cannot see what we have seen or feel what we have felt. If we can take someone to hear the same concert, or see the same view, or meet the same people, we do not need to rely on description. But when we can't do this, we try to capture an experience with a tape recorder, with photographs or with words. None of these is truly adequate, but they are the best substitutes we have when we want to share or re-create an experience.

But even with a photograph or a record we find ourselves—in words and gestures—adding the feelings we had during the experience, adding, sometimes, the thoughts we have as we relive the event, thoughts we may not have had at the time. In retrospect, as we tell or write, we put things together in order, or add our later understanding, or compare it with other experiences or sensations, which we were too busy to do when we had the experience in the first place.

A well-written description helps us become involved in a story. We "see" the place and the people; we feel drawn into the atmosphere; we enter the world of that story, even if that world is absolutely foreign to us. We feel what the author wants us to feel. We even share his or her opinions. How does the author manage to do this with only ink and paper? How can words become so alive that we can actually feel them and be moved by them?

The following paragraphs are descriptions written by well-known authors. After you read each one, write down, in just a few words, your first impression. Include the feelings you think are being conveyed and the feelings you have toward what is being described.

The first two selections describe animals—one a lamb, the other a bull. As you might imagine, the feelings and impressions of each description are quite different.

E. B. WHITE

FROM *Farm Paper*

1   I pulled on some cold clothes and stumbled out toward the barnyard. Before I got down to the shed where the sheep were I could hear a lamb blaring.* The sound seemed artificial, almost as though somebody were blowing short blasts on a cheap horn. I slowed my step and looked in at the door of the fold.* On the frozen ground just over the threshold a lamb lay dead. A coating of frost had formed on its stiff yellow fleece.* The ewe* stood just beyond, her stern* showing traces of blood, her eyes full of bewilderment. A few feet away there was another lamb, staggering about in small spasmodic* jerks, its little dung*-smeared body about the size of a turnip,* its woeful* voice strangely penetrating in the biting wind that blew in through the open door.

ERNEST HEMINGWAY

FROM *The Sun Also Rises*

2   I leaned way over the wall and tried to see into the cage. It was dark. Someone rapped* on the cage with an iron bar. Inside something seemed to explode. The bull, striking into the wood from side to side with his horns, made a great noise. Then I saw a dark muzzle* and the shadow of horns, and then, with a clattering* on the wood in the hollow box, the bull charged* and came out into the corral, skidding* with his forefeet in the straw as he stopped, his head up, the great hump of muscle on his neck swollen tight, his body muscles quivering* as he looked up at the crowd on the stone walls. The two steers* backed away against the wall, their heads sunken, their eyes watching the bull.

(1) **blare:** to sound loudly, as with a trumpet
(1) **fold:** an enclosure for sheep
(1) **fleece:** the coat of wool of a sheep or other wool-bearing animal
(1) **ewe:** female sheep (the male is called a ram)
(1) **stern:** the rear end, the tail part
(1) **spasmodic:** from **spasm**—an abnormal and involuntary contraction of muscles, often contracting and relaxing in quick alteration
(1) **dung:** animal excrement, bowel discharge
(1) **turnip:** a round, lightly colored fleshy root vegetable, often used in soup or stew
(1) **woeful:** distressed, pitiful, expressing grief
(2) **rapped:** knocked
(2) **muzzle:** the mouth of an animal
(2) **clatter:** to make repeated sharp sounds, usually by hitting objects that carry the sound
(2) **charge:** to rush suddenly and vigorously, often to attack
(2) **skid:** to slide, often as a result of putting on the brakes suddenly
(2) **quiver:** to shake or tremble
(2) **steer:** a young ox; in the cattle family, a male that has been castrated (desexed)

☐ QUESTIONS

---

1. What is the dominant visual impression in paragraph 1? What is the dominant emotion? What purely physical sensation do you feel? Now read the paragraph again and underline the words that portray this picture so clearly and that make you feel the sadness and the cold. How cold is it? How do you know? Why is that important? What does the description of the ewe add?
2. What is the dominant impression in paragraph 2? What adjectives come to your mind to describe the bull? How would you feel if you were in front of it? Notice that none of these adjectives appears in the paragraph. You came to these conclusions because of evidence shown to you. Again, underline the nouns and verbs that show you that bull, for example, words that describe his frightening strength and power.

CHARLES DICKENS

FROM *Great Expectations*

3   My sister, Mrs. Joe, with black hair and eyes, had such a prevailing redness of skin, that I sometimes used to wonder whether it was possible she washed herself with a nutmeg-grater* instead of soap. She was tall and bony, and almost always wore a coarse* apron, fastened over her figure behind with two loops, and having a square impregnable* bib* in front, that was stuck full of pins and needles. She made it a powerful merit in herself, and a strong reproach* against Joe, that she wore this apron so much. Though I really see no reason why she should have worn it at all; or why, if she did wear it at all, she should not have taken it off every day of her life.

☐ QUESTIONS

---

1. What is your impression of Mrs. Joe? Would you recommend her as the ideal mother? Wife? Why not? What details support your impression? (Underline the exact words.)
2. What else might you deduce about Mrs. Joe—her way of life, her way of acting, her way of handling a child—from these details?

(3) **nutmeg-grater:** a grater is an instrument with many sharply edged openings, upon which one rubs a hard piece of food (such as a carrot or hard cheese) to reduce it to very small particles; **nutmeg:** a hard, pleasant-smelling seed that is grated for use as a spice
(3) **coarse:** rough
(3) **impregnable:** not capable of being taken; firm and unyielding
(3) **bib:** the upper part of the apron
(3) **reproach:** a way of blaming him, of making him feel wrong

FRANZ KAFKA

FROM *The Metamorphosis*

4 As Gregor Samsa awoke one morning from uneasy dreams he found himself transformed in his bed into a gigantic insect. He was lying on his hard, as it were armor-plated,* back and when he lifted his head a little he could see his domelike brown belly divided into stiff arched segments on top of which the bed quilt* could hardly keep in position and was about to slide off completely. His numerous legs, which were pitifully thin compared to the rest of his bulk, waved helplessly before his eyes.

□ QUESTIONS

What was your feeling as you read this, the opening paragraph of a long story? Can you imagine what kind of story it will be or what life will be like for Gregor? Of course, people don't just turn into gigantic insects, but so clearly is this change described, and in so factual a manner, that it seems believable. What details convey the unmistakable reality of an insect? What details show us that the insect is clearly a human being so transformed? The facts presented in this selection combine to create a horror, yet nowhere is this horror stated. The unemotional, matter-of-fact treatment only increases the horror, making it seem like a very possible, quite ordinary occurrence.

What we need to know in each of these paragraphs can be reduced to the following:

Paragraph 1. It was very cold the morning the two lambs were born. One was dead, and the other did not look too good. It was very sad.

Paragraph 2. The bull came out of his cage, making a lot of noise. He came out quickly, looking strong, powerful, and frightening.

Paragraph 3. My sister, Mrs. Joe, is not too attractive, nor is she very warm and loving. It is hard to get close to her.

Paragraph 4. A man had turned into a gigantic insect overnight.

If you understand what has been lost in these summaries, you are well on the way to understanding the function and necessary elements of good description. We can summarize the qualities we have observed in the above paragraphs. The next step will be to write your own description, keeping these suggestions in mind.

---

(4) **armor-plated:** armor was the metal suit worn as protection in battle during the Middle Ages

(4) **quilt:** feather-filled bed cover

IN GENERAL, SHOW RATHER THAN TELL

If you give the reader a picture he can really see, and give him the necessary facts and evidence, he will form the impression you want him to form. Do not tell the reader what his opinion is supposed to be. Instead, create a situation, place, or personality in such a way that he will arrive at that opinion. *People are convinced by facts, not by other people's judgments.*

The following are five general rules for writing good descriptions.

1. *Avoid adjectives of judgment* (e.g., ugly, beautiful, good, stupid, mean). *Show* the reader the ugly features, the stupid words or actions, the mean treatment. The adjectives you use should make the reader see or feel something factual (e.g., yellow, coarse, hollow). If you occasionally do use judgmental adjectives, be sure to support them with substantial evidence.

2. *Depend upon nouns and verbs more than adjectives.* Notice that the words you marked in the preceding paragraphs, the words that best conveyed the scene or feeling, were primarily nouns and verbs. Not many adjectives were used, and those that were most "alive" and meaningful were derived from verbs or nouns; e.g., impregnable, bony, spasmodic, woeful, quivering, armor-plated, and arched.

3. *Appeal directly to the senses.* Appeal to one's senses of sight, sound, smell, touch, and taste. When the senses are engaged, the reader becomes more involved in your writing, adding his or her own experience to yours. This is also true of motion.

4. *Supply significant details.* Use concrete, factual details like those in the preceding paragraphs. These details, however, should not be chosen at random, but because they are significant. The author selected them to contribute to the intended impression. Other details that would clutter up the paragraph or add unnecessary information were omitted.

5. *Create a dominant impression.* Choose which major aspects of a situation or qualities of a person you wish to focus on. Then select and use those details and facts that best support the impression.

☐ SUGGESTIONS FOR COMPOSITION

Write *one* good descriptive paragraph following the previous suggestions. Choose something or someone you know well and write in such a way that the reader "sees" what you are describing. If you wish to convey feeling about what you describe, the composition will be still better, but remember to avoid the use of judgmental adjectives. Several composition suggestions follow.

1. Without sounding like a guidebook, describe a place in your part of the world to someone who has never been there. *Remember to include details.*

2. Describe a person's room in such a way that you characterize the individual who lives in it. *Supply details that tell us something about the person's interests,*

personality, and character. You may want to make this up out of your imagination.

3. Describe a person, choosing details or actions that illustrate his or her most outstanding quality. Let your feelings for this person, positive or negative, come through.

4. Describe a mechanical object, such as a kitchen gadget or a tool, so that someone unfamiliar with it would be able to visualize it.

The following excerpts are from a journal kept by the Irish writer John Millington Synge when he went to live for a while on the Aran Islands, located about thirty miles off the Irish coast. Synge went to the islands because he wanted to immerse himself in the old Gaelic language and the folklore of these people whose lives had barely been affected by the modern world.

The descriptions of the people and their way of life are so effective because of Synge's careful choice of details and because he makes connections between the descriptions and the human element: human life, human difficulties, human feelings. As we read these essays, we not only see what he describes, but also get the feel of a way of life.

JOHN MILLINGTON SYNGE

FROM *The Aran Islands*

Pampooties

1   Michael walks so fast when I am out with him that I cannot pick my steps, and the sharp-edged fossils* which abound* in the limestone have cut my shoes to pieces.

2   The family held a consultation on them last night, and in the end it was decided to make me a pair of pampooties, which I have been wearing today among the rocks.

3   They consist simply of a piece of raw cow-skin, with the hair outside, laced over the toe, and round the heel with two ends of fishing line that work round and are tied above the instep.*

4   In the evening, when they are taken off, they are placed in a basin* of water, as the rough hide cuts the foot and stocking if it is allowed to harden. For the same reason the people often step into the surf* during the day, so that their feet are continually moist.

5   At first I threw my weight upon my heels, as one does naturally in a boot, and was a good deal bruised; but after a few hours I learned the natural walk of man, and could follow my guide in any portion of the island.

(1) **fossils:** rock formations preserving traces of plant or animal life
(1) **abound:** are in great quantity
(3) **instep:** the upper surface of the arch of the foot, between the ankle and the toes
(4) **basin:** bowl
(4) **surf:** the waves of the sea breaking upon the shore

6   In one district below the cliffs, toward the north, one goes for nearly a mile jumping from one rock to another without a single ordinary step; and here I realized that toes have a natural use, for I found myself jumping towards any tiny crevice* in the rock before me, and clinging with an eager grip in which all the muscles of my feet ached from their exertion.

7   The absence of the heavy boot of Europe has preserved to these people the agile* walk of the wild animal, while the general simplicity of their lives has given them many other points of physical perfection.

The Time of Day

1   While I am walking with Michael someone often comes to me to ask the time of day. Few of the people, however, are sufficiently used to modern time to understand in more than a vague way the convention* of the hours, and when I tell them what o'clock it is by my watch they are not satisfied, and ask how long is left them before the twilight.

2   The general knowledge of time on the island depends, curiously enough, on the direction of the wind. Nearly all the cottages are built, like this one, with two doors opposite each other, the more sheltered of which lies open all day to give light to the interior. If the wind is northerly the south door is opened, and the shadow of the door-post moving across the kitchen floor indicates the hour; as soon, however, as the wind changes to the south the other door is opened, and the people, who never think of putting up a primitive dial, are at a loss.

3   This system of doorways has another curious result. It usually happens that all the doors on one side of the village pathway are lying open with women sitting about on the thresholds,* while on the other side the doors are shut and there is no sign of life. The moment the wind changes everything is reversed, and sometimes when I come back to the village after an hour's walk there seems to have been a general flight from one side of the way to the other.

4   In my own cottage the change of the doors alters the whole tone of the kitchen, turning it from a brilliantly lighted room looking out on a yard and laneway to a sombre* cell with a superb view of the sea.

5   When the wind is from the north the old woman manages my meals with fair regularity; but on the other days she often makes my tea at three o'clock instead of six. If I refuse it she puts it down to simmer* for three hours in the turf,* and then brings it in at six o'clock full of anxiety to know if it is warm enough.

6   The old man is suggesting that I should send him a clock when I go away.

(6) **crevice:** a narrow opening caused by a crack or a split
(7) **agile:** ready to move quickly and lightly, active, alert

(1) **convention:** custom, the way it is usually done
(3) **thresholds:** doorsills, places of entry
(4) **sombre:** dark and sad
(5) **simmer:** to keep at or just below the boiling point
(5) **turf:** a layer of earth with grass, sometimes used for fuel

He'd like to have something from me in the house, he says, the way they wouldn't forget me, and wouldn't a clock be as handy as another thing, and they'd be thinking on* me whenever they'd look on its face.

7   The general ignorance of any precise hours in the day makes it impossible for the people to have regular meals.

8   They seem to eat together in the evening, and sometimes in the morning a little after dawn, before they scatter for their work; but during the day they simply drink a cup of tea and eat a piece of bread, or some potatoes, whenever they are hungry.

The Wake* and the Keening*

1   After Mass* this morning an old woman was buried. She lived in the cottage next mine, and more than once before noon I heard a faint echo of the keen. I did not go to the wake for fear my presence might jar* upon the mourners, but all last evening I could hear the strokes of a hammer in the yard, where, in the middle of a little crowd of idlers, the next of kin* laboured slowly at the coffin. Today, before the hour for the funeral, poteen* was served to a number of men who stood about upon the road, and a portion was brought to me in my room. Then the coffin was carried out, sewn loosely in sailcloth, and held near the ground by three cross-poles lashed* upon the top. As we moved down to the low eastern portion of the island, nearly all the men, and all the oldest women, wearing petticoats over their heads came out and joined in the procession.

2   While the grave was being opened the women sat down among the flat tombstones, bordered with a pale fringe of early bracken,* and began the wild keen, or crying for the dead. Each old woman, as she took her turn in the leading recitative,* seemed possessed for the moment with a profound ecstasy* of grief, swaying to and fro, and bending her forehead to the stone before her, while she called out to the dead with a perpetually* recurring chant of sobs.

3   All round the graveyard other wrinkled women, looking out from under the deep red petticoats that cloaked them, rocked themselves with the same

(6) **on:** "on" here is *not* standard English; Synge has tried to approximate Gaelic idiom in indirectly quoting the islander

(Title) **wake:** an all-night watch over a corpse before burial, often with festivities (common among the Irish)
(Title) **keen:** a piercing lamentation or wailing (loud crying) over the dead body
(1) **Mass:** a church service
(1) **jar:** to have an irritating effect
(1) **next of kin:** nearest relatives
(1) **poteen:** in Ireland, homemade whiskey
(1) **lashed:** tied
(2) **bracken:** a fern, a type of green plant
(2) **recitative:** a type of singing that is almost like talking or reciting
(2) **ecstasy:** a feeling of being overpowered with emotion (usually used to mean great joy)
(2) **perpetually:** constantly, without stopping

rhythm and intoned the inarticulate* chant that is sustained by all as an accompaniment.

4   The morning had been beautifully fine, but as they lowered the coffin into the grave, thunder rumbled overhead and hailstones hissed among the bracken.

5   In Inishmaan one is forced to believe in a sympathy between man and nature, and at this moment, when the thunder sounded a death peal* of extraordinary grandeur above the voices of the women, I could see the faces near me stiff and drawn with emotion.

6   When the coffin was in the grave, and the thunder had rolled away across the hills of Clare, the keen broke out again more passionately than before.

7   This grief of the keen is no personal complaint for the death of one woman over eighty years, but seems to contain the whole passionate rage that lurks* somewhere in every native of the island. In this cry of pain the inner consciousness of the people seems to lay itself bare for an instant, and to reveal the mood of beings who feel their isolation in the face of a universe that wars on them with winds and seas. They are usually silent, but in the presence of death all outward show of indifference or patience is forgotten, and they shriek with pitiable despair before the horror of the fate to which they all are doomed.

8   Before they covered the coffin an old man kneeled down by the grave and repeated a simple prayer for the dead.

9   There was an irony in these words of atonement* and Catholic belief spoken by voices that were still hoarse with the cries of pagan* desperation.

10   A little beyond the grave I saw a line of old women who had recited in the keen sitting in the shadow of a wall beside the roofless shell of the church. They were still sobbing and shaken with grief, yet they were beginning to talk again of the daily trifles* that veil them from the terrors of the world.

☐ QUESTIONS

Answer the following questions in complete sentences.

1. Why was it easier for the author to walk among the rocks in pampooties?
2. Why are the pampooties kept in a basin of water when they are taken off (use "if" or "unless")?
3. What has been the effect of heavy boots upon the way people walk?
4. For what, besides the death of an eighty-year-old woman, were the mourners crying so passionately (use "not only")?

    (3) **inarticulate:** without understandable speech, unable to express in speech
    (5) **peal:** a loud ringing sound, as of bells, thunder, gunfire, laughter
    (7) **lurks:** lies hidden, waiting
    (9) **atonement:** being sorry for wrongdoing, coming back to God
    (9) **pagan:** refers to primitive religions believing in many gods
  (10) **trifles:** small, unimportant things

☐ FOCUS ON DESCRIPTIVE WRITING

For each of the journal entries, decide *what* it is you see and *how* you are made to see it.

1. "Pampooties"
   Can you picture the pampooties? Do you see just a type of shoe or people in motion? What kind of motion? In what kind of environment? Point out the specific nouns and verbs that convey the pictures and the action to you. What physical sensations are conveyed in this section?
2. "The Time of Day"
   What scenes do you picture? What causes the scenes to change? How do these changes affect mood and atmosphere? What specific words and details convey these different moods and atmospheres? How does the author illustrate the islanders' lack of understanding of clock time?
3. "The Wake and the Keening"
   a. Pretend you are filming this incident. Make a list of what you would focus your camera on, where you would show a close-up, where you would show a larger panoramic scene. Where would you leave the camera focused for a longer time, and where might you perhaps shift back and forth? How would you use sound? That is, what would be heard, and what would be the relationship among the sounds? Would you use black and white or color? Defend your choice. If color, what colors would predominate? How might different colors be effectively used to convey the incident and the feelings?
   b. What words convey the strength and depth of feeling expressed in this essay? Pick out the nouns, verbs, and adjectives that express passion.
   c. Is the return to daily trifles a letdown at the end? Why or why not?

☐ FOCUS ON SENTENCE VARIETY

Change the structure of each of the following sentences as directed.

1. Put into passive voice: "I cannot pick my steps, and the sharp-edged fossils . . . have cut my shoes to pieces." (paragraph 1, "Pampooties")
2. Put into active voice: "The family held a consultation on them last night, and . . . it was decided to make me a pair of pampooties. . . ." (paragraph 2, "Pampooties")
3. Use a noun clause as subject of this sentence: "The general ignorance of any precise hours in the day makes it impossible for the people to have regular meals." (paragraph 7, "The Time of Day")
4. Reconstruct sentence number 3 using an adverbial clause.
5. Use an introductory participial phrase: "They were still sobbing and shaken with grief, yet they were beginning to talk again of the daily trifles. . . ." (paragraph 10, "The Wake and the Keening")
6. Reconstruct sentence number 5 using an adverbial clause.

☐ SUGGESTIONS FOR COMPOSITION

1. Write a detailed description of some aspect of your country's way of life—a ceremony, a custom, a mode of dress, or an event. (Notice that the previous essays were about shoes, a funeral, time as it was perceived by the islanders.) Allow the humanity and the feelings to come through in your essay.
2. You may want to reverse this assignment and describe something about life in America as if you were writing to a friend at home, describing what you have chosen in such a way that he or she will fully understand it.

FIGURATIVE LANGUAGE

It is said that one picture is worth a thousand words. In the same way, an image, a mental picture created by words, can convey more in a few words than whole paragraphs of words that fail to touch our experiences or our senses. When the poet says "my love is like a rose," we respond consciously or unconsciously in several ways. The rose is a flower, beautiful to look at; it is also beautiful to smell; its petals are soft. To three senses, then, sight, smell, and touch, a rose is very appealing. We understand and feel more directly just *how* lovely a woman is when we think of her in comparison to a rose than when we simply hear her described as being "lovely." The poet may want to make other suggestions about the similarities between a rose and his beloved, suggestions that involve more complex emotions or a relationship of conflict. Roses have thorns; they lose their beauty very quickly; they may contain worms or beetles that cause them to rot from within; they eventually die. Guided by the way the writer develops the comparison, we bring our own experience with roses to our understanding of the writer's feelings. And we do so without necessarily thinking about it at all.

When we use an image to express something else, we are using a *metaphor*. We are making a comparison or drawing an analogy between the image we have used and what we are trying to express or explain.* Poets, of course, are very well aware of the power of good metaphors to radiate meaning, but all effective writers and speakers use metaphors to make their communication more real and more immediate to their audiences and to generate more feeling by calling upon what people see or feel. They use metaphors to bring abstract ideas and feelings within the range of our experience and to dramatize those feelings for which words are inadequate. Writers use them as a kind of shorthand—if you "see" the analogy, you understand the writer. When carefully used, figurative language can make writing much more colorful and alive.

Each of the following sentences uses metaphor quite effectively.

"The waves made little salaams to the shore."

(Vladimir Nabokov)

* You may have learned that a *simile* uses like or as to draw such an analogy. A simile is a type of metaphor and, in this discussion, will be included under the more general term *metaphor*.

The Jonny Walker wisdom ... [handwritten, illegible]

"It was as quiet as a leaf changing colors."

> (Musical composition, "As Quiet As . . .", by Michael Colgrass)

"The little girl wanted to speak, but the words stuck in her throat like peanut butter with no jelly."

"The boy's face was a clenched fist."

> (John Ciardi)

"It is a damp, drizzly November in my soul."

> (Herman Melville)

"Perhaps one day he will grow into his powerful position; now it hangs on his shoulders and threatens to trip him as he walks."

You may be able to sympathize with the man in the following selection, who, sent away from his native country, dreaded being in a land where he could not speak the language:

> And now my tongue's use is to me no more
> than an unstringed viol[in] or a harp
> or . . . [an] instrument . . . put into . . . hands
> that know no touch to tune the harmony.
> Within my mouth you have enjailed my tongue
> And . . . ignorance is made my jailor.

> (From *Richard II* by William Shakespeare)

☐ EXPERIMENTING WITH FIGURATIVE LANGUAGE

as disconcerting as a drawing by E... [handwritten, illegible]

1. Try to create your own metaphors. Choose a common adjective such as quiet, strong, weak, wild, or stupid and use it to create an "as . . . as" analogy (e.g., as wild as a summer storm). Or use the word *like* to write a metaphor modifying a noun (e.g., her eyes were like dying coals). Avoid using expressions you have heard frequently (such overused expressions are called trite expressions).
2. Think of idioms (e.g., Keep your shirt on!) or proverbs in English or in your own language that function figuratively, not literally. For example, "Trust in God, but tie up your camel" is not only meant for people who have camels.

☐ SUGGESTION FOR COMPOSITION

Choose a proverb, preferably one from your own country, and write about an experience that illustrates the truth of the proverb. Make clear the analogy between the proverb and your experience.

In the following essay, the descriptions of a landscape, a boy, and a train combine to transport us to a time past. Notice the careful use of metaphor throughout.

MARSHA RABE

Passages

1   There is land in central Illinois that is as flat as the floor. It does not roll and ripple* into hills, nor does it fill, lift, and erupt* like sails into mountains the way some land does. The most it grants, and this begrudgingly,* is to warp and buckle* where rare and subtle sorts of lumps appear; but these lumps are not hills and this land is very flat.

2   It happens more frequently of late* that when I imagine my father, I see him not as the large, soft, hazy* man I have always known, but as a boy of nine, standing on a dark spot in this flat Illinois land, standing near a railroad crossing. It is night and it is hot. Summer here is dreadful, windless. The air clots* and settles close to the ground, while the sky, smeared thick with stars, floats farther away than at other times of the year. It is cricket* season, baseball season.

3   My father's father was a passenger conductor on the Chicago and Alton Railroad. He had the best and fastest run from Chicago to St. Louis. It was 1915 when on Friday afternoon my grandfather, who had gone to Chicago on a morning train, phoned Walt Hempfing, the dispatcher in my father's hometown, and asked him to call my grandmother and tell her to pack an overnight bag and have Louis, my father, at the crossing that night at 11 o'clock so he could pick him up as his train swept through town. "The Cubs* are in St. Louis tomorrow, Walt. Jim Lavender is pitching. It's time Louis sees a big league game. It's time he sees the Cubs."

4   The signal switch near where my father stands lights and begins to swing back and forth. In the clockwork flashing back and forth, back and forth like a pendulum, I see that my father is a little boy. He is wearing baggy knickers* that bellow around his thick, straight legs like a cloud. Long, thin socks pucker* at his knees and tuck into high-button shoes cut just above his ankles. He also wears a loose, wrinkled white shirt, a long, thin tie, and a cloth-banded straw hat. From his left hand hangs a small suitcase, and in his right he holds a pocket watch. His head is bent—I cannot see his face for the flashing shadows and the brim of his hat—but I *can* see that he is looking into the palm of his right hand to check the time.

5   As I watch, the signal switch begins to clang and my father looks to his

---

(1) **ripple:** to make small waves
(1) **erupt:** burst out
(1) **begrudgingly:** giving without wanting to give
(1) **buckle:** bend
(2) **of late:** recently
(2) **hazy:** foggy, not clear
(2) **clots:** forms into lumps; coagulates
(2) **cricket:** an insect that begins in late summer to chirp loudly at night
(3) **Cubs:** Chicago baseball team
(4) **knickers:** boys' short trousers, gathered just below the knee; fashionable at that time
(4) **pucker:** fold, wrinkle

left. A train is coming. First to arrive is its whistle, a metallic honk like an elephant's call. Then its threading lights appear, bright across the cow pastures and corn fields, blinking on and off behind the trees and barns, scintillating,* seeming to shatter and then, miraculously, to heal and reappear, whole. My father watches, then notes the time. 10:58. It's on time.

6   So there he is and I see him, a little boy on a hot night, waiting on flat, adamant* land, while a huge, punctual monster uncoils toward him, rushing and rising up out of the dark, hurtling* across the still fields, frightening small animals and birds, shocking the earth itself. The train is the only thing with lights for miles around, and his father is bringing it to him. For a long time he watches, because the land is so flat and he can see so far, and all the time I watch him watching I try to imagine how grand he must feel, the object of all this roaring commotion,* of this hissing power.

7   Here it comes, closer, larger, louder. Brakes grind, out pours steam like a wet sigh. The engine chokes, jolts, and gently stops in front of him. Directly, deliberately in front of him. His father lowers a large hand and whisks him aboard. Sweaty smiles and grave excitement all around, and they are off, off to St. Louis, off to Jim Lavender, and off to the Cubs, who lost that game, my father tells me, 3 to 2.

☐ FOCUS ON DESCRIPTIVE WRITING

1. Make a list of the metaphors used in the preceding selection. Notice that *verbs* can also be used metaphorically, e.g., "smeared" (paragraph 2), "swept" (paragraph 3), and "uncoils" (paragraph 6).
2. What nouns and verbs, used literally, give you a clear picture of the scene and the boy?
3. What is the dominant impression of the train? How is this impression an important introduction to these sentences: "The train is the only thing with lights for miles around, and his father is bringing it to him. . . . I try to imagine how grand he must feel. . . ."? Besides a description of the event, what do these sentences convey?
4. This essay appeals to the ear as well as to the eye. Explain how the sounds of the following words contribute to the total description.
   a. "clang" (paragraph 5)
   b. "honk" (paragraph 5)
   c. "this hissing power" (paragraph 6)
   d. "out pours steam like a wet sigh" (paragraph 7)
5. In paragraph 4, "back and forth" is used three times. Why is this effective? Read this sentence aloud: "The engine chokes, jolts, and gently stops in front of

(5) **scintillating:** sparkling, flashing
(6) **adamant:** firm, hard, unyielding
(6) **hurtling:** coming forward with a crash, moving violently and noisily
(6) **commotion:** disorder, disturbance

him." How does the rhythm of successive one-syllable words contribute to the total impression?

6. Why is the essay written in the present tense? Why the *simple* present?

7. Why do we need the introductory description of the flat land?

☐ SUGGESTION FOR COMPOSITION

Choose an event from your childhood or from your recent past and present it, including a detailed description of the *place* and the *person*. Use metaphors, sounds, and sentence structures to reinforce the impression you want to create.

DESCRIPTIVE WRITING AND METAPHOR IN A POEM

Read the following poem, preferably out loud, and try to "see" the picture it "paints," hear the sound it makes, and feel what the speaker in the poem is feeling.

ROBERT FROST

Storm Fear

When the wind works against us in the dark,
And pelts* with snow
The lower-chamber window on the east,
And whispers with a sort of stifled* bark,*
The beast,
"Come out! Come out!"—
It costs no inward struggle not to go,
Ah, no!
I count our strength,
Two and a child,
Those of us not asleep subdued* to mark*
How the cold creeps as the fire dies at length—
How drifts are piled,
Dooryard and road ungraded,*
Till even the comforting barn grows far away,
And my heart owns* a doubt
Whether 'tis in us to arise with day
And save ourselves unaided.

pelts: strikes or beats heavily
stifled: smothered, kept in check, suppressed
bark: the sound dogs make
subdued: conquered, brought under control
mark: observe, pay attention to; to identify as by a mark
ungraded: *not* classifiable by distinct steps; *not* made level or sloped evenly for a roadway
owns: here, admits

□ QUESTIONS

1. Describe the scene in your own words.
2. To what senses does the poem appeal? Name the exact words that appeal to these senses.
3. Why is "the beast" introduced? How is it used as metaphor? What other words in the poem support the image of the beast? (Hint: look up the *noun* pelt in the dictionary.)
4. Read aloud the first six lines. What two sounds are repeated several times? How does repetition of these sounds intensify our experience of the storm?
5. What is the "strength" he counts? What does this "count" represent together with the house? To what extent can he count *on* (that is, rely on or depend on) this strength?
6. What is opposed to that strength? Which seems stronger? How do you interpret "unaided"? Notice that it is a past participle, implying a passive voice. This can always raise the question by whom or by what? Ask that question and give *your* view of the answer.
7. Explain the title. Of what is the speaker afraid? Is the fear justified? Explain, using specific details. Explain line 15; why is the barn "comforting"? How is it growing far away? How does that line contribute to the sense of insecurity?
8. Does the poem seem to have application beyond a single snow storm? What?
9. Notice that the first sentence (lines 1 through 8) has a logical structure: "When the wind . . ." then "it costs no inward struggle not to go." In other words, "it costs no inward struggle not to go" when the wind and storm are so terrible, so dangerous. Qualified as the sentence is by the when clause, what does the sentence imply about *other* times when "the beast" whispers "come out! come out!"? Can you attach a broader metaphorical association to beast other than simply the storm?

Now reread the poem out loud without stopping and allow its meaning to come together for you. Notice how it has become enriched by the possibilities of its meanings while it remains a vivid picture of a storm, a vivid emotion of fear.

□ CHALLENGING YOUR ABILITY TO DESCRIBE

1. Describe the painting (Figure 4) in such a way that a person who has never seen it will be able to visualize it.
   You may find that you are having a problem with it! Keep describing—*just* describing—what you see, without trying to explain or interpret it.
2. Now, if you like, try to explain the painting. The more closely you examine the painting, the more you may find that explanations are not really satisfactory. But remember, a painting is not a photograph. A painter can create his own version of reality.
3. Perhaps you would like to try interpreting what you have described. Could the painting possibly be a metaphor? Of what? How does it work? Why might someone find it difficult to see this painting as a metaphor?

Menil Foundation, Inc., Houston, Texas

4. The original French title of this painting is *La Lunette d'Approche*. In English this means "a small telescope." Does this knowledge help you, or does this just create new problems? If so, how do you resolve them?
5. This painting is by a Belgian surrealist painter named René Magritte. You may want to look up the meaning of surrealism or look at a book of Magritte's paintings—an unusual experience!

Description is seldom used for its own sake. Usually it contributes to our understanding of an event, a person, a situation, an emotion, a relationship, or a social or cultural phenomenon. As was stated at the beginning of this chapter, description helps us to get involved. In the following compositions, narrative is combined with description to give us a real feeling for the events, the situations, and the people who participate in them.

STUDENT COMPOSITIONS

The Coming of Tết

The day of happiness was coming. My family like millions of others were preparing for that important New Year day which we called "Tết." It is a most special celebration, and it represents the joy of the country like the idea of Christmas vacation.

When I was in sixth or seventh grade in high school, a few days before school was over, everyone in my class looked fatigued; my close friend, who was next to me, was already taking his vacation as he sank his head on the desk. On the board, even the "not-easy" math teacher also had stopped her monotonous voice and changed to the topic Tết. Suddenly 50 heads rose up at the same time, opening their eyes widely. The whole country was waking up after a long year of sleep. The noises of cannons could not be heard by anyone anymore; the soldiers had come home to their families.*

It was finally time for the school to close its iron gate. I ran quickly toward home throwing my books onto the shelf and mumbling to myself, "No more books for a while, no more home work, no more tests; I am free, free...!" Now you understand why I like Tết so much. My five brothers and sisters now were at home also. We began to "clean" our house to its absolute cleanest by definition of the dictionary: the floor, the walls, the corners were swept and mopped carefully. It was hard to see a single tiny spot of dust on the wall!

After lunch my mother took her most helpful children with her to the open-air market. I was lucky enough to be chosen. As we approached the crowd, we were completely surrounded by the laughing, the talking, and the noisy advertising. I ran in front of everyone in my family and stared at the delicious coconuts, dark purple prunes, red tomatoes, jams covered by thick white layers of sugar outside. Immediately, I pointed my finger in that direction to show my mother. We passed by a few stalls full of the newest clothes hanging everywhere. The fat lady, the seller, seemed to be covered by these new clothes; it was hard to recognize her, except for her round funny-looking face. We continued to search for goods and foods. On the way, I bought some new year greeting cards to send to my friends. Our next stop was at the watermelon stall; I saw a huge pyramid formed by giant solid

---

* Notice how simply we are told something very important. This sentence hasn't a single adjective or descriptive word in it. The facts are enough; they add another whole dimension of feeling and significance to the holiday.

green watermelons. Just looking at the red juicy sample which the seller showed to my mother was enough to make me thirsty.

Meanwhile, at home, my father, imagining himself in the army now, commanded my older brother to decorate the altar. On the floor, my youngest brother was happily working on his duty of cleaning the incense burners. In another corner of the living room, on the slender plant called "Mai" plant, my father was hanging the few dozen greeting cards sent by our family friends. The plant was very special, as its flowers only bloomed at the time of the New Year. My father, too, was pleased with his accomplishment; he walked back and forth watching the balance of the cards hanging in the air.

In the kitchen my mother was making food immediately after the shopping. I realized that she was making a special kind of cake, the New Year rice cake: it was eight inches square, and in the middle of the cake, my mother put meat, green beans, and seasonings surrounded by the sticky rice. Outside she used banana leaves to wrap the cake. . . .

My Relative's Wedding Party

In the summer of 1968, one of my relatives came to visit us on a huge brown donkey. It was the first time he had visited us in my life. I was surprised about the heavy clothes which he was wearing in the hot weather. He was wearing a *barnoce,* which was a piece of cloth made of sheep's wool, wide at the bottom, narrow at the top. It had a cowl at the top, and at the neck both sides were connected by a thread of silk in a beautiful Arabesque decoration. He said that he wore it all the time, and if he took it off, he would get sick. Besides that, he was also wearing wonderful pants which looked like the pants of the Arabs in the twelfth century. They had decoration on both sides from the bottom to the pockets. Those pants were also made of silk. He had a yellow turban covering his head making him look like someone who was injured on his head in an accident. He did not have shoes, but he had two pieces of leather under his feet, both of which were connected to his feet by a thread to protect them from the heat of the ground. Those were called *gaa.*

He stayed in our house two weeks. He told my father that he was going to make a party right after he got back, because his son was going to get married. He invited us to that party, and my father accepted his invitation.

The relative was living in the country. When we arrived, all the people came to welcome us. My relative's family took us to a big room where we noticed that all the women had tattooing on their faces and hands.

The party was two days later. They usually had the party before the bride was brought to it. It started in the afternoon. All the people were wearing new clothes with bright colors. The women were wearing long dresses and expensive jewelry. They were singing inside the house and playing drums. The men and the children were outside listening to the folk music which was played by two old men on an old instrument which looked like a reed. After one hour, they stopped playing. An old man started shouting that it was time for afternoon coffee. The people were divided into many groups. Each group contained six people. Then the coffee was brought in silver jugs and served with date cake. When everyone finished his coffee, the music started again until the sun set. They turned on some lights of petrol or olive oil. They started serving dinner for men first, which consisted of soup with traditional bread, couscous with lamb meat, vegetables, and summer fruit such as watermelon, grapes, and dates. When they finished serving dinner for men, they started serving it to the women and children, while the men were drinking coffee. When I finished my dinner, I went to where my father was sitting. While I was listening to the jokes between two old men, someone asked what time it was. An old man looked toward the sky and said it was 9:30. I was surprised. I looked at my father and asked him how he knew the time without a watch. My father told me that they used stars to know the time at night, and the shadow of the sun to know the time during the day.

Around 10 o'clock, the music started again. Some old men stood in two lines facing each other and they began playing a fantastic game called *fantazia*. They were carrying guns and they fired all of them simultaneously with a special movement. When they finished, some old women and men started dancing a kind of Old Bailey dance. The party lasted until 3 o'clock in the morning.

The next morning, a group of people, mostly young girls, went to bring the bride. Her home was just about ten minutes away from my relative's house. When they came back, and before they entered the house, a plate which consisted of some dates, wheat, and two eggs were brought, and the bride was asked to throw these on the people who were behind her. She did as she was asked; then the guns were fired. They took the bride to her new house, and started singing some special songs for her.

I was really so excited that summer that I hated to leave when my father told me to get ready to go home.

In the preceding composition, there was not as much sentence variety as there might have been because the student who wrote it was not advanced enough to handle this comfortably. This shows us, then, that even the less advanced student can write an exciting, vivid composition. Which details help us to share his experience and the environment with him?

You Can't Go Home Again

When I thought of my parents and brothers last summer I felt that I really missed them and I wanted to see them after two years in college. I went back during the first week of June and as the plane was landing I really felt excited about meeting and chatting with my family again. The first thing I noticed when I stepped off the plane was the smell of the country, which I had not noticed before. I remembered smelling America when I first came here and thought that only foreign countries have a distinguished smell.

A crowd of passengers was gathered around the conveyor belts that were bringing in all the luggage when I walked into the airport's arrival terminal. There was a larger crowd, waving their hands, beyond the immigration blockages. The children were jumping and running around with excitement while the adults were looking anxiously, and somehow they had a worried look on their faces. After my bags were checked I stepped out into the waiting crowd of people and suddenly I was surrounded by my family. That was the first instance that I had the funny feeling of being a stranger among my own family. It was not that any of them or I had changed so much physically but something deeper that I just couldn't place at that time.

We went home and I told them as much about America as I remembered. At 2:00 A.M. when everyone had gone to bed, which was about three hours after I first stepped into the house, I found that I still could not shake the strangeness that I felt. The smell of the house, the sound of the night insects, the feelings I felt were all very strange to me.

When I woke up, the sun was just rising in the eastern horizon and from my new bed I could see the strength and fierceness that it possesses. The "egg yolk"–like light seemed to tell me that I was at home and everything would be like the past. Just as the sun would rise again tomorrow, everything would be the same. A few days later the conversations I had with my family began to get shorter and shorter. The person with new information was beginning to run out of interesting stories and all the members of my family were getting back into their routine, normal life without me in it.

I decided to call up a friend about a week later and we went to a pub to talk. We carried out conversations that were totally out of character. He told me about how much he had done and what he had achieved, as if to show that he was as good as, if not better off than, I am by going to college in the United States. We talked about good times we had, but never good times we might have. When we talked about politics, his nationalistic feelings were never shared by me. I was glad that the evening came to an end as we were running out of things to say. The uncomfortable and uneasy feelings I am sure were mutually felt, and we parted on the note that we hoped to meet again sometime in the future.

In the house, I started to help my mother with the housework, like hanging the clothes to dry, washing vegetables, but most of all getting in her way. She has been doing all this routinely for so many years, and I was sure she would prefer my not helping. Like the rest of my family, my mother went out of her way to find things for me to do.

The communication level differences between my family and me were very distinct as the weeks passed, and somehow none of them really understood me. I had learned in the United States to be precise and straight to the point in my conversations, but they felt threatened and uneasy and often retaliated. I asked my brother one day why this was so and he advised me by saying, "In Malaysia do as the Malaysians do," as if I was a foreigner in Malaysia.

I guess when I left Malaysia for the United States two years ago I left a hole that my family had filled, and now that I return, there is no hole there for me. It didn't help that I left when I was a teenage boy and came home an adult. The change I went through in the transition was never shared by them and somehow it left a gap between us. I tried to dig a hole when I came back but the hole was different and I could never fit into it.

When I was waving goodbye to my family on my trip back to the United States, I saw my parents' faces and knew that they knew as well as I did that home for me was where I could dig a new hole and fit in it. I now understood that the worried faces on the parents waiting in the airport were that their children will never be the same anymore and that they will never be able to come home again.

☐   QUESTIONS

1. How has the student used figurative language to make his story more vivid? Find specific metaphors and comment on them. How about the title? Does the writer mean, literally, that he can't go back to the house he came from?
2. To what senses does this essay appeal? Find specific examples, and show how they make the scene and the feelings come alive for you.
3. The writer begins and ends at the airport. How does this serve to "frame" his story? Notice especially the reference to the facial expression of the waiting parents.

5

PROCESS ANALYSIS

When we describe how something was done, or explain how to do it, we use a form of writing called **process analysis.** *Process analysis is frequently used in scientific writing. For example, it can be used when writing implementation or methods in lab reports or when writing operating instructions.* Such writing proceeds in chronological order, outlining clearly the necessary steps or stages in sequence. While process analysis uses the same chronological techniques and transitions that narrative writing does, its focus and purpose are quite different. In narration we are most interested in what happened; we want to know more about the characters, their motives, the point of view, and the outcome. In process analysis, however, our main interest is the answer to the question *How?* How is a result achieved? Or, how can we accomplish the same goal or perform the same task?

Sometimes we are interested in information about a historical process (how events worked in the past) or a natural process (perhaps how plants or animals develop) or a technical process (how a device functions). These all invite discussions of the way specific things have been done in the past or the way they usually function in some generalized present.

Another type of process composition details the necessary steps one must take to do the process. This is *directional, instructional process* writing. Typical examples are instructions for putting something together or recipes, which tell the cook how to prepare a food. *In such directional process writing, you should rely on the imperative.*

The selection that follows is an example of process analysis telling how something was done—here, how sentence formulation, reading, and writing were taught to a girl who was both blind and deaf. Helen Keller, born in 1880 and struck blind and deaf by illness when nineteen months old, was taught to speak, read, and write by Anne Sullivan, a remarkable teacher who came to tutor Helen when she was seven years old. That was the beginning of a lifelong association. Still deaf and blind, Helen was able, with her teacher's help, to become educated at Harvard. She wrote books and articles and lectured widely, for she had become a famous woman and an inspiring example of what is possible in the face of overwhelming handicaps.

Anne Sullivan wrote of this teaching process in greater length and detail in her letters, but she made this shorter summary of her methods in her "Report to the Perkins Institution, 1887." At that time, the Perkins Institution of Boston was probably the greatest in the world for the teaching of blind children and their teachers.

At the beginning of the report, Miss Sullivan summarizes the way she taught Helen that "everything has a name" by spelling the name for everything into her hand. The great breakthrough in Helen's education came when she began to understand the relationship between words and things. (For a moving account of Helen's awakening to the meaning of language as she later wrote about it, see "Helen's Awakening to Language," pages 223–225.) The following excerpt begins *after* that point, showing how Helen's education progressed from simply understanding "naming" (that is, concrete nouns) to other parts of speech, sentences, reading, and writing.

ANNE SULLIVAN

Teaching Sentences, Reading, and Writing to Helen Keller

1   Everything she touched had to be named for her, and repetition was seldom necessary. Neither the length of the word nor the combination of letters seems to make any difference to the child. Indeed, she remembers *heliotrope** and *chrysanthemum** more readily than she does shorter names. At the end of August she knew 625 words.

2   This lesson was followed by one on words indicative of place-relations. Her dress was put in a trunk, and then on it, and these prepositions were spelled for her. Very soon she learned the difference between on and in, though it was some time before she could use these words in sentences of her own. Whenever it was possible she was made the actor in the lesson, and was delighted to stand on the chair, and to be put into the wardrobe.* In connection with this lesson she learned the names of members of the family and the word *is*. "Helen is in wardrobe," "Mildred is in crib," "Box is on table," "Papa is on bed," are specimens of sentences constructed by her during the latter part of April.

3   Next came a lesson on words expressive of positive quality.* For the first lesson I had two balls, one made of worsted,* large and soft, the other a bullet. She perceived the difference in size at once. Taking the bullet she made her habitual sign for *small*—that is, by pinching a little bit of the skin of one hand. Then she took the other ball and made her sign for *large* by spreading both hands over it. I substituted the adjectives *large* and *small* for those signs. Then her attention was called to the hardness of the one ball and the softness of the other, and she learned *soft* and *hard.* A few minutes afterward she felt of her little sister's head and said to her mother, "Mildred's head is small and hard." Next I tried to teach her the meaning of *fast* and *slow.* She helped me wind

(1) **heliotrope and chrysanthemum:** names of flowers
(2) **wardrobe:** large cupboard used for hanging clothes
(3) **positive quality:** modifiers, adjectives
(3) **worsted:** wool, to be used for knitting

some worsted one day, first rapidly and afterward slowly. I then said to her with the finger alphabet, "wind fast," or "wind slow," holding her hands and showing her how to do as I wished. The next day, while exercising, she spelled to me, "Helen wind fast," and began to walk rapidly. Then she said, "Helen wind slow," again suiting her action to the words.

4   I now thought it time to teach her to read printed words. A slip on which was printed, in raised letters, the word *box* was placed on the object; and the same experiment was tried with a great many articles, but she did not immediately comprehend that the label-name represented the thing. Then I took an alphabet sheet and put her finger on the letter A, at the same time making A with my fingers. She moved her finger from one printed character to another as I formed each letter on my fingers. She learned all the letters, both capital and small, in one day. Next I turned to the first page of the primer and made her touch the word *cat,* spelling it on my fingers at the same time. Instantly she caught the idea, and asked me to find *dog* and other words. Indeed, she was much displeased because I could not find her name in the book. Just then I had no sentences in raised letters which she could understand, but she would sit for hours feeling each word in her book. When she touched one with which she was familiar, a peculiarly sweet expression lighted her face, and we saw her countenance* growing sweeter and more earnest every day. About this time I sent a list of the words she knew to Mr. Anagnos,* and he very kindly had them printed for her. Her mother and I cut up several sheets of printed words so that she could arrange them into sentences. This delighted her more than anything she had yet done; and the practice thus obtained prepared the way for the writing lessons. There was no difficulty in making her understand how to write the same sentences with pencil and paper which she made every day with the slips, and she very soon perceived that she need not confine herself to phrases already learned, but could communicate any thought that was passing through her mind. I put one of the writing boards used by the blind between the folds of the paper on the table, and allowed her to examine an alphabet of the square letters such as she was to make. I then guided her hand to form the sentence, "Cat does drink milk." When she finished it she was overjoyed. She carried it to her mother, who spelled it to her.

5   Day after day she moved her pencil in the same tracks along the grooved* paper, never for a moment expressing the least impatience or sense of fatigue.

6   As she had now learned to express her ideas on paper, I next taught her the braille* system. She learned it gladly when she discovered that she could herself read what she had written; and this still affords* her constant pleasure.

(4) **countenance:** face
(4) **Mr. Anagnos:** director of the Perkins Institution
(5) **grooved:** lines cut or folded into the paper
(6) **braille:** the system of raised dots that allows the blind to read, using their fingers
(6) **affords:** gives

For a whole evening she will sit at the table writing whatever comes into her busy brain; and I seldom find any difficulty in reading what she has written.

The following is from Helen Keller's own writing, detailing some of this same process.

1   The next important step in my education was learning to read.

2   As soon as I could spell a few words my teacher gave me slips of cardboard on which were printed words in raised letters. I quickly learned that each printed word stood for an object, an act, or a quality. I had a frame in which I could arrange the words in little sentences; but before I ever put sentences in the frame I used to make them in objects. I found the slips of paper which represented, for example, "doll," "is," "on," "bed" and placed each name on its object; then I put my doll on the bed with the words *is, on, bed* arranged beside the doll, thus making a sentence of the words, and at the same time carrying out the idea of the sentence with the things themselves.

3   One day, Miss Sullivan tells me, I pinned the word *girl* on my pinafore and stood in the wardrobe. On the shelf I arranged the words, *is, in, wardrobe.* Nothing delighted me so much as this game. My teacher and I played it for hours at a time. Often everything in the room was arranged in object sentences.*

4   From the printed slip it was but a step to the printed book. I took my "Reader for Beginners" and hunted for the words I knew; when I found them my joy was like that of a game of hide-and-seek. Thus I began to read.†

☐ FOCUS ON PROCESS

---

1. List the steps in the process of teaching Helen, from naming to writing.
2. If you can remember how you were taught English, list the steps in *that* process. Are there similarities between Helen's educational process and your own? Are there differences? Discuss them.
3. Underline the transitional words that carry you from step to step as you read, especially words that keep you moving chronologically or that make the succession of steps clearer.
4. Notice that the verb *is* was introduced along with prepositions. How do you suppose other verbs were taught to Helen?

The essay that follows is an example of writing about a process in nature. The author has lived in wild habitats and worked in biological laboratories. This selection is only the first part of a longer article, which is part of a book entitled *Wild Heritage.*

(3) **object sentences:** sentences arranged using the objects themselves, rather than only the words for them

† In this same book, *The Story of My Life* by Helen Keller, are Helen's and Anne Sullivan's accounts of the way Helen learned the meaning of such abstractions as thought, love, death, and various religious ideas. The book provides some fascinating insights into language learning and also into a developing mind.

SALLY CARRIGHAR

FROM *Sex: The Silent Bell*

1   By the time that young animals reach maturity, most of them have absorbed from their parents' teaching, or from sharing adult activities, all they will need to know for their everyday living. But nothing has helped to prepare them for finding a mate. For each of the many animal species the mating customs are different. They are of dazzling* variety and in some species extremely elaborate. Dances, calls, and songs, special displays of fur, feathers, or pigmented skin: each detail is traditional; each step of a dance, note of a song, or seductive* movement has been decreed. Even more strict are the prohibitions, especially in regard to timing. The growing animal soon will perform all these rites,* and yet no one will tell him what he must do and must not do. No elder will give him advice, no companions share sexual secrets.

2   In a way he is fortunate. He has inherited no religious taboos,* and he won't have his natural way confused by fashions in loving—fashions, temporary and artificial, which are a pressure exerted on young human animals by movies, television, advertising, popular songs, and books. A wild creature does not have to reconcile* such conflicting notions of love as Casanova's* and Romeo's* or those of conflicting live models that he might want to copy. And no psychiatrist analyzes any animal's sexual difficulties, reducing to the small, precise dimensions of words what the lover probably feels as amorphous*—and dark and immense. Strictly, completely on their own are all animals, male and female, when sex overtakes them.

3   Yet they do have a guide, the one within: instinct. It does not shout, and some animals have to learn how to listen. The more complex, highly evolved* mammals may do more than a little fumbling* in their approach to first mates. We often assume that the coupling of animals is abrupt, brief, and fully effective from the beginning. That is not always true. And many of them go through a preliminary anguish* that would seem familiar to the parents of adolescents. A human father or mother would recognize the irritability, ten-

(1) **dazzling:** brilliant in an overpowering way; arousing admiration by brilliant display
(1) **seductive:** tempting; often used for tempting sexually
(1) **rites:** serious, ceremonial acts associated with religion or other formal customary observances or procedures; rituals
(2) **taboo:** something forbidden by the rules or conventions of that society
(2) **reconcile:** to bring (back) into agreement
(2) **Casanova:** legendary great lover who kept going from one woman to the next
(2) **Romeo:** hero of Shakespeare's *Romeo and Juliet* who killed himself because he thought his beloved was dead
(2) **amorphous:** shapeless; having no specified form
(3) **evolved:** here, higher on the evolutionary scale; developed gradually
(3) **fumbling:** handling awkwardly; failing to catch or hold properly
(3) **anguish:** great mental or physical pain

sions, and tantrums;* the strange eating habits, fasting one day and stuffing the next; the benumbed* attachment to one individual, who may appear even less prepossessing* than others. As some animals enter their breeding cycle, they show these signs of disturbed emotions. Nevertheless, they develop a responsiveness to the prompting of instinct that is almost incomprehensible to a human being. We who are human have lost the ear for those signals—to such an extent that the peak of the average civilized woman's receptiveness does not even come, now, at the time when she could conceive. Hers is a deafness that would have caused any other species to become extinct. Let us watch a porcupine,* one of the mammals who is most sensitive to the sound of her bell. She is necessarily so alert because her internal program allows her only a very brief time to mate.

4   This one is rather young, having had but one previous pregnancy. Now in July she is her normal self and could be described as a happy little creature with a considerable talent for amusing herself. She lives on a farm in New Hampshire, one abandoned these many years by its human owners. Here a company of a dozen porcupines have established several dens, in the cellar of the old house, in the barn, and in two or three rock piles. Although there are no close companions among them, the porcupines treat one another with tolerance, and they have flexible social habits. On one night a group of six or eight may sleep in one of the dens together; on the following night, three or four. Some like to sleep alone. Our female prefers a crevice* among the rocks into which, she has found, she just fits. But when the weather is stormy she may cuddle in with some others.

5   Food is no problem; the leaves and bark of the trees in the woodlot, and now in summer the soft green meadow plants, keep the colony nourished with only the effort of chewing up the fibers. And the porcupines fear no enemies. Dogs come around sometimes; if they could get to the porcupine flesh, they know by its scent they would find it delicious, but the porcupines have an easy defense. They just back up to a dog, raise their quills,* flip a barbed* tail in his face, and he runs away howling. The male porcupines enjoy wrestling, but they are careful to remain facing each other, there being no quills in the fine, soft fur of their bellies. They like to challenge the females, but when they do, they make sure that the game is welcome.

6   The one that concerns us will not often wrestle. She prefers other ways to let her energy boil up in play. Now in the moonlight she lies on her back

(3) **tantrum:** a violent outburst of anger
(3) **benumbed:** as if paralyzed
(3) **prepossessing:** pleasing; impressing favorably
(3) **porcupine:** an animal whose hair is mixed with long, stiff, sharp spines, the sharp points of which protect it from other animals
(4) **crevice:** narrow opening caused by a crack or split
(5) **quills:** sharp, pointed spines of the porcupine; stiff feathers of a bird, from which pens used to be made
(5) **barbed:** sharp; pointed

at the edge of the meadow, and with all four feet in the air she fools with* a stick. She bats it around, tugs* it, gnaws* it, and throws it away. Next she pretends to defeat an enemy: this old stump,* couldn't it be a dog? She backs up to it, raises her quills, and thrashes* her tail against it, enjoying the rattling, a warning, made by the quills.

7   This is one of her better nights. She will go and gnaw on an old rusty oil drum beside the drive. It makes a splendid loud clanging, and like all porcupines, this one delights in any resonant sound. She likes something else: rhythm. She stands upright and marks time with her hind feet, swaying from side to side and giving her own particular twist to the dance—a turn of one wrist and the other in time with her steps. Two of the porcupine colony join her. One keeps reaching down, also in time with his steps, as though he were lifting things. Another male walks past the dancers. He acts as if he were not seeing them; then he wheels suddenly, seizes the female, and holds her and bites her neck—gently, for this is not sex play, not in July. She wriggles* away from him. Sensing that she is not angry, he chases her in a little game, like a pup playing tag,* but more cautiously, never ignoring those quills.

8   A free season, now, with her young one looking after himself and the new mating program not yet beginning: a sweet season, but short.

9   By the middle of August the porcupine is becoming nervous. The ease, the lightness are gone from her mood. She still goes through some of the motions of playing, but now it is with an urgency. Even when she is well fed, she bites into sticks and the bark of trees, often impatiently. She climbs the trees for no reason, going up and coming right down again. She and the other porcupines do their dance several times a day, and faster. They do everything faster. A new whining* sound often is heard in the woodlot and meadow, a complaining about the mate-hunger that grows within them. The female whines are subdued;* the males' are more shrill and louder.

10   The hunger is generalized at first, a diffuse restlessness. The males fight rather frequently with each other, not ever now with the female. She won't stand for much. By the end of September the hunger is starting to be a torment.* It is more localized; our porcupine tries to get some relief by touching herself to the rocks, to the stump, to the ground. After she puts her scent on the ground, one of the males is likely to come by and pick up that

(6) **fools with:** plays around with
(6) **tugs:** pulls
(6) **gnaws:** chews
(6) **stump:** what is left in the ground when a tree has been cut down
(6) **thrashes:** beats against; tosses violently
(7) **wriggles:** twists and turns
(7) **tag:** a children's game in which the object is to touch those who are running away from you
(9) **whining:** a drawn-out sound, almost like crying, of complaint, as complaining little children sound
(9) **subdued:** tamed; made lower in force; conquered
(10) **torment:** torture, great pain, or suffering

bit of earth in his forepaw and smell it. But no male pursues her. They will leave her alone until she has given a sign that some one of them is acceptable.

11   Still the tension continues, the hunger increases. The porcupine has a new trick for relief. She goes around riding a stick, walking upright and dragging one end of the stick on the ground, between her hind legs, holding the other end in a forepaw. The males have similar, solitary diversions.

12   Why are the sexes so slow to approach each other? Are they stupid? No, they are very smart, exquisitely sensitive to the inner instructions. However difficult waiting is, they will delay till the final bell, which will ring for the female when her physical preparations are quite complete.

13   She now enters a different phase. She becomes very quiet, seeming unnaturally subdued. She stops eating. She "mopes,"* as one observer described her. It almost seems as if she had suffered some grief, but the explanation is otherwise: She has become still in order to let her emotions gather for one brief and explosive release.

14   It is November. Among the males in the colony she has made her choice. She spends most of the time sitting near him. But not for much longer.

15   At last the moment for coupling* arrives—almost inevitably, for it seems that there are few frigid* porcupines. The female takes the initiative, as she must since she is the one whose internal event sets the time. Rather suddenly she comes out of her waiting mood. She sniffs* the male in significant ways. He responds. They touch noses, retreat a few steps, rise on their hind feet, walk toward each other, and standing upright, touch noses again. This touch is the trigger. With the speed of a fire storm the female is down and the male is atop her.

16   With his mate armed so awesomely, he is brave indeed. She is cooperative. She has flattened her quills and has drawn her tail over her back so that he partly lies on its soft underside. Nevertheless, this is one time when the female, as Ernest Thompson Seton remarked, "has complete control of the situation." The male does not try to restrain her, as the males of some species do, by grasping the female's sides with their forelegs and taking the fur of her neck in their teeth. The porcupine female may end this embrace whenever she wishes . . . but she isn't impatient. It may last for as long as five minutes and be repeated, but only during a span of three to five hours. Then the female is through. She will no longer receive this male, or any other, until a year from now. So perfectly has she timed the coupling, however, that her pregnancy almost certainly is assured.

17   What seems most remarkable about porcupines is not the long emotional preparation for accepting the male, but the female's alertness which finally tells her that this is the day. For there will be only one day in all the year when

(13) **mopes:** is spiritless; inactive because of sadness or low spirits
(15) **coupling:** joining; connecting
(15) **frigid:** extremely cold; when said of women, sexually cold and unresponsive
(15) **sniffs:** breathes in through the nose, as if smelling something

receiving the male will result in a pregnancy with the assurance of perfectly formed young. She has, in fact, less than a day in which to note the signal, reveal her willingness to the male, carry out with him their brief mating ritual, and then come together. Yesterday would have been too soon; tomorrow would be too late. Only today will do, but there is little chance that she will make a mistake.

☐ FOCUS ON PROCESS

1. In which paragraph does the process—the step-by-step, stage-by-stage sequence—begin? *p 9*
2. Which words lead us forward, showing sequence from stage to stage? Consider transition words such as adverbial connectors, adverbs, and adverbial conjunctions. Notice prepositions and the use of "become" and "becoming."
3. Notice verb tenses: Most of the essay is written in the simple present with some future. Paragraphs 7 through 11, on the other hand, contain many verbs in the present continuous, with many present participles (-ing). Then the essay returns primarily to the simple present and future. What has made the difference in paragraphs 7 through 11?

☐ QUESTIONS FOR DISCUSSION

1. What is the "silent bell"? Why is it so important? What does the author mean by saying: "Hers [the civilized woman's] is a deafness that would have caused any other species to become extinct"? (paragraph 3)
2. In what ways are mammals similar to the human adolescent?

☐ SUGGESTIONS FOR COMPOSITION

1. Choose another animal and trace the process of its breeding. (You may have to look this up in the library if there are no animals with which you are sufficiently familiar.) You need not confine yourself to mammals. Some fish and insects have interesting breeding patterns as well, especially the salmon or the bee. In the complete article "Sex: The Silent Bell," the author also speaks of the long courtship of elephants and the discourtesy of some species of monkeys. You may wish to look this up in her book *Wild Heritage* or in the periodical *The Atlantic* (March 1965).
2. Trace another kind of natural process: the life cycle of a plant, the nitrogen cycle, the formation of clouds and rain, to mention only a few.
3. Describe a process in nature and show how it is analogous (similar) to something in human life, development, emotion, or thought.

4. Another kind of process is the mental process of decision making. Think about a decision you have had to make, the decision to come to the United States to attend a university, for example. Describe the step-by-step process that led you to your decision.

In the following selection, Samuel H. Scudder, whose scientific contributions were in the studies of butterflies and insects, tells about his days as a student of the famous Harvard natural scientist, Louis Agassiz.

SAMUEL H. SCUDDER

Take This Fish and Look at It

1   It was more than fifteen years ago that I entered the laboratory of Professor Agassiz, and told him I had enrolled my name in the Scientific School as a student of natural history. He asked me a few questions about my object in coming, antecedents* generally, the mode in which I afterwards proposed to use the knowledge I might acquire, and, finally, whether I wished to study any special branch. To the latter I replied that, while I wished to be well grounded in all departments of zoology,* I purposed to devote myself specially to insects.

2   "When do you wish to begin?" he asked.

3   "Now," I replied.

4   This seemed to please him, and with an energetic "Very well!" he reached from a shelf a huge jar of specimens in yellow alcohol. "Take this fish," he said, "and look at it; we call it a haemulon;* by and by I will ask what you have seen."

5   With that he left me, but in a moment returned with explicit instructions as to the care of the object entrusted to me.

6   "No man is fit to be a naturalist,"* said he, "who does not know how to take care of specimens."

7   I was to keep the fish before me in a tin tray, and occasionally moisten the surface with alcohol from the jar, always taking care to replace the stopper tightly. Those were not the days of ground-glass stoppers and elegantly shaped exhibition jars; all the old students will recall the huge neckless glass bottles with their leaky, wax-besmeared corks, half eaten by insects, and begrimed* with cellar dust. Entomology* was a cleaner science than ichthyology,* but the

(1) **antecedents:** whoever or whatever came before
(1) **zoology:** the scientific study of animals
(4) **haemulon:** a species of fish
(6) **naturalist:** an expert in natural history, i.e., the study of organisms such as plants or animals and their interrelationships
(7) **begrimed:** very dirty
(7) **entomology:** the scientific study of insects
(7) **ichthyology:** the scientific study of fish

example of the Professor, who had unhesitatingly plunged to the bottom of the jar to produce the fish, was infectious; and though this alcohol had a "very ancient and fishlike smell," I really dared not show any aversion* within these sacred precincts,* and treated the alcohol as though it were pure water. Still I was conscious of a passing feeling of disappointment, for gazing at a fish did not commend itself to an ardent* entomologist. My friends at home, too, were annoyed when they discovered that no amount of eau-de-Cologne would drown the perfume which haunted me like a shadow.

8   In ten minutes I had seen all that could be seen in that fish, and started in search of the Professor—who had, however, left the Museum; and when I returned, after lingering* over some of the odd animals stored in the upper apartment, my specimen was dry all over. I dashed the fluid over the fish as if to resuscitate* the beast from a fainting fit, and looked with anxiety for a return of the normal sloppy appearance. This little excitement over, nothing was to be done but to return to a steadfast* gaze at my mute* companion. Half an hour passed—an hour—another hour; the fish began to look loathsome.* I turned it over and around; looked it in the face—ghastly;* from behind, beneath, above, sideways, at a three-quarters' view—just as ghastly. I was in despair; at an early hour I concluded that lunch was necessary; so, with infinite relief, the fish was carefully replaced in the jar, and for an hour I was free.

9   On my return, I learned that Professor Agassiz had been at the Museum, but had gone, and would not return for several hours. My fellow-students were too busy to be disturbed by continued conversation. Slowly I drew forth that hideous fish, and with a feeling of desperation again looked at it. I might not use a magnifying glass; instruments of all kinds were interdicted.* My two hands, my two eyes, and the fish: It seemed a most limited field. I pushed my finger down its throat to feel how sharp the teeth were. I began to count the scales in the different rows, until I was convinced that was nonsense. At last a happy thought struck me—I would draw the fish; and now with surprise I began to discover new features in the creature. Just then the Professor returned.

10   "That is right," said he, "a pencil is one of the best eyes. I am glad to notice, too, that you keep your specimen wet, and your bottle corked."

11   With these encouraging words, he added:

(7) **aversion:** intense dislike, a feeling of revulsion, a desire to turn away from
(7) **sacred precincts:** holy places
(7) **ardent:** having great feeling or passion
(8) **lingering:** delaying, moving slowly, putting off going on
(8) **resuscitate:** bring back to life or consciousness
(8) **steadfast:** unchanging, constant, loyal
(8) **mute:** unable to speak, silent in the sense of not speaking
(8) **loathsome:** making one feel extreme dislike
(8) **ghastly:** frightening, repellent, suggestive of ghosts or death
(9) **interdicted:** forbidden

12   "Well, what is it like?"

13   He listened attentively to my brief rehearsal* of the structure of parts whose names were still unknown to me; the fringed gill-arches and movable operculum*; the pores* of the head, fleshy lips and lidless eyes; the lateral line, the spinous fins and forked tail; the compressed and arched body. When I finished, he waited as if expecting more, and then, with an air of disappointment:

14   "You have not looked very carefully; why," he continued more earnestly, "you haven't even seen one of the most conspicuous* features of the animal, which is plainly before your eyes as the fish itself; look again, look again!" and he left me to my misery.

15   I was piqued*; I was mortified.* Still more of that wretched fish! But now I set myself to my task with a will, and discovered one new thing after another, until I saw how just the Professor's criticism had been. The afternoon passed quickly; and when, towards its close, the Professor inquired:

16   "Do you see it yet?"

17   "No," I replied, "I am certain I do not, but I see how little I saw before."

18   "That is next best," said he, earnestly, "but I won't hear you now; put away your fish and go home; perhaps you will be ready with a better answer in the morning. I will examine you before you look at the fish."

19   This was disconcerting.* Not only must I think of my fish all night, studying, without the object before me, what this unknown but most visible feature might be; but also, without reviewing my discoveries, I must give an exact account of them the next day. I had a bad memory; so I walked home by Charles River in a distracted state, with my two perplexities.*

20   The cordial greeting from the Professor the next morning was reassuring; here was a man who seemed to be quite as anxious as I that I should see for myself what he saw.

21   "Do you perhaps mean," I asked, "that the fish has symmetrical* sides with paired organs?"

22   His thoroughly pleased "Of course! Of course!" repaid the wakeful hours of the previous night. After he had discoursed most happily and enthusiastically—as he always did—upon the importance of this point, I ventured to ask what I should do next.

---

(13) **rehearsal:** retelling, a reciting
(13) **operculum:** gill cover; lid, flap, or shell covering an opening in an animal
(13) **pores:** tiny openings in the skin, serving as outlet for perspiration; in leaves, to absorb moisture
(14) **conspicuous:** obvious, easy to see
(15) **piqued:** annoyed, resentful, feeling hurt pride
(15) **mortified:** humiliated, shamed
(19) **disconcerting:** upsetting, frustrating
(19) **perplexities:** puzzles, condition of being complicated
(21) **symmetrical:** correspondence of form and arrangement of parts on opposite sides of a boundary, here, the fish's two sides being exactly alike

23   "Oh, look at your fish!" he said, and left me again to my own devices.* In a little more than an hour he returned, and heard my new catalogue.

24   "That is good, that is good!" he repeated; "but that is not all; go on"; and so for three long days he placed that fish before my eyes, forbidding me to look at anything else, or to use any artificial aid. "Look, look, look," was his repeated injunction.*

25   This was the best entomological lesson I ever had—a lesson whose influence has extended to the details of every subsequent study; a legacy* the Professor had left to me, as he has left it to so many others, of inestimable value, which we could not buy, with which we cannot part. . . .

26   The fourth day, a second fish of the same group was placed beside the first, and I was bidden* to point out the resemblances and differences between the two; another and another followed, until the entire family lay before me, and a whole legion* of jars covered the table and surrounding shelves; the odor had become a pleasant perfume; and even now, the sight of an old, six-inch, worm-eaten cork brings fragrant memories.

27   The whole group of haemulons was thus brought in review; and, whether engaged upon the dissection of the internal organs, the preparation and examination of the bony framework, or the description of the various parts, Agassiz's training in the method of observing facts and their orderly arrangement was ever accompanied by the urgent exhortation* not to be content with them.

28   "Facts are stupid things," he would say, "until brought into connection with some general law."

29   At the end of eight months, it was almost with reluctance that I left these friends and turned to insects; but what I had gained by this outside experience has been of greater value than years of later investigation in my favorite groups.

☐ FOCUS ON PROCESS

---

1. What is the process that the author seems to be going through? What are its stages?
2. How is the essay organized?
3. Underline the words or phrases that serve to move the process forward from one paragraph to the next. Note, for example: "With that" (paragraph 5); "I was to keep" (paragraph 7); "In ten minutes" (paragraph 8).

(23) **left me . . . to my own devices:** left me to do as I pleased, to be independent
(24) **injunction:** command
(25) **legacy:** something valuable handed down, like an inheritance
(26) **bidden:** ordered, commanded
(26) **legion:** an army unit, a large number
(27) **exhortation:** strong advice, urgent appeal

□ QUESTIONS FOR DISCUSSION

1. Since Scudder had come to study insects, why did Professor Agassiz start him on a fish?
2. The author says: "This was the best entomological lesson I ever had." What had he learned?
3. Analyze Professor Agassiz's methods of teaching. Do you feel he did too little actual teaching? Why or why not?
4. Note the steps of the "lesson." Analyze their order. Pay particular attention to paragraphs 18 to 22. What had Scudder's answer (paragraph 21) to do with this order?
5. Draw analogies between this lesson in science and elements of writing. How about painting?
6. How well does Scudder really know the characteristics of a fish? What are the limitations of his knowledge? How does his knowledge differ from that of a fisherman?

□ SUGGESTIONS FOR COMPOSITION

1. Trace the process by which you learned or taught an important lesson. Try to include the rationale for teaching it in that order.
2. Using Louis Agassiz's saying "facts are stupid things until brought into connection with some general law," do one of the following:
   a. Discuss the relationship between generalization and specific facts or examples in writing, and illustrate with examples.
   b. Using your own selection of facts or specifics, show how these are related to some "general law."

INFORMATIONAL PROCESS: PASSIVE VOICE OR ACTIVE VOICE

As a rule, good writing is active writing. That is, sentences are in the active voice with a clear sense of who is doing what. The student solved the problem rather than *the problem was solved by the student*. In process writing (especially in scientific writing), however, the passive voice is frequently used. Overuse of the passive will yield dull, boring, lifeless writing, no matter what the type or reason, but in some cases use of the passive in scientific writing is appropriate. (The use of the passive to create the impression that the writer's opinions are the product of scientific observation, rather than pure conjecture, is inappropriate because the writer is attempting to attribute scientific credence to mere opinion.)

what does this say about science?

Review of the Passive Voice

The passive voice, as you already know, puts into the *subject position* the noun that would be in the *direct object position* of the active voice sentence. In the preceding example, the direct object is *problem, problem* is what is *acted upon*. To make the sentence passive, *problem* becomes the subject, but a subject that *does not act* (hence *not active*) but *is acted upon* (passive).

The problem <u>was</u> <u>solved</u> by the student.

As you have learned, the passive is formed by using the auxiliary verb *be* with the past participle. The causer, or agent (in this case, the one who did the solving), is expressed using the preposition *by*.

Since a sentence may be complete with a subject and verb, it is a grammatically complete sentence without the agent.

The problem <u>was</u> <u>solved</u>.

The agent, the one who did the solving, can be eliminated from the sentence. In this case, we know what happened to the problem, but not who or what caused it to happen (thought of the solution). Deleting the agent by means of the passive voice can be merely sloppy or dull. But it can also be done because the writer wants to keep the reader in ignorance, hoping nobody will bother to ask "who did it?" This is a use of the passive we must watch out for.

Example
Your wife was being kissed in a restaurant.

Notice the *agent* is missing. *By whom* was she being kissed? Or, in the active sentence, *who* kissed her? An active sentence would have to specify *who kissed her?* The passive sentence can leave this information out. Before the husband becomes angry, he should ask that question.

Another example
Your composition was thought to be really terrible.

By whom? Your professor? A failing student? The garbage man? One who disagrees with you? It *matters* whose opinion it was; therefore you should ask, *"who* thought so?"

A truly legitimate use of the passive voice, of the deletion of the agent, is the sentence wherein it truly does not matter who performed the action. The action or function and what was acted upon are the important points, not who did it.

In the following sentence, we are given the information we need in order to understand what went on in a laboratory: *The test tube was heated.* We do not care who heated the test tube, for it could be heated over and over again using the same process and producing the same results no matter who is doing it. Removing of the agent gives the process a kind of scientific objectivity. Unless that individual is describing a new discovery, *how* he did it and *what happened* are important, *not who* did it.

Furthermore, by putting *test tube* at the beginning of the sentence (in passive voice the object acted upon moves to the subject, or front, position), the emphasis is on the test tube, which is the focus the scientist wants. In general, when the focus is on the way something works (the equipment in an experiment, the working of a machine) the passive is appropriate. If the emphasis is on how the experimenter or "doer" performed the process, the active voice is appropriate. There is, related to all this, another reason the passive is used: to remove the "I." This can be done because of modesty—that is, not wanting to sound self-centered or self-congratulatory—or because of the desire to sound detached and objective. Objectivity can also be maintained using an impersonal third person such as "the experimenter," "one," or the first person plural, "we." Where you are describing the way you did something, though, the particular way *you* did it, where you are *not* just writing a scientific experiment or process, you need not be so afraid to use "I," as long as you do not overdo it. Keep in mind that frequent uses of "I think" or "in my opinion" can distract the reader from the subject matter at hand.

☐ ANALYZING EXAMPLES OF ACTIVE OR PASSIVE SENTENCES

Let us now go back to the two selections you have already read, paying particular attention to the author's choices of active or passive constructions. Let us decide if the author chose appropriately and, if so, why that choice is appropriate.

"Teaching Sentences, Reading, and Writing to Helen Keller"

1. In paragraph 2, notice that the first two sentences are written in the passive voice and that the rest of the paragraph is written in the active voice. Why the difference?
2. In paragraph 4, the writer keeps changing from active to passive. Why? Do you agree with these changes?
3. Rewrite the sentence in which Ms. Sullivan refers to Mr. Anagnos, leaving out "Mr. Anagnos" (paragraph 4).
4. Is this selection mainly active or passive writing? Would it be better or worse written the other way? Why?

"Sex: The Silent Bell"

1. Is the essay primarily in the active or passive voice? Why is this appropriate?

☐ PRACTICING THE PASSIVE

Change the passive sentences to active sentences. (Where there is no agent you may have to use the word *someone* or "invent" an agent.) Change the active sentences to passive sentences. In some cases, an active sentence will have *no direct object* or have an *intransitive* verb. (We went home early.) Such sentences cannot be made passive. Mark these sentences *No Passive.*

1. Somebody was being chased down the street by a large black dog.
2. The Smith family went to the park every day last summer.
3. Everyone had been told what to do by the policeman.
4. Susan was singing that song over and over again, until we all thought we would go crazy!
5. It's too bad that we won't see Yellowstone National Park while we're here.
6. The pie was put into the oven to bake.
7. Those clothes should be taken to the dry cleaner by one of you.
8. All the decorations fell down within about ten minutes.
9. One hundred students took Professor Wong's chemistry exam.
10. The dean will give the students diplomas at the commencement next Wednesday.

THREE ESSAYS ON THE PROCESS OF MAKING WINE

The following three essays explain the wine-making process. The first one instructs us in how to make wine; the second one is an advertisement for a brand of wine; the third is the beginning of a chapter called "The Corpse" from a book entitled *Mortal Lessons* by Richard Selzer, a physician. As you read these process essays, try to determine the differences in the ways they are written and the reasons for those differences.

Instructions for Making Wine

1   To make wine, begin with grapes that have not been washed. (This is important because the skin contains a natural yeast which will aid in the fermentation process.) In a crock* crush the grapes by hand so that the skins crack and the juice runs out. Leave the grapes at room temperature (or slightly warmer) to begin fermenting. Cover the crock, to keep fruit flies from getting into the wine. In a day or two the pulp should be at the top and the juice at the bottom. Stir, so that pulp and juice are mixed. At the end of five days, press the mass so that the liquid remains, and the solids are removed. If you have no winepress, you can squeeze the mass through cheesecloth (a material full of fine holes, like a screen), wringing the juice out of the cloth by hand. At this point, if you want sweet wine add one or two pounds of sugar per gallon of wine, and let it dissolve in the juice.

2   The liquid will now continue to ferment. Bubbles will be forming. The crock should now be covered so that no air can get in. A tube leading to a device known as a water lock permits the gas to escape from the crock into a jar of water, causing the water to bubble. When the water stops bubbling the fermentation is complete.

3   At this point you may open the crock, but the wine will be muddy looking. Gradually the sediment will drop to the bottom, leaving the clear

(1) **crock:** a deep earthenware container

wine behind. Look at the wine and taste it. When it looks clear and tastes good, it is ready for drinking. Siphon off the clear wine and put it into bottles or barrels.

E. & J. GALLO WINERY

Fermentation: The Birth of a Fine Red Wine

1   Despite the wealth of sophisticated equipment available today, there is no substitute for the judgment and care of a dedicated winemaker.

2   At no time is this more apparent than during the critical days of fermentation, for it is at this stage, the birth of the wine, that taste, character, aroma, body, and color are in large part determined.

3   When the grapes arrive at our crusher, a State Agricultural Inspector measures sugar content and physical condition. But, in addition, our winemaker checks and tastes for grape quality.

4   Those grapes which he approves move directly to our "crusher-stemmer," which removes the stems and then gently "crushes" the fruit.

5   Since fermentation results from the natural interaction of yeast with the sugars and acids in the juice, the selection of the right yeast from the many available to our winemaker is crucial.

6   The winemaker must select exactly the right yeast, in exactly the proper quantity, to yield a wine whose flavor is true to the grape, with all the desirable taste characteristics in balance.

7   Now begins a vigil* that will remain unbroken for 72 to 95 hours.

8   Because fermentation creates heat, temperature must be carefully controlled.

9   As the liquid ferments in the presence of the skins, each passing hour brings changes in flavor, in color, in aroma, and in body which the winemaker monitors constantly, partially with sophisticated instruments but primarily through his own highly developed senses of taste and smell. At each tasting, our winemaker must be able to call to mind all the various vintages of his past and how they tasted at each particular stage. . . . This talent we have found to be more than an acquired skill; it is, rather, a rare gift.

10   As the juice ferments, skins and pulp float to the top, forming a "cap" vital to the wine's development.

11   If the wine is to achieve its true peak of flavor, color, body, and aroma, the cap must not be permitted to dry out and harden. Therefore, we designed a system that circulates the fermenting wine over the entire surface of the cap. The winemaker must determine exactly how often and for what duration the fermenting wine will be circulated over the cap.

12   When his tasting tells him the wine is fermented to the precise degree that augurs* a superb Zinfandel, he halts the process by lowering the tem-

(7) **vigil:** a purposeful watch, especially one that requires staying awake to do so
(12) **augurs:** foretells, tells of the future

perature. He then has the wine carefully drawn off and removed to the cooperage* for aging.

13   Now, finally, the wine can rest. And so, for the moment, can our winemaker.

RICHARD SELZER

You Are Wine

1   Shall I tell you once more how it happens? Even though you know, don't you?

2   You were born with the horror stamped upon you, like a fingerprint. All these years you have lived you have known. I but remind your memory, confirm the fear that has always been prime. Yet the facts have a force of their insolent* own.

3   Wine is best made in a cellar, on a stone floor. Crush grapes in a barrel such that each grape is burst. When the barrel is three-quarters full, cover it with a fine-mesh* cloth, and wait. In three days, an ear placed low over the mash will detect a faint crackling,* which murmur, in two more days, rises to a continuous giggle.* Only the rendering* of fat or a forest fire far away makes such a sound. It is the song of fermentation! Remove the cloth and examine closely. The eye is startled by a bubble on the surface. Was it there and had it gone unnoticed? Or is it newly come?

4   But soon enough more beads gather in little colonies, winking and lining up at the brim. Stagnant* fluid forms. It begins to turn. Slow currents carry bits of stem and grape meat on voyages of an inch or so. The pace quickens.* The level rises. On the sixth day, the barrel is almost full. The teem* must be poked down with a stick. The air of the cellar is dizzy with fruit flies and droplets of smell. On the seventh day, the fluid is racked into the second barrel for aging. It is wine.

5   Thus is the fruit of the earth taken, its flesh torn. Thus is it given over to

---

(12) **cooperage:** barrels

(2) **insolent:** rude, insulting, showing disrespect for authority, showing no consideration for others

(3) **mesh:** open space; little holes, like a screen

(3) **crackling:** making short, sudden noises, as when something cracks or burns

(3) **giggle:** a laugh with quick high-pitched sounds, suggesting silliness or nervousness

(3) **rendering:** melting down

(4) **stagnant:** without motion or current; dirty and smelly from lack of movement, especially referring to water or other fluid

(4) **quickens:** in addition to speeding up, quickens refers to coming to life

(4) **teem:** refers to that which is full, overflowing, fertile, newly produced life; a swarm (as of many, many flies)

standing, toward rot.* It is the principle of corruption,* the death of what is, the birth of what is to be.

6   You are wine.

☐ QUESTIONS ON "INSTRUCTIONS FOR MAKING WINE"

1. Notice that the verbs are, for the most part, in the *imperative,* assuming a "you" to which the instructions "speak." Someone is giving you instructions, telling you what to do. Why is this better than the passive?
2. Are the instructions clear? Do you understand what you are to do? Do you understand all the terminology?

☐ SUGGESTIONS FOR COMPOSITION

Try writing simple directions for preparing a food or operating a device. Be clear and use the imperative.

☐ QUESTIONS ON "FERMENTATION: THE BIRTH OF A FINE RED WINE"

1. The advertisement is certainly an informational process composition, but it is not neutral, as a lab report is supposed to be. This ad tries to convince us to buy Gallo wine, even though it never explicitly says so. How does it do this? Be specific.
2. Is the writing mainly in the passive voice or the active voice? Why?
3. The verbs telling of the process are mainly active; this means they must have subjects causing, doing. Find the subjects of the active verbs showing process. Who is the primary causer of the action in this process?
4. Would it have been better to have left the causer out of this process analysis? Does it make a difference that this is an ad trying to convince us to buy Gallo wine, rather than a neutral report of how the process was done? Explain your answer. (*Hint:* Go back to the reasons given for wanting to delete the "causer." Then explain why this writer decided to keep putting the causer/subject in the ad.)

☐ QUESTIONS ON "YOU ARE WINE"

1. What is the major difference between this process composition and the preceding ones? Is the major purpose of this process analysis to teach us winemaking? If not, what is the major purpose and how is winemaking used?

(5) **rot:** decay; decomposition
(5) **corruption:** decay; a change for the worse; another meaning, possibly intended here: wickedness, badness, impurity

2. Notice the choices of active or passive verbs. The process begins with a passive sentence: "Wine is best made . . . on a stone floor." The rest of the paragraph uses some imperatives, giving instructions. What happens, though, in the next paragraph (4) and why?

3. Make a list of the subjects and verbs in paragraph 4 *before* the sixth day. Why are there so many subjects? Why is the paragraph so "active"? What is the relationship between the activity of this paragraph and the sentence from paragraph 2 that reads: "Yet the facts have a force of their insolent own"?

4. What does the author mean when he says: "You are wine"? The process of fermentation is obviously being linked to "process" in life—the cyclical relationship linking birth, decay, and death. Explain this analogy. (See Chapter 7 for a fuller treatment of analogy.)

5. Analyze word choice in this essay. Besides using the active voice, the author has chosen nouns and verbs associated with active animal or human life. We almost forget that we are being told about fermenting grapes. Find the nouns and verbs usually associated with animals or human beings.

6. Why is the passive voice again used in speaking of the sixth and seventh days?

☐   SUGGESTIONS FOR COMPOSITION

Write a composition in which you draw an analogy between a process and a fundamental fact of life: some thought you are illustrating by means of analogy with a process. You may choose a process in nature, but you may also use a scientific process, a cooking process, or a mechanical process—whatever serves your purpose.

A Few Words About Purpose

In each of the preceding essays, the author's purpose had a significant effect on the way he wrote the essay—the choice of the imperative, the active or passive voice, and the choice of words. Having a purpose for writing and keeping that purpose in mind as you write will always yield a more unified and convincing essay, no matter what the kind of writing.

☐   WRITING CLEAR INSTRUCTIONS

The following sentences give instructions and warnings about the use of an electric garden tool called an edger, which is used to cut grass where it borders on pavement or driveways. You will notice that the sentences are not very well written. They are wordy and repetitious; they have dangling or misplaced participles; they are awkward and unclear; they use long, pretentious words instead of simple, common ones. Rewrite these directions being as clear, simple, and concise as possible *without eliminating any essential information.* (Remember that the imperative is usually the best verb form for giving instructions.)

hw/k

1. If you want your lawn (grass) to look neat, you will be happier if you own an electric cutting tool that cuts clean edges along your walks, driveway, and curbs. This tool, called an edger, will be one that will be able to allow the job to be done well by you. The job will be easy with this high-speed tool.
2. The operator or user should be cognizant of the fact that it is a good idea that safety goggles (glasses) be worn when your edger is being utilized.
3. Wearing long pants to protect your legs, your face, hands and feet should be kept away from the cutting area. Do this every time.
4. You wouldn't want an electric shock, so in order to prevent it, utilization should be made of an extension cord that is suitable for using outside.
5. It is important to remember that the cord should not be abused. It should not be pulled hard from the receptacle. It is imperative that it be kept from heat, oil, and sharp edges.
6. Provide assurance that the power cord be kept from the blade while it is moving.
7. The edger should be disconnected while cleaning or removing blades.
8. When it is raining outside, the edger should not be used, being wet outside, and damp locations are not advantageous or safe for tools operated electrically.
9. The edger should be kept away from children locked in a dry place.
10. Being a motor that might spark, it is unwise to employ a tool such as this in an atmosphere that has gaseous or explosive content, the fact being that fumes might be ignited by the sparks.

S T U D E N T   C O M P O S I T I O N S

How to Study for a Test

I'm going to write about how I prepared myself for the test I just took—the test on "Articles."

The first thing I did was to find out what the test was really about. Although it seems ridiculous, it isn't. I know many students who prepared themselves for the wrong test.

After knowing what the test was on, I got some books and copied down all the information given on a piece of paper. The next thing was getting the materials organized. I put all we had to know about indefinite articles on one page and the second page was for the article *the*. Then I sat down and memorized all the *exceptions*.

Practicing and using them came next. I did some of the exercises given in the book and some articles in the newspaper and explained to myself the reasons for using the articles in each case.

Then last but not least was sleeping enough the night before. I think it is the most important thing to sit for an exam with a relaxed body and an easy mind.

How to Make a Child Hate School

I have a brother. He is a nice and kind boy. He is also a good brother for me. I like him more than a brother because I understand some of the problems he has and nobody has really helped him and understood him. He was five years old when my father took him to enroll him in an elementary school. The first day of school is not really interesting, especially for the children in primary school. I don't really know what his problem was when he came back home that day. I thought he would get used to it little by little. I suppose he was not old enough for first grade. (I mentioned he was only five.) When the classes began, everything seemed difficult to him. Everybody, including him, thought everything would be all right after a few weeks, but he never liked the school. He was young, younger than other students. He also wasn't a genius. He still needed more freedom and comfort before entering a school. Anyway, his first grades were not good.

Then the advice of parents began. After that, sisters and brothers did the same. I did not really agree with the opinions of my parents, sisters, and brothers about him. Sometimes I thought deeply about him and his problems. I guessed that probably other people didn't understand him. I extended this assumption to teachers and other students. The time a teacher wanted him to bring my father to school about his situation, my brother was affected terribly. When my father came back home that night, he tried to advise my brother and make every thing clear for him, like what is important in education and what is the purpose of it.

More and more everybody used to make fun of him because of his grades. Even in the school, some of the students didn't behave in a friendly way to him. I blame the teachers more than anybody else. They were the main dreams in his life. He had expected more than this from a teacher whom he had heard so much about. I had hoped that the teachers would solve his problems but unfortunately I was wrong. Most of them couldn't really understand a child, and didn't know the psychology of a child.

Eventually the insults and reproaches, the behavior of the teachers and parents were going to make him hate school. Sometimes when he wanted to buy a toy or a book, he had to get a good grade; consequently his life and childish dreams had been related to grades and this made him hate those grades. He couldn't watch TV because my mother made him study. I know he studied, but he didn't have a great capacity for everything.

Now all of a sudden without a logical reason he was deprived of a lot of things. We used to go to picnic some weekends, but he couldn't come with us because my parents believed that study is more important and he had to finish his homework at home. After nine months of restrictions and reproaches, strictness, being deprived of recreation, being made fun of, with no one understanding him, he came to hate school. The thought of school as a nice place for training and preparing for the better future had been killed in his mind.

The preceding composition was written by a student who still needs a lot of work on his English. Originally there were many errors, and the vocabulary and sentence structure are not very advanced; however, there is nothing "simple" about this student's ability to analyze a complex situation. One need not, as you can see, be perfect in English in order to write a sensitive analysis in English.

☐   QUESTION

How would you combine some of the sentences to make the composition read more smoothly?

The following has been excerpted from a lab report in electrical engineering. The students were making electronic Ping-Pong games.

An Electronic Ping-Pong Game

The main objective of this lab is to implement and design the "famous" Ping-Pong game by using eight LEDs to represent the position of the ball in motion. To make this game work, four interrupts were used. Those were RST6, RST7, RST6.5, and RST7.5.

Two of those, RST6 and RST7, combined with switches, $5\omega_2$ and $5\omega_0$, were used as players' paddles. . . .

To start the game, first select the skill level by flipping one of the eight switches, then push VECTR-INTR key. The action of the latter will cause the scoreboard, the seven-segment window, to display for both players and the eight LEDs, which display the position of the ball in motion, to be blanked. Then the ball will be served by one player, for example, the right player, and it will travel to the left. . . .

As the game goes on, the score will be displayed on the seven-segment window. Whoever faults will serve the ball. If the game is reset by pushing VECTR-INTR button the initial server must change.

As the players get more proficient in a lower skill level, they could try to go to a higher skill level. (The leftmost switch of the eight switches will give lower skill level and the rightmost switch would allow higher skill level.) This skill level may be changed dynamically, i.e., it could be altered in the middle of a point. This will allow interesting strategy for either player. The game itself will last until one player reaches 21.

What follows is not really a process composition, but so well does it discuss the beginning steps in the process of acculturation (getting used to another culture) that it will surely be of interest to you. It is also an excellent example of a student's willingness to experiment with new words. The beginning of the composition has been omitted.

FROM *Being Away*

I have noted to myself that the dorm environment was different in its styles and assumptions from my own family environment, and that in order to survive I would have to make a choice, at least temporarily, between both worlds. It seemed to me that, up to a point, everything I had known before I moved here was irrelevant to the situation. I had the strange feeling that remembering most of what my culture had provided me was a disadvantage. I felt that the temporary disposal of most of the past and its cultural values was inevitable, and even more, necessary.

When I could not imitate American pronunciations or master the slangy dialect of the dorms, when I was plainly uninterested in ethnic customs and could not naturally master a special handshake that most students often use with one another, they knew I was different. I began hearing sounds that were new, harder, less friendly. Hearing people speak to me in English troubled me and constantly emphasized that I was foreign. The language was a high obstacle to the normal development of my social life; ineluctably I felt in an alien world. The situation intensified the absence of my family, girlfriend, friends, places I used to go. Feelings of depression came occasionally but forcefully. My Spanish thoughts started to be the only link with my past. I found myself floating in probably the most difficult dilemma that I had had in my life, but after intense moments of thinking, I decided to challenge myself and draw the sword against the situation. There was no point in going back.

After the initial awkwardness of transition, I committed myself, fully and freely, to the culture of the place. And it was then that a sense of loss started to develop inwardly as I moved away from my identifications and models. In addition, education seemed to mean not only a gradual dissolving of familial ties but also a change of social identity. My fears now have turned to the possible disconnection from my roots, and the rupture with my family and its customs and orientations.

6

ORGANIZATION

Up to this point, organizing a paper has not presented too great a problem. Narration and process are usually organized chronologically; description is often organized spatially, accompanied by a record of what the senses take in. Unity has been important, but it has been achieved in such ways as focusing on an incident, a scene, a point of view, or a limited process.

When we are trying to establish an idea, answer a question, or prove a point, we may use narration, description, or process to help us do so, but the unifying principle of our discussion is the point we are trying to make. The entire paper will be a development or substantiation of that point. If we are to produce an essay that is readable and convincing, it will have to be logical and well organized, leading the readers easily from paragraph to paragraph. It will have to end in such a way that the reader feels the writer knew exactly where he intended to lead him.

Of course it goes without saying that writers cannot accomplish all of this if they themselves do not know where they are going and how they plan to arrive there. Too often papers are just an accumulation of thoughts, ideas, and illustrations, each added as the writer thinks of it. This may be a good way to record ideas for a paper, like notes, but it is the beginning, not the end, of the process. As has been said before (see Chapter 1), you may find yourself writing drafts of the composition at this stage, or possibly paragraphs that will eventually be a part of the paper. Some people prefer working this way, but for a longer paper, or one that makes a point and develops it, it is more efficient to put thoughts down in the form of random notes, as sketchy or as detailed as you like, allowing ideas to flow freely from your mind onto the paper. This is the stage of invention. What will you be writing about? What do you have to say about the subject? From this "laundry list" of thoughts, facts, and ideas, you will select, rearrange, and draw together. When you do this you are planning, organizing. Whether this process takes place mentally or on paper, whether the paper comes out perfectly formed the first time or needs several rewritings, somewhere along the way *the well-written, well-organized paper has been thought out and planned before it was written in its final form.*

When writing a paper of *any length,* ask yourself the following questions at some point.

1. What general topic am I writing about?
2. What more specific topic, or what aspect of the general topic, will be the subject of my paper?
3. What am I saying about that subject?
4. How will I develop the idea?
5. What information will I include?
6. How is this information best organized?

Asking these questions and working thoughtfully to answer them constitute the basic steps in planning a paper.

TOPIC SENTENCES AND THESIS SENTENCES

No matter what you have decided to choose as your subject (questions 1 and 2), you will then have to decide what it is you want to say about it. This is related to the importance of the sentence as a unit of communication. It is important to the paper, just as it is important to the grammar, because a sentence *says* something, makes a statement. If you cannot state what you are talking about, *if you cannot put it into a sentence,* chances are *the point you wish to make is not yet clear in your mind.* * Your ability to state a point clearly is an indication that you have clarified your thinking and focused it. The inability to do this is a symptom that your idea is not yet focused and clear.

A **thesis sentence** is a sentence that states the main idea of your paper and controls it. Since the thesis sentence is an indication of clarity of thought and focus, it is understandable that you may have difficulty in arriving at it. You may have a lot of ideas, but no *clear* thesis sentence. It is important to realize that such a focusing sentence may not come about automatically or easily. It often takes considerable effort to arrive at a good thesis statement, but it is worth the effort. Let us practice finding the main idea in another person's writing and using thesis sentences to focus our own writing.

What the *thesis sentence* is to an entire paper, a *topic sentence* is to a paragraph. It is the sentence that best states the main idea of the paragraph. It can be found at the beginning of the paragraph, at the middle, or at the end. Often, it is not stated at all, but from reading the paragraph, *you* could supply the topic sentence that is implied.

☐   PRACTICE WITH TOPIC SENTENCES

Read each of the following paragraphs. If you find a topic sentence, underline it. If not, write one yourself that sums up the paragraph's message or states its point.

* David Belasco, a great American theatrical producer, once said: "If you can't write your idea on the back of my calling card, you don't have a clear idea."

CAROLYN KANE
___

FROM *Thinking: A Neglected Art*

1   Thinking does require time and effort. It is a common misconception that if a person is "gifted" or "bright" or "talented," wonderful ideas will flash spontaneously into his mind. Unfortunately, the intellect does not work in this way. Even Einstein had to study and think for months before he could formulate his theory of relativity. Those of us who are less intelligent find it a struggle to conceive even a moderately good idea, let alone a brilliant one.

ALBERT C. BAUGH
___

FROM *A History of the English Language*

2   Toward the close of the Old English period an event occurred which had a greater effect on the English language than any other in the course of its history. This event was the Norman Conquest* in 1066. What the language would have been like if William the Conqueror had not succeeded in making good his claim to the English throne can only be a matter of conjecture. It would probably have pursued much the same course as the other Teutonic* languages, retaining perhaps more of its inflections* and preserving a preponderatingly* Teutonic vocabulary, . . . incorporating much less freely words from other languages. In particular it would have lacked the greater part of that enormous number of French words which today make English seem on the side of vocabulary almost as much a Romance* as a Teutonic language. The Norman Conquest changed the whole course of the English language.

JOHN HOLT
___

FROM *Why Children Fail*

3   The bright child is patient. He can tolerate uncertainty and failure, and will keep trying until he gets an answer. When all his experiments fail, he can even admit to himself and others that for the time being he is not going to get an answer. This may annoy him, but he can wait. Very often, he does not want to be told how to do the problem or solve the puzzle he has struggled with, because he does not want to be cheated out of the chance to figure it out for

(2) **Norman Conquest:** the conquest of England by William of Normandy (a French-speaking country)
(2) **Teutonic:** Germanic; the family of languages to which English belongs
(2) **inflections:** changes in the form of verbs to correspond with number, gender, or person
(2) **preponderatingly:** mostly
(2) **Romance:** language family deriving from Latin; e.g., French, Italian, or Spanish

himself in the future. Not so the dull child. He cannot stand uncertainty or failure. To him, an unanswered question is not a challenge or an opportunity, but a threat. If he can't find the answer quickly, it must be given to him, and quickly; and he must have answers for everything. Such are the children of whom a second-grade teacher once said, "But my children *like* to have questions for which there is only one answer." They did; and by a mysterious coincidence, so did she.

You would be correct in having marked the first sentence of paragraph 1 as the topic sentence. The main idea of paragraph 2 is best expressed in the last sentence, though it is introduced in the first two, almost as if the paragraph is "framed," beginning and end, with its main idea.

Paragraph 3 is more difficult. The first sentence might seem like the topic sentence. It is the type of sentence that *could* easily be a topic sentence. But does it really cover the ideas expressed in the paragraph? What important elements does it exclude? This paragraph is one that makes a point but does not directly state it in one sentence. We could do so, however. The topic sentence would have to include the bright child's enjoyment of a challenge as opposed to the dull child's reaction to it as a threat. A possible topic sentence might be: *To a bright child a puzzle or unanswered question is a challenge, whereas to a dull child it is a threat.* (Holt, incidentally, is making the point that unchallenging education is producing "dull" children, who are *not born* dull.)

Now analyze the following paragraphs by yourself. Where you cannot find the topic sentence (either in the beginning, middle, or end) write your own.

ASHLEY MONTAGU

FROM *The American Way of Life*

4   Because of the narrowness of vision of so many scientists, science has become far too important and dangerous an activity to leave to the scientists. Just as war is too important to leave to the generals and it is therefore necessary that they be under the control of the Secretary of the Army, so, until they can take care of themselves, scientists should be under the control of a Secretary for Humanity, who sees to it that their work is not misused. Of course, the best protection for the scientists, and for us all, is a basic education of everyone, including the would-be scientists, in the humanities, in *humanitas*.*

(4) **humanitas:** in Latin, a liberal education

JACOB BRONOWSKI

FROM *The Ascent of Man*

5   Salt is not an element in the modern sense. Salt is a compound of two elements: sodium and chlorine. This is remarkable enough, that a white fizzy metal like sodium, and a yellowish poisonous gas like chlorine, should finish up by making a stable structure, common salt. But more remarkable is that sodium and chlorine belong to families. There is an orderly gradation of similar properties within each family: sodium belongs to the family of alkali metals, and chlorine to the active halogens. The crystals remain unchanged, square and transparent, as we change one member of a family for another. For instance, sodium can certainly be replaced by potassium: potassium chloride. Similarly in the other family the chlorine can be replaced by its sister element bromine: sodium bromide. And, of course, we can make a double change: lithium fluoride, in which sodium has been replaced by lithium, chlorine by fluorine. And yet all the crystals are indistinguishable by the eye.

BETTY FRIEDAN

QUOTED IN *The Feminine Mystique*

6   The tragedy was, nobody ever looked us in the eye and said you had to decide what you want to do with your life, besides being your husband's wife and children's mother. I never thought it through until I was thirty-six, and my husband was so busy with his practice that he couldn't entertain me every night. The three boys were in school all day. I kept on trying to have babies despite an Rh discrepancy. After two miscarriages, they said I must stop. I thought that my own growth and evolution were over. I always knew as a child that I was going to grow up and go to college, and then get married, and that's as far as a girl has to think. After that, your husband determines and fills your life. It wasn't until I got so lonely as the doctor's wife and kept screaming at the kids because they didn't fill my life that I realized I had to make my own life. I still had to decide what I wanted to be. I hadn't finished evolving at all. But it took me ten years to think it through.

JOHN CIARDI

FROM *Another School Year—Why?*

7   Assume, for example, that you want to be a physicist. You pass the great stone halls of, say, M.I.T., and there cut into the stone are the names of the master scientists. The chances are that few if any of you will leave your names to be cut into those stones. Yet any one of you who managed to stay awake

through part of a high school course in physics, knows more about physics than did many of these great makers of the past. You know more because they left you what they knew. The first course in any science is essentially a history course. You have to begin by learning what the past learned for you. Except as a man has entered the past of the race he has no function in civilization.

E. B. WHITE

FROM *Unity*

8   We hold arms so that, in the event of another nation's breaking its word, we will have something to fall back on, something by which we can command respect, enforce our position, and have our way. Modern arms are complicated by their very destructiveness, their ability to turn and bite whoever unleashes them. That is why everyone is pleased by the prospect of disarming and why there is a great hue and cry raised against arms. And how are we to disarm? By signing a treaty. And what is a treaty? A treaty is a document that is generally regarded as so untrustworthy we feel we must hold arms in order to make sure we're not disadvantaged by its being broken. In other words, we are seriously proposing to sign an agreement to abandon the very thing we will need in the event that the agreement itself fails to stick. This seems a queer program to me.

PETER FARB

FROM *Word Play*

9   Some twenty-five hundred years ago, Psamtik, an Egyptian pharaoh, desired to discover man's primordial tongue. He entrusted two infants to an isolated shepherd and ordered that they should never hear a word spoken in any language. When the children were returned to the pharaoh several years later, he thought he heard them utter *bekos,* which means "bread" in Phrygian, a language of Asia Minor. And so he honored Phrygian as man's "natural" language. Linguists today know that the story of the pharaoh's experiment must be apocryphal.* No child is capable of speech until he has heard other human beings speak, and even two infants reared together cannot develop a language from scratch. Nor does any single "natural" language exist. A child growing up anywhere on earth will speak the tongue he hears in his speech community, regardless of the race, nationality, or language of his parents.

(9) **apocryphal:** legendary, not history or sacred truth

HENRY DAVID THOREAU

FROM *Walden*

10   Why should we be in such desperate haste to succeed and in such desperate enterprises? If a man does not keep pace with his companions, perhaps it is because he hears a different drummer. Let him step to the music which he hears, however measured or far away. It is not important that he should mature as soon as an apple tree or an oak. Shall he turn his spring into summer?

☐ SUGGESTION FOR COMPOSITION

Choose one of the above topic sentences and use it to develop a paragraph of your own.

☐ FINDING THE POINT AND STATING THE POINT

Cartoons serve a variety of purposes—to amuse, to ridicule, to make a political opinion known. The cartoons that appear on pages 100 and 101 have been chosen because they make a point, though they do so in an amusing way. It will be up to you to *state the point in words*. In order to do this, it will first be necessary to *understand* the point. The next step will be to write down what is happening in the cartoon. This may take several sentences. (In such an exercise, it is easier to write several sentences than to write one that crystallizes the idea.) The final step is to express the general point that is being made in one clear sentence. Do not, at this stage, *include any of the particulars of the cartoon's dramatic situation.* You are trying to state a general principle. This will not be easy! It will be interesting to then compare your statements with those of your classmates.

☐ SUGGESTION FOR COMPOSITION

Choose one of the sentences you have written and use it as a controlling or thesis statement for a composition of your own. Illustrate or explain it by using your own examples, not the cartoonist's.

Creating Your Own Thesis Sentence

Let us assume that you have decided on your subject, that you may possibly have written an exploratory draft, that you may even have decided upon a title for your composition. It is important to remember that *neither a title nor a subject/topic is a thesis sentence.* (As a title, you may simply name your topic or subject, or you may choose a more catchy title, one that sounds more interesting. These are not usually in

"Poor things!"

Drawing by Stan Hunt; © 1969 The New Yorker Magazine, Inc.

sentence form.) To demonstrate this and to show that a title or topic designation is very general and leaves a topic wide open while a thesis sentence directs and controls it, let us begin with a topic (or subject) name and proceed to possible thesis sentences.

Subject/Topic: My Childhood
Possible thesis sentences:

1. I had a terrible childhood.
2. My childhood prepared me well for my life as an adult.
3. My childhood was so carefree that I was unprepared for the chores and responsibilities of adult life.
4. My childhood seems, on the surface, to have been like anyone else's.
5. My childhood can be divided into three parts.
6. Looking back, I realize I had no childhood.
7. My childhood was a time of magic—of benevolent angels and fiery dragons, bearded giants and handsome princes.
8. My childhood ended on a cold day in December.

"It's some odd-ball* salesman."

Drawing by George Price; © 1966 The New Yorker Magazine, Inc.

9. My childhood was very different from my sister's.
10. My childhood on the farm seemed to be directed by the rhythm of the seasons.

There are many hypothetical thesis sentences we could derive from this topic. Perhaps you can supply some of your own.

Notice that each of the sentences expresses a different point of view, a different feeling, opinion, or experience. Notice, too, that some sentences lead us to expect a narrative, some a description, some a series of examples. Sentence 9 introduces a comparative essay, as could sentence 4, which implies that surface appearance contrasts with an unseen reality. Sentence 3 could begin an analysis of cause and effect. A thesis sentence, then, not only focuses the subject, but controls its method of development.

☐   FROM TITLE TO THESIS SENTENCE

For each of the following subject/topics, write at least *two* thesis sentences, showing different points of view, opinions, or modes of development.

1. The view from my window
2. Nuclear weapons
3. Abortion
4. Being eighteen

* **odd-ball:** weird, strange, crazy

5. Playing soccer
6. The value of English
7. Violence on TV
8. My car
9. My first job
10. Last summer
11. Memory
12. The _____ International Airport
13. What every child needs
14. Communication
15. Love

Any of these subjects/topics would answer the question: "What are you writing about?" But it requires a sentence to answer the question *"What are you saying* about that subject?" When you can answer this question clearly, you are well on your way to writing a unified composition.

ORGANIZING: DIVIDING AND CLASSIFYING

A paper that is at least several paragraphs long requires some kind of plan, once you have arrived at the controlling idea. The topic has to be *divided* into manageable parts, and the information, data, examples, or other specifics you use have to be classified so that each item will be used where it belongs. Each subdivision should be a logical part of the whole. The ways you divide and classify will be determined by the point you are making. You may find that once you have done your classifying you are left with items that do not fit anywhere or that are unimportant; these items can be left out.

☐ PRACTICE IN CLASSIFYING

Before we attempt to organize a paper or classify information, it may be helpful to practice the variety of ways one can classify. The following items are arranged alphabetically.

1. Organize the list into groups of items that belong together. It may help to write each item on a slip of paper and arrange these separate papers in piles as you classify. Be prepared to justify the unifying principle of each group of items. (A group can be as few as two items.)

an athlete	carrots	a hammer
a baseball	a cook	the juice of an orange
a baseball bat	a drill	lettuce
a bed	an egg beater	a librarian
boards	a gardener	lime soda
a book with a green cover	a grassy piece of land	a mahogany dining table
a carpenter	a green tablecloth	maple syrup

milk	a rose	a sweater of red wool
movies before color film	a salesman	table salt
nails	a screwdriver	a tree
a newspaper	a sheep	a TV set
an oak bookshelf	snow	an unripe apple
an orange	a snowball	a white sheet
peas	a stove	a zebra

2. Now *rearrange* the items. Change the principles of classification and, once more, be prepared to defend your choices. Every item has *at least* two possibilities. Keep rearranging the items as often as you can.
3. You may find that some of your groups are very large and general. If so, *subdivide* your group of items. Or see if you can put two or more smaller groups together as subdivisions of a larger category. Name the smaller groups and the larger one.

Let us now apply principles of division and classification to the organization of an essay. Before we attempt to plan an essay to be written, let us analyze the organization of an essay that has already been written. Dr. Elisabeth Kübler-Ross is well known for her studies of terminally ill patients (patients suffering from an illness that leads to death) and her suggestions of ways the living can and should be helpful to them. Besides being an important article, one well worth discussing for its content, it is also a good example of a well-organized essay that really says something.

ELISABETH KÜBLER-ROSS, M.D.

Facing Up to Death

1   People used to be born at home and die at home. In the old days, children were familiar with birth and death as part of life. This is perhaps the first generation of American youngsters who have never been close by during the birth of a baby and have never experienced the death of a beloved family member.

2   Nowadays when people grow old, we often send them to nursing homes. When they get sick, we transfer them to a hospital, where children are usually unwelcome and are forbidden to visit terminally ill patients—even when those patients are their parents. This deprives the dying patient of significant family members during the last few days of his life and it deprives the children of an experience of death, which is an important learning experience.

3   At the University of Chicago's Billings Hospital, some of my colleagues and I interviewed and followed approximately 500 terminally ill patients in order to find out what they could teach us and how we could be of more benefit, not just to them but to the members of their families as well. We were most impressed by the fact that even those patients who were not told of their serious illness were quite aware of its potential outcome. They were not only able to say that they were close to dying, but many were able to predict the approximate time of their deaths.

4   It is important for next of kin and members of the helping professions to understand these patients' communications in order to truly understand their needs, fears, and fantasies. Most of our patients welcomed another human being with whom they could talk openly, honestly, and frankly about their predicament.* Many of them shared with us their tremendous need to be informed, to be kept up-to-date on their medical condition, and to be told when the end was near. We found out that patients who had been dealt with openly and frankly were better able to cope with the imminence* of death and finally to reach a true stage of acceptance prior to death.

5   Two things seem to determine the ultimate adjustment to a terminal illness. When patients were allowed hope at the beginning of a fatal illness and when they were informed that they would not be deserted "no matter what," they were able to drop their initial shock and denial rather quickly and could arrive at a peaceful acceptance of their finiteness.*

6   Most patients respond to the awareness that they have a terminal illness with the statement, "Oh no, this can't happen to me." After the first shock numbness,* and need to deny the reality of the situation, the patient begins to send out cues that he is ready to "talk about it." If *we*, at that point, need to deny the reality of the situation, the patient will often feel deserted, isolated, and lonely and unable to communicate with another human being what he needs so desperately to share.

7   When, on the other hand, the patient has one person with whom he can talk freely, he will be able to talk (often for only a few minutes at a time) about his illness and about the consequences of his deteriorating* health, and he will be able to ask for help. Sometimes, he'll need to talk about financial matters; and, toward the end of the life, he will frequently ask for some spiritual help.

8   Most patients who have passed the stage of denial will become angry as they ask the question, "Why me?" Many look at others in their environment and express envy, jealousy, anger, and rage toward those who are young, healthy, and full of life. These are the patients who make life difficult for nurses, physicians, social workers, clergymen, and members of their families. Without justification they criticize everyone.

9   What we have to learn is that the stage of anger in terminal illness is a blessing, not a curse. These patients are not angry at their families or at the members of the helping professions. Rather, they are angry at what these people represent: health, pep, energy.

10   Without being judgmental, we must allow these patients to express their anger and dismay. We must try to understand that the patients have to ask,

(4) **predicament:** situation, especially a distressing or embarrassing situation
(4) **imminence:** likely to happen soon, closeness
(5) **finiteness:** not being infinite, having definable limits; here, that one's being alive has a limit, an end
(6) **numbness:** state in which one cannot feel sensation; deadness, frozenness
(7) **deteriorating:** getting worse

"Why me?" and there is no need on our part to answer this question concretely. Once a patient has ventilated* his rage and envy, then he can arrive at the bargaining stage. During this time, he's usually able to say, "Yes, it is happening to me—*but.*" The *but* usually includes a prayer to God: "If you give me one more year to live, I will be a good Christian (or I'll go to the synagogue every day)."

11   Most patients promise something in exchange for prolongation* of life. Many a patient wants to live just long enough for the children to get out of school. The moment they have completed high school, he may ask to live until the son gets married. And the moment the wedding is over, he hopes to live until the grandchild arrives. These kinds of bargains are compromises, the patient's beginning acknowledgement that his time is limited, and an expression of finiteness, all necessary in reaching a stage of acceptance. When a patient drops the *but,* then he is able to say, "Yes, me." At this point, he usually becomes very depressed. And here again we have to allow him to express his grief and his mourning.

12   If we stop and think how much we would grieve if we lost a loved spouse,* it will make us realize what courage it takes for a man to face his own impending* death, which involves the loss of everyone and everything he has ever loved. This is a thousand times more crushing than to become a widow or a widower.

13   To such patients, we should never say, "Come on now, cheer up." We should allow them to grieve, to cry. And we should even convey to them that "it takes a brave person to cry," meaning that it takes courage to face death. If the patient expresses his grief, he will feel more comfortable, and he will usually go through the stage of depression much more rapidly than he will if he has to suppress it or hide his tears.

14   Only through this kind of behavior on our part are our patients able to reach the stage of acceptance. Here, they begin to separate themselves from the interpersonal* relationships in their environment. Here, they begin to ask for fewer and fewer visitors. Finally, they will require only one beloved person who can sit quietly and comfortably near.

15   This is the time when a touch becomes more important than words, the time when a patient may simply say one day, "My time is very close now, and it's all right." It is not necessarily a happy stage, but the patient now shows no more fear, bitterness, anguish,* or concern over unfinished business. People who have been able to sit through this stage with patients and who have experienced the beautiful feeling of inner and outer peace that they show will

(10) **ventilated:** discussed openly; literally, ventilate is to circulate fresh air, to allow release of stale air
(11) **prolongation:** lengthening
(12) **spouse:** husband or wife
(12) **impending:** about to happen, threatening
(14) **interpersonal:** among people; between themselves and others
(15) **anguish:** great mental or physical pain

soon appreciate that working with terminally ill patients is not a morbid,* depressing job but can be an inspiring experience.

16   The tragedy is that in our death-denying society, people grow up uncomfortable in the presence of a dying patient, unable to talk to the terminally ill and lost for words when they face a grieving person.

17   We tried to use dying patients as teachers. We talked with these patients so they could teach our young medical students, social work students, nurses, and members of the clergy about one part of life that all of us eventually have to face. When we interviewed them, we had a screened window setup in which we were able to talk with them in privacy while our students observed and listened. Needless to say this observation was done with the knowledge and agreement of our patients.

18   This teaching by dying patients who volunteered this service to us enabled them to share some of their turmoil and some of their needs with us. But perhaps more important than that, they were able to help our own young students to face the reality of death, to identify at times with our dying patients, and to become aware of their own finiteness.

19   Many of our young students who originally were petrified* at the thought of facing dying patients were eventually able to express to us their own concerns, their own fears, and their own fantasies about dying. Most of our students who have been able to attend one quarter or perhaps a semester of these weekly death-and-dying seminars have learned to come to grips with* their own fears of death and have ultimately become good counselors to terminally ill patients.

20   One thing this teaches us is that it would be helpful if we could rear* our children with the awareness of death and of their own finiteness. Even in a death-denying society, this can be and has been done.

21   In our hospital we saw a small child with acute leukemia. She made the rounds and asked the adults, "What is it going to be like when I die?" The grown-ups responded in a variety of ways, most of them unhelpful or even harmful for this little girl who was searching for an answer. The only messages she really received through the grown-ups' response was that they had a lot of fear when it came to talking about dying.

22   When the child confronted the hospital chaplain with the same question, he turned to her and asked, "What do you think it's going to be like?" She looked at him and said, "One of these days I'm going to fall asleep and when I wake up I'm going to be with Jesus and my little sister." He then said something like "That should be very beautiful." The child nodded and happily returned to play. Perhaps this is an exaggerated example, but I think it conveys how children face the reality even of their own death if the adults in

(15) **morbid:** as if from a sick state of mind, horrible
(19) **petrified:** very, very frightened; literally, changed to stone, made stiff
(19) **come to grips with:** to face, to try to cope with; struggle with
(20) **rear:** raise; educate

their environment don't make it a frightening, horrible experience to be avoided at all costs.

23   The most forgotten people in the environment of the dying patient are the brothers and sisters of dying children. We have seen rather tragic examples of siblings* who were terribly neglected during the terminal illness of a brother or a sister. Very often those children are left alone with many unanswered questions while the mother attends the dying child in the hospital and the father doesn't come home from work because he wants to visit the hospital in the evening.

24   The tragedy is that these children at home not only are anxious, lonely, and frightened at the thought of their sibling's death, but they also feel that somehow their wish for a sibling to "drop dead" (which all children have at times) is being fulfilled. When such a sibling actually dies, they feel responsible for the death, just as they do when they lose a parent during the preschool years. If these children receive no help prior to, and especially immediately after, the death of a parent or a sibling, they are likely to grow up with abnormal fears of death and a lot of unresolved conflicts that often result in emotional illness later on in life.

25   We hope that teachers are aware of the needs of these children and can make themselves available to them in order to elicit* expression of their fears, their fantasies, their needs. If they're allowed to express their anger for being neglected and their shame for having "committed a crime," then these children can be helped before they develop permanent emotional conflict.

26   A beautiful example of death eduation in an indirect way is expressed in a letter I received from a man who became aware of my work and felt the need to convey some of his life experiences to me. I will quote his letter verbatim* because it shows what an early childhood memory can do for a man when he's faced with the imminent death of his own father.

27   Dear Dr. Ross: May I commend you and your colleagues who took part in the Conference on "death. . . ."

        I am a production-line brewery worker here in Milwaukee who feels strongly on this subject. Because of your efforts, maybe one day we can all look death in the eye. . . . In reading and rereading the enclosed account of your meeting, I found myself with the urge to relate to you a personal experience of my own.

28   About six years ago, my dad was a victim of terminal cancer. He was a tough, life-loving 73-year-old father of 10 with 10 grandchildren who kept him aglow* and always on the go. It just couldn't be that his time had come. The last I saw him alive was the result of an urgent

(23) **siblings:** brothers and sisters
(25) **elicit:** draw forth
(26) **verbatim:** word for word, in exactly the same words
(28) **aglow:** full of joy

phone call from my sister. "You'd better come home as soon as possible; it's Pa."

29   The 500-mile drive to northern Minnesota wasn't the enjoyable trip that so many others had been. I learned after I arrived that he wasn't in the hospital, but at home. I also learned that "he didn't know." The doctor told the family that it was up to us to tell or not tell him. My brother and sisters who live in the area thought it best "not to" and so advised me.

30   When I walked in on him, we embraced as we always did when we'd visit about twice or so each year. But this time it was different— sort of restrained and lacking the spirit of earlier get-togethers; and each of us, I know, sensed this difference.

31   Then, some hours later, after the usual kinds of questions and answers and talk, it was plain to me that he appeared so alone and withdrawn, almost moody or sulking.* It was scary to see him just sitting there, head in hand, covering his eyes. I didn't know what to say or do. I asked if he'd care for a drink—no response. Something had to give. It all seemed so cruel. So I stepped into the kitchen and poured me a good one—and another. This was it, and if he didn't "know," he would now.

32   I went over and sat down beside and sort of facing him, and I was scared. I was always scared of my father, but it was a good kind of fear, the respectful kind. I put one hand on his shoulder and the other on his knee. I said, "Pa, you know why I came home, don't you? This is the last time we will be together." The dam burst. He threw his arms around me, and just hung on.

33   And here's the part I'll never forget and yet always cherish. I remember when our tears met, I recalled, in a sort of vivid flashback, a time 30 years before when I was five or six and he took me out into the woods to pick hazelnuts. My very first big adventure! I remembered being afraid of the woods. Afraid of bears or monsters or something that would eat me up. But even though I was afraid, I at the same time was brave, because my big strong daddy was with me.

34   Needless to say, thanks to that hazelnut hunt, I knew how my dad was feeling at that moment. And I could only hope that I gave him some small measure of courage; the kind he had given me. I do know he was grateful and appreciated my understanding. As I remember, he regained his composure and authority enough to scold* *me* for crying. It was at the kitchen table, after a couple or three fingers of brandy, that we talked and reminisced* and planned. I would even guess he was eager to start a long search for his wife, who also had known how to die.

(31) **sulking:** showing resentment or bad mood by quiet, withdrawn behavior
(34) **scold:** to find fault with, to speak to with disapproval
(34) **reminisced:** remembered, spoke of times past

35   What I am trying to convey is that everything depends on the way we rear our children. If we help them to face fear and show them that through strength and sharing we can overcome even the fear of dying, then we will be better prepared to face any kind of crisis that might confront them, including the ultimate reality of death.

☐ FOCUS ON ORGANIZATION

Before we examine the organization of the whole essay, let us first focus on that part of it that divides into stages the period between the awareness of the terminal illness and the death itself (paragraphs 6 through 15). How many stages are there? Make a list, identifying each stage and including a few notes that explain or characterize each stage.

While this section is a major part of the essay, it is not the entire essay. It is a part of a larger topic. Can you, at this point, write a thesis sentence that tells us the point or statement of the entire essay? If you cannot do this yet, you should be able to do it by the time you have finished analyzing the total structure. Sometimes we can begin with this main point, but sometimes we need to arrive at it after we have examined the minor points and items of information.

☐ NOTING THE IDEAS

The first step in analyzing structure (as in creating your own structure for an essay) is often to make a list of the points that are made, including statements, examples, opinions, and other data. Make such a list from this essay.

☐ CLASSIFYING THE IDEAS

The next step is to determine which points and information go together or are part of a larger unified idea. Each of these groups will, in turn, form a major division of the overall essay.

Relating Major Ideas to a Thesis Sentence

The major divisions of an essay are divisions of the main idea, that idea which we try to formulate in a thesis sentence.

Whether one works from the main idea down to the details or from the details up through to the main idea is not important. This will vary from paper to paper. What is important is that there *be* a main idea and that the parts be related to it, and to each other, in a logical fashion. There are various ways to diagram such a relationship, for example, a center and its radii (Figure 5a) or a tree diagram (Figure 5b).

A very good way to show these relationships is the Standard Harvard outline. While practiced writers often arrive at their own systems of organization, many use

FIGURE 5

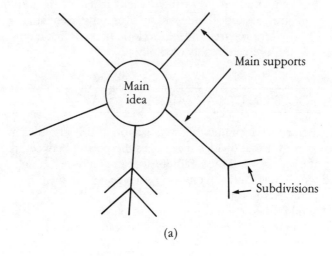

(a)

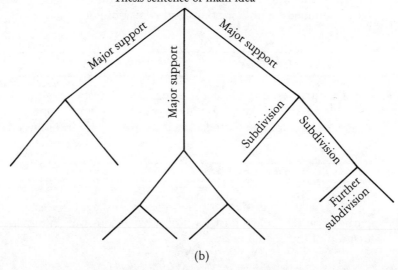

(b)

some version of this form, especially when doing expository writing. Some courses and types of writing require its use. Most students benefit from learning such a method of structuring, even though they might not need to use it for all their writing. Whether or not you have already learned the form of the Standard Harvard outline, a review may be helpful.

Major divisions are signaled by means of roman numerals (I, II, III, IV, V). Subdivisions of a major category are indicated by capital letters (A, B, C, D), which are indented under the roman numeral division. Should further breakdown and detail be desired, the next indented subdivision, under the capital letters, is in arabic numerals

FIGURE 6

Thesis Sentence Stated at the Top
(this governs everything that follows):

I. First major point or division
    A. First point belonging to above division
    B. Second point under I
II. Second major point or division
    A.
    B.
    C.
III. Third major point or division
    A. First point belonging to this division
        1. ⎫
        2. ⎬ details belonging to Point A
        3. ⎭
            a. ⎫
            b. ⎬ finer details belonging to 3
            c. ⎭
                (1) ⎫
                (2) ⎬ still finer details belonging to c
                (3) ⎭
    B.

(1, 2, 3, 4, 5). Under that are small letters (a, b, c, d) and, rarely, further divisions into arabic numerals in parentheses [(1), (2), (3)], and then small letters in parentheses [(a), (b), (c)]. Set up properly, the outline graphically shows the major and subordinate points of an essay. The outline should look like Figure 6.

Notice the way you can see, at a glance, the three major divisions and their subordinate points, and how those subordinate points relate to the whole scheme. Some important things to keep in mind include the following.

1. *All like points should have approximately equal importance and be of similar length.*
2. *One cannot divide into fewer than two.* Therefore, a I must have a II; an A must have a B; a 1 must have a 2, etc.
3. *The items must be expressed in parallel structure.* All items must be sentences or phrases beginning with nouns, or gerunds, or verbs, etc. Now practice *both* the skill of using the outline form and the *more important* skill of recognizing major and subordinate divisions by making an outline of Dr. Kübler-Ross's essay. Begin with the thesis sentence and follow the pattern just given to you.

☐ QUESTIONS FOR DISCUSSION

1. The author speaks of this generation of Americans as a "death-denying" society. What does she mean? Is your society similar or different? Discuss.

2. Ashley Montagu writes in "The Cult of Youthfulness": "The emphasis on youthfulness is an evidence of insecurity, a fear of aging ... and ultimately an unwillingness to face the fact of human mortality." Is there a connection between this cult of youthfulness and any of the points Dr. Kübler-Ross makes? What is it? Do you think there is a relationship between a society's attitude toward its aged and its attitude toward death? If so, explain.

3. Do you think people are better off dying at home or in a good hospital? How about the families? Consider the pros and cons (the arguments for and against) of each position as part of your answer.

4. Why should one not say "Come on now, cheer up" to a dying patient? Explain in some detail, using examples if you can.

5. What are the special problems of the siblings (brothers and sisters) of dying children? What suggestions would you have for dealing with them?

6. Relate the letter at the end to the author's point. Notice that this letter is used by way of conclusion, leading to Ross's concluding remarks.

Creating Your Own Organization

Let us now plan a hypothetical paper, taking it through the various planning stages we have been discussing. Whether you are doing this alone, as a small group, or as a class, you should follow the basic steps we have been discussing.

1. Choose your general topic.
2. Write down your ideas.
3. Narrow your topic to a more specific subject.
4. Focus the subject by writing a thesis sentence.
5. Decide what specific information you want to include.
6. Organize the information with an outline.

Sometimes the organization of your paper comes to mind first, after which you can think about specific examples; sometimes the specific examples or information are on your mind before you focus the paper. *The main thing is to go through all the steps* in whichever order comes to you more naturally, given the topic you have chosen.

1. Choosing a general topic. You and your class could begin with any broad topic you wish. On one topic, however, you will have some knowledge and experience in common: your university. Let us use your university as an example of a general topic that you will be able to break down into many subjects.

2. Narrowing down to a more specific subject. Make a list of aspects of your university about which you could possibly write a paper. Try to make the topics as diverse as possible. Here are some examples:

Social life at _____ University
Academic pressure
The faculty

The food at _____ University
International student activities and services
Life in the dorm
One day at _____ University
Laboratory and research opportunities
The cost of attending _____ University

3. Choose three or four of the subjects and, for each one, create a thesis sentence. For example: The Cost of Attending _____ University.

   a. It requires a lot of money to attend _____ University, or
   b. _____ University is more expensive than _____
      University, or
   c. Coming to study at _____ University is worth the various costs
      of having come.

Organizing topic b will require comparison of data. (How to organize a comparison/contrast paper will be taken up in a separate chapter.) Sentence a will likewise be dependent on factual data to support the main idea. How would you classify this data? Perhaps by types of expenses:

  I. Academic expenses
 II. Living expenses
III. Travel expenses
IV. Entertainment expenses

Perhaps the topic could be directed toward sources of aid. Restated, the thesis sentence might read:

The high cost of _____ University requires many students to be subsidized.

  I. Academic expenses
 II. Living expenses
III. Travel and entertainment
IV. Possible sources of aid

Using the two preceding outlines, fill in the A, B, C subdivisions. Choose one such subdivision and subdivide it further into 1, 2, and 3.

Sentence c is less dependent on factual data and more dependent on weighing various factors such as personal experiences and priorities in order to arrive at an evaluation. It might be outlined as follows:

Coming to study at _____ University is worth the various costs of having come.

  I. Financial costs
    A. Academic costs
       1. Tuition
       2. Books
       3. Lab fees

B. Living costs

C. Travel

II. Emotional costs

    A. Distance from family and friends

    B. Distance from a familiar way of life

    C. Difficulties in adjusting to American campus life

        1. Language

        2. Culture

        3. Social adjustment

III. Worthwhile gains

    A. Personal development

        1. Better education

        2. Broader understanding of the world as a result of the experience

        3. Friendships with kinds of people I never would have met at home

        4. More maturity and self-confidence as a result of living so far from home

    B. More secure future

        1. Better pay

        2. More prestige

Any one of the preceding major divisions could be developed into a paper. To make an entire paper out of any one division would require rewriting the thesis sentence and going into more detail, for the minor points would become major points to be divided further.

☐ SUGGESTED ASSIGNMENT

Choose two topics (either on the subject of the university or on a subject of your own choosing). For each one, go through the planning stages discussed in this chapter. You should have a thesis sentence and an outline, at least to the A/B level.

Do not divide the paper into only two major divisions. Papers divided only into I and II tend to fall in half, to be like two subjects taped together.

Do not have too many roman numeral divisions. More than five major divisions usually indicates that not every division is really a major one. If you find yourself with too many such divisions, reexamine them and try to find common headings for some, grouping them as A/B under the more inclusive heading.

You should get into the habit of using this system of outlining the papers you will be writing. To learn the system is to learn order in writing and in thinking. It is the difference between putting together lumber, bricks, nails, pipes, and plumbing fixtures at random, hoping the end result will be a house, and beginning with a sketch of the finished house and a blueprint to follow. However, simply putting the materials from each source together—all the lumber together, all the nails together, all the pipes together, all the bricks together—will bring you no closer to a finished house. All buildings must follow a design, and the materials must be combined in a logical manner that works toward a desired end. My house will look different from yours and have different financial and spatial priorities, but both buildings will definitely be houses, not bridges or stores. It is not too far-fetched to compare structure in building to structure in writing. In both cases, the well-planned structure is more functional and more beautiful.

BASIC ORGANIZATIONAL STRUCTURES

One kind of paper will state its main point at the beginning. This could very well serve as the introduction. The paper then goes on to illustrate the point, to bring proof of it in the form of facts, evidence, or analysis. In the case of the illustrative paper, a thesis sentence may begin *there is* or *there are* (see Figure 7). The analysis presented this way might be stated as *The causes of* _____ *were,* as in Figure 7.

Another way to structure a paper is to proceed toward the main idea. This type of paper builds toward its thesis, as illustrated in Figure 8.

The Body of the Paper

The body of the paper really is the paper; that is, organizing the body is organizing the paper (introductions and conclusions come easy when you understand that principle).

The body of the paper is what we are talking about when we talk of organizing a paper into three or so parts. All too often, students who have been taught that papers have an introduction, a body, and a conclusion assume that this forms a natural three-part division. What could be simpler! The problem is that such simplicity avoids the whole question of organization, treating the body as a single unit when it should comprise most of the paper. Such a division also makes it seem as if the body were one-third of the paper. Were that true, the paper would be grossly out of balance. If that were not true, the outline would not represent the true structure of the paper and would therefore be of no help.

FIGURE   7

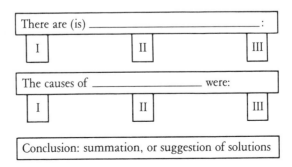

FIGURE 8

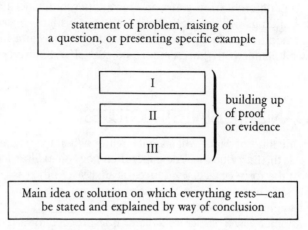

Too often conclusions are obviously "tacked on" because students have heard a teacher say every paper must have one. As a result they are often artificial, repetitious. A genuine conclusion means that something has really been concluded—the point you are making. It grows out of the paper organically or is basic to it. If you make a point and stick to it, what you write will draw the paper to its natural end. Your job will be much easier and the ending will sound much more natural. *A truly well-organized paper, whose organization arises from a thesis sentence, a sense of purpose, will not be difficult to introduce, and it will arrive naturally at a conclusion.*

How naturally introductions and conclusions become part of a paper when it is well organized and when it makes a point! Certainly one wants to arrest the attention of readers as they begin the first paragraph and leave them feeling satisfied at the end. But, unless the conclusion genuinely concludes and unless the introduction is interesting and naturally leads us into the paper, the writer has not been successful. Doing these things successfully depends on control of one's subject—knowing, organizing, and communicating one's purpose.

Suggestions on Introductions

What are some effective ways to begin a paper?

1. Pose the question or state the problem your paper is meant to answer. Let it reflect your own interest—what made you curious about it, why you chose it. Even if you leave yourself out of the problem, your questions, concerns, and curiosities can be presented so that the reader shares them.
2. Present facts or statistics in evidence of your point, especially if the facts will arouse the reader's concern or interest. However, be sure the facts you present are true and relevant to your point.
3. Begin by illustrating your point with a narrated incident. Focusing on a specific

person, an incident, or a dramatic event or conflict is an almost certain way to interest readers. Again, of course, your example must be appropriate.

4. An appropriate quotation, either on the subject or relevant to it, is another good way to begin.

5. You may need to provide background information on the subject you have chosen so that readers can understand the point of your paper. Be careful to keep this information brief. Your background material should not exceed 15 to 20 percent of your paper.

6. As has already been said, stating the point of the paper first is a perfectly acceptable way to begin.

If you still are uncertain how to begin your paper, move to the body and start writing. When you finish, read what you have written from the beginning. Does the first paragraph sound like the beginning or does it need something else to get it started? If it seems to be missing something, use one of the preceding methods of introducing a paper. If it leads clearly and interestingly into your subject, consider your paper well begun!

7

ILLUSTRATION

One of the most common ways to develop an idea is by providing examples to illustrate it. Saying "for instance" or "for example" comes very naturally to us when we are explaining something. We also usually ask others for examples when they are trying to convey ideas to us. As students, we welcome examples in our texts. We learn material and abstract concepts more easily when our teachers provide examples. If we still do not understand or if we find something difficult to believe, we ask for still another example.

If there is anything you have heard from your teachers of composition, it is "be specific!" Providing specific examples makes your writing better in several ways.

1. Examples make writing more convincing. If you support your general statement with examples, the reader will have more respect for the validity of your opinion. You will seem to know what you are talking about. The reader may know of other examples with which he or she could oppose yours, but it will be an opposition based on information and respect for your knowledge and experience. Making assertions with no support, simply stating opinions or generalities, is not going to convince anyone.
2. Such writing is also boring. Examples make writing more interesting. Examples provide details that add life to your composition. There is no life in generalities; there is life in the particular.
3. Examples make your meaning clear. The examples you provide show exactly the way you are using a concept, the way you interpret a word or idea. The reader will also better understand what you are trying to explain.

Without examples, writing would be vague as well as dull. Specific examples connect ideas with reality. On the other hand, using all examples with no abstract ideas or generalizations is pointless, more like a list than a paper. *The general and the particular must work together.* Without the general, a paper has no point, no purpose for its examples, nothing tying the examples together. Without the specific, a paper sounds vague, empty, and dull.

Of course it goes without saying that examples must be relevant and appropriate. They must support your point and be examples to which a reader can relate. There must also be some judgment exercised in the *number* of examples you use. Readers should not feel they are reading one example after another without moving forward to other ideas.

What you have already learned about narration and description will be very useful in writing examples, for examples sometimes take the form of narration and description. A description or narration can be *an example* to illustrate the point you are making.

WAYS OF USING AND ORGANIZING EXAMPLES

1. General to particular or particular to general. One way of organizing a discussion with examples is to state the point or generalization, then follow it with examples. Very often, however, you will find very well-written essays that capture your interest by starting with the particular examples, and then generalizing from these. It doesn't matter which pattern you follow, as long as you have both the general and the specific, and as long as there is a relationship between them.

2. Enumeration or extension. There are basically two methods of illustrating with example: providing a list of examples, one after the other, which is known as **enumeration;** and fully developing a single example, which is called an **extended example.** Often the two methods are combined.

The essay that follows *enumerates* its examples. Notice the relationship between statements and examples and notice the way the whole essay is organized. William Fulbright, a former United States senator, was chairman of the Senate Foreign Relations Committee from 1959 to 1974.

J. WILLIAM FULBRIGHT

We're Tongue-Tied

1   Our heritage and our culture have caused most Americans to assume not only that our language is universal but that the gestures we use are understood by everyone. We do not realize that waving goodbye is the way to summon a Filipino to one's side, or that in Italy and some Latin-American countries, curling the finger in a beckoning* motion is a pantomime* of farewell.

2   Those private citizens who sent packages to our troops occupying Germany after World War II and marked them GIFT to escape duty payments did

(1) **beckoning:** motioning to come
(1) **pantomime:** acting out without using words; using only motions, gestures, facial expressions

not bother to find out that *Gift* means poison in German. Moreover, we like to think of ourselves as friendly, yet we prefer to be at least 3 feet or an arm's length away from others. Latins and Middle Easterners like to come closer and touch, which makes Americans uncomfortable.

3   Our linguistic and cultural myopia* and the casualness with which we take cognizance*—when we do—of the developed tastes, mannerisms, mores* and languages of other countries, are losing us friends, business and respect in the world.

4   Even here in the United States, we make few concessions* to the needs of foreign visitors. There are no information signs in four languages on our public buildings or monuments; we do not have multilingual* guided tours at Mt. Vernon or in Arlington National Cemetery. Very few restaurant menus have translations, and multilingual waiters, bank clerks and policemen are rare. Our transportation systems have maps in English only and often we ourselves have difficulty understanding them.

5   When we go abroad, we tend to cluster in hotels and restaurants where English is spoken. The attitudes and information we pick up are conditioned by* those natives—usually the more affluent*—who speak English. Our business dealings, as well as the nation's diplomacy, are conducted through interpreters.

6   For many years, America and Americans could get by with cultural blindness and linguistic ignorance. After all, America was the most powerful country of the free world, the dispenser* of needed funds and commodities, the peacemaker, the "top banana" in the global cast.

7   But all that is past. American dollars no longer buy all good things, and we are slowly beginning to realize that our proper role in the world is changing. A 1979 Harris poll reported that 55 percent of Americans want this country to play a more significant role in world affairs; we want to have a hand in the important decisions of the next century, even though it may not always be the upper hand.

8   It is clear that in order to play a significant role, more of us will have to know languages and understand cultural differences. In 1976, only 4 percent of high-school graduates had spent two years learning a foreign language; in 1977, only 9 percent of degree-credit college students were enrolled in foreign-language courses. In the same year, it was found that only 14.3 percent of college freshmen could speak a second language, no matter how

(3) **myopia:** nearsightedness; inability to see things distinctly
(3) **take cognizance of:** notice, be aware of, recognize
(3) **mores:** ways of living of a group that its members consider important for their welfare; customs that have the force of law in that society
(4) **concessions:** giving in, yielding, granting
(4) **multilingual:** in many languages
(5) **conditioned by:** we are made used to them, influenced by
(5) **affluent:** rich
(6) **dispenser:** one who gives out, distributes

many courses they had absorbed. Two years of study gives a student only a taste of the basics of a language. The fact that fewer than one in twenty recent graduates from public high schools have studied any foreign language for more than two years shows the limitations of our linguistic achievement.

9   Unfortunately, foreign-language and cultural studies have often been discouraged at the high-school level because many guidance counselors believe that this kind of knowledge has little commercial value. But this perception is obsolete:* already one out of eight jobs in industry and one out of five in agriculture depend on international trade. Many more positions may soon require the secondary skill of a foreign language.

10   The general feeling is that language skills can be purchased as needed. This is a strange notion if one can visualize the rapid-fire talk and signals used when a contract is being negotiated, and gauge* the handicap under which an American competes with foreigners facing him at a conference table. The foreigners are usually capable of communicating quickly with one another while the American must rely on the accuracy of an interpreter from another culture.

11   Americans are similarly handicapped in conducting foreign policy. In recent years, our graduate centers for international and area studies have received less and less Federal money, which has resulted in declining enrollments in international studies at the undergraduate level. Just when our need for diplomatic skills is most intense, we are failing to train generations of diplomats to fill many overseas posts.

12   In Teheran in 1978, only 9 of the 60 Foreign Service officers could speak Persian. In Pakistan, only 5 of America's 32 diplomatic officials are required to be proficient* in Urdu. In Kenya, only 1 officer of 22 in the American Embassy is required to speak Swahili. It is very difficult to find in the service a bilingual interpreter of Chinese or Japanese.

13   For the important work of international affairs, long years of study are required to thoroughly master a language and to acquire in-depth knowledge of the societies the student wishes to enter. The President's Commission on Foreign Language and International Studies is considering how Americans can become better citizens of the world. To teach languages to youngsters— the younger the better—and to greatly expand educational exchange programs would seem to be logical steps.

14   In Jamaica, N.Y., there is a high school which offers nine languages, including Hebrew, Chinese, Russian and Greek. The school provides a two-year career course to selected students who wish to enter the fields of international trade, tourism or diplomacy. It is one of the few high schools to offer international studies along with the appropriate languages. There should be many more such schools.

(9) **obsolete:** no longer in use, out of date
(10) **gauge:** measure, estimate
(12) **proficient:** very skilled, able

15   Georgetown University has already received a grant, recommended by Congress and administered by the International Communication Agency, to provide administrative costs for a program that would permit paying students at the university to exchange places with foreign counterparts in any of 40 universities in eight nations.

16   If the pilot program at Georgetown is successful, it is expected that Congress will recommend that it be repeated at other American universities. We need all the versions of international cultural and educational interchange we can create if the growing parochialism* of Americans, both old and young, is to be replaced with knowledge and understanding.

☐ FOCUS ON USING EXAMPLES

---

1. Underline each of the general statements or points Mr. Fulbright makes. How convincing would Mr. Fulbright's argument be if his essay consisted only of the general statements you have underlined?
2. Now mark the examples that substantiate each point.

Notice how many facts have been used. To enumerate, as Fulbright has done, you need to use many examples, many facts. Perhaps you will need to go to the library or to some other source of information to gather the facts you will need. Sometimes you can find enough examples from your own experience, depending, of course, on your topic.

☐ QUESTIONS FOR DISCUSSION

---

1. Explain the author's use of the term "linguistic and cultural myopia." Is myopia a good word choice? Why? Do you agree or disagree with Mr. Fulbright? Support your view with examples.
2. Do you find "parochialism" to be a characteristic of the American students you know? Of most of them? All of them? Any of them? Are they more parochial than the people in your own country or less so? Are they parochial in a different way? Have you known people of other nationalities who are just as parochial? In what ways are they parochial?
3. Could you advance any theories that might explain the "linguistic and cultural myopia" of the United States?
4. How do you feel about the study of foreign languages in high school and college? Of what value is such study? If you were American, what language or languages would you want to study? Why? Would you avoid the study of a foreign language? Why or why not?
5. What values of language study does Fulbright seem to miss altogether? Discuss.

    (16) **parochialism:** narrowness of thought, interest, activity; interest restricted to small area or scope; provincialism

☐ SUGGESTIONS FOR COMPOSITION

1. How do you feel about studying a foreign language in high school? How well did your high school English course enable you to manage in the United States? What advice would you give your teachers now? Your younger friends and relatives back home? Use examples from your experience.

2. Read the following quotation on learning a second language from Mina P. Shaughnessey's book *Errors and Expectations..*

> To the extent that he *is* motivated to learn about his common errors, he is usually negatively motivated, that is, he wishes to avoid the punishment of a bad grade.... Such motivation carries a student through the beginning of a course but not always to the end of it. If, in addition to this kind of motive, however, the student has a career goal that calls for writing skill ... he usually has the fuel he needs to get through the course. Nonetheless, the strongest learning energies are generated by the desire rather than the obligation to learn something. Gardner and Lambert in their research on attitudes and motivation in second-language learning distinguish between ... the recognition of a practical use for the language and ... an active desire to identify with the cultural group that uses the language. While both attitudes will serve the language learner, the authors conclude that "learners who identify with the cultural group represented by a foreign or second language are likely to enjoy an advantage in attempts to master that language. Their motivation to learn the language appears to stem from and be sustained by the desire to identify."

Write a composition in which you comment on the preceding passage. For example: Is "punishment" a good language teacher? To what extent are career goals an important factor in having learned your English lessons well? How important is attitude toward an English-speaking culture? Use examples from your own experience or that of your friends.

The following essay uses both extended examples and enumeration to illustrate the point that in every culture there are nonverbal ways of sending and receiving messages, systems we may not even be conscious of using. Edward Hall's books, *The Silent Language* and *The Hidden Dimension,* are very well known and draw upon Mr. Hall's combined expertise in anthropology (the study of different kinds of human societies) and linguistics (the science of language).

EDWARD AND MILDRED HALL

The Sounds of Silence

1   Bob leaves his apartment at 8:15 A.M. and stops at the corner drugstore for breakfast. Before he can speak, the counterman says, "The usual?" Bob nods yes. While he savors* his Danish,* a fat man pushes onto the adjoining stool and overflows into his space. Bob scowls* and the man pulls himself in as much as he can. Bob has sent two messages without speaking a syllable.

2   Henry has an appointment to meet Arthur at 11 o'clock; he arrives at 11:30. Their conversation is friendly, but Arthur retains a lingering* hostility. Henry has unconsciously communicated that he doesn't think the appointment is very important or that Arthur is a person who needs to be treated with respect.

3   George is talking to Charley's wife at a party. Their conversation is entirely trivial,* yet Charley glares at them suspiciously. Their physical proximity* and the movements of their eyes reveal that they are powerfully attracted to each other.

4   Jose Ybarra and Sir Edmund Jones are at the same party, and it is important for them to establish a cordial relationship for business reasons. Each is trying to be warm and friendly, yet they will part with mutual distrust and their business transaction will probably fall through. Jose, in Latin fashion, moved closer and closer to Sir Edmund as they spoke, and his movement was miscommunicated as pushiness to Sir Edmund, who kept backing away from this intimacy, and this was miscommunicated to Jose as coldness. The silent languages of Latin and English cultures are more difficult to learn than their spoken languages.

5   In each of these cases, we see the subtle power of nonverbal communication. The only language used throughout most of the history of humanity (in evolutionary terms, vocal communication is relatively recent), it is the first form of communication you learn. You use this preverbal language, consciously and unconsciously, every day to tell other people how you feel about yourself and them. This language includes your posture, gestures, facial expressions, costume, the way you walk, even your treatment of time and space and material things. All people communicate on several different levels at the same time but are usually aware of only the verbal dialog and don't realize that they respond to nonverbal messages. But when a person says one thing and really believes something else, the discrepancy between the two can usually be sensed. Nonverbal-communication systems are much less subject

(1) **savors:** enjoys the taste or smell of
(1) **Danish:** a type of yeast pastry, especially popular for breakfast
(1) **scowls:** looks severe or angry, frowns
(2) **lingering:** remaining
(3) **trivial:** small and unimportant
(3) **proximity:** nearness, closeness

to* the conscious deception* that often occurs in verbal systems. When we find ourselves thinking, "I don't know what it is about him, but he doesn't seem sincere," it's usually this lack of congruity* between a person's words and his behavior that makes us anxious and uncomfortable.

6   Few of us realize how much we all depend on body movement in our conversation or are aware of the hidden rules that govern listening behavior. But we know instantly whether or not the person we're talking to is "tuned in" and we're very sensitive to any breach* in listening etiquette.* In white middle-class American culture, when someone wants to show he is listening to someone else, he looks either at the other person's face or, specifically, at his eyes, shifting his gaze from one eye to the other.

7   If you observe a person conversing, you'll notice that he indicates he's listening by nodding his head. He also makes little "Hmm" noises. If he agrees with what's being said, he may give a vigorous nod. To show pleasure or affirmation, he smiles; if he has some reservations, he looks skeptical by raising an eyebrow or pulling down the corners of his mouth. If a participant wants to terminate the conversation, he may start shifting his body position, stretching his legs, crossing or uncrossing them, bobbing his foot or diverting* his gaze from the speaker. The more he fidgets,* the more the speaker becomes aware that he has lost his audience. As a last measure, the listener may look at his watch to indicate the imminent* end of the conversation. . . .

8   The language of the eyes—another age-old way of exchanging feelings— is both subtle and complex. Not only do men and women use their eyes differently but there are class, generation, regional, ethnic,* and national cultural differences. Americans often complain about the way foreigners stare at people or hold a glance too long. Most Americans look away from someone who is using his eyes in an unfamiliar way because it makes them self-conscious. If a man looks at another man's wife in a certain way, he's asking for trouble, as indicated earlier. But he might not be ill mannered or seeking to challenge the husband. He might be a European in this country who hasn't learned our visual mores.* Many American women visiting France or Italy are acutely embarrassed because, for the first time in their lives, men really look at them—their eyes, hair, nose, lips, breasts, hips, legs, thighs, knees, ankles,

(5) **subject to:** controlled by

(5) **deception:** an act of misleading or making a person believe what is not true

(5) **congruity:** agreement, harmony, suitability

(6) **breach:** break

(6) **etiquette:** the forms, manners, and ceremonies established as acceptable in a society

(7) **diverting:** turning aside

(7) **fidgets:** is restless; makes quick, restless movements of the body because of nervousness or discomfort

(7) **imminent:** about to happen

(8) **ethnic:** referring to a group of people as distinguished by their customs, characteristics, language

(8) **mores:** ways of living of a group that its members consider important for their welfare; customs that have the force of law in that society

feet, clothes, hairdo, even their walk. These same women, once they have become used to being looked at, often return to the United States and are overcome with the feeling that "No one really looks at me anymore." . . .

9   The eye is unlike any other organ of the body, for it is an extension of the brain. The unconscious pupillary reflex* and the cast of the eye have been known by people of Middle Eastern origin for years—although most are unaware of their knowledge. Depending on the context, Arabs and others look either directly at the eyes or deeply *into* the eyes of their interlocutor.* We became aware of this in the Middle East several years ago while looking at jewelry. The merchant suddenly started to push a particular bracelet at a customer and said, "You buy this one." What interested us was that the bracelet was not the one that had been consciously selected by the purchaser. But the merchant, watching the pupils of the eyes, knew what the purchaser really wanted to buy. Whether he specifically knew *how* he knew is debatable. . . .

10   One common situation for most people involves the use of the eyes in the street and in public. Although eye behavior follows a definite set of rules, the rules vary according to the place, the needs and feelings of the people, and their ethnic background. For urban whites, once they're within definite recognition distance (16–32 feet for people with average eyesight), there is mutual avoidance of eye contact—unless they want something specific: a pickup, a handout or information of some kind. In the West and in small towns generally, however, people are much more likely to look at and greet one another, even if they're strangers.

11   It's permissible to look at people if they're beyond recognition distance; but once inside this sacred zone, you can only steal a glance at strangers. You *must* greet friends, however; to fail to do so is insulting. Yet, to stare too fixedly* even at them is considered rude and hostile. Of course, all of these rules are variable. . . .

12   Another very basic difference between people of different ethnic backgrounds is their sense of territoriality* and how they handle space. This is the silent communication, or miscommunication, that caused friction between Mr. Ybarra and Sir Edmund Jones in our earlier example. We know from research that everyone has around himself an invisible bubble of space that contracts and expands depending on several factors: his emotional state, the activity he's performing at the time and his cultural background. This bubble is a kind of mobile territory that he will defend against intrusion.* If he is accustomed to close personal distance between himself and others, his bub-

(9) **pupillary reflex:** the pupil is the black-looking center of the eye; the pupillary reflex, the involuntary expanding and contracting of the pupil due to external stimuli such as light

(9) **interlocutor:** one who participates in a conversation or dialogue

(11) **fixedly:** without moving one's eyes

(12) **territoriality:** being of, or state of belonging to, a specific territory; here, a possessive attitude toward one's own space

(12) **intrusion:** act of pushing oneself in without being invited or wanted; with no invitation or right to be there (*intrude* is the verb form)

ble will be smaller than that of someone who's accustomed to greater personal distance. People of North European heritage—English, Scandinavian, Swiss and German—tend to avoid contact. Those whose heritage is Italian, French, Spanish, Russian, Latin American or Middle Eastern like close personal contact.

13   People are very sensitive to any intrusion into their spatial bubble. If someone stands too close to you, your first instinct is to back up. If that's not possible, you lean away and pull yourself in, tensing your muscles. If the intruder doesn't respond to these body signals, you may then try to protect yourself, using a briefcase, umbrella or raincoat. Women—especially when traveling alone—often plant their pocketbook in such a way that no one can get very close to them. As a last resort, you may move to another spot and position yourself behind a desk or a chair that provides screening. Everyone tries to adjust the space around himself in a way that's comfortable for him; most often, he does this unconsciously.

14   Emotions also have a direct effect on the size of a person's territory. When you're angry or under stress, your bubble expands and you require more space. New York psychiatrist Augustus Kinzel found a difference in what he calls Body-Buffer zones between violent and nonviolent prison inmates. Dr. Kinzel conducted experiments in which each prisoner was placed in the center of a small room and then Dr. Kinzel slowly walked toward him. Nonviolent prisoners allowed him to come quite close, while prisoners with a history of violent behavior couldn't tolerate his proximity and reacted with some vehemence.*. . .

15   Unfortunately, there is little detailed information about normal people who live in highly congested* urban areas. We do know, of course, that the noise, pollution, dirt, crowding, and confusion of our cities induce feelings of stress in most of us, and stress leads to a need for greater space. The man who's packed into a subway, jostled* in the street, crowded into an elevator and forced to work all day in a bull pen* or in a small office without auditory* or visual privacy is going to be very stressed at the end of his day. He needs places that provide relief from constant overstimulation of his nervous system. Stress from overcrowding is cumulative and people can tolerate more crowding early in the day than later; note the increased bad temper during the evening rush hour as compared with the morning melee.* Certainly one factor in people's desire to commute by car is the need for privacy and relief from crowding (except, often, from other cars); it may be the only time of the day when nobody can intrude.

16   In crowded public places, we tense our muscles and hold ourselves stiff,

(14) **vehemence:** action or feelings of great force, characterized by intense feeling and passionate expression
(15) **congested:** overcrowded
(15) **jostled:** pushed, as in a crowd
(15) **bull pen:** an office in which there are many desks in one large room
(15) **auditory:** pertaining to hearing or being heard
(15) **melee:** confusion, a mixed or confused mass

and thereby communicate to others our desire not to intrude on their space and, above all, not to touch them. We also avoid eye contact, and the total effect is that of someone who has "tuned out." Walking along the street, our bubble expands slightly as we move in a stream of strangers, taking care not to bump into them. In the office, at meetings, in restaurants, our bubble keeps changing as it adjusts to the activity at hand.

17   Most white middle-class Americans use four main distances in their business and social relations: intimate, personal, social and public. Each of these distances has a near and a far phase and is accompanied by changes in the volume of the voice. Intimate distance varies from direct physical contact with another person to a distance of six to eighteen inches and is used for our most private activities—caressing* another person or making love. At this distance, you are overwhelmed by sensory* inputs from the other person— heat from the body, tactile* stimulation from the skin, the fragrance of perfume, even the sound of breathing—all of which literally envelop you. Even at the far phase, you're still within easy touching distance. In general, the use of intimate distance in public between adults is frowned on. It's also much too close for strangers, except under conditions of extreme crowding.

18   In the second zone—personal distance—the close phase is one and a half to two and a half feet; it's at this distance that wives usually stand from their husbands in public. If another woman moves into this zone, the wife will most likely be disturbed. The far phase—two and a half to four feet—is the distance used to "keep someone at arm's length" and is the most common spacing used by people in conversation.

19   The third zone—social distance—is employed during business transactions or exchanges with a clerk or repairman. People who work together tend to use close social distance—four to seven feet. This is also the distance for conversations at social gatherings. To stand at this distance from someone who is seated has a dominating effect (e.g., teacher to pupil, boss to secretary). The far phase of the third zone—seven to twelve feet—is where people stand when someone says, "Stand back so I can look at you." This distance lends a formal tone to business or social discourse.* In an executive office, the desk serves to keep people at this distance.

20   The fourth zone—public distance—is used by teachers in classrooms or speakers at public gatherings. At its farthest phase—twenty-five feet and beyond—it is used for important public figures. Violations of the distance can lead to serious complications. During his 1970 U.S. visit, the president of France, Georges Pompidou, was harassed* by pickets* in Chicago, who were permitted to get within touching distance. Since pickets in France are kept

(17) **caressing:** touching and stroking lovingly and gently
(17) **sensory:** of the senses
(17) **tactile:** referring to touch or feeling
(19) **discourse:** communication of ideas in speech or writing
(20) **harassed:** worried, made tired, annoyed
(20) **pickets:** here, demonstrators carrying signs of protest

behind barricades a block or more away, the president was outraged by this insult to his person, and President Nixon was obliged to communicate his concern as well as offer his personal apologies. . . .

21   Touch also is an important part of the constant stream of communication that takes place between people. A light touch, a blow, a caress are all communications. In an effort to break down barriers among people, there's been a recent upsurge in group-encounter activities, in which strangers are encouraged to touch one another. In special situations such as these, the rules for not touching are broken with group approval and people gradually lose some of their inhibitions.

22   Although most people don't realize it, space is perceived and distances are set not by vision alone but with all the senses. Auditory space is perceived with the ears, thermal space with the skin, kinesthetic space with the muscles of the body and olfactory space with the nose. And, once again, it's one's culture that determines how his senses are programmed—which sensory information ranks highest and lowest. The important thing to remember is that culture is very persistent. In this country, we've noted the existence of culture patterns that determine distance between people in the third and fourth generations of some families, despite their prolonged contact with people of very different cultural heritages.

23   Whenever there is great cultural distance between two people, there are bound to be problems arising from differences in behavior and expectations. An example is the American couple who consulted a psychiatrist about their marital problems. The husband was from New England and had been brought up by reserved parents who taught him to control his emotions and to respect the need for privacy. His wife was from an Italian family and had been brought up in close contact with all the members of her large family, who were extremely warm, volatile* and demonstrative.

24   When the husband came home after a hard day at the office, dragging his feet and longing for peace and quiet, his wife would rush to him and smother* him. Clasping his hands, rubbing his brow,* crooning over his weary head, she never left him alone. But when the wife was upset or anxious about her day, the husband's response was to withdraw completely and leave her alone. No comforting, no affectionate embrace, no attention—just solitude. The woman became convinced her husband didn't love her and, in desperation, she consulted a psychiatrist. Their problem wasn't basically psychological but cultural.

25   Why has man developed all these different ways of communicating messages without words? One reason is that people don't like to spell out certain kinds of messages. We prefer to find other ways of showing our feelings. This is especially true in relationships as sensitive as courtship. Men don't like to

(23) **volatile:** changeable, full of spirit
(24) **smother:** prevent from breathing or getting air
(24) **brow:** forehead (also eyebrow)

be rejected and most women don't want to turn a man down bluntly. Instead, we work out subtle ways of encouraging or discouraging each other that save face and avoid confrontations.

26   How a person handles space in dating others is an obvious and very sensitive indicator of how he or she feels about the other person. On a first date, if a woman sits or stands so close to a man that he is acutely conscious of her physical presence—inside the intimate-distance zone—the man usually construes it to mean that she is encouraging him. However, before the man starts moving in on the woman, he should be sure what message she's really sending; otherwise, he risks bruising his ego. What is close to someone of North European background may be neutral or distant to someone of Italian heritage. Also, women sometimes use space as a way of misleading a man and there are few things that put men off more than women who communicate contradictory messages—such as women who cuddle up and act insulted when a man takes the next step.

27   How do people learn body language? The same way they learn spoken language—by observing and imitating people around them as they're growing up. Little girls imitate their mothers or an older female. Little boys imitate their fathers or a respected uncle or a character on television. In this way, they learn the gender signals appropriate for their sex. Regional, class and ethnic patterns of body behavior are also learned in childhood and persist throughout life. . . .

28   The way we walk, similarly, indicates status, respect, mood and ethnic or cultural affiliation. The many variants of the female walk are too well known to go into here, except to say that a man would have to be blind not to be turned on by the way some women walk—a fact that made Mae West* rich before scientists ever studied these matters. To white Americans, some French middle-class males walk in a way that is both humorous and suspect. There is a bounce and looseness to the French walk, as though the parts of the body were somehow unrelated. Jacques Tati, the French movie actor, walks this way; so does the great mime, Marcel Marceau.

29   Blacks and whites in America—with the exception of middle- and upper-middle-class professionals of both groups—move and walk very differently from each other. To the blacks, whites often seem incredibly stiff, almost mechanical in their movements. Black males, on the other hand, have a looseness and coordination that frequently makes whites a little uneasy; it's too different, too integrated, too alive, too male. Norman Mailer has said that squares walk from the shoulders, like bears, but blacks and hippies walk from the hips, like cats.

30   All over the world, people walk not only in their own characteristic way but have walks that communicate the nature of their involvement with whatever it is they're doing. The purposeful walk of North Europeans is an im-

(28) **Mae West:** an old-time movie star

portant component of proper behavior on the job. Any male who has been in the military knows how essential it is to walk properly (which makes for a continuing source of tension between blacks and whites in the Service). The quick shuffle of servants in the Far East in the old days was a show of respect. On the island of Truk, when we last visited, the inhabitants even had a name for the respectful walk that one used when in the presence of a chief or when walking past a chief's house. The term was *sufan,* which meant to be humble and respectful. . . .

31   Once identified and analyzed, nonverbal-communication systems can be taught, like a foreign language. Without this training, we respond to nonverbal communications in terms of our own culture; we read everyone's behavior as if it were our own, and thus we often misunderstand it.

☐ FOCUS ON THE USE OF EXAMPLES

1. Do the Halls go from the general to the particular, the particular to the general, or both? Compare the opening paragraphs of this essay with those of the Fulbright essay.
2. Find examples of enumeration and of extended examples at least one paragraph long.

☐ QUESTIONS FOR DISCUSSION

1. In their essay, the Halls not only give examples of behavior, but also interpret those examples. For example, they assert that "women sometimes use space as a way of misleading a man . . ." (paragraph 26). Give other possible interpretations of the behavior the Halls describe.
2. In *The Hidden Dimension,* Hall writes of misunderstanding and friction between two roommates, one English and one American, that had their origin in different customs and experiences with space. Americans, accustomed to private bedrooms and offices, go into a room and close the door when they want to be alone with their thoughts, the closed door meaning "do not disturb." The British, unaccustomed to private rooms and offices, "have in effect internalized a set of barriers [made up of subtle clues] which they erect and which others are supposed to recognize." The Englishman was irritated because, as he said, "I'm walking around the apartment and it seems that whenever I want to be alone my roommate starts talking to me. Pretty soon he's asking 'What's the matter?' and wants to know if I'm angry. By then I am angry. . . ." For an American, who goes into a room alone when he wants to be alone, such refusal to talk while in the same room signaled rejection and displeasure.
   Can you recall a similar misunderstanding or irritation because of a

seeming lack of tact or good manners on the part of a person not of your culture? If so, try to analyze it on the basis of "cultural language" differences.

3. Are there *architectural* differences between your country and the United States that reflect different values or ways of interacting? How does your culture view the need for privacy? How do you achieve privacy when you want it?

4. How does your culture show the following?
   a. respect to an elder
   b. you are listening
   c. you are impatient to terminate the conversation
   d. you are a boy who wants to attract the attention of a girl
   e. you are a girl who wants to attract the attention of a boy
   f. you are a girl who wants to discourage the attention of a boy without embarrassing or hurting him unnecessarily
   g. you are a boy who wants to discourage the attention of a girl without embarrassing or hurting her unnecessarily
   h. you are meeting someone for the first time
   i. you are greeting a very good friend of the same age
   j. you want your hostess to know you enjoyed the meal or the party
   k. you want to convey: "I want to be left alone to think, please."

5. Reread the Halls' descriptions of the four main distances used by most white middle-class Americans (paragraphs 17–20). Try to determine the distances used by the people of your culture in the same relationships and situations.

☐ SUGGESTIONS FOR COMPOSITION

1. Give an example from your own experience of having sensed a discrepancy between a person's words and his or her behavior (paragraph 5) that made you doubt his or her sincerity. If possible, give one example based on your experience in the United States or with Americans and one example based on an experience in your own country or among your countrymen.

2. In *The Silent Language,* Hall makes the point that culture "hides most effectively from its own participants." (That is, its own participants are so used to what has been taught to them and take their own behavior so for granted that they are unaware of this "language" and "the extent to which it controls their lives.") He feels that "the best reason for exposing oneself to foreign ways" is to become more aware of one's own culture—"to generate a sense of vitality and awareness—an interest in life which can only come when one lives through the shock of contrast and difference."

   Think about this carefully and be prepared to discuss (or write about) your own greater awareness of aspects of your culture and system of social behavior since encountering a different culture. Think about the ways in which your culture handles, for example, time, space, or eye communication differently from the American culture.

□ A LOOK AT SENTENCE STRUCTURE

1. Notice the sentence pattern of the following sentences:
   a. "... it's usually this lack of congruity between a person's words and his behavior that makes us anxious and uncomfortable" (paragraph 5).
   b. "... it's one's culture that determines how his senses are programmed ..." (paragraph 22).

   Using the same pattern, complete the following sentences:
   c. It is my family's feeling about the importance of education that ...
   d. It is his lack of studying that ...
   e. It was her stubbornness that ...
   f. It is our love of food that ...

2. The following sentences use noun clauses. Identify the noun clause and name its function in the sentence. (Note: There can be more than one noun clause in a sentence.)
   a. "What interested us was that the bracelet was not the one that had been consciously selected by the purchaser" (paragraph 9).
   b. "How a person handles space in dating others is an obvious and very sensitive indicator of how he or she feels about the other person" (paragraph 26).
   c. "What is close to someone of North European background may be neutral or distant to someone of Italian heritage" (paragraph 26).
   d. "We do know, of course, that the noise, pollution, dirt, crowding, and confusion of our cities induce feelings of stress in most of us ..." (paragraph 15).

3. Participial phrases are used in the following sentences. Rewrite them, using adverbial clauses or simple sentences instead.
   a. "... the merchant, watching the pupils of the eyes, knew what the purchaser really wanted to buy" (paragraph 9).
   b. "Clasping his hands, rubbing his brow, crooning over his weary head, she never left him alone" (paragraph 24).
   c. "Once identified and analyzed, nonverbal-communication systems can be taught ..." (paragraph 31).

ANALOGY

An **analogy** is a similarity in one or more important features between two things. Perhaps you have taken a test that uses analogy to test some combination of vocabulary and reasoning ability. For example:

cow : milk   ::   chicken : _____

The correct answer, of course, is "eggs." Milk and eggs are both food products we get from these living animals. While analogy is basically a comparison, it is often very useful as illustration, especially when one wants to explain a complex or abstract concept. Then a concrete analogy can illustrate and clarify a point for us. For example, the heart is often likened to a pump, the brain to a computer. At one time, the universe was explained in terms of a giant clock. (Of course, one must always be aware that, despite similarities between the two objects being compared, there are always *differences.* Illustrating an aspect of a complex idea or system by analogy is fine, but reasoning by analogy can lead to faulty reasoning when it ignores differences. See Chapter 12 on Logical Fallacies.)

The following selection is an example of the way analogy can help us understand complex ideas. In this case, we are shown the ways in which a story is analogous to psychological reality.

Fairy tales are stories—mostly of folk origin—that are told to children. They are often about magic, or magical beings capable of doing harm (wicked witches, trolls, dragons,* child-eating giants) or good (fairies, fairy godmothers, animals who give good advice). "Cinderella," "Little Red Riding Hood" (or Red Cap), "Jack and the Bean Stalk," "Snow White," "Beauty and the Beast" are examples of such tales in Western literature. *The Arabian Nights* and the geniis (djinns) in such tales as "Ali Baba and the Forty Thieves" come to us from the East, as do the "Scheherezade" stories. A study of folk tales from around the world shows that there are basic patterns common to cultures that are otherwise worlds apart: the marriage of the beautiful princess or handsome prince; dead parents replaced by wicked step-parents; three brothers (or sisters), the youngest, weakest, and simplest of whom wins the princess or the riches; children deserted or sent out to die; animals who were really people put under a wicked spell; clever young people outwitting greedy, rich old people. Fear, jealousy, and romantic love are emotional elements common to all tales from all countries. That there are such similar patterns leads to theories not only that stories travel (the German Cinderella has its origins in a Chinese tale) but that there are psychological elements in these tales to which all cultures respond because, as human beings, we have much in common *psychologically* no matter what our geographical location, no matter what our particular customs.

In his book *The Uses of Enchantment: The Meaning and Importance of Fairy Tales,* Bruno Bettelheim, a clinical psychologist and noted writer, explains the psychological benefit to children provided by these tales. The defeat of the wicked stepmother by the actions of the good fairy godmother corresponds to the child's perception of his mother as wicked and cruel at times yet ultimately good and giving. The young, simple son out-achieving his brothers and showing his father that he can be strong and rich corresponds to the child's need for reassurance that even though he feels stupid (or ugly, or deserted, or afraid of being left alone), things will come out right in the end—usually with the aid of a little magic.

Dr. Bettelheim points out that children, of course, do not understand psychology—they do not always realize their fears consciously, either. But working *subconsciously* (that is, without their being aware or conscious of it), these stories do help children deal with their *subconscious* fears and desires as well as their conscious ones.

---

* Western dragons, unlike Eastern dragons, are fire-breathing, destructive, evil.

skip   find better example   analogy = extended metaphor

BRUNO BETTELHEIM

"The Three Languages": Building Integration

1   If we want to understand our true selves, we must become familiar with the inner workings of our mind. If we want to function well, we have to integrate the discordant* tendencies which are inherent in our being. Isolating these tendencies and projecting them into separate figures, as illustrated by "Brother and Sister" and "The Two Brothers," is one way fairy tales help us visualize and thus better grasp what goes on within us.

2   Another fairy-tale approach to showing the desirability of this integration is symbolized by a hero who encounters these various tendencies one at a time and builds them into his personality until all coalesce* within him, as is necessary for gaining full independence and humanity. The Brothers Grimm's "The Three Languages" is a fairy story of this type. It has a history reaching quite far back, and versions were found in many European and some Asian countries. Despite its antiquity,* this timeless fairly tale reads as if it could have been written for the adolescent of today about his conflicts with his parents, or about parents' inability to understand what moves their adolescent children.

3   The story begins: "In Switzerland there once lived an old count* who had only one son, but he was stupid and couldn't learn anything. So the father said, 'Listen, my son, I can't get anything into your head, as hard as I try. You've got to get away from here. I'll turn you over to a famous master; he shall have a try with you.' " The son studied with this master for a year. When he returned, the father was disgusted to hear that all he had learned was "what the dogs bark." Sent out for another year of study with a different master, the son returned to tell that he had learned "what the birds speak." Furious that his son had again wasted his time, the father threatened, "I'll send you to a third master, but if again you learn nothing, I shall no longer be your father." When the year was over, the son's reply to the question of what he had learned was "what the frogs croak."* In great rage, the father cast his son out, ordering his servants to take the son into the forest and do away with him. But the servants had pity on the son, and simply left him in the forest.

4   Many fairy-tale plots begin with children being cast out,* an event which occurs in two basic forms: prepubertal* children who are forced to leave on

(1) **discordant:** not in harmony, disagreeing
(2) **coalesce:** grow together, unite
(2) **antiquity:** being very, very old; from ancient times
(3) **count:** a nobleman (this is a title, like lord, or duke, or baron)
(3) **croak:** the deep sounds frogs make
(4) **cast out:** thrown out
(4) **prepubertal: puberty** is that time of physical development when it becomes possible to bear children or beget them (the male begets when he causes a female to become pregnant); sexual development; the legal age of puberty is usually 12 for girls, 14 for boys. **Prepubertal:** an age younger than that of puberty; **pubertal:** the age of puberty

their own ("Brother and Sister") or are deserted in a place from which they cannot find their way back ("Hansel and Gretel"); and pubertal or adolescent youngsters who are handed over to servants ordered to kill them, but are spared because the servants take pity and only pretend to have murdered the child ("The Three Languages," "Snow White"). In the first form the child's fear of desertion is given expression; in the second, his anxiety about retaliation.*

5   Being "cast out" can unconsciously be experienced either as the child wishing to be rid of the parent, or as his belief that the parent wants to be rid of him. The child's being sent out into the world, or deserted in a forest, symbolizes both the parent's wish that the child become independent and the child's desire for, or anxiety about, independence.

6   The young child in such tales is simply deserted—like Hansel and Gretel—for the anxiety of the prepubertal age is "If I am not a good, obedient child, if I give trouble to my parents, they will no longer take good care of me; they might even desert me." The pubertal child, more confident that he might be able to take care of himself, feels less anxious about desertion and thus has more courage to stand up to his parent. In the stories where the child is handed over to a servant to be killed, he has threatened the parent's dominance or self-respect, as Snow White does by being more beautiful than the queen. In "The Three Languages" the count's parental authority is put into question by the son's so obviously not learning what the father thinks he should.

7   Because the parent does not murder his child but entrusts the evil deed to a servant, and because the servant releases the child, this suggests that on one level the conflict is not with adults in general, but only with the parents. The other adults are as helpful as they dare to be, without coming directly into conflict with the authority of the parent. On another level this indicates that, despite the adolescent's anxiety about the parent holding power over his life, this is not so—because, as outraged as the parent is, he does not vent* his anger directly on the child, but has to use an intermediary* such as the servant. Since the parent's plan is not carried out, this shows the inherent impotence* of the parent's position when he tries to misuse his authority.

8   Maybe if more of our adolescents had been brought up on fairy tales, they would (unconsciously) remain aware of the fact that their conflict is not with the adult world, or society, but really only with their parents. Further, threatening as the parent may seem at some time, it is always the child who wins out in the long run, and it is the parent who is defeated, as the ending of all these tales makes amply clear. The child not only survives the parents but surpasses them. This conviction, when built into the unconscious, permits

(4) **retaliation:** getting back at, taking revenge; here, fear of its being done to him
(7) **vent:** let out
(7) **intermediary:** one who goes between; that is, having another deal with someone for you
(7) **impotence:** powerlessness, lacking strength

the adolescent to feel secure despite all the developmental difficulties from which he suffers, because he feels confident about his future victory.

9   Of course, if more adults had been exposed to the messages of fairy tales as children and profited from them, they might as adults have retained some dim recognition of how foolish any parent is who believes he knows what his child ought to be interested in studying, and who feels threatened if the adolescent goes against his will in this respect. A particularly ironic twist of "The Three Languages" is that it is the father himself who sends his son away to study and selects the masters, only to be outraged* by what they teach his son. This shows that the modern parent who sends his child to college and then is furious about what he learns there, or about how it changes his child, is by no means a new arrival on the scene of history.

10   The child both wishes and fears that his parents will be unwilling to accept his striving for independence and will take revenge. He wishes this because it would demonstrate that the parent cannot let go, which proves the child's importance. To become a man or a woman really means to stop being a child, an idea which does not occur to the prepubertal child, but which the adolescent realizes. If a child wishes to see his parent stop having parental power over him, in his unconscious the child also feels he has destroyed the parent (since the child wants to remove parental powers) or is about to do so. How natural for him to think that the parent wishes to seek retaliation.

11   In "The Three Languages" a son repeatedly goes against his father's will, and asserts himself in doing so; and at the same time he defeats his father's paternal* powers through his actions. For this, he fears his father will have him destroyed.

12   So the hero of "The Three Languages" goes off into the world. On his wanderings he comes first to a land in deep trouble because the furious bark of wild dogs permits nobody to rest; and, worse, at certain hours a man must be handed over to the dogs to be devoured. Since the hero can understand the dogs' language, the dogs talk to him, telling why they are so ferocious,* and what must be done to pacify* them. When this is done, they leave the country in peace, and the hero stays there awhile.

13   After some years the hero, who has grown older, decided to travel to Rome. On his way, croaking frogs reveal his future to him, and this gives him much to think about. Arriving in Rome, he finds that the Pope* has just died and the cardinals* cannot make up their minds whom to elect as the new Pope. Just as the cardinals decide that some miraculous token should designate the future Pope, two snow-white doves settle on the hero's shoulders.

---

 (9) **outraged:** made extremely angry
(11) **paternal:** pertaining to a father, fatherly
(12) **ferocious:** violently cruel, savage
(12) **pacify:** calm, make peaceful
(13) **Pope:** the head of the Roman Catholic Church, a branch of the Christian religion
(13) **cardinals:** high position in the Catholic church; the Pope is chosen from among the cardinals, and it is the cardinals who elect the Pope

Asked whether he would be Pope, the hero does not know if he is worthy; but the doves counsel him to accept. Thus, he is consecrated,* as the frogs had prophesied. When the hero has to sing Mass* and does not know the words, the doves, which continually sit upon his shoulders, tell him all the words in his ears.

14   This is the story of an adolescent whose needs are not understood by his father, who thinks his son is stupid. The son will not develop himself as the father thinks he should, but stubbornly insists on learning instead what *he* thinks is of real value. To achieve his complete self-realization, the young man first has to become acquainted with his inner being, a process no father can prescribe even if he realizes the value of it, as the youth's father does not.

15   The son of this story is youth in search of itself. The three different masters in faraway places to whom the son goes to learn about the world and himself are the up-to-now-unknown aspects of the world and himself which he needs to explore, something he could not do as long as he was tied too closely to his home.

16   Why did the hero first learn to understand the language of dogs, then that of birds, and finally of frogs? . . . Water, earth, and air are the three elements in which our life unfolds. Man is a land animal, and so are dogs. Dogs are the animals living in closest proximity* to man. They are the animals which to the child seem most like man, but they also represent instinctual freedom—freedom to bite, to excrete in an uncontrolled way, and to indulge sexual needs without restraint—and at the same time they stand for higher values such as loyalty and friendship. Dogs can be tamed to control their aggressive biting and trained to control their excretions.* So it seems natural that learning dog language comes first and easiest. It would seem that dogs represent the ego* of man—that aspect of his personality closest to the surface of the mind, since it has as its function the regulation of man's relation to others and to the world around him. Dogs have since prehistory* served somewhat this function, aiding man in fending off* enemies as well as showing him new ways of relating to savage and other beasts.

17   Birds which can fly high into the sky symbolize a very different free-

---

(13) **consecrated:** dedicated to a holy job or high purpose

(13) **Mass:** Catholic church service (these Christian terms are surely used to represent a spiritual dimension of his development)

(16) **proximity:** nearness

(16) **excretions:** waste that comes out of the body (here obviously referring to urine and bowel discharge)

(16) **ego:** the self, the individual as aware of himself. In the terminology of psychology, the psyche (mind) has three parts: the ego, the id, and the superego. The *ego* is that part of the mind which experiences the external world through the senses, and consciously controls the impulses of the *id,* that part of the psyche that is the source of instinct, desire for pleasure, impulse. The *superego* controls the *id un*consciously—a sort of conscience (voice of right and wrong) of the unconscious; it is often associated with higher ethical or moral principles

(16) **prehistory:** before recorded history

(16) **fending off:** keeping away, preventing from entering

dom—that of the soul to soar,* to rise seemingly free from what binds us to our earthly existence, so appropriately represented by the dogs and frogs. Birds stand in this story for the superego,* with its investment in high goals and ideals, its soaring flights of fancy and imagined perfections.[†]

18   If birds stand for the superego, and dogs for the ego, so frogs symbolize the most ancient part of man's self, the *id*.* It might seem a remote connection to think that the frogs stand for the evolutionary process in which land animals, including man, in ancient times moved from the watery element onto dry land. But even today we all begin our life surrounded by a watery element, which we leave only as we are born. Frogs live first in water in tadpole* form, which they shed and change as they move to living in both elements. Frogs are a form of life developed earlier in the evolution of animal life than either dogs or birds, while the id is that part of the personality which exists before ego and superego.

19   Thus, while on the deepest level frogs may symbolize our earliest existence, on a more accessible level they represent our ability to move from a lower to a higher stage of living. If we want to be fanciful,* we could say that learning the language of the dogs and the birds is the precondition for gaining the most important ability: to develop oneself from a lower into a higher state of existence. The frogs may symbolize both the lowest, most primitive, and earliest state of our being, and the development away from it. This can be seen as similar to the development from archaic* drives seeking the most elemental* satisfactions, to a mature ego able to use the vast resources of our planet for its satisfactions.

20   This story also implies that simply learning to understand all aspects of the world and our existence in it (earth, air, water) and of our inner life (id, ego, superego) does little for us. We profit from such understanding in meaningful ways only as we apply it to our dealings with the world. To know the language of dogs is not enough; we must also be able to deal with that which the dogs represent. The ferocious dogs whose language the hero has to learn before any higher humanity becomes possible, symbolize the violent, aggressive, and destructive drives in man. If we remain alienated from these drives, then they can destroy us as the dogs devour* some men.

(17) **soar:** fly high

(17) **superego:** see (16) *ego*

(18) **id:** see (16) *ego*

(18) **tadpole:** the first stage of a frog, when it has gills, a tail, no legs, and lives only in water; this change in form is called *metamorphosis,* another example of which is the change from caterpillar to butterfly or moth

(19) **fanciful:** using our imagination, imaginative

(19) **archaic:** ancient, very old, from an early time

(19) **elemental:** basic, primal, forces such as hunger and sex, natural forces

(20) **devour:** eat greedily, destroy

[†] White doves are a peace symbol, but they also are used as a spiritual symbol in Christianity.

21   The dogs are closely linked to ... possessiveness* because they watch over a great treasure, which explains their ferociousness. Once these violent pressures are understood, once one has become conversant with them (as symbolized by having learned the language of the dogs), the hero can tame them, which brings immediate benefit: the treasure the dogs so savagely protected becomes available. If the unconscious is befriended and given its due—the hero brings food to the dogs—then that which was so fiercely kept hidden, the repressed,* becomes accessible* and, from being detrimental,* turns beneficial.

22   Learning the language of the birds follows naturally from having learned that of the dogs. The birds symbolize the higher aspirations of the superego and ego ideal. Then after the fierceness of the id and ... possessiveness ... have been overcome, and his superego has been established (learning the language of the birds), the hero is ready to cope with the ancient and primitive amphibian. This also suggests the hero's mastering sex, which in fairy-tale language is suggested by his mastering the language of frogs. (Why frogs, toads, etc., represent sex in fairy tales is discussed later in considering "The Frog King."†) It also makes sense that frogs, which in their own life cycle move from a lower to a higher form, tell the hero of his impending* transformation to a higher existence, his becoming Pope.

23   White doves ... inspire and enable the hero to achieve the most exalted position on earth; he gains it because he has learned to listen to the doves and do as they bid him. The hero has successfully gained personality integration, having learned to understand and master his id (the ferocious dogs), listen to his superego (the birds) without being completely in its power, and also pay attention to what valuable information the frogs (sex) have to give him.

24   I know of no other fairy tale in which the process of an adolescent

---

(21) **possessiveness:** unwillingness to give up what is ours, holding on to something, wanting to keep what is ours to ourselves

(21) **repressed:** kept down; in psychology, that which is kept unconscious, or forgotten because to recognize it would be painful. (It is considered healthier psychologically to face these things and come to terms with them, because that which is repressed—that is, kept *un*conscious—can cause unexplained anxiety. Better to face what is unpleasant and deal with it or control it consciously.)

(21) **accessible:** obtainable; can be gotten, reached, entered

(21) **detrimental:** harmful

(22) **impending:** coming soon

† The reference is to a story in which a repulsive frog turns into a handsome prince. In discussing this story, Bettelheim points out its similarity to the change from childhood to adulthood with respect to feelings about sex: what may have seemed "disgusting" or "dirty" to the child becomes beautiful to the adult as he becomes mature enough to understand it. That a frog undergoes metamorphosis (change in form) from youth to maturity is one reason it is used as a symbol for sexual development. Physically and emotionally, sexual development is the great "metamorphosis" from childhood to adulthood. Correspondingly, our attitude toward sex undergoes a metamorphosis as well.

reaching his fullest self-actualization* within himself and also in the world is described so concisely. Having achieved this integration, the hero is the right person for the highest office on earth.

☐   QUESTIONS

Complete the following sentences (the necessary information is in the paragraphs indicated):

1. Disgusted with what his son had learned _____.

   (paragraph 3)

2. The servants took pity on the son, and simply left him in the forest, despite

   _____. (paragraph 3)

3. Had _____ brought up on fairy tales, they might have

   realized their conflict was only with their parents. (paragraph 8)

4. To wish to see his parents stop having parental power over him is

   unconsciously _____. (paragraph 10)

5. That frogs stand for the evolutionary process _____.

   (paragraph 18)

☐   QUESTIONS FOR DISCUSSION

---

1. Explain the basic analogy between the story and real life.
2. Find the analogies *within* the larger analogy, for example, the different "languages," animals, and environments.
3. Bettelheim makes the point, using the intervention of the servant, that the struggle between generations is really a struggle against the *father,* not against the older generation (paragraphs 7 and 8). How do *you* feel about this point?
4. Discuss Bettelheim's point regarding the irony that the father sent the son to three masters, and then was outraged by what the son had learned (paragraph 9). Are you learning "languages" that neither you nor your parents expected you to learn? Discuss.
5. Are Bettelheim's analogies completely consistent? Are there places where the dogs and the frogs, the *ego* and the *id* are given characteristics that are shared rather than kept distinguished from one another? For example, he associates dogs at one point with the *ego,* at another point with the *id.* Is there a way to reconcile the contradictory elements?

(24) **self-actualization:** becoming that which one really is, being true to oneself in what one does and is, self-fulfillment and realization

---

☐   SUGGESTIONS FOR COMPOSITION

---

1. Tell a story you remember from your childhood. It can be a "fairy tale" such as the ones mentioned above or, better yet, a folk tale out of your own tradition.
2. Relate a tale to actual life situations, showing in what ways it is analogous to actual experience or psychological states. (It may be interesting to compare tales told by students from different parts of the world to see whether there are similarities among them.)
3. Choose a process in nature or a natural phenomenon and describe it *in such a way that we understand that you are using this as analogy.* You may spell out the message or the analogy. You may, on the other hand, record it and then leave it for us to define.
4. Do the same with something mechanical, showing how its operation or function is analogous to some larger, more abstract concept in life.
5. Relate an incident in your life or an observation you have made that seemed somehow symbolic or that taught you something. Show how your mind perceived the analogy between the specific experience and the larger idea.

STUDENT   COMPOSITIONS

The following composition, "Going Home," is effective, realistic, and moving because of the many concrete examples the writer gives us. This essay is a good example of illustration by *enumeration*—listing many examples.

Going Home

Where is home to me? England? America? To me, home is where I am brought up, where I can find similar ways of life, where my culture lies and, most important, where people of my nationality live. Before I left my own country, I thought of home as a place where I could stay at night. Having been in America for three years, my view of home has changed. It is not only a place where I can sleep but a place that has laughter and sorrow, a place that involves passions and emotions. It is all the memories that I miss in being away.

My home is situated in a very small country called the "Pearl of the Orient."* In the "Pearl" is a twenty-story apartment building, where lies my home. Living on the eighteenth floor, I can see ferries in the harbor, planes coming in or taking off at Kai Tak Airport, and, last but not least, the busy

---

* Hong Kong

traffic down the street. Having been in the urban area, my home is filled with polluted air. There are no trees or grass around, but only tall buildings. It is noisy because of the people in the apartment and the frustrated drivers who keep pushing the car horns in the street. There is never a time of silence in my home.

At home, I can find security. Whenever I have problems, there is always somebody whom I can talk to and whom I can trust to give me good advice. Being with my parents and brothers, I have a feeling of unity. We solve problems together, and we experience joy and sadness together because we understand each other's feelings. It is a place where I can never feel lonely. Away from home, I have to be independent in thought and in action. Being a minority in America, I cannot find a person that I can go to for problems. Since we are brought up in a different environment, with different ways of life and views, I feel left out in this alien place. Nobody ever cares for me here. At home, I have a sense of belonging, but not in America.

Home is where I can find similar ways of life. When I go shopping, I can find clothes that Chinese people wear. I can buy things that are related to my culture. At home, I can speak my own language. I can express myself better. Communicating with others in my own language gives me a sense of closeness. This is also true when I listen to Chinese songs on the radio. Sometimes the songs move me. When I turn on the television set, I can see familiar faces—black hair and dark eyes. I can see people of my own origin—in culture and in nationality. The movies reflect the real life of Chinese people and I enjoy watching them.

Home reminds me of the delicious Chinese food that my mom cooks. She is always willing to cook us whatever we like to eat. Home also reminds me of Chinese New Year when all my relatives and friends come over to our apartment for dinner. That day is busy for my mom. My brother and I help her to make pastries but it only gets her mad when we throw them at each other. For New Year's dinner, everybody has to wear new clothes. We wish each other good fortune. Those who got married have to give money to the children. We laugh and joke till dawn. It is such a happy evening and is such an unforgettable memory.

At home, I can find peace. It is a place we can rest and talk with friends. I can picture my father sitting in a rocking chair reading a newspaper, my mother sewing, my brother and I playing Chinese checkers on the floor. It is such a good place to be. I am glad that I am going home this summer. After three years of an alien life, I deserve a break, and this is best done by going home!

The following composition uses an *extended example:* one detailed example to illustrate the main idea. It is also an example of the development of a thesis sentence by example. The title expresses the thesis.

The One Who Increases Knowledge Increases Sorrow

Living in a country where we were supposed to close our eyes and look at the facts blindly, I have experienced this fact myself.

I was just sixteen years old when I found *the* teacher. He taught literature in my high school, and I was lucky enough to take a course with him. I remember, at that age, I had a very optimistic point of view toward everything: life, society, politics. My only source of information was the common magazines which could be found everywhere, in which you could read about the marvelous country that we had. I should admit that I was happy to live in a country where there was no racism or inequality or war; that was my point of view when I met him.

The first week of classes passed and it was in the middle of the second week when I found that he had a tendency to draw our attention toward politics. Having an army officer father, I found his comments very interesting. One day I saw him outside of class and told him that I wanted to know more about his views of the country's politics. He asked my age; then he said, "Young man, I don't think it is the right time to expose you to the truth," and he went to class. I was so curious that I met him out of class again. Finally, when he saw my ambitions, he consented to help me, even though he knew it would be a big risk (at that time, the government was extremely against those people who were opposing the ruling power).

It was the middle of the school year when I was reading the "forbidden" magazines. All the truths were marching in front of me and very soon I found that my interest in politics was taking over my studying time. I told my teacher that I wanted to stop getting more involved; he simply answered: "Whatever you wish, but you have already been exposed to the truth and you will never be able to close your eyes again."

I finished that school year with highest honor, but nevertheless I was not feeling happy as I used to feel. My parents knew that there was something wrong with me but they were not sure of what it was.

One day in the middle of July I received a phone call from my teacher. He wanted to see me immediately. I was so happy about it that I told him I would visit him in his office. When I saw him, he asked me if I was still interested in the group. I nodded happily. Now I was being exposed to newer and more serious information. This was the case until I entered the university. By that time my parents were really worried about me. My father was beginning to get suspicious about my political point of view and my mother was worried about my health. On the other hand, I felt it much easier to talk about politics in the university. One day I was called by the secret police. When my father found out, he said that I should stop my political opposition. He was trying to help me, while he himself did not believe in the ruling power (he had himself retired the same year). He told me: "I admit that there are a lot of faults in our politics, but you should stop thinking about them."

But how could I "stop" my thought when I was already being exposed to the truth?

This was three years ago. I never regained my sixteen-year-old feeling. That might have brought me sorrow but I never regret those moments. My parents decided to send me to the United States a week after my decision to accept anything, but never close my eyes again.

☐ SUGGESTION FOR COMPOSITION

Write an extended example narrating an experience of your own to illustrate a statement or perhaps a famous quotation.

Illustration by *analogy* as well as by personal example is used by the student writer of the following essay.

Education by Questions or Education by Statements?

If I had to choose between being educated with questions or being educated with statements, I would definitely choose the questions because they force the mind to think about the "why's," while the statements are taken in by the mind without effort, but always with agreement. Jesus once said: "If you find somebody hungry, do not give him fish; *teach* him to fish."* Speaking with metaphors, the statements are the fish; they do not teach us to think because they are the answer. I learned this by myself; in my country the teaching system is with statements, always with statements. Then, if the students have good memories to catch all the statements, they are considered "good students." The problems that this method carries are very great: (1) the ability of the students to think for themselves is reduced by more than half; (2) consequently, the ability to think out the solution to problems in their lives after school is reduced too. And all this is just because the teachers don't want to spend a little more time with their students, deducing some statement; they just say "This is it, this person said so in that year and that is it." I think a lot of problems would be solved if the teachers took more time and changed the system from statements to questions. I had a very bad experience when I came to the university in America. I felt like a stupid kid of sixth grade because I could not think for myself; I was used to being given all the statements without thinking why they were what they were. . . . I feel particularly frustrated because I think about all the students from my country; they could do almost anything if they were taught with questions. Our dependence on foreign technology would be reduced . . . and life for all of us would

---

* There is a very similar Chinese proverb: "Give a man a fish, and you feed him for a day; teach a man to fish, and you feed him for a lifetime."

be easier, healthier, and happier. This may be just a dream that perhaps will never happen, but I will always hope. This is what I think now, when I am starting to develop my own ability to think.

☐ SUGGESTION FOR COMPOSITION

Do you agree with the student? Point out the statements with which you agree and with which you disagree. Write a composition of your own (1) using the same title, (2) discussing the method of education in your country, or (3) comparing ways of teaching in your country with ways of teaching in the United States.

See Figure 3, pages 8–9, for another student example of analogy.

The following essay incorporates all the above methods of illustration in a fascinating picture of an Indonesian custom.

Puppets

When you glance at a map of Indonesia, you will know the location of Indonesia. To know where Indonesia is, is very simple, but to understand the Indonesians' behavior and actions is quite difficult and puzzling. The only solution to this difficulty is by knowing and understanding their culture.

In *wayang kulit* (leather puppets) the richness of Javanese culture is manifested. For Indonesians, especially Javanese, the significance of *wayang kulit* is very great. An endless variety of human characters are portrayed in *wayang,* from men to demons, from deities to animals, from half humans to half animals. These varieties of characters which have found their expression in *wayang* offer ample opportunity for the Javanese to choose among the characters for their own models to achieve their goals.

A *dalang,* puppeteer, is the one who manipulates the puppets and narrates the stories. The position of *dalang* is usually handed down from father to son. A nonmember of the family can become a *dalang* as long as he learns the trade from a *dalang.* Every *dalang* has to know Javanese literature, such as poetic verse in old Javanese and middle Javanese; he must know how to read prosaic verse in modern Javanese, and he must be able to sing *suluks* (mood songs) and perform *janturans* (melodious narration). Mostly every *dalang* has power upon his audience. To acquire this power he has to perform fasting for forty days and also *tapa* (meditation) during that time.

When darkness comes, the smell of burning *dupa* (sweet-scented wood) fills the air surrounding the stage. As the shadow of the night is cast on the earth so are the shadows of puppets on the *kelir* (screen). The *dalang* manipulates his puppets skillfully and the oscillation of *blencong* (coconut oil lamps) makes the shadows come alive. Then the story of either Mahabharata, the great Bharata families, or Ramayana is cast on the screen from early dusk until dawn.

The battle of Mahabharata started over a disputed kingdom as follows: Long ago in the kingdom of Astina lived a king who had three sons. Destarata was his eldest son. Since Destarata was blind, he rejected the throne. Hence, Pandu, the second son, inherited the throne. During his reign, Pandu had five sons. The five of them were called the "Pandawa." Suddenly Pandu was ill and he died very soon when his sons were still too young to inherit the throne. The blind Destarata, as the uncle of the Pandawa, took care of the throne temporarily.

After many years Destarata was influenced by his *guru* (teacher), named Durna, to pass the throne to his son, named Suyudana. The sons of Destarata were called the "Kurawa." To solve the dispute both the Pandawa and the Kurawa agreed to take a bet on dice numbers. Since the Pandawa lost their bets they went into exile, and they built their own kingdom, called Amarta. But the Kurawa claimed that the land of Amarta belonged to them. Hence the *Gala Yudha* (big fight) of Mahabharata started which lasted for eighteen days. The losses on both sides were very heavy. On the last day of the *Yuda* (fight), Suyudana, the king of Kurawa, died at the hands of Yudisdira, the king and eldest of the Pandawa, giving the Pandawa both kingdoms.

To the Javanese, almost every aspect of *wayang* is filled with symbolic meaning. The public does not attend a *wayang* performance for entertainment alone, but also enjoys uncovering the hidden meaning concealed in the *lakon,* or play. The ideal character emphasized by *wayang* covers such aspects in life as *dharma* (duty) towards society and country, respect for elders, restraint and moderation in desire, passion, anger and joy as well as detachment from worldly temptation.

As dawn comes, the *lakon,* play, ends. When the first purple streak rises on the east, the *dalang* finishes his *lakon* and all the evil *wayang,* puppets, are defeated by the good *wayang.* With this, the people of Indonesia, Java in particular, hope that the prosperous era will come.

The *wayang* performance is a living tradition which is held in high esteem by the people. People of Java always look back at their *wayang lakons* in almost everything they do. Hence their behavior and actions can be interpreted by *wayang* characters. Therefore to comprehend Javanese behavior and actions is to understand the *lakons* in a *wayang* show.

Let us look back for a moment at the different ways illustration works in this essay. The entire essay illustrates the idea that one must know something about a nation's culture to understand the behavior of its people. The student then goes on to develop his explanation of *wayang* as an important example of Javanese culture. He then gives us a legendary story as an example of *wayang* and, finally, he explains the way in which the whole *wayang* tradition is used analogically in Indonesian culture for the purpose of teaching and influencing behavior and values. Throughout the essay the writer enumerates details and defines terms so that we can learn about a rich cultural tradition and picture it in our minds.

C H A P T E R
8
COMPARISON/CONTRAST

Consciously or unconsciously, we are always making comparisons: One girl is prettier than another; one apartment is more expensive than another; one country is very different from another; one student gets better grades than another. Sometimes we have to make choices based on comparison: which girl to call for a date, which apartment to rent, which country to study in, which student to accept. While such decisions are often made impulsively, a rational decision would include weighing the relative advantages and disadvantages of each, ultimately choosing the one that outweighs the other in those ways that are important to us.

Even when we are not comparing in order to choose, we often need to compare in a reasoned way. Sometimes we need to communicate to others the similarities and differences we see or feel in two people, places, or ideas. Sometimes we need to compare to understand something better or to define it even for ourselves. The result may be a decision, but more often it will be increased understanding.

Notice we have said similarities *and* differences, that is, comparison *and* contrast. While contrast emphasizes the differences between two terms, and comparison emphasizes the similarities, to compare really means to compare and contrast. Were there no differences, the two terms would be identical and there would be nothing to compare. Were there no similarities, there would be no connection between the two and, likewise, no basis of comparison.

BASIS OF COMPARISON

You have known since childhood that you can't add apples and eggs, that only like things can be added, subtracted, or compared. In order to decide whether 3/4 is larger than 2/3, you had to find the common denominator; only then, when you were comparing 9/12 to 8/12, could you decide which was larger. If you had six apples and your friend had eight pears, you had no basis of comparison if you were trying to determine who had more apples. But if the question put the apples and pears into the common denominator "fruit," you could say that your friend had two more pieces of fruit than you. If you were eating a cheese sandwich and your friend was eating only fruit, you would need still another common denominator to determine who had more to eat—perhaps weight or number of calories. If your interest were in whose meal was more expensive, you would add the cost of each item and compare total costs. In changing common factors, we have changed the context (the background or situation relevant to our subject, the larger whole and its relationship to the parts) from apples to fruit, to food value or amount, to cost. We see that changing the context is directly related to changing the purpose of the comparison from an interest in amount to an interest in cost. It would be still different if we were to compare these foods with respect to nutritional or chemical content.

These same principles hold true when we contrast because the contrast must be between common factors if we are to find it logical or appropriate. Capitalism and communism are considered opposites or at least opposed. To show how they differ, however, one would have to show how they differ on common factors such as ideology, economic assumptions, or relationship of government to industry. In setting up a comparison/contrast situation (whether in an essay or in a conversation), therefore, it is up to you, the one making the comparison, to decide on what bases you are making the comparison, in what context you are making it, and, with this in mind, whether a comparison is appropriate.

PURPOSE OF COMPARISON

When making a comparison, it will help to keep in mind the purpose for making it. A purpose not only will help you create a context and find common factors, but it will make the comparison more unified, more logical, and more interesting. It will also help in determining whether two items are genuinely comparable. Suppose you had to compare two young women: One is slim, pretty, and graceful in her movements; the other is fat and has a wooden leg. Were you hiring a dancer for a musical production in your theater, there would be "no comparison." Except for their both being young women, they are not comparable. If you were hiring a teacher, however, other factors or bases of comparison would come into play, and the two women could be quite comparable. You might choose the fat one for her superior education, her personal warmth, and her proven ability to teach well and to get along with children.

A car and a bicycle have little in common except that they are both wheeled modes of transportation. But if one must take fuel shortage, costs of upkeep, and availability of parking into greater account than speed, comfort, and distance to travel, these two seemingly incomparable modes of transportation become genuinely comparable. Clocks and cars seem to have nothing in common and would, therefore, not be compared. If, however, you were interested in the way gears work, you might choose to discuss gears in clocks as compared and contrasted with gears in cars. Even when comparing two like items, two cars for example, there must be common factors that you compare and contrast: gas mileage, horsepower, total weight, design, leg room. The reader must feel that there has been some purpose to the comparison and that some kind of conclusion has been drawn.

In the two reading selections that follow, try to determine what common factors unite the terms being compared, what similarities and differences are presented, what conclusions the writers draw, and what purposes there have been for the comparison. (Remember that understanding, clarifying, and communicating our feelings and insights are legitimate purposes for comparison.)

SUZANNE BRITT JORDAN

That Lean and Hungry Look

1   Caesar was right. Thin people need watching.* I've been watching them for most of my adult life, and I don't like what I see. When these narrow fellows spring at me, I quiver* to my toes. Thin people come in all personalities, most of them menacing. You've got your "together" thin person, your mechanical thin person, your condescending* thin person, your tsk-tsk thin person, your efficiency-expert thin person. All of them are dangerous.

2   In the first place, thin people aren't fun. They don't know how to goof off, at least in the best, fat sense of the word. They've always got to be adoing. Give them a coffee break, and they'll jog around the block. Supply them with a quiet evening at home, and they'll fix the screen door and lick S&H green stamps. They say things like "there aren't enough hours in the day." Fat people never say that. Fat people think the day is too damn long already.

3   Thin people make me tired. They've got speedy little metabolisms* that cause them to bustle briskly.* They're forever rubbing their bony hands together and eyeing new problems to "tackle." I like to surround myself with sluggish,* inert, easygoing fat people, the kind who believe that if you clean it up today, it'll just get dirty again tomorrow.

4   Some people say the business about the jolly fat person is a myth, that all of us chubbies* are neurotic, sick, sad people. I disagree. Fat people may not be chortling* all day long, but they're a hell of a lot *nicer* than the wizened

(1) **Julius Caesar,** the Roman emperor, was murdered by a conspiracy of Romans who were afraid he was getting too powerful for the good of the Republic. In Shakespeare's play, *Julius Caesar,* Caesar, who knows nothing of the conspiracy, says of Cassius, the leader of the conspiracy:

> Let me have men about me that are fat;
>
> . . . .
>
> Yond Cassius has a *lean and hungry look;*
> He thinks too much: such men are dangerous.

(1) **quiver:** shake or tremble
(1) **condescending:** dealing with others as if they are inferior
(3) **metabolisms:** chemical and physical processes in which food is built up, used, and broken down within the living organism
(3) **briskly:** quickly
(3) **sluggish:** slow-moving, lacking energy
(4) **chubbies:** fatties
(4) **chortling:** a laughing and snorting sound

and shriveled.* Thin people turn surly,* mean and hard at a young age because they never learn the value of a hot-fudge sundae for easing tension. Thin people don't like gooey* soft things because they themselves are neither gooey nor soft. They are crunchy* and dull, like carrots. They go straight to the heart of the matter while fat people let things stay all blurry and hazy* and vague, the way things actually are. Thin people want to face the truth. Fat people know there is no truth. One of my thin friends is always staring at complex, unsolvable problems and saying, "The key thing is . . ." Fat people never say that. They know there isn't any such thing as the key thing about anything.

5   Thin people believe in logic. Fat people see all sides. The sides fat people see are rounded blobs,* usually gray, always nebulous* and truly not worth worrying about. But the thin person persists. "If you consume more calories than you burn," says one of my thin friends, "you will gain weight. It's that simple." Fat people always grin when they hear statements like that. They know better.

6   Fat people realize that life is illogical and unfair. They know very well that God is not in his heaven and all is not right with the world. If God was up there, fat people could have two doughnuts and a big orange drink anytime they wanted it.

7   Thin people have a long list of logical things they are always spouting off* to me. They hold up one finger at a time as they reel off* these things, so I won't lose track. They speak slowly as if to a young child. The list is long and full of holes. It contains tidbits* like "get a grip on yourself," "cigarettes kill," "cholesterol clogs," "fit as a fiddle," "ducks in a row," "organize" and "sound fiscal management."* Phrases like that.

8   They think these 2,000-point plans lead to happiness. Fat people know happiness is elusive* at best and even if they could get the kind thin people talk about, they wouldn't want it. Wisely, fat people see that such programs are too dull, too hard, too off the mark.* They are never better than a whole cheesecake.

(4) **wizened and shriveled:** dried out
(4) **surly:** bad-tempered
(4) **gooey:** sweet and sticky
(4) **crunchy:** when bitten, makes a noisy, crackling sound (nuts, potato chips, and celery, for example)
(4) **blurry, hazy:** indistinct, not seen clearly
(5) **blobs:** drops or lumps
(5) **nebulous:** unclear, vague
(7) **spouting off:** (slang) shooting out the words, often said of one who shows off superior knowledge
(7) **reel off:** tell fluently, easily
(7) **tidbits:** little "goodies"
(7) **sound fiscal management:** managing money well (in business)
(8) **elusive:** always escaping, hiding from one
(8) **off the mark:** (slang) wrong

9   Fat people know all about the mystery of life. They are the ones acquainted with the night,* with luck, with fate, with playing it by ear. One thin person I know once suggested that we arrange all the parts of a jigsaw puzzle* into groups according to size, shape and color. He figured this would cut the time needed to complete the puzzle by at least 50 percent. I said I wouldn't do it. One, I like to muddle through.* Two, what good would it do to finish early? Three, the jigsaw puzzle isn't the important thing. The important thing is the fun of four people (one thin person included) sitting around a card table, working a jigsaw puzzle. My thin friend had no use for my list. Instead of joining us, he went outside and mulched the boxwoods.* The three remaining fat people finished the puzzle and made chocolate, double-fudge brownies to celebrate.

10   The main problem with thin people is they oppress. Their good intentions, bony torsos, tight ships,* neat corners, cerebral machinations and pat solutions loom like dark clouds over the loose, comfortable, spread-out, soft world of the fat. Long after fat people have removed their coats and shoes and put their feet up on the coffee table, thin people are still sitting on the edge of the sofa, looking neat as a pin, discussing rutabagas.* Fat people are heavily into fits of laughter, slapping their thighs and whooping it up, while thin people are still politely waiting for the punch line.*

11   Thin people are downers. They like math and morality and reasoned evaluation of the limitations of human beings. They have their skinny little acts together. They expound, prognose, probe* and prick.

12   Fat people are convivial.* They will like you even if you're irregular and have acne.* They will come up with a good reason why you never wrote the great American novel. They will cry in your beer with you. . . . Fat people will gab, giggle, and guffaw,* gallumph, gyrate and gossip. They are generous, giving, and gallant.* They are gluttonous* and goodly and great. What you want when you're down is soft and jiggly, not muscled and stable. Fat people know this. Fat people have plenty of room. Fat people will take you in.

(9) **acquainted with the night:** night is being used here in the sense of loneliness, depression; the reference is to a poem by Robert Frost (see "Storm Fear," Chapter 4)

(9) **jigsaw puzzle:** a picture, mounted on cardboard and cut into irregular shaped pieces; the object of the puzzle is to put the pieces back together to form the picture or design

(9) **muddle through:** to succeed in spite of apparent confusion

(9) **mulched the boxwoods:** boxwood is a species of tree; to mulch is to put straw, leaves, or other loose material around a plant

(10) **tight ship:** reference is to a well-run ship; well organized, strictly disciplined

(10) **rutabagas:** a kind of vegetable

(10) **punch line:** the last line of a joke—the funny part

(11) **probe:** to search to the bottom, investigate with great thoroughness

(12) **convivial:** fond of eating, drinking, and good company

(12) **acne:** blemishes or pimples on the face, especially common among adolescents

(12) **guffaw:** laugh loudly

(12) **gallant:** high spirited, showing great courtesy to women, brave, grand

(12) **gluttonous:** given to excessive eating

MARK TWAIN

Reading the River

1   The face of the water, in time, became a wonderful book—a book that was a dead language to the uneducated passenger but which told its mind to me without reserve,* delivering its most cherished secrets as clearly as if it uttered them with a voice. And it was not a book to be read once and thrown aside, for it had a new story to tell every day. Throughout the long twelve hundred miles there was never a page that was void of interest.* . . . The passenger who could not read it was charmed with a peculiar sort of faint dimple* on its surface (on the rare occasions when he did not overlook it altogether) but to the pilot that was an *italicized* passage;* indeed it was more than that, it was a legend of the largest capitals with a string of shouting exclamation-points at the end of it, for it meant that a wreck or a rock was buried there that could tear the life out of the strongest vessel that ever floated. It is the faintest and simplest expression the water ever makes, and the most hideous* to a pilot's eye. In truth, the passenger who could not read this book saw nothing but all manner of pretty pictures in it, painted by the sun and shaded by the clouds, whereas to the trained eye these were not pictures at all, but the grimmest* and most dead-earnest of reading matter.

2   Now when I had mastered the language of this water, and had come to know every trifling* feature that bordered the great river as familiarly as I knew the letters of the alphabet, I had made a valuable acquisition. But I had lost something too. I had lost something which could never be restored to me while I lived. All the grace, the beauty, the poetry, had gone out of the majestic* river! I still kept in mind a certain wonderful sunset which I witnessed when steamboating was new to me. A broad expanse of the river was turned to blood; in the middle distance the red hue* brightened into gold, through which a solitary log came floating, black and conspicuous;* in one place a long, slanting mark lay sparkling upon the water; in another the surface was broken by boiling, tumbling rings, that were as many-tinted as an opal; where the ruddy* flush was faintest, was a smooth spot that was covered

(1) **without reserve:** without holding anything back, openly and freely
(1) **void of interest:** of no interest, empty of interest
(1) **dimple:** a slight dent or depression in the cheek, usually noticeable when the person smiles
(1) **italicized passage:** portion of the printed matter in *italics* (*print of this kind*), often used for emphasis
(1) **hideous:** very ugly, horrible to look at
(1) **grim:** hard and unyielding, threatening, dealing with unpleasant subjects
(2) **trifling:** unimportant, of small value, small
(2) **majestic:** like a king, royal, the manner of kings
(2) **hue:** color
(2) **conspicuous:** easy to see, obvious
(2) **ruddy:** reddish in color; a healthy-looking reddish color, if applied to complexions

with graceful circles and radiating lines, ever so delicately traced; the shore on our left was densely wooded, and the somber* shadow that fell from this forest was broken in one place by a long, ruffled trail that shone like silver; and high above the forest wall a clean-stemmed dead tree waved a single leafy bough that glowed like a flame in the unobstructed* splendor that was flowing from the sun. There were graceful curves, reflected images, woody heights, soft distances; and over the whole scene, far and near, the dissolving lights drifted steadily, enriching it every passing moment with new marvels of coloring.

3   I stood like one bewitched.* I drank it in,* in a speechless rapture.* The world was new to me, and I had never seen anything like this at home. But as I have said, a day came when I began to cease from noting the glories and the charms which the moon and the sun and the twilight wrought* upon the river's face; another day came when I ceased altogether to note them. Then, if that sunset scene had been repeated, I should have looked upon it without rapture, and should have commented upon it, inwardly, after this fashion: "This sun means that we are going to have wind tomorrow; that floating log means that the river is rising, small thanks to it;* that slanting mark on the water refers to a bluff reef* which is going to kill somebody's steamboat one of these nights, if it keeps on stretching out like that; those tumbling 'boils' show a dissolving bar* and a changing channel* there; the lines and circles in the slick* water over yonder* are a warning that that troublesome place is shoaling up* dangerously; that silver streak in the shadow of the forest is the 'break' from a new snag,* and he has located himself in the very best place he could have found to fish for steamboats; that tall dead tree, with a single living branch, is not going to last long, and then how is a body* ever going to get through this blind place at night without the friendly old landmark?"

4   No, the romance and beauty were all gone from the river. All the value any feature of it had for me now was the amount of usefulness it could furnish toward compassing the safe piloting of a steamboat. Since those days, I have

(2) **somber:** dark and sad
(2) **unobstructed:** not blocked, nothing in the way of a view
(3) **bewitched:** as if put under a spell by a witch—fascinated, charmed
(3) **drank it in:** (idiom) absorbed it all with great enthusiasm
(3) **rapture:** ecstasy, great joy and excitement
(3) **wrought:** formed, made, decorated
(3) **small thanks to it:** (idiom) we are *not* thankful for that—it is not good for us
(3) **bluff reef:** *reef:* a line or ridge of sand or rock lying at or near the surface of the water; *bluff:* steep and having a broad, flat front
(3) **bar:** here, a bank of sand, gravel, or earth at the mouth of a river or harbor that obstructs it or makes it difficult to enter or cross
(3) **channel:** bed of a river or stream, the course of the water's flow
(3) **slick:** slippery, oily
(3) **over yonder:** over there (not usually used in modern speaking or writing)
(3) **shoaling up:** (idiom) becoming shallow
(3) **snag:** sharp point that sticks out
(3) **a body:** here, anybody

pitied doctors from my heart. What does the lovely flush in a beauty's cheek mean to a doctor but a "break" that ripples above some deadly disease? Are not all her visible charms sown thick* with what are to him the signs and symbols of hidden decay? Does he ever see her beauty at all, or doesn't he simply view her professionally and comment upon her unwholesome condition all to himself? And doesn't he sometimes wonder whether he has gained most or lost most by learning his trade?

ORGANIZING THE COMPARISON/CONTRAST ESSAY

Both Mark Twin and Suzanne Britt Jordan have established major contrasts in their essays, and in both it is on common bases of comparison that contrasts are made. Were you to outline these two essays, however, you would find that they are organized very differently. Jordan lists many points of contrast by giving the general category and then specific examples and, *at the point of each example,* she contrasts her fats with her thins.

I. Attitude toward activity
   A. Fats goof off
   B. Thins keep very busy
II. Temperament
   A. Fats are nicer
   B. Thins are mean and hard
III. Attitude toward truth
   A. Fats are more realistic—life is unclear
   B. Thins want to face truth logically

The list could go on through the end of the essay and be broken down into specific examples, but the pattern is the same. Each example serves as a common basis of contrast, and the contrast is made before the next example is given.

Mark Twain uses a different pattern. He, too, establishes contrasts, the "uneducated" view as opposed to the knowledgeable view, around common factors. However, he first shows his "uneducated" view of the scene in its entirety before contrasting the knowledgeable view against it. Such organization runs the risk of becoming two separate essays, with the common factors not established or not kept clearly in the reader's mind. In the hands of Mark Twain, however, they are absolutely clear. The views are two perceptions of the same scene, kept parallel by using the same objects in the same order.

I. Earlier "uneducated" view
   A. Red sunset
   B. Floating log
   C. Slanting mark
   D. Rings and lines

(4) **sown thick:** full of; literally, thickly planted, as if seeds were *sown* (planted)

    E. Wooded shore and silver trail in its shadow
    F. Dead tree

 II. Later knowledgeable view
    A. Red sunset
    B. Floating log
    C. Slanting mark
    D. Rings and lines
    E. Shadow of shore and silver trail
    F. Dead tree

Having shown the contrasts, Twain then goes on to:

III. Conclusion: Knowledge works against beauty and robs it of romance

In drawing a conclusion, he further unifies his two perceptions so that we feel they are part of a single essay, a single idea. We feel there has been a purpose in showing the two views.

    Study these two basic organizational patterns carefully. When you write a comparison/contrast paper, choose one or the other. Either way, you will be comparing and contrasting like factors and doing so in an order that is easy for the reader to follow. While some of the other essays in this section combine these techniques or use them more subtly, these basic methods of comparison are definitely there. The less experienced writer would do better to follow the basic organization more strictly, remembering that somewhere in the essay the reader should sense that there is a purpose to the essay—some reason for the comparison, some point to be communicated by means of the comparison. When constructing outlines for your own essays, be sure to include a genuine conclusion. Even Jordan's obviously exaggerated and humorous essay has an underlying serious purpose—perhaps a need to justify one's overeating or a plea for liking the fat person. One can certainly sense that the writer is "plump."

☐ QUESTIONS ON "READING THE RIVER"

Answer the following questions in your own words, using complete sentences.

1. Why is a "dimple" on the water's surface "hideous to a pilot's eye"?
2. What is the basic difference between the untrained passenger's view of the river and that of the trained eye?
3. When did Mark Twain begin to view the river differently?
4. Summarize how he looked at the same sunset scene after his training.
5. What was the only value any feature of the river had for him now?

☐ SENTENCE VARIETY

Form a single sentence from each group of simple sentences. After you have finished, compare your sentences with the author's.

1. Some passengers could not read the river. They were charmed with a dimple on the river's surface. (paragraph 1)
2. The face of the water became a wonderful book. That took time. The book was a dead language to the uneducated passenger. It told me its mind. It held nothing back. It delivered it secrets. The secrets were cherished. It told the secrets clearly. It seemed to have a voice. (paragraph 1)
3. Now I had made a valuable acquisition. I had mastered the language of this water. I had come to know its every feature. Many features bordered the great river. They were familiar to me. The letters of the alphabet were familiar to me too. I had also lost something. (paragraph 2)

☐ QUESTIONS FOR DISCUSSION

1. Express Mark Twain's thesis statement or conclusion in one sentence.
2. What else, besides two views of the river, is being compared? (Think of the larger context, the more universal comparison of which the river comparison is just one example.)
3. In writing about "reading the river" the author compares the river to a book. He is using a book as a metaphor (see Chapter 4), that is, he is drawing an analogy or comparison between the river and a book. What specific words relating to books and reading does he use to carry out his analogy? Are they consistent with it?
4. Do you feel that the "poetry" had to go out of the sunset? What about a rainbow when you have learned what causes it? What about the moon, now that you know men have walked on it?
5. Do you feel that Mark Twain has gained or lost more? How about the surgeon? How about you? Is it better that one "learns to read"? Is ignorance preferable? Always? Ever? Sometimes?

☐ SUGGESTIONS FOR COMPOSITION

1. Using your own experience as an example, discuss question 5 above. You may discuss some specific knowledge that has made you feel gain and loss as well. You may draw a comparison between the way you looked at something before and after you really understood it.
2. Write a comparison/contrast essay comparing your view of the United States before you came here with your more experienced view now. Compare the vision with the reality, including what may have disappointed you or what may have turned out better than you expected. Don't forget that to do this, you should keep in mind the ways to organize a comparison/contrast paper as discussed above.
3. "_____ in time became a wonderful book to me." Choose something out of your experience to fill in the blank and write about it in detail.

☐   QUESTIONS ON "THAT LEAN AND HUNGRY LOOK"

Using Negative and Positive Words.   Notice the negative or positive ways the following words are used in the essay. Use each word or phrase in a sentence that changes the feeling Jordan gave it. If Jordan uses it in a positive way, use it in a negative or neutral manner; if she uses it in a negative way, use it in a positive or neutral manner. (Numbers in parentheses refer to the paragraphs in which the words can be found.)

> people who tackle problems (3)
> gooey (4)
> crunchy (4)
> carrots (4)
> gray, rounded blobs (5)
> sound fiscal management (7)
> classifying into parts according to size, shape, and color (9)
> putting one's feet on the table (10)
> gossip (12)
> crying in one's beer (12)

Making Writing More Alive.   This essay provides very good examples of the way concrete, specific words make writing more effective. In this case, the author keeps naming foods, not only because the essay is about the love of food, but because these words will appeal to the reader's taste, the reader's own love of food, and thus to his sympathy.

In the following examples, notice how much better the original sentences are than the rewritten ones, even though the rewritten ones convey the same ideas:

1. *Rewrite:* Thin people turn surly, mean and hard at a young age because they never learn that eating helps to relieve tension.
   Original: "Thin people turn surly, mean and hard at a young age because they never learn the value of a hot-fudge sundae for easing tension."
2. *Rewrite:* They know that God is not in his Heaven and all is not right with the world. If God was up there, eating would not make people fat.
   Original: "They know very well that God is not in his Heaven and all is not right with the world. If God was up there, fat people could have two doughnuts and a big orange drink anytime they wanted it."
3. *Rewrite:* They are dull and hard and boring.
   Original: They are crunchy and dull, like carrots.
4. *Rewrite:* Such programs are too dull, too hard. They are never better than having fun.
   Original: ". . . such programs are too dull, too hard. . . . They are never better than a whole cheesecake."

Creating Lively Sentences.   Complete the following sentences using specifics in the way Jordan does.

1. Some students turn surly, mean and hard at a young age because they never learn . . .
2. Some professors are boring and dry like . . .
3. Fun-loving students know that if God was up in his heaven . . .
4. Americans are always in a hurry. They haven't learned . . .

Compare the characteristics of some people you know to foods, plants, or animals and show why. Avoid trite comparisons such as "My girlfriend is like a flower" or "My roommate is a rat."

☐ SUGGESTIONS FOR COMPOSITION

---

1. Choose two "types" as Jordan has done, and compare them in a humorous essay. You may want to use types of students (the fraternity man, the nerd, the grub, the Romeo) or types of professors. You may want to compare Americans with another nationality group. (Note: In this case you are using the stereotype *humorously;* you should not expect to be taken seriously. *In serious writing that attempts legitimate arguments and points, of course, stereotyping must be avoided.*)
2. Begin your composition as follows: "The world is divided into two kinds of people." (You may choose, for example, to divide the world into those who squeeze the toothpaste tube wherever their fingers happen to be and those who roll it carefully from the bottom.) Then develop your composition accordingly, assigning words, actions, and characteristics appropriate to each type.

In the essay that follows, two men are contrasted: Diogenes, a Greek philosopher of the fourth century B.C.; and Alexander the Great, the Macedonian conqueror who spread Greek culture throughout the civilized world of his time. The author has combined comparison/contrast with narrative but, even so, we are always aware of the fact that two men are being compared. Despite the dramatic effect of the narrative, it is still possible, though a little more difficult, to follow the comparison.

GILBERT HIGHET

The Philosopher and the Conqueror

1   Lying on the bare earth, shoeless, bearded, half-naked, he looked like a beggar or a lunatic.* He was one, but not the other. He had opened his eyes with the sun at dawn, scratched, done his business* like a dog at the roadside, washed at the public fountain, begged a piece of breakfast bread and a few olives, eaten them squatting on the ground, and washed them down with a few handfuls of water scooped from the spring. (Long ago he had owned a

---

(1) **lunatic:** crazy man
(1) **done his business:** relieved himself; gone to the bathroom, of course with no bathroom

rough wooden cup, but he threw it away when he saw a boy drinking out of his hollowed hands.) Having no work to go to and no family to provide for, he was free. As the marketplace filled up with shoppers and merchants and gossipers and sharpers* and slaves and foreigners, he had strolled* through it for an hour or two. Everybody knew him, or knew of him. They would throw sharp questions at him and get sharper answers. Sometimes they threw jeers,* and got jibes;* sometimes bits of food, and got scant thanks; sometimes a mischievous pebble, and got a shower of stones and abuse. They were not quite sure whether he was mad or not. He knew they were mad, all mad, each in a different way; they amused him. Now he was back at his home.

2   It was not a house, not even a squatter's* hut. He thought everybody lived far too elaborately, expensively, anxiously. What good is a house? No one needs privacy: natural acts are not shameful; we all do the same things, and need not hide them. No one needs beds and chairs and such furniture: the animals live healthy lives and sleep on the ground. All we require, since nature did not dress us properly, is one garment to keep us warm, and some shelter from rain and wind. So he had one blanket—to dress him in the daytime and cover him at night—and he slept in a cask.* His name was Diogenes. He was the founder of the creed called Cynicism* (the word means "doggishness"); he spent much of his life in the rich, lazy, corrupt Greek city of Corinth, mocking and satirizing* its people, and occasionally converting one of them.

3   His home was not a barrel made of wood: too expensive. It was a storage jar made of earthenware, something like a modern fuel tank—no doubt discarded because a break had made it useless. He was not the first to inhabit such a thing: the refugees* driven into Athens by the Spartan invasion had been forced to sleep in casks. But he was the first who ever did so by choice,* out of principle.

4   Diogenes was not a degenerate* or a maniac.* He was a philosopher who wrote plays and poems and essays expounding* his doctrine; he talked to those who cared to listen; he had pupils who admired him. But he

(1) **sharpers:** cheaters
(1) **strolled:** walked in a slow and leisurely way
(1) **jeers, jibes:** mocking laughs
(2) **squatter:** an idiom for one who lives on unsettled or public land without any title to it or any right to do so
(20 **cask:** barrel
(2) **cynicism:** usually used to mean a view of life that is not trusting, one that questions people's sincerity, motives, actions (**cynic:** a person with this view of life; **cynical:** having this view of life)
(2) **satirizing:** the verb from the noun *satire,* a literary work in which wrongdoing or stupidity is laughed at
(3) **refugees:** people who have fled a dangerous place to find safety (**refuge**) in another
(3) **by choice:** because he chose to do so; he wanted to
(4) **degenerate:** a person who has gone down to a worse or abnormal state
(4) **maniac:** a wildly crazy person, a madman
(4) **expounding:** explaining

taught chiefly by example. All should live naturally, he said, for what is natural is normal and cannot possibly be evil or shameful. Live without conventions,* which are artificial and false; escape complexities and super-fluities and extravagances:* only so can you live a free life. The rich man believes he possesses his big house with its many rooms and its elabo-rate furniture, his pictures and his expensive clothes, his horses and his servants and his bank accounts. He does not. He depends on them, he worries about them, he spends most of his life's energy looking after them; the thought of losing them makes him sick with anxiety. They possess him. He is their slave. In order to procure* a quantity of false, perishable goods he has sold the only true, lasting good, his own inde-pendence.

5   There have been many men who grew tired of human society with its complications, and went away to live simply—on a small farm, in a quiet village, in a hermit's* cave, or in the darkness of anonymity. Not so Diogenes. He was not a recluse,* or a stylite, or a beatnik. He was a missionary. His life's aim was clear to him: it was "to restamp the currency." . . . to take the clean metal of human life, to erase the old false conventional markings, and to imprint it with its true values.

6   The other great philosophers of the fourth century before Christ taught mainly their own private pupils. In the shady groves* and cool sanctuaries of the Academy, Plato* discussed to a chosen few on the unreality of this contingent* existence. Aristotle,* among the books and instruments and spec-imens and archives and research-workers of his Lyceum, pursued investiga-tions and gave lectures that were rightly named *esoteric** "for those within the walls." But for Diogenes, laboratory and specimens and lecture halls and pupils were all to be found in a crowd of ordinary people. Therefore he chose to live in Athens or in the rich city of Corinth, where travelers from all over the Mediterranean world constantly came and went. And, by design,* he publicly behaved in such ways as to show people what real life was. He would constantly take up their spiritual coin, ring it on a stone, and laugh at its false superscription.*

7   He thought most people were only half-alive, most men only half-men. At bright noonday he walked through the marketplace carrying a lighted lamp

(4) **conventions:** accepted ways of living and doing things

(4) **superfluities and extravagances:** excesses, great shows, too much

(4) **procure:** get

(5) **hermit, recluse:** one who leaves society and lives alone, away from others

(6) **groves:** small woods, pleasant groups of trees

(6) **Plato, Aristotle:** great Greek philosophers of the fourth century, B.C. Plato had been a student of Socrates; Aristotle, a pupil in Plato's Academy; Alexander, a pupil of Aristotle

(6) **contingent:** dependent, accidental, not necessarily real

(6) **esoteric:** understood only by a select few

(6) **by design:** by intention

(6) **spiritual coin . . . superscription:** Notice the way he uses the metaphor of genuine and false currency (also in paragraph 5) to express the difference between genuine value and false exteriors or what is stamped on the surface (**superscribed**)

and inspecting the face of everyone he met. They asked him why. Diogenes answered, "I am trying to find a *man.*"

8 To a gentleman whose servant was putting on his shoes for him, Diogenes said, "You won't be really happy until he wipes your nose for you: that will come after you lose the use of your hands."

9 Once there was a war scare so serious that it stirred even the lazy, profit-happy Corinthians. They began to drill, clean their weapons, and re-build their neglected fortifications. Diogenes took his old cask and began to roll it up and down, back and forward. "When you are all so busy," he said, "I felt I ought to do *something!*"

10 And so he lived—like a dog, some said, because he cared nothing for privacy and other human conventions, and because he showed his teeth and barked at those whom he disliked. Now he was lying in the sunlight, as contented as a dog on the warm ground, happier (he himself used to boast) than the Shah of Persia. Although he knew he was going to have an important visitor, he would not move.

11 The little square began to fill with people. Page boys* elegantly dressed, spearmen speaking a rough foreign dialect, discreet secretaries, hard-browed officers, suave* diplomats, they all gradually formed a circle centered on Diogenes. He looked them over, as a sober man looks at a crowd of tottering drunks, and shook his head. He knew who they were. They were the atten-dants of the conqueror of Greece, the servants of Alexander, the Macedonian king, who was visiting his newly subdued realm.*

12 Only twenty, Alexander was far older and wiser than his years. Like all Macedonians he loved drinking, but he could usually handle it; and toward women he was nobly restrained and chivalrous.* Like all Macedonians he loved fighting; he was a magnificent commander, but he was not merely a military automaton. He could think. At thirteen he had become a pupil of the greatest mind in Greece, Aristotle. No exact record of his schooling survives. It is clear, though, that Aristotle took the passionate, half-barbarous boy and gave him the best of Greek culture. He taught Alexander poetry: the young prince slept with the *Iliad* under his pillow and longed to emulate Achilles,* who brought the mighty power of Asia to ruin. He taught him philosophy, in particular the shapes and uses of political power: a few years later Alexander was to create a supranational empire that was not merely a power system but a vehicle for* the exchange of Greek and Middle Eastern cultures.

(11) **page boys:** uniformed, often aristocratic, boys serving a person of high rank
(11) **suave:** worldly, sophisticated, smooth in speech and action
(11) **newly subdued realm:** recently conquered kingdom or land
(12) **chivalrous:** having the qualities of an ideal knight: courage, courtesy, honor, fairness, and respect for women and the poor
(12) **emulate:** imitate as an ideal, an example of the kind of a person he wanted to be
(12) **Iliad . . . Achilles:** The *Iliad* is one of the two great epic poems of ancient Greece written by Homer; Achilles was the name of its great hero
(12) **vehicle for:** a means by which ideas are expressed and made known

13   Aristotle taught him the principles of scientific research: during his invasion of the Persian domains Alexander took with him a large corps of scientists, and shipped hundreds of zoological specimens back to Greece for study. Indeed, it was from Aristotle that Alexander learned to seek out everything strange which might be instructive. . . .

14   Now, Alexander was in Corinth to take command of the League of Greek States which, after conquering them, his father Philip had created as a disguise for the New Macedonian Order. He was welcomed and honored and flattered.* He was the man of the hour, of the century: he was unanimously appointed commander-in-chief of a new expedition against old, rich, corrupt Asia. Nearly everyone crowded to Corinth in order to congratulate him, to seek employment with him, even simply to see him: soldiers and statesmen, artists and merchants, poets and philosophers. He received their compliments* graciously.* Only Diogenes, although he lived in Corinth, did not visit the new monarch. With that generosity which Aristotle had taught him was a quality of the truly magnanimous* man, Alexander determined to call upon Diogenes. Surely Dio-genes, the God-born, would acknowledge the conqueror's power by some gift of hoarded* wisdom.

15   With his handsome face, his fiery glance, his strong supple* body, his purple and gold cloak, and his air of destiny,* he moved through the parting crowd, toward the Dog's kennel. When a king approaches, all rise in respect. Diogenes did not rise, he merely sat up on one elbow. When a monarch enters a precinct, all greet him with a bow or an acclamation. Diogenes said nothing.

16   There was a silence. Some years later Alexander speared his best friend to the wall, for objecting to the exaggerated honors paid to His Majesty; but now he was still young and civil.* He spoke first, with a kindly greeting. Looking at the poor broken cask, the single ragged garment, and the rough figure lying on the ground, he said: "Is there anything I can do for you, Diogenes?"

17   "Yes," said the Dog, "stand to one side. You're blocking the sunlight."

18   There was silence, not the ominous* silence preceding a burst of fury, but a hush of amazement. Slowly, Alexander turned away. A titter* broke out from the elegant Greeks, who were already beginning to make jokes about

(14) **flattered:** praised; told he was wonderful, whether or not it was true, in order to be on his good side

(14) **compliments:** words of praise

(14) **graciously:** in a kind, polite, friendly manner

(14) **magnanimous:** very generous

(14) **hoarded:** stored away, saved secretly

(15) **supple:** flexible, easy-moving

(15) **air of destiny:** quality of having a great fate, of being the one appointed to change and influence the world greatly

(16) **civil:** polite

(18) **ominous:** expecting something terrible

(18) **titter:** short, nervous laugh

the Cur that looked at the King. The Macedonian officers, after deciding that Diogenes was not worth the trouble of kicking, were starting to guffaw* and nudge one another. Alexander was still silent. To those nearest him he said quietly, "If I were not Alexander, I should be Diogenes." They took it as a paradox,* designed to close the awkward little scene with a polite curtain line.* But Alexander meant it. He understood Cynicism as the others could not. Later he took one of Diogenes' pupils with him to India as a philosophical interpreter.... He was what Diogenes called himself, a *cosmopolitēs,* "citizen of the world." Like Diogenes, he admired the heroic figure of Hercules, the mighty conqueror who labors to help mankind while all others toil* and sweat only for themselves. He knew that of all men then alive in the world only Alexander the conqueror and Diogenes the beggar were truly free.

☐ QUESTIONS

Answer or complete the following, using complete sentences.

1. What was Diogenes' purpose in remaining in society rather than living as a recluse in the country?
2. How did Diogenes feel about our "need" for privacy?
3. When the people of Corinth were busily preparing for war, Diogenes mocked them by _____. (Complete the sentence.)
4. In what ways were Diogenes and Alexander similar (use "in that" in your sentence)?
5. Not only was Alexander a magnificent commander, _____. (Complete the sentence.)
6. Besides a corps of soldiers, Alexander took with him a corps of scientists _____. (Complete the sentence showing purpose.)

☐ SENTENCE VARIETY

Form a single sentence from each group of sentences. After you have finished, compare your sentences with the author's.

1. He had no work to go to. He had no family to provide for. He was free.
2. We do not require much. We need some shelter from rain and wind. We need one garment. It has to keep us warm. Nature did not dress us properly.

(18) **guffaw:** laugh in a loud and ridiculing way
(18) **paradox:** something that seems contradictory or unbelievable, but which may, in fact, be true
(18) **to close the awkward little scene with a polite curtain line:** taken from the theater; it means to end the scene of the play with an appropriate line or speech
(18) **toil:** work very hard

3. His home was not a house. It was not a squatter's hut. It was not a barrel of wood. It was a storage jar made of earthenware. It had probably been cracked.
4. He knew he was going to have an important visitor. He would not move (use "despite").

☐ QUESTIONS FOR DISCUSSION

1. How does the author use narration to dramatize the comparison and contrast? How does the meeting serve to unify the essay? Can you outline this essay?
2. The contrasts between Diogenes and Alexander are obvious, and the meeting dramatizes these differences, but what do they have in common? Why does Alexander say, "If I were not Alexander I should be Diogenes"?
3. This essay compares different methods of teaching. What are they?
4. Diogenes would say: "I am trying to find a *man.*" Define what it was he was looking for as you see it.
5. Notice the short simple sentences in paragraph 2. Why are they appropriate?

☐ SUGGESTIONS FOR COMPOSITION

1. Compare two people in history or two people whom you know who, on the surface, seem very different, but who have fundamental qualities or views in common.
2. Compare two different ideologies, emphasizing what they have in common.
3. Choose a personal or historical confrontation between two people. Build up to it by giving the background of each person. Then show how the two people view each other and treat each other in the confrontation. The confrontation could be between a father and son, two generals making peace or war, two heads of state, or two friends who have been apart for a long time, having led different kinds of lives in the meantime.

USEFUL SIGNALS TO USE IN COMPARISON/CONTRAST WRITING

The following words are very useful when making comparisons. They help the writer make his connections and transitions clear. Using these words to connect clauses, sentences, or paragraphs will give coherence to the comparison and thus allow the reader to follow the writer's train of thought easily.

Likeness	Difference	
in the same way	whereas	although
similarly	unlike	however
likewise	on the other hand	yet
then	on the contrary	instead
accordingly	in contrast	different from
too	conversely	then again
also	nevertheless	despite
correspondingly	but	while (not in the
equally		sense of time)
like ⎫ *		
as ⎭		

Write pairs of sentences or clauses using these words as connectors. Refer to this list when you write your own compositions of comparison and contrast.

Other Ways to Signal Contrast

Skillful and experienced writers have found additional ways to make comparisons. They have learned ways to structure contrasts without always using these words. In this way they produce more varied, less mechanical comparisons. They make the contrasts clear and pointed, but they leave it to the reader to see the connection.

☐   EXERCISES

In the following examples, explain the ways in which contrast is made clear without use of the preceding transitional words:

1. "Long after fat people have removed their coats and shoes and put their feet up on the coffee table, these people are still sitting on the edge of the sofa, looking neat as a pin. (Jordan, paragraph 10)
2. "It [a dimple] is the faintest and simplest expression the water ever makes, and the most hideous to a pilot's eye." (Twain, paragraph 1)
3. "They were not quite sure whether he was mad or not. He knew they were mad, all mad, each in a different way." (Highet, paragraph 1)
4. "Sometimes they threw jeers, and got jibes." (Notice here how the use of the same sound at the beginning of the contrasting words, called alliteration, heightens the contrast.) (Highet, paragraph 1)
5. "The rich man believes he possesses his big house with its many rooms and its elaborate furniture. . . . He does not. He depends on them. . . . They possess him. He is their slave." (Highet, paragraph 4)

---

* Remember that *like* is a preposition and *as* is a conjunction. This means that *like* is followed by a noun or pronoun object, and *as* is followed by a whole clause. *Examples:* "He looks like his mother." "This mechanic does things as I like them to be done."

(In examples 3 and 5, stress is an important feature of establishing contrasts. Read the passages aloud, stressing the words that you feel should be stressed to indicate contrast, or underline the words that you feel should be stressed.)

S T U D E N T   C O M P O S I T I O N S

He

I still remember him as he was looking at a mirror to straighten his uniform before he went to school every morning. I still remember him as he hesitated and was unsure of what to do with the two women whom he had fallen in love with. I was proud of him when he yelled at friends, teachers, and parents, saying that he was going to support the welfare program for the people of Korea when he became a medical doctor. I was proud of him because he was a faithful Christian who preached the gospel to his friends and other people; who yelled at his friends to go to church; who yelled to people on a street on Sunday to go to church. I was proud of him as he asked for students' rights and resisted the orders of teachers and principals—who caused a great deal of trouble because he was standing against them.

I still remember him, but I am not proud of him anymore. He seems to have changed completely into another person within a lapse of time.

He does not look at a mirror before he goes to school in the morning. He does not even care how he looks anymore. He no longer hesitates as to what he does with the two women whom he had fallen in love with. He does not yell to his friends, teachers, and parents that he is going to support the welfare program, but he is thinking only of being rich himself when he becomes a medical doctor. He does not argue with teachers or principals anymore but he is worrying about his grades. He is worrying because he was rejected from Johns Hopkins University for having had a lower grade point average once. He does not go to church on Sunday any more. When he wakes up at about 12 o'clock on Sunday, he points at people who are going to church and says that they are crazy for going to church. One thing, however, that he does not understand himself is that he is still reading the Bible.

Now, he only wishes that time were revocable so that he could go back to who he was two years ago. He curses time, which caused him to change, and curses himself for having changed.

Cultural Differences in Nonverbal Communication: The United States and Japan

After having spent ten years in the United States, my return to Japan showed me how really different the countries are and how the people communicate these differences nonverbally. While I was in Japan for a visit, I often felt embarrassed because I smiled, almost like a conditional reflex, after I made accidental eye contact with someone I didn't know. Because I had been living both in the United States and Europe for so many years, I came to observe the Japanese and to react to their behavior often with a foreign sense.

When I get on the elevator at University Hospitals in Cleveland, I almost always greet other passengers. I may even have a harmless little talk with them, like "It's a cold day, isn't it?" or "Did you watch the Super Bowl yesterday?" The same thing happens almost everywhere—at offices, at banks, or at bus stops. The Americans appear to be very friendly and casual, but this is not the way people are in Japan. When I get on the elevator there, I stand in the corner or lean against the wall, keeping my glance away from anybody else's. I may watch the ceiling or floor so that I can avoid accidental eye contact. No greeting nor chat. The Japanese seem to be reserved, formal, and somewhat unfriendly.

The handling of personal space is another area of nonverbal behavioral differences. In the United States, at movie theaters or at concerts, if I come a little late, I find myself embarrassed. I have to keep saying, "Excuse me," "Pardon me," or "Sorry, Sir," just in order to reach my seat at the end of the row. This is because I have to touch the strangers and intrude on their space, thus annoying them. At restaurants at a prime lunch hour crowded with office workers, I have to wait for a long time to find a seat because Americans don't want to share a table with strangers. They are very reluctant to do so. On a train or on a bus I tense my muscles and hold myself stiff, trying hard not to touch anybody, and if I ever touch anyone I apologize.

But in Japan I feel that all of the above matters are more easy and loose. In a big Japanese terminal at rush hour, trains keep arriving, bringing in numerous commuters from nearby suburbs. They rush to the doors to get out of the train and dash up and down the stairs to another line. They are shoving and pushing. They hustle and jostle. Even in less crowded situations, when a train arrives, people all move toward the doors and scramble and rush for seats. They touch or push each other on the shoulders or other parts of their bodies. But I hardly hear anybody say "Sorry," "Pardon," or "Excuse me." As the train moves on, it swings on the curb. A man standing next to me loses his balance and leans toward my body. Although he eventually moves back to his first position, he does not offer any apology, and just keeps silent as if nothing has happened.

While the handling of space between strangers differs between the two countries, I also find it is quite significant that the expression of emotion between persons of a close relationship also varies. In the United States I see wives and husbands walk hand in hand and kiss each other to show their affection no matter where it is, in private or in public. Their ways of expressing affection are more passionate. Although it is changing lately among the young people, Japanese people don't show much of their emotions, especially in public. Suppose a husband has been gone for a month or even longer for a business trip, and his wife is waiting at the gate of the airline to meet him. Here he comes out of the plane. They both recognize each other and make a sparkling eye contact. If they were American they would rush to one another and hug and kiss. Yet, as Japanese their reaction is quite different. They do not rush to each other. There is no passionate embrace or hug. No rain of kisses is seen. They merely exchange a casual but cordial greeting like "Welcome back!" or "How was your flight?" They hardly seem very excited.

I guess all these differences in nonverbal communication between the countries are cultivated over many years by an intricately constructed mixture of cultural, historical, and racial differences. Because the United States is a melting pot of different races, a young country made up of a diversity of immigrants, people unconsciously feel a need to present themselves as harmless to others. On the other hand, Japan is an unusually homogeneous society; the same language is used all over the country; we have the same ancestral origin, and the same dark black hair and dark eyes. One does not really need to communicate with others to show what kind of person he is, or that he is not an enemy. Everyone understands one another; thus they may comfortably assume an air of indifference. This may be important in understanding their use of eye contact, and might be an element in the use of body space as well.

With respect to space, a few other ideas come to mind: The United States is a huge land, which used to be a frontier. Pioneers who came to the new world fought for a piece of land and declared it as their own property. It is their nature to defend their own space from intruders. They are used to living in a spacious land comfortably. On the other hand, Japan is a heavily populated country. People overflow everywhere, especially in big cities. Therefore the Japanese get used to crowds. Because of this, they have no control of their personal space; they can not avoid body contact. At the same time, however, because of the homogeneous characteristics I mentioned before, the Japanese seem to lack a protective nature. Indeed there are far fewer social crimes than in the United States.

All in all, the Japanese seem shy and reserved, unless you get to know them well. They are also often trained not to show but to control their emotions and to be rather passive and quiet, as the result of the Confucian influences, whereas Americans show their feelings straightforwardly. Understanding the meaning of such unintentional differences in nonverbal communication is certainly important from the point of view of customs and manners, and is essential in all our attempts to understand another society.

☐ QUESTIONS

---

1. What is the basic organizational pattern of "He"? What is the basic organizational pattern of "Cultural Differences in Nonverbal Communication"?
2. Do you agree with the analysis of the way Americans behave? How does the Japanese way compare with yours? The American way? Comment on the student's analysis of the differences between Americans and Japanese.

Then and Now in Saudi Arabia

During the last thirty years, Saudi Arabia had undergone a modernization period that changed the country completely. Surprisingly enough, the Saudis did not retain the same virtues they had had before industrialization affected the way people thought and dealt with others.

Before oil was discovered, the people were simple Bedouins who lived by tending camels and sheep. The desert was hot and rain was scarce. They had to keep moving in the desert to find water. Their life was tough, but they were very close to each other. Loyalty was an essential characteristic of theirs. They were known to die to protect their friends. They were also so trusting that they would lend large amounts of money and refuse to take any written proof of the lending. They used to welcome strangers coming from far away places and invite them to stay overnight. Strangers were not even required to declare their names. The Saudis were very simple and natural.

The discovery of oil was the beginning of a new era in the history of Saudi Arabia. Industry found its way into the country, and Saudis had to advance. This required them to give up the free life they had before. They had to be in offices and factories which required following a time schedule. They also started working with advanced machinery. Almost everyone in the country was involved in the industrialization process.

Their efforts were very rewarding. Now Saudi Arabia is a different country. In place of the old yellow clay houses there are huge tall buildings, and where the black herds of sheep used to graze, there are factories that blow smoke out of their long chimneys. Instead of the camels and white Arabian horses, there now are long green buses that can take forty people at one time. Many things have changed.

During this transitional period, the Saudis have not remained the same. The industries occupied their time. People had appointments to keep and jobs to do. They did not have much time to spend with their families and neighbors. They started meeting people of different cultures, and they did not trust every stranger as they had done before. Papers and signatures were needed for commerce since the handshaking was not a guarantee anymore. People became more cautious in their relations with other people and more devoted to the new industries.

The modernization Saudi Arabia went through has changed the people, and now they are "not like they used to be."

☐ QUESTIONS

---

1. Can you tighten this composition by eliminating some of the repetition or combining sentences more effectively? (See paragraph 2 especially.)

2. Would you think that the student prefers life now or would he have preferred life then? (Classes have been divided on this subject. What in the essay could convey preference for the past? What could convey preference for the present? Be specific.)
3. Is the student being realistic about the past?

C H A P T E R

9

DEFINITION

When we want to know what a word means or what something is, we are asking for a definition. To define is to answer the questions: *What does that word mean? What is it?*

How would you define the word *table?* What is wrong with the following definition? *A table is something on which you eat.* First of all, a table is not only used for eating. Also, not everyone eats on a table. Some people have their food served on trays, and some eat it on the floor.

Going further, can we do better than "thing"? All concrete nonhuman nouns are "things." Tables, carrots, dolls, hammers, and bottles are all things. Is there a class of things to which *table* belongs? Yes, furniture: A table is a piece of furniture.

We still have a problem, for a table is only one kind of furniture. This definition would apply equally to a bed, a chair, or a couch. To define *table,* it is necessary to show how it *differs* from other objects in the same class: "A table is a piece of furniture consisting of a flat top set horizontally on legs."*

We see that to define is to set up an equation:

$$\rule{3cm}{0.4pt} = \rule{3cm}{0.4pt}.$$

The definition consists of the larger class to which the word belongs and those characteristics that make it different from other items in that class.

The process is similar to the biologist's division of animals into genus and species. The more specialized one is, the more precise his or her definitions need to be, and the further into subspecies he or she will want to classify. For example, the furniture dealer (or the person shopping for furniture) will want to differentiate among dining tables, coffee tables, and work tables, for each has a different function and a correspondingly different height and design. There may be elegant tables that rest, not on legs, but on unusual pedestals. The standard short definition of *table* is the most *usual* one, the one not necessarily specialized. As we will see, an *expanded definition* will allow for greater detail and individual interpretation.

---

* As given in *Webster's New Twentieth Century Dictionary of the English Language,* Unabridged, Second Edition.

You may also have seen the word *table* used in your textbooks when you are referred to "Table 1" for a graphic presentation of a set of figures. This is a completely different use of the word. Or is it? Look up *table* in a good dictionary. What was its original meaning? How is this meaning common to both modern definitions?

☐   EXERCISE

Write your own definitions of the following words. Use the following formula as a guide:

Word = Larger class + that which differentiates it from other members of that class

bed	book
fish	tree
tuna	cup
hammer	freedom
kindness	water

Now look up the words in your dictionary and compare your definitions with the dictionary's. *Do you have any criticisms of the dictionary definitions?* Be specific. Go back to the definition for *table,* for example. Is it adequate? How would you differentiate between a table and a stool?

What if your dictionary defines *kindness* as: "the state or quality of being kind"? What is the problem? Such a definition is circular; it uses a form of the word in its own definition. In creating definitions, therefore, *do not use a word (or a form of it) in its own definition.* It is also important to realize that a *synonym,* while it can help us understand a word, *is not a definition.* Neither is its equivalent in another language!

EXTENDED DEFINITION

There are times when we want to do more than define a word in the most simple and concise way. Perhaps we are using an abstract word like democracy that is open to many interpretations. Perhaps we want someone to understand the way we are using a word that has a very deeply felt meaning or value for us. Or perhaps it is a term we are trying to make as clear as possible to an audience we want to inform or teach. Whatever the motive for its use, an extended definition will increase understanding and make communication more accurate.

To enlarge upon a definition, you can use modes of writing you have already studied such as description, example, or comparison/contrast. Even concise dictionary definitions sometimes use description or explanation of an object's function. In an extended definition, then, you can go into greater detail about the way this thing or person looks, functions, and acts; you can list its characteristics; you can give examples to support your definition; you can even make your definition clearer by writing what it is *not,* how it differs from terms that might be confused with the one you are discussing, what this thing or person does *not* do. In some cases a historical approach is appropriate: How was this term thought of in the past? How has its meaning or use changed? How are you using it? Sometimes the easiest way to write an extended definition is by beginning with the dictionary definition and then enlarging upon it.

In the example below, the writer defines a friend. He obviously did not feel the need to supply a dictionary definition, assuming we all know what a friend is. He tries to communicate what *he* considers a friend, friendship as he has experienced it. His perception and experience, hence his definition, may be quite different from anyone else's.

ELIE WIESEL

FROM *The Gates of the Forest*

1   He was a friend. And what is a friend? More than a father, more than a brother: a traveling companion, with him, you can conquer the impossible, even if you must lose it later. Friendship marks a life even more deeply than love. Love risks degenerating* into obsession,* friendship is never anything but sharing. It is to a friend that you communicate the awakening of a desire, the birth of a vision or a terror, the anguish* of seeing the sun disappear or of finding that order and justice are no more. That's what you can talk about with a friend. Is the soul immortal, and if so why are we afraid to die? If God exists, how can we lay claim to freedom, since He is its beginning and its end? What is death, when you come down to it? The closing of a parenthesis, and nothing more? And what about life? In the mouth of a philosopher, these questions may have a false ring, but asked during adolescence or friendship, they have the power to change being: a look burns and ordinary gestures tend to transcend* themselves. What is a friend? Someone who for the first time makes you aware of your loneliness and his, and helps you to escape so you in turn can help him. Thanks to him you can hold your tongue* without shame and talk freely without risk. That's it.

☐ QUESTIONS FOR DISCUSSION

1. Does the author ever get around to a formal definition of "a friend"? When? What is the definition?
2. According to this author, what are the characteristics of a friend? Of friendship? List them.
3. What different modes of writing are used in this extended definition? Identify them specifically.

(1) **degenerating:** sinking below its former condition, getting worse
(1) **obsession:** the state of being totally preoccupied by an idea or emotion, as if ruled by it
(1) **anguish:** extreme pain of mind or body
(1) **transcend:** go beyond the limits of, be superior to, exceed
(1) **hold your tongue:** keep quiet, not talk

4. The preceding definition does more than make clear for us what a word means to the writer. It expresses great feeling and does so with beauty. How? What specific choices of examples and words make this definition moving and beautiful?

In his book *The Art of Loving,* psychologist Erich Fromm develops his theory that love is an active, mature, giving art—one that requires knowledge and effort, like any other art. He speaks of the difference between infantile love ("I love you because I need you") and mature love ("I need you because I love you"). He examines types of love, among them the love between parent and child, and the ways in which motherly and fatherly love contribute to the child's development into a mature adult, truly capable of loving.

ERICH FROMM

Motherly and Fatherly Love

1 Motherly love by its very nature is *unconditional.** Mother loves the newborn infant because it is her child, not because the child has fulfilled any specific condition, or lived up to any specific expectation. (Of course, when I speak here of mother's and father's love, I speak of the "ideal types" . . . and do not imply that every mother and father loves in that way. I refer to the fatherly and motherly principle, which is represented in the motherly and fatherly person.) Unconditional love corresponds to one of the deepest longings, not only of the child, but of every human being; on the other hand, to be loved because of one's merit, because one deserves it, always leaves doubt; maybe I did not please the person whom I want to love me, maybe this or that—there is always a fear that love could disappear. Furthermore, "deserved" love easily leaves a bitter feeling that one is not loved for oneself, that one is loved *only* because one pleases, that one is, in the last analysis, not loved at all but used. No wonder that we cling to the longing for motherly love, as children and also as adults. Most children are lucky enough to receive motherly love (to what extent will be discussed later). As adults the same longing is much more difficult to fulfill. In the most satisfactory development it remains a component of normal erotic* love; often it finds expression in religious forms, more often in neurotic forms.

2 The relationship to father is quite different. Mother is the home we come from, she is nature, soil, the ocean; father does not represent any such natural home. He has little connection with the child in the first years of its life, and his importance for the child in this early period cannot be compared with that of mother. But while father does not represent the natural world, he represents the other pole of human existence; the world of thought, of manmade

(1) **unconditional:** with no conditions attached, absolute
(1) **erotic:** referring to sexual love

things, of law and order, of discipline, of travel and adventure. Father is the one who teaches the child, who shows him the road into the world.

3   Closely related to this function is one which is connected with socioeconomic development. When private property came into existence, and when private property could be inherited by one of the sons, father began to look for that son to whom he could leave his property. Naturally, that was the one whom father thought best fitted to become his successor, the son who was most like him, and consequently whom he liked the most. Fatherly love is conditional love. Its principle is "I love you *because* you fulfill my expectations, because you do your duty, because you are like me." In conditional fatherly love we find, as with unconditional motherly love, a negative† and a positive aspect. The negative aspect is the very fact that fatherly love has to be deserved, that it can be lost if one does not do what is expected. In the nature of fatherly love lies the fact that obedience becomes the main virtue, that disobedience is the main sin—and its punishment the withdrawal of fatherly love. The positive side is equally important. Since his love is conditional, I can do something to acquire it, I can work for it; his love is not outside of my control as motherly love is.

4   The mother's and the father's attitudes toward the child correspond to the child's own needs. The infant needs mother's unconditional love and care physiologically as well as psychically.* The child, after six, begins to need father's love, his authority and guidance. Mother has the function of making him secure in life, father has the function of teaching him, guiding him to cope with those problems with which the particular society the child has been born into confronts him. In the ideal case, mother's love does not try to prevent the child from growing up, does not try to put a premium on helplessness. Mother should have faith in life, hence not be overanxious, and thus not infect the child with her anxiety. Part of her life should be the wish that the child become independent and eventually separate from her. Father's love should be guided by principles and expectations; it should be patient and tolerant, rather than threatening and authoritarian. It should give the growing child an increasing sense of competence and eventually permit him to become his own authority and to dispense with that of father.

5   Eventually, the mature person has come to the point where he is his own mother and his own father. He has, as it were, a motherly and a fatherly conscience. Motherly conscience says: "There is no misdeed, no crime could deprive you of my love, of my wish for your life and happiness." Fatherly conscience says: "You did wrong, you cannot avoid accepting certain consequences of your wrongdoing, and most of all you must change your ways if

---

(4) **psychically:** for the mind, the emotional state

† Fromm discusses the negative aspect of unconditional motherly love on a previous page in his book: Since it is unconditional and does not depend on deserving, it cannot be earned. The child may feel "If it is there, it is like a blessing; if it is not there, . . . there is nothing I can do to create it."

I am to like you." The mature person has become free from the outside mother and father figures, and has built them up inside. In contrast to Freud's concept of the superego, however, he has built them inside not by *incorporating* mother and father, but by building a motherly conscience of his own capacity for love, and a fatherly conscience on his reason and judgment. Furthermore, the mature person loves with both the motherly and the fatherly conscience, in spite of the fact that they seem to contradict each other. If he would only retain his fatherly conscience, he would become harsh and inhuman. If he would only retain his motherly conscience, he would be apt to lose judgment and to hinder himself and others in their development.

6   In this development from mother-centered to father-centered attachment, and their eventual synthesis, lies the basis for mental health and achievement of maturity.

☐ QUESTIONS

Answer the following questions according to Fromm, using complete sentences.

1. What is the basic difference between motherly love and fatherly love?
2. What is the relationship between private property and fatherly love?
3. What has happened to the mother and father figures by the time a person is mature?
4. Why does a person need both a fatherly and a motherly conscience? (Use "without.")

☐ QUESTIONS FOR DISCUSSION

1. As Fromm sees it, what are the characteristics of motherly love? Functions? Advantages? Disadvantages?
2. As Fromm sees it, what are the characteristics of fatherly love? Functions? Advantages? Disadvantages?
3. How does Fromm account for the difference between motherly and fatherly love? In what does each originate?
4. In the context of the capacity to love, how does Fromm seem to define the mature person? Formulate a definition from what Fromm implies. Do you agree?
5. What is your opinion of Fromm's definitions of motherly and fatherly love? (Notice that he has said these terms refer to "ideal types," *principles,* not necessarily to every mother or every father. Either parent could be capable of either type of love; one person may be capable of both kinds.) How close does he come to your own experience?

6. Do you feel Fromm's definitions depend on a given culture or are they universal?

☐ SUGGESTION FOR COMPOSITION

Analyze child-rearing practices in your country *and the ways in which these practices contribute to the development of the adult your society wants and needs.* You might consider the following: What is the ideal role played by mother? By father? At what point does the child begin to move closer to father? Is this true of both sexes? How do mother's role and father's role seem to influence the way in which the adult becomes his "own mother and father"? When does this happen? Has this happened with you yet? Perhaps it does not happen as long as the parents are alive. Perhaps these parental voices are transferred to another person or institution, such as the religious leader or the state. Think about the qualities your society values most and then try to remember how these were taught to you. How strict was the discipline? If it was strict, what form did it take? At what age did it begin? Which parent was the strict disciplinarian? Were you raised any differently from a sibling (brother or sister) of the opposite sex? Is the eldest child raised differently from the others? You may not have thought of all this before, but it should be interesting for you to look back and make the analysis. Remember to choose a focus and organize before you begin writing.

☐ SUGGESTIONS FOR WRITING EXTENDED DEFINITIONS

Write your own extended definition of a term, using the techniques of development we have discussed. You may use a role or type of person, as did Wiesel in his definition of a friend, or you may define abstract concepts, as did Fromm in his definition of motherly love and fatherly love. In the case of qualities or roles, you should allow your values to come through. For example, what is a *real* friend or mother? What is love as it really should be? If you like, you may choose from the list below.

Roles	*Feelings, qualities, or concepts*
mother	love
father	happiness
brother	security
sister	discipline
husband	ignorance
wife	education
friend	music
teacher	art
doctor	poverty
religious leader or teacher	wealth
student	success

Feelings, qualities, or concepts	nerd
power	the cool person
faith	artist
trust	scientist
loyalty	
fear	*Institutions*
worry	school
guilt	university
	religious institution
Types around campus	hospital
slob	government
grub	types of political systems
jock	(choose one)
creep	ruler (choose one type)

KALVERO OBERG

Culture Shock and the Problem of Adjustment in New Cultural Environments

1   Culture shock might be called an occupational disease of people who have been suddenly transplanted abroad. Like most ailments,* it has its own symptoms and cure.

2   Culture shock is precipitated* by the anxiety that results from losing all our familiar signs and symbols of social intercourse.* Those signs or cues* include the thousand and one ways in which we orient ourselves to the situation of daily life: when to shake hands and what to say when we meet people, when and how to give tips, how to make purchases, when to accept and when to refuse invitations, when to take statements seriously and when not. These cues, which may be words, gestures, facial expressions, customs, or norms,* are acquired by all of us in the course of growing up and are as much a part of our culture as the language we speak or the beliefs we accept. All of us depend for our peace of mind and our efficiency on hundreds of these cues, most of which we do not carry on the level of conscious awareness.

3   Now when an individual enters a strange culture, all or most of these familiar cues are removed. He or she is like a fish out of water. No matter how broad-minded or full of good will you may be, a series of props* have been

(1) **ailments:** mild illnesses
(2) **precipitated:** caused
(2) **social intercourse:** social dealing and communication between groups or persons
(2) **cues:** signals reminding one or prompting one to act; hints, suggestions
(2) **norms:** ways things are typically done in a given group, standards or models for that group
(3) **props:** supports, that which helps to hold something up

knocked from under you, followed by a feeling of frustration and anxiety. People react to the frustration in much the same way. First they reject the environment which causes the discomfort. "The ways of the host country are bad because they make us feel bad." When foreigners in a strange land get together to grouse* about the host country and its people, you can be sure they are suffering from culture shock. Another phase of culture shock is regression.* The home environment suddenly assumes a tremendous importance. To the foreigner everything becomes irrationally glorified. All the difficulties and problems are forgotten and only the good things back home are remembered. It usually takes a trip home to bring one back to reality.

4   Some of the symptoms of culture shock are excessive washing of the hands; excessive concern over drinking water, food dishes, and bedding; fear of physical contact with attendants; the absent-minded stare; a feeling of helplessness and a desire for dependence on long-term residents of one's own nationality; fits of anger over minor frustrations; great concern over minor pains and eruptions of the skin;* and finally, that terrible longing to be back home.

5   Individuals differ greatly in the degree in which culture shock affects them. Although not common, there are individuals who cannot live in foreign countries. However, those who have seen people go through culture shock and on to a satisfactory adjustment can discern steps in the process. During the first few weeks most individuals are fascinated by the new. They stay in hotels and associate with nationals who speak their language and are polite and gracious to foreigners. This honeymoon* stage may last from a few days or weeks to six months, depending on circumstances. If one is very important, he or she will be shown the show places, will be pampered and petted,* and in a press interview will speak glowingly about good will and international friendship.

6   But this mentality does not normally last if the foreign visitor remains abroad and has seriously to cope with real conditions of life. It is then that the second stage begins, characterized by a hostile and aggressive attitude toward the host country. This hostility evidently grows out of the genuine difficulty which the visitor experiences in the process of adjustment. There are house troubles, transportation troubles, shopping troubles, and the fact that people in the host country are largely indifferent to all these troubles. They help, but they don't understand your great concern over these difficulties. Therefore, they must be insensitive and unsympathetic to you and your worries. The result, "I just don't like them." You become aggressive, you band together

(3) **grouse:** complain, grumble
(3) **regression:** a going backward; returning to an earlier, usually worse, condition; becoming more childlike
(4) **eruptions of the skin:** breaking out, as in pimples or rashes
(5) **honeymoon:** the earliest period of marriage, the holiday taken by a new couple, the early period of a relationship when everything still seems just fine
(5) **Pampered and petted:** taken very good care of, made to feel important and good

with your fellow countrymen and criticize the host country, its ways, and its people. But this criticism is not an objective appraisal. Instead of trying to account for the conditions and the historical circumstances which have created them, you talk as if the difficulties you experience are more or less created by the people of the host country for your special discomfort.

7   You take refuge* in the colony of your countrymen which often becomes the fountainhead* of emotionally charged labels known as stereotypes. This is a peculiar kind of offensive shorthand which caricatures* the host country and its people in a negative manner. The "dollar grasping American" and the "indolent* Latin Americans" are samples of mild forms of stereotypes. The second stage of culture shock is in a sense a crisis in the disease. If you come out of it, you stay; if not, you leave before you reach the stage of a nervous breakdown.

8   If the visitor succeeds in getting some knowledge of the language and begins to get around by himself, he is beginning to open the way into the new cultural environment. The visitor still has difficulties but he takes a "this is my problem and I have to bear it" attitude. Usually in this stage the visitor takes a superior attitude to people of the host country. His sense of humor begins to exert itself. Instead of criticizing, he jokes about the people and even cracks jokes about his or her own difficulties. He or she is now on the way to recovery.

9   In the fourth stage, your adjustment is about as complete as it can be. The visitor now accepts the customs of the country as just another way of living. You operate within the new surroundings without a feeling of anxiety, although there are moments of social strain. Only with a complete grasp of all the cues of social intercourse will this strain disappear. For a long time the individual will understand what the national is saying but he is not always sure what the national means. With a complete adjustment you not only accept the food, drinks, habits, and customs, but actually begin to enjoy them. When you go home on leave, you may even take things back with you; and if you leave for good, you generally miss the country and the people to whom you became accustomed.

☐ QUESTIONS FOR DISCUSSION

---

1. What different modes of writing are used in this extended definition of culture shock? Identify them specifically.
2. Discuss Oberg's picture of culture shock: Do you find it exaggerated? Accurate? Incomplete?

(7) **take refuge:** find safety
(7) **fountainhead:** source
(7) **caricatures:** represents with exaggerations of its distinctive features in a humorous or negative manner
(7) **indolent:** lazy

☐ SUGGESTIONS FOR COMPOSITION

---

1. Write your own extended definition of culture shock, using whatever modes of writing best suit your purposes.
2. Discuss your own adjustment (or problems with adjusting) in light of Oberg's definition and description. At which stage are you?

DEFINITION BY MEANS OF CONCRETE ASSOCIATIONS

An informal, often creative way to explain the meaning a word has for you is to list the kinds of experiences you associate with that word, the specific ways in which that concept makes itself felt.

Excellent examples of this type of unconventional (or informal) definition were created by the cartoonist Charles Schulz through his *Peanuts* characters. He published a series of illustrated books defining *security, happiness,* and *love.* In one of them, *Security Is a Thumb and a Blanket* (complete with a cartoon of a child sucking his thumb and holding his blanket), he gives many such definitions by association. Another one is: "Security is writing down your locker combination." In these examples, we are not given formal definitions; rather, we are reminded very specifically of the kinds of acts we associate with the need for security, the things that make us feel more secure.

☐ EXERCISE

Try writing some of your own unconventional definitions—remembering the little things, the *concrete, specific* acts, things, and feelings you associate with the following:

Security is . . . .
Happiness is . . . .
Love is . . . .
Guilt is . . . .
Fear is . . . .
Poverty is . . . .
Wealth is . . . .

Do as many for each as you can. It will be interesting to see what others have written. Remember to be specific—and human!

While this kind of definition can be creative and humorous, it can also serve as the basis for a serious, extended definition paper. Jo Goodwin Parker writes a definition of poverty that depends on concrete situations to make the fortunate try to understand what poverty is. Each of her "poverty is . . ." sentences begins a paragraph of specific examples developing that one idea. Some of them are the following: "Poverty is getting up every morning from a dirt- and illness-stained mattress." "Poverty is being tired." "Poverty is asking for help." The following is an example of one of her developed paragraphs.

JO GOODWIN PARKER

FROM *Poverty*

1   Poverty is dirt. You say in your clean clothes coming from your clean house, "Anybody can be clean." Let me explain about housekeeping with no money. For breakfast I give my children grits* with no oleo* or cornbread without eggs and oleo. This does not use up many dishes. What dishes there are, I wash in cold water and with no soap. Even the cheapest soap has to be saved for the baby's diapers. Look at my hands, so cracked and red. Once I saved for two months to buy a jar of Vaseline for my hands and the baby's diaper rash. When I had saved enough, I went to buy it and the price had gone up two cents. The baby and I suffered on. I have to decide every day if I can bear to put my cracked, sore hands into the cold water and strong soap. But you ask, why not hot water? Fuel costs money. If you have a wood fire it costs money. If you burn electricity, it costs money. Hot water is a luxury. I do not have luxuries.

Another example is the composition a foreign student wrote defining "racism." Each of the following sentences began a paragraph of concrete examples:

Racism is not being able to protect yourself from another "superior" group because you have no choice but to obey. . . .

Racism is an excessive and irrational feeling of superiority on the part of a given group, people, or nation on racial grounds alone. . . .

Racism is being the envy of another race because of successful achievements. . . .

Racism is insulting somebody because of his racial background. . . .

Racism is difference based on skin color.

☐   SUGGESTION FOR COMPOSITION

Using the above method of extending definition, go back to the preceding list of abstract concepts and choose one to "define." You may, of course, choose a concept that is not on the list.

"IT ALL DEPENDS ON WHAT YOU MEAN BY—"

You may already have heard teachers tell you to *define your terms.* Abstract terms, words that have values and judgments attached to them, need to be defined in your context when you use them. A sharp reader or listener will pick up on your

(1) **grits:** grain, coarsely ground, like a cereal
(1) **oleo:** margarine

generalization or your term and ask, "What do you mean by that word?" "How are you using that term?" "What's your definition of that word?"

The following essay was written by Benjamin Franklin (1706–1790), American statesman, author, printer, scientist, and inventor of the lightning rod. He helped to draft the Declaration of Independence and participated in the Convention to frame the American Constitution. He was a diplomat who helped negotiate peace with Great Britain following the American Revolution and was the first U.S. Ambassador to France.

If you detect some irony and even sarcasm in his "Remarks on the Politeness of the Savages of North America," you will be quite right! Much of it depends upon calling into question what we mean by terms such as "savage," "rude," "polite," "education," and "truth."

BENJAMIN FRANKLIN

Remarks on the Politeness of the Savages of North America

1   Savages we call them, because their manners differ from ours, which we think the perfection of civility;* they think the same of theirs.

2   Perhaps, if we could examine the manners of different nations with impartiality,* we should find no people so rude,* as to be without any rules of politeness; nor any so polite, as not to have some remains of rudeness.

3   The Indian men, when young, are hunters and warriors; when old, counsellors; for all their government is by the counsel or advice of the sages; there is no force, there are no prisons, no officers to compel obedience, or inflict punishment. Hence they generally study oratory,* the best speaker having the most influence. The Indian women till* the ground, dress the food, nurse and bring up the children, and preserve and hand down to posterity* the memory of public transactions. These employments of men and women are accounted natural and honorable. Having few artificial wants, they have abundance of leisure for improvement by conversation. Our laborious manner of life, compared with theirs, they esteem slavish* and base,* and the learning, on which we value ourselves, they regard as frivolous* and useless. An instance of this occurred at the treaty of Lancaster, in Pennsylvania, *anno** 1744, between the government of Virginia and the Six Nations.* After the principal business was settled, the commissioners from Virginia acquainted the Indians by a speech,

(1) **civility:** courtesy, politeness
(2) **impartiality:** without bias; fairness
(2) **rude:** without good manners, vulgar, lacking refinement, untaught
(3) **oratory:** the art of making speeches
(3) **till:** cultivate, prepare for crops
(3) **posterity:** the future, for succeeding generations
(3) **slavish:** like slaves
(3) **base:** low
(3) **frivolous:** of little value or importance, silly
(3) ***anno:*** (Latin) in the year
(3) **the Six Nations:** refers to a group of Indian tribes

that there was at Williamsburg a college, with a fund for educating Indian youth; and that, if the chiefs of the Six Nations would send down half a dozen of their sons to that college, the government would take care that they should be well provided for, and instructed in all the learning of the white people. It is one of the Indian rules of politeness not to answer a public proposition the same day that it is made; they think it would be treating it as a light matter, and that they show it respect by taking time to consider it, as of a matter important. They therefore deferred* their answer till the day following; when their speaker began, by expressing their deep sense of the kindness of the Virginia government, in making them that offer; "for we know," says he, "that you highly esteem* the kind of learning taught in those colleges, and that the maintenance of our young men, while with you, would be very expensive to you. We are convinced, therefore, that you mean to do us good by your proposal; and we thank you heartily. But you, who are wise, must know that different nations have different conceptions of things; and you will therefore not take it amiss,* if our ideas of this kind of education happen not to be the same with yours. We have had some experience of it; several of our young people were formerly brought up at the colleges of the northern provinces; they were instructed in all your sciences; but, when they came back to us, they were bad runners, ignorant of every means of living in the woods, unable to bear either cold or hunger, knew neither how to build a cabin, take a deer, nor kill an enemy, spoke our language imperfectly, were therefore neither fit for hunters, warriors, nor counsellors; they were totally good for nothing. We are however not the less obliged by your kind offer, though we decline accepting it; and, to show our grateful sense of it, if the gentlemen of Virginia will send us a dozen of their sons, we will take great care of their education, instruct them in all we know, and make *men* of them."

4   Having frequent occasions to hold public councils, they have acquired great order and decency in conducting them. The old men sit in the foremost ranks, the warriors in the next, and the women and children in the hindmost. The business of the women is to take exact note of what passes, imprint it in their memories (for they have no writing), and communicate it to their children. They are the records of the council, and they preserve the tradition of the stipulations* in treaties a hundred years back; which, when we compare with our writings, we always find exact. He that would speak, rises. The rest observe a profound silence. When he has finished and sits down, they leave him five or six minutes to recollect,* that, if he has omitted any thing he intended to say, or has any thing to add, he may rise again and deliver it. To interrupt another, even in common conversation, is reckoned highly inde-

(3) **deferred:** postponed (to deter to: to yield with courtesy)
(3) **esteem:** value, respect
(3) **take it amiss:** take it the wrong way, be insulted, misunderstand
(4) **stipulations:** agreements, conditions
(4) **recollect:** remember

cent. How different this is from the conduct of a polite British House of Commons, where scarce a day passes without some confusion, that makes the speaker hoarse in calling *to order;* and how different from the mode of conversation in many polite companies of Europe, where, if you do not deliver your sentence with great rapidity, you are cut off in the middle of it by the impatient loquacity* of those you converse with, and never suffered to* finish it!

5   The politeness of these savages in conversation is indeed carried to excess, since it does not permit them to contradict or deny the truth of what is asserted in their presence. By this means they indeed avoid disputes; but then it becomes difficult to know their minds, or what impression you make upon them. The missionaries who have attempted to convert them to Christianity, all complain of this as one of the great difficulties of their mission. The Indians hear with patience the truths of the Gospel* explained to them, and give their usual tokens of assent* and approbation;* you would think they were convinced. No such matter. It is mere civility.

6   A Swedish minister, having assembled the chiefs of the Susquehanna Indians, made a sermon to them, acquainting them with the principal historical facts on which our religion is founded; such as the fall of our first parents* by eating an apple, the coming of Christ to repair the mischief, his miracles and suffering, &c. When he had finished, an Indian orator stood up to thank him. "What you have told us," says he, "is all very good. It is indeed bad to eat apples. It is better to make them all into cider.* We are much obliged by your kindness in coming so far, to tell us those things which you have heard from your mothers. In return, I will tell you some of those we have heard from ours. In the beginning,* our fathers had only the flesh of animals to subsist on;* and, if their hunting was unsuccessful, they were starving. Two of our young hunters, having killed a deer, made a fire in the woods to broil some parts of it. When they were about to satisfy their hunger, they beheld a beautiful young woman descend from the clouds, and seat herself on that hill, which you see yonder among the Blue Mountains. They said to each other, it is a spirit that perhaps has smelt our broiling venison,* and wishes to eat of it; let us offer some to her. They presented her with the tongue; she was pleased with the taste of it, and said, 'Your kindness shall be rewarded; come

(4) **loquacity:** talkativeness
(4) **suffered to:** allowed to
(5) **the Gospel:** the teachings of Jesus
(5) **assent:** agreement
(5) **approbation:** approval
(6) **our first parents:** Adam and Eve
(6) **cider:** drink made from apples
(6) **In the beginning:** an echo of the first sentence of the Bible: "In the beginning God created the Heavens and the Earth."
(6) **subsist on:** live on, eat in order to live
(6) **venison:** the meat of the deer

to this place after thirteen moons, and you shall find something that will be of great benefit in nourishing you and your children to the latest generations.' They did so, and, to their surprise, found plants they had never seen before; but which, from that ancient time, have been constantly cultivated among us, to our great advantage. Where her right hand had touched the ground, they found maize;* where her left hand had touched it, they found kidney-beans; and where her backside had sat on it, they found tobacco." The good missionary, disgusted with this idle tale, said, "What I delivered to you were sacred truths; but what you tell me is mere fable, fiction, and falsehood." The Indian, offended, replied, "My brother, it seems your friends have not done you justice in your education; they have not well instructed you in the rules of common civility. You saw that we, who understand and practice those rules, believed all your stories; why do you refuse to believe ours?"

7   When any of them come into our towns, our people are apt to crowd around them, gaze upon them, and incommode* them, where they desire to be private; this they esteem great rudeness, and the effect of the want of instruction in the rules of civility and good manners. "We have," they say, "as much curiosity as you, and when you come into our towns, we wish for opportunities of looking at you; but for this purpose we hide ourselves behind bushes, where you are to pass, and never intrude* ourselves into your company."

☐ QUESTIONS

Answer the following questions using complete sentences.

1. How can we see that women were esteemed in this Indian tribe?
2. Why did the Indians wait until the following day to answer on the subject of the government scholarship for six Indian boys?
3. If the Indians were not convinced about the Gospel, why did they show assent? (Begin with "despite.")
4. How did the beautiful spirit reward the young Indian hunters? (Use "by" in your answer.)
5. How do the Indians act when the white people come into their town? (Use "so that" in your answer.)

☐ QUESTIONS FOR DISCUSSION

1. Be able to give extended definitions (that is, with examples) of the following words as the Indians understood them and as the "white men" did: *education, rudeness, politeness, truth.*

(6) **maize:** corn
(7) **incommode:** bother, inconvenience, give trouble to
(7) **intrude:** push in where not welcome

2. Show by similarly extended definitions how *you* understand these terms.
3. The Indians of North America were called "savages" by the "white men." The term was used as the opposite of "civilized." Look up the word *savage*. What is Franklin's tone in using the term? (See especially the first sentence.) Define *civilized*. Were the American Indians of that time civilized? Be able to defend your answer.
4. Look up *rude* in a dictionary that shows the older meaning of the word. How rude were the Indians in Franklin's examples? Do you know other examples of Indian behavior that you would consider "rude," "uncivilized," or "savage"? In Westerns, for example? How about the behavior of the "white man"?
5. What potential problems could be caused by the excessive politeness mentioned in paragraph 5? What might be more important than politeness in avoiding misunderstanding and loss of trust?
6. What potential is there for misunderstanding in paragraph 7?

□ SUGGESTIONS FOR COMPOSITION

1. Write an imaginary account of a traveller reporting on the behavior or customs of a group different from his own, showing how their definitions of terms and values differ. (Examples might be: hospitality, polite manners, education, or religious observance.)
2. Write a true account of the ways in which your culture differs from that of the United States with respect to good manners.
3. Write an account of an experience or an event here in the United States as if you were showing its "'strangeness" to someone who has never seen such a thing.
4. Do the same with an event in your country, taking the point of view of an American traveller to whom it may seem strange.

□ FOCUS ON SENTENCE VARIETY

In each sentence below, change the participial phrase to an adverbial clause.

1. "Having frequent occasions to hold public councils, they have acquired great order and decency in conducting them." (paragraph 4)
2. "A Swedish minister, having assembled the chiefs of the Susquehanna Indians, made a sermon to them. . . ." (paragraph 6)
3. "Two of our young hunters, having killed a deer, made a fire in the woods to broil some parts of it." (paragraph 6)

In each of the following sentences, change the subordinate clause to a participial or absolute phrase.

1. "After the principal business was settled, the commissioners from Virginia acquainted the Indians by a speech, that there was at Williamsburg a college, with a fund for educating Indian youth." (paragraph 3)
2. "... several of our young people ... were instructed in all your sciences; but, when they came back to us, they were bad runners" (paragraph 3)
3. "When they were about to satisfy their hunger, they beheld a beautiful young woman descend from the clouds." (paragraph 6)

S T U D E N T   C O M P O S I T I O N S

The following student compositions illustrate different kinds of definitions. "The Sarong" focuses quite simply on an object and explains what it is, using description and giving us some interesting information about function, as well. "Success" shows how one person defines his terms and shows us a beautiful idea and a beautiful relationship. "To Be a Foreigner" is a still more extended definition, one that may seem familiar to you.

The Sarong

In daily life, people in my country, especially the ones who live in the villages, wear a kind of clothing called "sarong." A sarong is made from two pieces of cotton cloth about 2½ square meters, which is sewn at each edge so that it makes the form of a cylinder. The pattern and color of the sarong is very special. It's just like the pattern and color of batik.

People like to wear sarongs because they are practical and comfortable. It's very easy to use; all you have to do is just slip into it and roll the upper edge so that it makes a kind of belt. A sarong can be used whether it is the cold or hot season in my country. If it's warm or hot, the sarong will make us feel cool, and if it is cold outside, wearing a sarong will make us warm.

A sarong is made by hand; usually the old people do it because patience is needed to make a sarong. It must be sewn and painted very carefully. The sarong is made in Java, Bali, and Sumatra, but the pattern and color of the sarong made in Java is different from the ones made in Bali. So are the ones made in Sumatra. The sarong which is made in Java usually has a dark color and simple pattern. The material used in Java is a cheap one. But the sarong which is made in Bali and Sumatra has a bright color and beautiful pattern. Sumatran sarongs usually have an abstract pattern and reddish color. Balinese sarongs have a special pattern. The pattern is about the story of their Gods. (People in Bali have more than one God.)

A sarong is not only used in daily life. On the *Hari Raya,* a Moslem holy day, people also wear sarongs. Of course on that day people wear the expensive ones.

Success

Before I came to the United States, my father told me that he wanted to talk with me. He said, "Son, maybe we will not find enough time to talk again; you are going to study in a country far away from here; you will stay there four or five years; you are going to build your life and your future; you are looking for your success. Son, I can say after 56 years experience that success is not money as you may think. It is not power as you might have heard. It's not status as you might feel. Success is happiness. You are as successful as you are happy. I know a lot of people who have power or money or status, but they are not happy in their lives because money, power, or status is their goal in life. They always see people who have more power or money than they so they push to get more and more; they never get their success. These things must be your instruments, not your goals.

"Son, I have said that there are always people who have more than you in some thing; I am telling you that there are always people who possess less than you, so smile when you have problems because I am sure that there is somebody who is in worse trouble than you. Son, if I ask you to improve your life, I ask you also to be content with your life.

"Son, to live your life is like being in a garden after a rain storm. You might look at the mud as something bad; but you might look at the flowers as the secret of the happiness, making you the successful man.

"Son, do not forget this conversation if you want to be a successful man. I pray that God may take care of you."

I have not forgotten it, Dad. That's why I can write it now as my opinion in the definition of the word success.

☐ QUESTIONS ON "SUCCESS"

1. What is your opinion of this definition of success?
2. What is your definition of success?

To Be a Foreigner

Far above and beyond the dictionary definition of *foreigner,* which refers to a person who has loyalty to another country, the word probably has a different meaning to every individual. To the native, the word can range from something exotic to something threatening; and to the foreigner—a stranger in a strange land—the word has endless meaning too. For each visitor in another country the experience is affected by the land from which he came, his skill with the language, his purpose for coming, his expectations of the country to which he is travelling. Add to that all the complicated mental and emotional factors which made us different and clearly every foreigner acts and reacts from his own point of reference. Within this context it becomes clear that generalizations are difficult, but there are some common bonds that I believe most foreigners in America share with me.

The enormous size of this country can be overwhelming. Concepts of time and distance need to be completely readjusted and relearned, and one is often left feeling like a child, trying to grasp the ideas of time and space. There is the variety of people which is unique to this country. With such a representation of nationalities, a foreigner has difficulty deciding what is "typically" American.

What does seem to be typically American is that because of the size and variety of the country, its people can satisfy their desire for space and privacy. A disadvantage of this luxury is that it allows for each man to be an "island."

Early in this century, the word *America* meant economic freedom to most Europeans; today, it means political freedom. For many foreigners the freedoms of democracy, the civil liberties, can undoubtedly be an exciting experience.

Perhaps the American who has been a tourist in another country has some understanding of the frustration of trying to communicate in a foreign tongue. The tourist, however, is often sheltered by his status; his needs are basic, and thus the level of communication is simpler. The frustration which an adult can experience when trying to communicate with natives can be so diminishing and demoralizing that it actually shakes one's self-confidence. The result is a reluctance to speak and a withdrawal that may be misunderstood and interpreted as lack of friendliness and enthusiasm.

As the foreigner's time in America passes, and he learns to adapt to his environment, he is often filled with a desire to become just another "face in the crowd." But this, too, becomes impossible the moment he speaks. His accent gives him away. It is like the mark of Cain—he is a "foreigner."

But in spite of all the tensions, the frustrations, and the painful experiences that the foreigner may suffer, the total experience of living, learning, and adapting to a new environment cannot but enrich* and enlarge a person. He becomes much more a citizen of the world.

☐ QUESTIONS ON "TO BE A FOREIGNER"

1. The writer speaks of common bonds that other foreigners in America share with him. What common bonds, if any, do *you* feel with him?
2. Discuss the writer's analysis of the effect of size and space on Americans. Do you agree? Do you have a similar view of America's "enormous size"? To what extent do you think your reaction to size depends on the size of your country relative to the United States?

* **cannot but enrich:** must enrich

CHAPTER

10

CAUSAL ANALYSIS

Whenever we ask "why," we are asking for an explanation of **cause.** When we answer the question "why," when we try to explain the *reasons* for something—a phenomenon, an event in history, a choice, a feeling—we are trying to analyze the cause. We try to identify the factors that had a part in the effect we are observing or discussing.

If we canceled the picnic because it was raining, we can say the rain caused the cancellation of the picnic.

Cause　　　　　　　　　　　　　　　　　　　　*Effect*
Rain ————————————————————————→ Picnic canceled

When we begin with the cancellation of the picnic (effect) and ask "why did this happen?" we are looking for *cause*—for *cause in the past*.

Effect (picnic canceled)

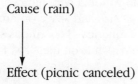
　　　Why?

Cause (rain)

Suppose, however, we were to begin with the possibility of rain and look to the future: If it rains, what will happen? What will be the *effect* of rain? In this kind of question, we are asking about **consequence.** *Rain will cause cancellation of the picnic.* Notice that we are still examining the general patterns:

Cause (rain)

Effect (picnic canceled)

But now, instead of working backward from effect to cause, we are working *forward from cause to effect.*

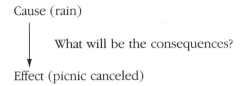

Cause (rain)

What will be the consequences?

Effect (picnic canceled)

Whether we look back from effect to cause and ask "why?" or forward from cause to effect and ask "what will be the consequence?" we are analyzing the relationship between cause and effect.

The above example is simple: one clear cause, one clear effect. It is an example of *sufficient cause:* The rain, by itself, was *sufficient* (was cause enough) to cancel a picnic. One can expect that, at any time, rain would have the effect of spoiling plans for a picnic. One can predict this relationship of cause and effect with some *uniformity.* In a laboratory, we can establish predictable relationships between cause and effect and can reproduce effects over and over again, given the same causes.

It is when we move out of the laboratory, when we move away from *simple cause → simple, predictable effect* that we must be aware that in most of life—social situations, personal motivations, politics, or history—events very seldom have simple causes or simple consequences. When more than one cause contributes to an effect, we call each one a **contributing cause.** To say that World War I was caused by the assassination of a crown prince in Serbia is to ignore all the *other* factors that led to the war. We do not have a world war, or any war necessarily, *every time* a prince is shot. This cause is not *sufficient,* it did not *by itself* cause a war.

Figure 9 illustrates the more usual patterns of complex cause and effect situations. Part A demonstrates how several causes may contribute to a single effect and a single cause may have several effects. Another type of complex causation is the *chain reaction,* illustrated in part B. Let us suppose that there is a riot in a small town. What has caused it? Looking at the faces of the people who are rioting, we could say they rioted because they were unhappy, discontented, or full of anger. To give no further analysis than that, however, seems very shallow and unsatisfying. We would like to know *why* they are angry. We may find that the cause of their anger is unemployment, so to complete our understanding of the situation, we would want to know what caused the unemployment. We may find that the principal industry of the town shut down. It may or may not be relevant to the analysis to discuss reasons for the shutdown of the factory. We could keep going back, cause by cause, until we lose sight of the riot for which we are trying to find the cause. We are interested in **immediate causes,** closer or **proximate causes,** and some causes further back, **remote causes.** But unless we are doing an economic or historical analysis, we do not want to get *too* remote. We must try to be fair and honest in an analysis, but at the same time we must decide what our subject is and not go back further than the subject warrants. A summary of important remote factors may help. Let us return to the chain causation diagram and apply it to the riot, as in part C.

One could, of course, look to the future and predict what the *consequences* of the riot might be, as in part D.

FIGURE 9

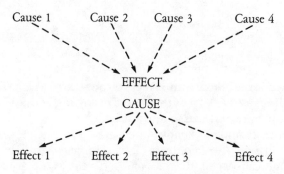

Part A. Multiple Causes or Effects

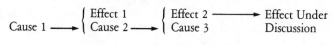

Part B. Chain Reaction

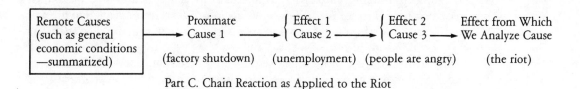

Part C. Chain Reaction as Applied to the Riot

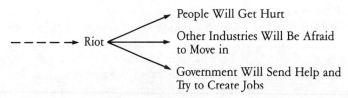

Part D. Consequences

NECESSARY CONDITION OR CAUSE?

The ringing of a telephone (plus your curiosity, plus your possible feeling of obligation to answer a caller, plus, possibly, your expecting a particular call) causes you to answer it. There are certain conditions, however, that must be met if that ring is to result in your answering the telephone. For example, you must have heard it ring; your arms and legs must operate well enough to get your hand to it; the telephone must be in an accessible place. All of these are conditions necessary to the answering of the telephone, yet none are reasons for answering it.

Suppose you were to write an essay analyzing why you came to the United States to study. There probably are several reasons, several *contributory causes.* The ability to pay for that education—whether by scholarship, or money you or your parents can afford to spend, or loans from the bank—is a *necessary condition* for your getting the education. Without some financial support, you would not be able to study abroad, but having the financial means is not the reason you came. Condition and cause operate together, but they are not the same.

BEING CAREFUL IN CAUSAL ANALYSIS

Most problems are complex. Human behavior, whether individual or societal, past or present, is very complex. Complex situations never have simple causes or simply one cause. One must not oversimplify. It is important to remember this when you are writing, but also when you are reading and listening, so that you think critically and objectively, whether you are giving the analysis or receiving it. The person who finds *one* cause to explain a complex situation is not a reliable analyst of cause.

If we are realistic, we know that we do not completely understand exactly why complex situations exist or how to solve them easily by getting rid of a cause. We must limit ourselves to what we feel competent to analyze. On the other hand, we do have minds, experience, insights, and education that allow us to hypothesize. We *try* to understand the "why's" of our world; we try to explain situations to ourselves and others—and we should! *Evidence* to back up our analysis is very important; so is the attitude that we are limited—but trying sincerely to understand the situation, trying to identify the relevant factors and their relationship to one another, trying to be fair and objective. We also must use our judgment in selecting relevant data and in including the factors that go back beyond the immediate causes, but only as far as they remain relevant to the topic we have chosen to discuss.

Ashley Montagu, a well-known physical and cultural anthropologist, was born in London, England, but is now a citizen of the United States. The following is a selection from a book of essays entitled *The American Way of Life.*

ASHLEY MONTAGU

Masculine Expression of Emotion

1   American men don't cry because it is considered unmasculine to do so. Only sissies* cry. Crying is a "weakness" characteristic of the female, and no American male wants to be identified with anything in the least weak or feminine. Crying, in our culture, is identified with childishness, with weakness and dependence. No one likes a crybaby, and we disapprove of crying

(1) **sissies:** a slang term usually used for boys (but also sometimes for girls) who seem weak or cowardly (afraid, fearful, not brave)

even in children, discouraging it in them as early as possible. In a land so devoted to the pursuit of happiness as ours, crying really is rather un-American. Adults must learn not to cry in situations in which it is permissible for a child to cry. Women being the "weaker" and "dependent" sex, it is only natural that they should cry in certain emotional situations. In women, crying is excusable. But in men, crying is a mark of weakness. So goes the American credo* with regard to crying.

2   "A little man," we impress on our male children, "never cries. Only sissies and crybabies do." And so we condition* males in America not to cry whenever they feel like doing so. It is not that American males are unable to cry because of some biological time clock within them which causes them to run down in that capacity as they grow older, but that they are trained not to cry. No "little man" wants to be like that "inferior creature," the female. And the worst thing you can call him is a sissy or crybaby. And so the "little man" represses* his desire to cry and goes on doing so until he is unable to cry even when he wants to. Thus we produce a trained incapacity* in the American male to cry. And this is bad. Why is it bad? Because crying is a natural function of the human organism which is designed to restore the emotionally disequilibrated person to a state of equilibrium.* The return of the disequilibrated organ systems of the body to steady states or dynamic stability is known as homeostasis. Crying serves a homeostatic function for the organism as a whole. Any interference with homeostatic mechanisms is likely to be damaging to the organism. And there is good reason to believe that the American male's trained incapacity to cry is seriously damaging to him.

3   It is unnecessary to cry whenever one wants to cry, but one should be able to cry when one ought to cry—when one needs to cry. For to cry under certain emotionally disequilibrating conditions is necessary for the maintenance of health.

4   On these matters we are strangely confused in our culture. Consider, for example, the behavior of husband and wife when a sudden catastrophe or bereavement* befalls the family. The wife is likely to be prostrated* with grief, shedding virtual waterfalls of tears. Having consumed all the linen in the household and having resorted to the bathroom mat, in the attempt to stanch* the flood, she will furtively* glance out of the corner of her eye admiringly at the heroic creature she married. So different from herself! There he stands,

(1) **credo:** a statement of belief, usually religious belief; profession of faith in a principle
(2) **condition:** here, a verb meaning to make them accustomed to, to get them used to
(2) **represses:** puts down, holds back, prevents natural expression of
(2) **incapacity:** inability, lack of the power to do
(2) **disequilibrated ... equilibrium:** *equilibrium* is a state of balance or adjustment; *disequilibrated* refers to the opposite state
(4) **bereavement:** a state of terrible loss, as of a friend or loved one by death
(4) **prostrated:** to be fallen or lying down flat
(4) **stanch:** stop the flow
(4) **furtively:** in a hidden manner, done without being seen

godlike, strong, silent, and with stiff upper lip,* puffing away intrepidly* at his pipe, without betraying a sign of the inner turmoil* which is so outwardly visible in herself. What a noble creature is the male!

5   There indeed he may stand, but the truth is that he isn't standing* the situation anywhere nearly as well as his wife is managing it horizontally. For in his marmoreal* ineffectuality, not only is the male being useless to everyone for miles around, but he is also perhaps being most useless to himself. For while his wife is doing what she ought, weeping away and thus restoring herself to a state of equilibrium as soon as possible, her husband, being utterly incapable of expressing his emotions through tears, is nevertheless expressing his emotions in the manner to which he has been accustomed by those who have trained him in his incapacity to cry. He turns his emotions into his body. Instead of expressing them overtly,* he expresses them covertly,* he interiorizes them; he somatizes them—that is to say, he expresses them through his body. Instead of weeping through his lachrymal* apparatus he now begins to weep vicariously,* either through his skin in the form of some sort of dermatological* eruption, such as urticaria, psoriasis, boils, and itching. Or he turns his emotions into his respiratory system and comes up with a variety of asthmatoid* conditions and begins to wheeze* and whine and cough. Or he expresses himself through his gastrointestinal* tract in the form of peptic ulcers of the stomach or duodenum or hyperirritability of the intestines or inflammation of the colon. Or he may express himself by expediting his emotions into his upper story and there begin to develop bats in his belfry* in the form of a nervous breakdown. Or it may all go into his cardiovascular* system, and there he may begin to develop heart or hypertensive* symptoms. And so on most unmerrily, not to say unprofitably—except, of course, to the medical profession.

6   And there lies his grief-stricken wife, peeping worshipfully out of the

(4) **stiff upper lip:** an idiom referring to putting on a brave front, refusing to be discouraged under difficulties, not showing emotion or weakness in these circumstances

(4) **intrepidly:** fearlessly, bravely

(4) **turmoil:** disturbance, tumult, confusion

(5) **standing:** in this second meaning, an idiom: bearing, managing, tolerating

(5) **marmoreal:** like marble

(5) **overtly:** openly, outwardly

(5) **covertly:** secretly, in a hidden or disguised way, inwardly

(5) **lachrymal:** pertaining to tears

(5) **vicariously:** by substitution; a function performed by other than the usual organ

(5) **dermatological:** referring to skin diseases

(5) **asthmatoid:** like asthma—a condition of choking cough, shortness of breath; a suffocating feeling

(5) **wheeze:** to breathe with a whistling sound

(5) **gastrointestinal:** digestive

(5) **upper story . . . bats in his belfry:** slang expression for mental or emotional problems; go crazy

(5) **cardiovascular:** heart and circulatory system

(5) **hypertensive:** high blood pressure

corner of a moist eye at her seemingly composed husband, admiring him and depreciating herself for all the wrong reasons in the world. For it is he who is doing the wrong thing and she who is doing the right. The male by his stolid* behavior is succeeding in damaging himself further, while the female is succeeding in restoring herself to a state of equilibrium and to continuing health. And this, supposedly, is why women are the weaker vessels and men are strong and resilient!* The very opposite is the truth.

7   Women, by virtue of the availability of such outlets as crying for the expression of pent-up* emotion, are likely to suffer from fewer psychosomatic* disturbances than men.

8   I know of no studies on the expression of the emotions in business-women. But the increase in psychosomatic disorders among women in recent years—for example, the rise in the peptic ulcer rate—suggests that women in business may be attempting to restrain the normal expression of their emotions. If so, I would say that this is not good. Women in business who believe that in order to succeed, they must imitate men are barking up the wrong tree.

9   I am not suggesting that every time the boss bawls one out* or every time one runs into a major frustration, one ought to assume the supine* position and have a good cry. I think this would be silly. Crying should be reserved for the appropriate situation, and that is whenever one's organism indicates the ·necessity. In this respect the American male has a great deal to learn from the American female—whether in business or out of it. In business the emotions that are likely to be called into play are not those which usually lead to the desire to cry. On the contrary, they tend to be the angry emotions, and crying is not a natural way of expressing such emotions, nor is it being suggested that they should—even if they could—be so expressed. Opportunities to blow off steam* in ways appropriate to the occasion should be provided until such time as we have contrived to produce human beings who have learned to deal with their frustrations in a constructive manner.

10   It would be absurd to suggest that the psychosomatic disorders from which men suffer in America are the result of the fact that they do not cry. The inability to cry is but one reflection of many indicating that the American male has not been taught how to use his emotions efficiently, and it is this general inefficient use of his emotions, rather than one particular expression of them; that is principally at fault. Nevertheless, it is agreed by most authorities that crying is a beneficial means of relieving the person of tensions which seek

(6) **stolid:** without emotion, unexcitable, dull
(6) **resilient:** bouncing or springing back; recovering strength, spirit, or humor quickly
(7) **pent-up:** shut in, confined
(7) **psychosomatic:** psychological or emotional problems showing themselves through a physical disturbance or illness or pain
(9) **bawls one out:** reprimands, shouts at to make behave or criticizes, as one would to correct a child, in an angry voice
(9) **supine:** lying on back
(9) **blow off steam:** (idiom) give expression to anger

expression in this particular manner. It is far better that the energies which seek release in such emotional expression find an outlet in weeping than that they should be pent up to seek adventitious* expression through the body.

11   Tears have been likened* to the clarifying and beneficent effects of the rain which comes after a thunderstorm on a sultry* summer day. It was Charles Dickens, a man, who wrote: "Heaven knows we need never be ashamed of our tears, for they are rain upon the blinding dust of earth, overlying our hard hearts." Indeed, the evidence on all sides supports the view that under the conditions which call for it, a good cry is a wonderful restorative. Hence, it may be concluded that although crying would hardly be a solution to all the difficulties of the American male, it would certainly be a help in some.

12   Perhaps it would be helpful if instead of so wholeheartedly pursuing the ideals of life, liberty, and happiness, we modified our orientation in the direction of life, liberty, and the pursuit of homeostasis. Perhaps, also, the institution of the wailing wall is not such a bad idea. In any event, and quite seriatim,* it is high time that parents realized that being a tender, gentle, warm, loving human being who can cry as well as laugh is not incompatible* with being a man. The taboo* on tenderness which is placed in the way of the American male's healthy development is something which we shall have to remove before American men are able to cry as and when they should. Italian and French men do not hesitate to cry whenever they feel like it, and I am sure that they are much the better off for being able to do so.

13   To be human is to weep. The human species is the only one in the whole of animated nature that sheds tears. The trained inability of any human being to weep is a lessening of his capacity to be human—a defect which usually goes deeper than the mere inability to cry. And this, among other things, is what American parents—with the best intentions in the world—have achieved for the American male. It is very sad. If we feel like it, let us all have a good cry—and clear our minds of those cobwebs of confusion which have for so long prevented us from understanding the ineluctable* necessity of crying.

☐ FOCUS ON CAUSAL ANALYSIS

---

1. The author begins with the statement: "American men don't cry," and proceeds to explain why. He then goes on to explain the consequences of this conditioning. What are the causes, according to Mr. Montagu? What are the consequences?

(10) **adventitious:** away from its natural position
(11) **likened:** compared, showing similarity
(11) **sultry:** very hot, close, humid
(12) **seriatim:** seriously
(12) **incompatible:** inconsistent, not in harmony with, not in agreement with or able to come to agreement
(12) **taboo:** something forbidden by the rules or conventions of that society
(13) **ineluctable:** not to be avoided

2. Are there other "whys" he explains? (Look at the discussion of women.)
3. What is his solution to the problem? How does it relate to cause?
4. Montagu considers that an inability to cry is not simply a result and cause for further "bad" effects; he also finds it to be *symptomatic* of a deeper wrong in American views and assumptions. What wrong?

☐ QUESTIONS FOR DISCUSSION

1. Explain the statement in the final paragraph: "To be human is to weep." If this is true, how would you complete the sentence "Not to weep. . . ."? Explain.
2. He contrasts men and women. Analyze the difference in this context.
3. In what way are the women as wrong as the men? How do they contribute to the men's problem?
4. What is Montagu's main point? In one sentence, write the essay's message. (How do you know in paragraph 1 that he disagrees with the American view?)
5. Do you agree or disagree with his views? Discuss.
6. How does your culture view crying by men? Do you feel your way is similar to the American way? More "macho"? More like what Montagu advocates? Do you feel the attitude in your culture is healthier than that in American society? (It must be made clear that there are many "subcultures" in American society, some of which view masculine expression of emotion as Montagu does. More and more, even among "typical" Americans, this "macho" ideal is being questioned, along with all other male/female stereotypes.)

☐ SUGGESTIONS FOR COMPOSITION

1. Using the basic structure of this essay, illustrated in Figure 10, construct an essay of your own in which you begin with a situation, trace its causes, show its consequences, and recommend (or show) its solution.
2. Use a difficult incident in your own experience, in that of people you know, or in something you have read, to show how emotion was handled. Show the manner in which it was expressed or hidden and comment on it, showing your feelings about whether it was handled in a healthy or an unhealthy way.
3. Montagu dramatizes a contrast between men and women with respect to showing emotion by means of tears. What do *you* consider basic differences between men and women? Are these *learned* or *innate* (inborn) differences? Defend your opinion.

FIGURE 10

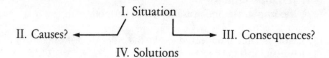

I. Situation

II. Causes? ← / ⌐ → III. Consequences?

IV. Solutions

4. This essay touches on a subject larger than just different ways of showing emotion. It touches on what a man thinks it means "to be a man." Montagu criticizes the view that "to be a man" means to be tough and outwardly unfeeling. When Americans say "Be a man!" its connotations (see Chapter 11 for a full discussion of "connotation") are "Be brave, be tough." In other languages, however, its connotations are "Have moral courage, integrity, strength. Be worthy of respect based on character." What are its connotations (those nonliteral, emotional meanings that become associated with words) in your language? Begin with that and go on to write your personal definition of "manhood." (See Chapter 9 on "Definition.")

PARALLELISM AND ANTITHESIS

You have no doubt been corrected for faulty parallelism or told to use parallelism correctly. This means that when you connect words with coordinate conjunctions or words in a series, the words you connect must be the same (parallel) in structure: Nouns must be connected with nouns, verbs with verbs, clauses with clauses. Verbs must also be in the same form.

Wrong: We went swimming, hiking, and we caught fish.
Right: We went swimming, hiking, and fishing.
          or
          We swam, we hiked, and we caught fish.
Wrong: He hoped for rain and that the temperature would drop.
Right: He hoped for rain and a drop in the temperature.
          or
          He hoped that it would rain and that the temperature would drop.

Let us now look at parallelism not simply as a potential problem in structure, but also as an asset in effective writing style. *Go back and reread the sentence you have just read.* Show how parallelism is used to emphasize the point. What are the coordinators, the *correlatives* (paired coordinates) that strengthen the parallel effect?

Useful correlatives for creating parallel structures are

Both . . . and
Either . . . or
Neither . . . nor
Not only . . . but also
Not . . . but

Antithesis is an opposition or contrast of thoughts expressed in parallel structure. This can be very effective in writing. The following two examples are famous for their simplicity, their beauty, and their effectiveness.

1. From the opening paragraph of *A Tale of Two Cities* by Charles Dickens, these lines express the tension and the possibilities of the days just before the French Revolution in 1792.

   It was the best of times, it was the worst of times, it was the age of wisdom, it was the age of foolishness, it was the epoch of belief, it was the epoch of incredulity, it was the season of Light, it was the season of Darkness, it was the spring of hope, it was the winter of despair, we had everything before us, we had nothing before us.

2. These lines have been selected from *Ecclesiastes,* a book in the Bible that is often attributed to King Solomon.

> To every thing there is a season, and a time to every purpose under the heaven:
>> A time to be born, and a time to die;
>> A time to plant, and a time to pluck up that which is planted;
>> A time to break down, and a time to build up;
>> A time to weep, and a time to laugh;
>> A time to mourn, and a time to dance;
>> A time to keep, and a time to cast away;
>> A time to keep silence, and a time to speak;
>> A time to love, and a time to hate;
>> A time for war, and a time for peace.

Ashley Montagu uses parallelism very effectively to show contrast; that is, he uses antithesis. Examine the structure and effectiveness of the following sentences:

1. *"It is not that* American males are unable to cry . . . *but that* they are trained not to cry." (paragraph 2)
2. *"It is* unnecessary to cry whenever one wants to cry, *but* one should be able to cry when one ought to cry. . . ." (paragraph 3)
3. *". . . not only* is the male being useless to everyone for miles around, *but* he is *also* perhaps being most useless to himself." (paragraph 5)
4. *"Instead of* expressing them overtly, he expresses them covertly. . . ." (paragraph 5) (Note that "instead of," being a preposition, requires an object; therefore, the verb is in the *gerund* form, while the antithesis follows the usual subject plus verb pattern.)
5. *". . . it is he who* is doing the wrong thing and *she who* is doing the right." (paragraph 6)
6. "The male . . . is succeeding in damaging himself further, *while* the female is succeeding in restoring herself to a state of equilibrium. . . ." (paragraph 6)
7. *"To* be human *is to* weep." (paragraph 13)

☐ USING ANTITHESIS

Let us now try to create our own sentences using these patterns. In (A), half of the sentence is given to you; complete that sentence. In (B), create your own sentence, using the same pattern.

1. (A) It is not that I don't like spaghetti, but that . . .
   (B) It is not that . . .
       but that . . .
2. (A) It is silly to get upset over every grade below A, but one should . . .

(B)   It is . . .
       but . . .
3. (A) Not only did she want to order steak for dinner, but she also . . .
   (B) Not only . . .
        but . . . also . . .
4. (A) Instead of changing the tire himself, he . . .
   (B) Instead of _____, she . . .
5. (A) It is the student who is doing all the work, and . . . who . . .
   (B) It is . . . who . . .
        and . . . who . . .
6. (A) . . . while the rich fly around in their jets.
   (B) . . . while . . .
7. (A) To be mature is to . . .
   (B) To . . . is to . . .

The following essay is a moving example of the way in which analyzing one's own situation can help a person come to terms with it, how clarifying it to others can help clarify it to oneself. Out of the experiences and feelings he expresses in this essay, the author has recently written a book entitled *Hunger of Memory: The Education of Richard Rodriguez.*

RICHARD RODRIGUEZ

FROM *Going Home Again: The New American Scholarship Boy*

1   At each step, with every graduation from one level of education to the next, the refrain* from bystanders was strangely the same: "Your parents must be so proud of you." I suppose that my parents were proud, although I suspect, too, that they felt more than pride alone as they watched me advance through my education. They seemed to know that my education was separating us from one another, making it difficult to resume familiar intimacies. Mixed with the instincts of parental pride, a certain hurt also communicated itself—too private ever to be adequately expressed in words, but real nonetheless.

2   The autobiographical facts pertinent to this essay are simply stated in two sentences, though they exist in somewhat awkward juxtaposition* to each other. I am the son of Mexican-American parents, who speak a blend of Spanish and English, but who read neither language easily. I am about to receive a Ph.D. in English Renaissance literature.* What sort of life—what tensions, feelings, conflicts—connects these two sentences? I look back and remember my life from the time I was seven or eight years old as one of constant movement away from a Spanish-speaking folk culture toward the

(1) **refrain:** in a song or poem, phrases or verses that keep getting repeated
(2) **juxtaposition:** placing side by side or close together
(2) **English Renaissance literature:** English literature at about the time of Shakespeare and Queen Elizabeth I, about the sixteenth century

world of the English-language classroom. As the years passed, I felt myself becoming less like my parents and less comfortable with the assumption of visiting relatives that I was still the Spanish-speaking child they remembered. By the time I began college, visits home became suffused with* silent embarrassment: there seemed so little to share, however strong the ties of our affection. My parents would tell me what happened in their lives or in the lives of relatives; I would respond with news of my own. Polite questions would follow. Our conversations came to seem more like interviews.

3   A few months ago, my dissertation* nearly complete, I came upon* my father poking through my bookcase. He quietly fingered the volumes of Milton's tracts and Augustine's theology* with that combination of reverence* and distrust those who are not literate sometimes show for the written word. Silently, I watched him from the door of the room. However much he would have insisted that he was "proud" of his son for being able to master the texts, I knew, if pressed further, he would have admitted to complicated feelings about my success. When he looked across the room and suddenly saw me, his body tightened slightly with surprise, then we both smiled.

4   For many years I kept my uneasiness about becoming a success in education to myself. I did so in part because I wanted to avoid vague feelings that, if considered carefully, I would have no way of dealing with; and in part because I felt that no one else shared my reaction to the opportunity provided by education. When I began to rehearse my story of cultural dislocation* publicly, however, I found many listeners willing to admit to similar feelings from their own pasts. Equally impressive was the fact that many among those I spoke with were *not* from non-white racial groups, which made me realize that one can grow up to enter the culture of the academy* and find it a "foreign" culture for a variety of reasons, ranging from economic status to religious heritage. But why, I next wondered, was it that, though there were so many of us who came from childhood cultures alien to the academy's, we voiced our uneasiness to one another and to ourselves so infrequently? Why did it take *me* so long to acknowledge publicly the cultural costs I had paid to earn a Ph.D. in Renaissance English literature? Why, more precisely, am I writing these words only now when my connection to my past barely survives except as nostalgic* memory?

5   Looking back, a person risks losing hold of the present while being

(2) **suffused with:** filled with
(3) **dissertation:** doctoral thesis, a requirement for the Ph.D. degree
(3) **came upon:** (idiom) met by accident, found
(3) **Milton's tracts and Augustine's theology:** Milton, a great British poet of the seventeenth century, wrote religious tracts (or essays); Augustine, a Christian saint, was famous for his writings
(3) **reverence:** deep respect, as for something holy
(4) **dislocation:** being out of place, its order upset
(4) **the academy:** here, higher education
(4) **nostalgic:** causing a longing to go back in time or back home, a longing for something far away or long ago

confounded by the past. For the child who moves to an academic culture from a culture that dramatically lacks academic traditions, looking back can jeopardize* the certainty he has about the desirability of this new academic culture. Richard Hoggart's description, in *The Uses of Literacy,* of the cultural pressures on such a student, whom Hoggart calls the "scholarship boy,"* helps make the point. The scholarship boy must give nearly unquestioning allegiance* to academic culture, Hoggart argues, if he is to succeed at all, so different is the milieu* of the classroom from the culture he leaves behind. For a time, the scholarship boy may try to balance his loyalty between his concretely experienced family life and the more abstract mental life of the classroom. In the end, though, he must choose between the two worlds: if he intends to succeed as a student, he must, literally and figuratively, separate himself from his family, with its gregarious* life, and find a quiet place to be alone with his thoughts.

6   After a while, the kind of allegiance the young student might once have given his parents is transferred to the teacher, the new parent. Now without the support of the old ties and certainties of the family, he almost mechanically acquires the assumptions, practices, and style of the classroom milieu. For the loss he might otherwise feel, the scholarship boy substitutes an enormous enthusiasm for nearly everything having to do with school.

7   How readily I read my own past into the portrait of Hoggart's scholarship boy. Coming from a home in which mostly Spanish was spoken, for example, I had to decide to forget Spanish when I began my education. To succeed in the classroom, I needed psychologically to sever my ties with Spanish. Spanish represented an alternate culture as well as another language—and the basis of my deepest sense of relationship to my family. Although I recently taught myself to read Spanish, the language that I see on the printed page is not quite the language I heard in my youth. That other Spanish, the spoken Spanish of my family, I remember with nostalgia and guilt: guilt because I cannot explain to aunts and uncles why I do not answer their questions any longer in their own idiomatic language. Nor was I able to explain to teachers in graduate school, who regularly expected me to read and speak Spanish with ease, why my very ability to reach graduate school as a student of English literature in the first place required me to loosen my attachments to a language I spoke years earlier. Yet, having lost the ability to speak Spanish, I never forgot it so totally that I could not understand it. Hearing Spanish spoken on the street reminded me of the community I once felt a part of, and still cared deeply about. I never forgot Spanish so thoroughly, in other words, as to move outside the range of its nostalgic pull.

(5) **jeopardize:** put in danger

(5) **scholarship boy:** one who, because of his academic ability, is given a scholarship; that is, he will not have to pay for his education and thus is given an opportunity his family could not afford to give him

(5) **allegiance:** loyalty, as to one's country, ruler, principle, or religion

(5) **milieu:** (French) environment

(5) **gregarious:** sociable, people coming together in a friendly way

8   Such moments of guilt and nostalgia were, however, just that—momentary. They punctuated the history of my otherwise successful progress from *barrio** to classroom. Perhaps they even encouraged it. Whenever I felt my determination to succeed wavering,* I tightened my hold on the conventions of academic life.

9   Spanish was one aspect of the problem, my parents another. They could raise deeper, more persistent doubts. They offered encouragement to my brothers and me in our work, but they also spoke, only half jokingly, about the way education was putting "big ideas" into our heads. When we would come home, for example, and challenge assumptions we earlier believed, they would be forced to defend their beliefs (which, given our new verbal skills, they did increasingly less well) or, more frequently, to submit to our logic with the disclaimer,* "It's what we were taught in our time to believe. . . ." More important, after we began to leave home for college, they voiced regret about how "changed" we had become, how much further away from one another we had grown. They partly yearned for* a return to the time before education assumed their children's primary loyalty. This yearning was renewed each time they saw their nieces and nephews (none of whom continued their education beyond high school, all of whom continued to speak fluent Spanish) living according to the conventions and assumptions of their parents' culture. If I was already troubled by the time I graduated from high school by that refrain of congratulations ("Your parents must be so proud . . ."), I realize now how much more difficult and complicated was my progress into academic life for my parents, as they saw the cultural foundation of their family erode,* than it was for me.

10   Yet my parents were willing to pay the price of alienation and continued to encourage me to become a scholarship boy because they perceived, as others of the lower classes had before them, the relation between education and social mobility.* Lacking the former themselves made them acutely aware of its necessity as prerequisite for the latter. They sent their children off to school with the hopes of their acquiring something "better" beyond education. Notice the assumption here that education is something of a tool or license—a means to an end, which has been the traditional way the lower or working classes have viewed the value of education in the past. That education might alter children in more basic ways than providing them with skills, certificates of proficiency, and even upward mobility, may come as a surprise for some, but the final cost is usually tolerated.

(8) **barrio:** (Spanish) neighborhood
(8) **wavering:** showing doubt, moving one way and then the other
(9) **disclaimer:** denial, saying one is not responsible
(9) **yearned for:** longed for, desired
(9) **erode:** wear down, wear away, disintegrate
(10) **social mobility:** ability to move upward in social status or rank, bettering oneself in society

.   .   .   .

11   Only when I finished my course work in graduate school and went off to England for my dissertation did I grasp how far I had traveled from my cultural origins. My year in England was actually my first opportunity to write and reflect upon the kind of material that I would spend my life producing. It was my first chance, too, to be free simultaneously of the distractions of course-work and of the insecurities of trying to find my niche* in academic life. Sitting in the reading room of the British Museum, I no longer doubted that I had joined academic society. Ironically, this feeling of having finally arrived allowed me to look back to the community whence I came. That I was geographically farther away from my home than I had ever been lent a metaphorical resonance to the cultural distance I suddenly felt.*

12   But the feeling was not pleasing. The reward of feeling a part of the world of the British Museum was an odd one. Each morning I would arrive at the reading room and grow increasingly depressed by the silence and what the silence implied—that my life as a scholar would require self-absorption. Who, I wondered, would find my work helpful enough to want to read it? Was not my dissertation—whose title alone would puzzle my relatives—only my grandest exercise thus far in self-enclosure? The sight of the heads around me bent over their texts and papers, many so thoroughly engrossed* that they wouldn't look up at the silent clock overhead for hours at a stretch, made me recall the remarkable noises of life in my family home. The tedious prose* I was writing, a prose constantly qualified by footnotes, reminded me of the capacity for passionate statement those of the culture I was born into commanded—and which, could it be, I had now lost.

13   As I remembered it during those gray English afternoons, the past rushed forward to define more precisely my present condition. Remembering my youth, a time when I was not restricted to a chair but ran barefoot under a summer sun that tightened my skin with its white heat, made the fact that it was only my mind that "moved" each hour in the library painfully obvious.

14   I did need to figure out where I had lost touch with my past. I started to become alien to my family culture the day I became a scholarship boy. In the British Museum the realization seemed obvious. . . . I am not suggesting that an academic cannot reestablish ties of any kind with his old culture. Indeed, he can have an impact on the culture of his childhood. But as an academic, one exists by definition in a culture separate from one's nonacademic roots

---

(11) **niche:** (French) a place or position especially suitable for the person in it

(11) **that I . . . felt:** in other words, the actual *geographic* distance was also a metaphor (see Analogy, Chapter 4), a kind of symbol, for the *cultural* distance he felt

(12) **engrossed:** absorbed, their attention completely taken

(12) **prose:** the ordinary form of spoken or written language, without rhyme or meter; not poetry

and, therefore, any future ties one has with those who remain "behind" are complicated by one's new cultural perspective.

. . . . . .

15   Paradoxically,* the distance separating the academic from his non-academic past can make his past seem, if not closer, then clearer. It is possible for the academic to understand the culture from which he came "better" than those who still live within it. In my own experience, it has only been as I have come to appraise* my past through categories and notions derived from the social sciences that I have been able to think of Chicano life in cultural terms at all. Characteristics I took for granted or noticed only in passing—the spontaneity, the passionate speech, the trust in concrete experience, the willingness to think communally* rather than individually—these are all significant phenomena to me now as aspects of a total culture. (My parents have neither the time nor the inclination* to think about their culture as a culture.) Able to conceptualize* a sense of Chicano culture, I am now also more attracted to that culture than I was before. The temptation now is to try to preserve those traits of my old culture that have not yet, in effect, atrophied.

. . . . . .

16   Although people intent upon social mobility think of education as a means to an end,* education does become an end: its culture allows one to exist more easily in a society increasingly anonymous and impersonal. The truth is, the academic's distance from his own experience brings the capacity for communicating with bureaucracies and understanding one's position in society. . . .

17   At this time when we are so keenly aware of social and economic inequality, it might seem beside the point* to warn those who are working to bring about equality that education alters culture as well as economic status. And yet, if there is one main criticism that I, as a minority group student, must make of minority group leaders in their past attacks on the "racism" of the academy, it is that they never distinguished between my right to higher education and the desirability of my actually entering the academy—which is another way of saying again that they never recognized that there were things I could lose by becoming a scholarship boy.

(15) **paradoxically:** in a manner contrary to belief, self-contradictory, seemingly contradictory but actually true
(15) **appraise:** judge, evaluate
(15) **communally:** as a community, as a member of a group
(15) **inclination:** leaning toward, having a preference for
(15) **conceptualize:** to imagine, to form a mental impression
(16) **end:** here, a goal
(17) **beside the point:** not relevant, not part of the idea being discussed

18   Certainly, the academy changes those from alien cultures more than it is changed by them. While minority groups had an impact on higher education, largely because of their advantage in coming as a group, within the last few years students such as myself, who finally ended up certified as academics, also ended up sounding very much like the academics we found when we came to the campus. I do not enjoy making such admissions. But perhaps now the time has come when questions about the cultural costs of education ought to be delayed no longer. Those of us who have been scholarship boys know in our bones that our education has exacted a large price* in exchange for the large benefits it has conferred upon* us. And what is sadder to consider, after we have paid that price, we go home and casually change the cultures that nurtured* us. My parents today understand how they are "Chicanos" in a large and impersonal sense. The gains from such knowledge are clear. But so, too, are the reasons for regret.

☐ FOCUS ON CAUSAL ANALYSIS

---

1. Before attempting a causal analysis of the entire essay, the relationship between Rodriguez's education and the person he became as an adult, let us focus on the more specific "whys" that are part of the larger question. Answer the following questions in complete sentences. Be clear in your answers.
   a. Why were visits home embarrassing? (paragraph 2)
   b. Why did Rodriguez keep his uneasiness to himself? (paragraph 4)
   c. Why must a student choose between two worlds? (paragraph 5)
   d. Why is a scholarship boy so enthusiastic about school? (paragraph 6)
   e. Why does he remember his "family Spanish" with guilt? (paragraph 7)
   f. Why was his academic progress difficult for his parents? (paragraph 9)
   g. Why were his parents "willing to pay the price of alienation"? (paragraph 10)
2. In your own words, explain what happened to Richard Rodriguez as a result of his having been a "scholarship boy." Starting with the beginning of his education, show the *consequences* of his education. (Somewhere in your analysis, also show what the necessary conditions were.)
3. Beginning with the feelings he was having while writing his dissertation at the British Museum (paragraphs 11 and onward), *go back* and trace the *causes* for those feelings.
4. What were the additional consequences of his having received an education so culturally removed from his roots?

(18) **exacted a large price:** asked a large price in payment, made us pay a large price (here, not literally in money, but emotionally and culturally: something was given up other than money)
(18) **conferred upon:** given
(18) **nurtured:** fed, nourished, raised, caused to grow

☐ THEMATIC QUESTIONS

Answer the following as briefly as possible. Try to express answers in *clear* sentences.

1. In paragraph 2 Rodriguez writes: "The autobiographical facts pertinent to this essay are simply stated in two sentences, though they exist in somewhat awkward juxtaposition to each other. I am the son of Mexican-American parents, who speak a blend of Spanish and English, but who read neither language easily. I am about to receive a Ph.D. in English Renaissance literature." From the "juxtaposition" of these sentences, create in your own words a sentence that explains the relationship. It will probably express the underlying conflict of the essay. Next, write a sentence that generalizes upon the first sentence; the result should be a thesis statement from which another essay by another person could be written—perhaps by *you!*
2. What were the mixed and complicated feelings Rodriguez's parents had about his success? (paragraphs 1 through 4)
3. In paragraph 4 Rodriguez refers to the "culture of the academy." Try to define it and list its characteristics.
4. In paragraph 17 the author makes a distinction between his *right* to a higher education and the *desirability* of it. Explain.

☐ QUESTIONS FOR DISCUSSION

1. In paragraphs 12 and 13, Rodriguez contrasts two scenes. Discuss in your own words the physical contrasts and then explain briefly and clearly what each scene represents. Notice, too, the contrast in styles of language that the author speaks of in paragraph 12 and the way in which this is all part of a major contrast. Contrast two scenes in your life that "stand for" different environments, symbolizing totally different value systems and worlds.
2. As Rodriguez has shown us, one need not travel thousands of miles to experience cultural dislocation and distance from one's home and family. The following is taken from the autobiography of a well-known writer and editor:

> One of the longest journeys in the world is the journey from Brooklyn to Manhattan [both are in New York City]—or at least from certain neighborhoods in Brooklyn to certain parts of Manhattan. I have made that journey, but it is not from the experience of having made it that I know how very great the distance is, for I started on the road many years before I realized what I was doing, and by the time I did realize it, I was for all practical purposes already there. At so imperceptible a pace did I travel, and with so little awareness, that I never felt footsore or out of breath or weary at the thought of how far I still had to go. Yet whenever anyone who has

remained back there where I started . . . [enters] the world in which I now live with such perfect ease, I can see that in his eyes I have become a fully acculturated citizen of a country as foreign to him as China and infinitely more frightening.

That country is sometimes called the upper middle class. . . . I am a member of that class less by virtue of my income than by virtue of the way my speech is accented, the way I dress, the way I furnish my home . . . the way I educate my children—the way, quite simply, I look and live. It appalls me to think what an immense transformation I had to work on myself in order to become what I have become: if I had known what I was doing I would surely not have been able to do it . . . there was a kind of treason in it: treason toward my family, treason toward my friends.*

In what ways has his experience been similar to that of Rodriguez? In what ways different? You may prefer to make the same comparison with your experience thus far.

3. Comment on the following, including your opinion as to whether it is true:

For a time, the scholarship boy may try to balance his loyalty between his concretely experienced family life and the more abstract mental life of the classroom. In the end, though, he must choose between the two worlds: if he intends to succeed as a student, he must literally and figuratively separate himself from his family, with its gregarious life, and find a quiet place to be alone with his thoughts.

4. In paragraph 8 Rodriguez establishes a strong connection between language and culture. Do you agree with his statements? Discuss, using your own experience as an example. Notice that he makes a distinction between the written language and the language spoken at home.

5. Education is often viewed by those who do not have it as a passport to higher economic and social status, but it is not seen as an end or a value *in itself.* Rodriguez writes (paragraph 10): "That education might alter [change] children in more basic ways . . . may come as a surprise for some. . . ." Which way do you view your education? Have your views on education changed since you entered college?

6. How did distance (in time, place, and culture) help Rodriguez better understand his own culture? Make a list, as he did (paragraph 15), of the characteristics of your native culture. Do you also see it more clearly by contrast with life in an American university? Why or why not? (Relate this to question 5, p. 212.)

---

* Norman Podhoretz, *Making It* (New York: Random House, 1967), pp. 3–4. Reprinted by permission of the author.

☐ SUGGESTIONS FOR COMPOSITION

1. "Looking back, a person risks losing hold of the present while being confounded by the past." Explain this sentence (paragraph 5) and then write an essay either agreeing with it or disagreeing with it, that is, establishing that "A person risks losing the past while being confounded by the present."

2. In his last paragraph Rodriguez says: "Those of us who have been scholarship boys know in our bones that our education has exacted a large price in exchange for the large benefits it has conferred upon us." Using your own experience as an example, discuss the price and the benefits. You should reach some kind of conclusion, even if it is tentative, even though it cannot be reduced to a simple "yes, it's worth it" or "no, it's not worth it."

3. Discuss your views on any of the following ideas or combination of them. Make a point and illustrate it by means of example.

   > Are we forever children to older persons? . . . What an incredible task it is for these young and talented students to return during . . . vacation to the rooms and persons of their childhood; . . . [one] predicament confronting the child at these times is to help his parents resolve the problems that occur when the young out-achieve their elders. . . . Regardless of their attainments, son and daughter want to remain in the child's role, at least in this one context.*

4. Despite the changes students have noticed in themselves and their previous relationships, most students are very excited about going home at vacation time, even when excitement is mixed with anxiety or conflict. Write an essay entitled "Going Home" in which you show in some detail what it feels like, what it looks like, what it smells like, and what it tastes like to go home. Or, if you prefer, if you find it more appropriate, you may discuss your mixed feelings or your conflicts about "going home." If you like, you may leave yourself out of the paper altogether and discuss the question hypothetically, as long as you remember to support your generalizations with examples or explanations.

5. Write about your own experiences in two different "worlds" (for example, two different countries, home and school, small town and big city).

☐ SENTENCE VARIETY

Notice the *absolute construction* in this sentence from the preceding essay.

> A few months ago, my dissertation nearly complete, I came upon my father poking through my bookcase.

---

* Thomas J. Cottle, "Parent and Child—The Hazards of Equality," *Saturday Review* (1 February 1969).

Rewrite this sentence, forming a complex sentence of two clauses. Rewrite the following sentences, using the absolute construction.

1. The party was over; I decided it was time to give up and go home.
2. After the dishes were washed, there was time for TV.

Notice the following use of "would" to indicate repeated, habitual action in the past.

> My parents would tell me what happened in their lives or in the lives of relatives; I would respond with news of my own. Polite questions would follow.

Write a sentence like this of your own, using "would" in this manner.

☐ COMPOSITION SUGGESTIONS FOR CAUSAL ANALYSIS

The list that follows may give you *other* ideas for compositions of causal analysis, *other* topics that interest you more. Choose one of the suggested topics or let these ideas stimulate your own thinking and choosing of a topic. Some topics may be analyzed by seeking causes, others by discussing consequences or further effects, still others by analyzing both causes and further consequences. Some topics may require research.

Science and nature
The changing of color in leaves in the fall
What causes a rainbow
Thunder and lightning
Soil erosion
The tide coming in and going out
Heart attacks

History, politics, economics
A particular war or revolution that interests you
The election of a particular candidate for political office
The advance or decline of a particular society or civilization
A depression, a financial failure, an economic success

Education
The large number of people going to universities
A student cheating
Why I like (or do not like) _____ (choose a subject)
Why I like (or do not like) _____ (choose a professor)
Students are not as well read as they used to be
Students have problems writing well—even in their native language
Student depression

Society today
Television

Rising crime rates
Overpopulation
Pollution
Increased number of divorces

Personal reasons

Why I like _____ (person, place, work of art, book—anything you
  choose)
Why I chose _____
Why I believe in _____
Why I do not believe in _____
Why I consider _____ to be valuable (or beautiful, or important)
Why I am here

S T U D E N T   C O M P O S I T I O N S

Changing

During the last two years, I had my education at a competitive high
school and a demanding university in the United States. Analysis of people
and matter was a basic element of my education during these two years.
Before that, schoolwork was very little and simple and I did not have to do
much analysis. But the "good" education I had in the last two years made me
look differently at my relations with people around me.

Before I came to the United States, I lived at home, Saudi Arabia. Just like
any other person, I liked some things and disliked others. Although I loved
my family, I constantly had arguments with my parents which made me
dislike being home; however, I enjoyed being with my friends all the time. My
best friend was a "funny guy" who made jokes of many things. I never
questioned my relations with my family nor my friends, nor did I try to
analyze this behavior.

However, the education I had after leaving home was very analytical.
Studying chemistry, for example, taught me to analyze matter. When studying
an element, I had to analyze its reactions and relations with other elements
and know why it behaves in a certain way. In English, analysis was applied
more toward people. I had to read stories and articles and try to analyze the
behavior of the people in these stories. My education gave me the skill of
analyzing and trying to understand my surroundings.

Being home last Christmas was not like being at home before I came to
the United States. It was more than rejoining my family and meeting old
friends. I was home with a new skill, analyzing. I tried to understand and find
reasons for the behavior of people around me. I found out the reason for the
arguments I had always had with my parents. They had always wanted to give
me advice but I had refused any interference in my life. I also realized that the

only reason they had been advising me was because they wanted my benefit. During Christmas, I started accepting their advice and, maybe after a peaceful discussion, did what they advised me to do. Things between my parents and me started going very well and I did not have a single argument with any of them during that Christmas vacation.

During the time I was with my friends at Christmas, I tried to analyze their behavior too. I noticed for example that my best friend, the "funny guy," made his jokes about authority in general and parents in particular. Knowing that he had severe problems with his parents, I related his jokes to these severe problems. I also realized that I had found his jokes funny because they made fun of parents at a time when I had had a bad relation with my own. During Christmas, his jokes were not as funny as they used to be. My problems with my parents were solved and I had no reason to find his jokes about parents funny any more. At the same time his jokes reminded me of the severe problem he still had with his parents, which made me feel sorry for him every time he told a joke. We did not enjoy the time we spent together as much as we used to do and we both knew that our friendship would never be the way it had been before.

The reason for the changes that occurred to my relations with people during Christmas was my education. It taught me, and made me used to analyzing my surroundings. This helped me understand people and my relationship with them and hence make some change in these relationships. Although that cost me a few relationships with people I enjoyed being with, it helped bring me closer to the people who cared about me the most.

Why Does the Shape of the Moon Change?

It is apparent that the shape of the moon changes in a regular cycle. As seen from earth, the shape of the moon changes in regular steps: dark, crescent, half, full, and back to dark again. The explanation of these changes of shape is quite simple.

The change of the shape of the moon is related to its revolution or orbiting motion around the earth. The moon goes through a set of phases (varying shapes of the lighted part of the moon) approximately once every month. The actual period of the phases, the interval between a particular phase of the moon and its next repetition, is approximately one month. This period can vary by as much as thirteen hours. The explanation of the phases with respect to the position of the moon in relation to the earth is quite simple.

The moon is a sphere, and at all times the side that faces the sun is lighted and the side that faces away from the sun is dark. This is visible because we all know that the moon does not have its own light. The phase of the moon that we see from the earth, as the moon revolves around the earth, depends on the relative orientation of three bodies or planets: sun, moon, and earth.

Basically, when the moon is almost exactly between the earth and the sun, the dark side of the moon faces us. We call this a "new moon." A few days later, we see a sharp fragment of the lighted side of the moon and call this a "crescent." This happens because the phase of the moon depends on the relative orientation of three bodies: sun, moon, and earth. We see the crescent because the moon, the earth, and the sun are not exactly between each other anymore. The sun, as the center of the solar system, does not revolve. The moon revolves around the earth, and its position after the new-moon phase makes an angle with respect to the position of the earth and the sun. As a result, the sun lights a small part of the moon, which is visible to an observer on earth as a crescent.

As the month wears on, the crescent gets bigger. At about seven days after the new moon, half of the face of the moon that is visible to us is lighted. We sometimes call this a "half moon." But actually, the lighted half that we see is only one-fourth of the whole moon. So for convenience, that is more properly called the "first-quarter moon."

When over half of the moon's surface is visible, we then have a "gibbious" moon. One week after the first-quarter moon, the moon enters its second-quarter phase. The moon is exactly on the opposite side of the earth from the sun. The entire face that is visible to us is lighted. This is called a "full moon."

We notice that the changes of phases—from dark to one-fourth lighted, half moon and full moon—take about fourteen days or approximately half a month. The rest of the half month is needed by the moon to revolve around the earth back to its initial position as a dark moon. Thus, one week after the full-moon phase we will have a "third-quarter moon," where we will see the other half side of the moon which had been dark at the first-quarter phase. Then, one week after the third-quarter phase, we will have a new moon again. This cycle then repeats.

We can conclude that the changes of the face of the moon as seen from the earth depend on the moon's revolution around the earth. And the cycles repeat once every month, from an entirely dark surface to a full moon and back to an entirely dark surface.

☐   QUESTIONS

1. In "Changing," do you find the student's analysis of his "changing" convincing? Why or why not? How does it compare with your feelings or experiences?
2. In "Changing," how is narration used in conjunction with causal analysis?
3. Has the student made clear to you the phenomena he discusses in "Why Does the Shape of the Moon Change?" How has he succeeded in doing so? If not, how would you improve upon his explanation? His organization?

11

THINKING ABOUT LANGUAGE

WORDS AND MEANING

> What's in a name? That which we call a rose
> By any other word would smell as sweet.

If that which we call, in English, a rose were presented to your class, if each person in the class were to name it in his or her own language, and if all of you learned to say each other's word for that flower, the flower would remain unchanged, whatever its label. Were you to close your eyes so as not to see the rose, it would presumably smell as sweet: Whatever the word and whatever the sight, the smell of the rose would not change, nor would its form or texture.

The famous lines that began this chapter are part of a passionate argument expressed by Juliet in Shakespeare's *Romeo and Juliet*. As you probably know, Romeo and Juliet are children of enemy families whose members have, for a long time, been killing one another. Romeo, of the Montague family, and Juliet, of the Capulet family, fall in love before they know each other's names. An agonized Juliet cries out against Romeo's *name*, wishing he could change it.

> Deny thy father and refuse thy name

> .   .   .   .

> Tis but thy name that is my enemy,
> Thou art thyself. . . .
> What's Montague? it is nor hand nor foot
> Nor arm nor face. . . .
> What's in a name? that which we call a rose
> By any other word would smell as sweet.
> So Romeo would were he not Romeo called.

Romeo agrees, telling her to call him "Love" from that time on, for to the young lovers, the word Love is more true than the words Romeo Montague, a name that means Enemy to Juliet's family.

But a cousin of Juliet's, one who sees Romeo not as Love but as Romeo of the house of Montague, attacks him, and Love is drawn into a fight in which he kills Juliet's cousin. Juliet's argument can be used against her now. That which we call an enemy by any other name would kill as tragically. What's in a name? Names are not hands and feet, she says. They are not concrete. They have no substance. In that she is right. *Words are not things, but they symbolize things.* To Juliet's father, the name Montague symbolized Enemy, Killer of my Family. To Juliet such symbolism was meaningless, for to her this boy was Love. Yet when Romeo goes back into the world where Montague and Capulet are enemies, he is attacked by one who knows him as Enemy, and then he is a true Montague. It is not his name that draws the sword; it is he. He is not only called Montague, he *is* one; he acts like one. "Thou art thyself," Juliet says. And what is that? It is Love to Juliet, Enemy to Capulet. His two names symbolize his two relationships, both of which are true.

A name is a useful means of identifying a thing. We must both know John Smith in order to talk about him, but he can be one kind of person to you and another to me. We can each have a different name for the flower that in English is called rose, but if that flower is not in front of us when we are talking about it, we will not be able to understand each other unless we both know the word or name by which we are calling it.

Still, a name is not the thing. The thing itself has, as we have seen in the Romeo example, many qualities; those qualities may be in conflict, but they do not cancel each other out. The better we understand the complexity of the thing we name, the more its name will symbolize for us. Like any other symbol, words have the power to generate associations and emotions, even conflicting ones. Likewise, we can come to blows if we have different associations, different shades of meaning, or different values for the same word.

Roses smell sweet, but they also eventually rot and die. They have thorns that prick the one who tries to pick them. To know a rose well is to know its various qualities.

What's in a name? A name includes everything we associate with it. It is only when we have the same names for things that we can communicate in words, realizing, of course, that the differences we bring to the words hold the possibility of misunderstanding. This obliges us to clarify our meaning of words and to try to understand what others mean by them.

In *Huckleberry Finn,* Mark Twain has created a humorous situation arising from the absurdity of using a word without knowing its meaning. Tom Sawyer, a child who gets all his ideas on life from books on adventure, forms a gang of boys based on the fantastic lives of his book friends. Keep in mind as you read this passage, what the word *ransom* really means, the sum or money demanded by a kidnapper for returning his prisoner to those willing to pay the price (the ransom) for his safe return.

MARK TWAIN
***

Ransom

Then they all stuck a pin in their fingers to get blood to sign with, and I made my mark on the paper.

"Now," says Ben Rogers, "what's the line of business of this Gang?"

"Nothing only robbery and murder," Tom said.

"But who are we going to rob?—houses, or cattle, or—"

"Stuff! Stealing cattle and such things ain't robbery; it's burglary," says Tom Sawyer. "We ain't burglars. That ain't no sort of style. We are highwaymen. We stop stages and carriages on the road, with masks on, and kill the people and take their watches and money."

"Must we always kill the people?"

"Oh, certainly. It's best. Some authorities think different, but mostly it's considered best to kill them—except some that you bring to the cave here, and keep them till they're ransomed."

"Ransomed? What's that?"

"I don't know. But that's what they do. I've seen it in books; and so of course that's what we've got to do."

"But how can we do it if we don't know what it is?"

"Why, blame it all, we've *got* to do it. Don't I tell you it's in the books? Do you want to go to doing different from what's in the books, and get things all muddled up?"

"Oh, that's all very fine to *say,* Tom Sawyer, but how in the nation are these fellows going to be ransomed if we don't know how to do it to them?— that's the thing *I* want to get at. Now, what do you *reckon* it is?"

"Well, I don't know. But per'aps if we keep them till they're ransomed, it means that we keep them till they're dead."

"Now, that's something *like*. That'll answer. Why couldn't you said that before? We'll keep them till they're ransomed to death; and a bothersome lot they'll be, too—eating up everything, and always trying to get loose."

"How you talk, Ben Rogers. How can they get loose when there's a guard over them, ready to shoot them down if they move a peg?"

"A guard! Well, that *is* good. So somebody's got to set up all night and never get any sleep, just so as to watch them. I think that's foolishness. Why can't a body take a club* and ransom them as soon as they get here?"

"Because it ain't in the books so—that's why. Now, Ben Rogers, do you want to do things regular, or don't you—that's the idea. Don't you reckon that the people that made the books knows what's the correct thing to do? Do you reckon *you* can learn 'em anything? Not by a good deal. No, sir, we'll just go on and ransom them in the regular way."

---

(1) **club:** a heavy stick

In another fantasy by Lewis Carroll, *Alice in Wonderland* and *Through the Looking Glass,* Alice, a child heroine, has many strange experiences, including the following argument with Humpty Dumpty. Remember that "glory" means great honor and admiration won by doing something important, high achievement highly praised, or magnificence.

LEWIS CARROLL

Humpty Dumpty on Meaning

Alice couldn't help smiling as she took out her memorandum-book, and worked the sum for him:

$$\begin{array}{r} 365 \\ 1 \\ \hline 364 \end{array}$$

Humpty Dumpty took the book and looked at it carefully. "That seems to be done right—" he began.

"You're holding it upside down!" Alice interrupted.

"To be sure I was!" Humpty Dumpty said gaily as she turned it round for him. "I thought it looked a little queer. As I was saying, that *seems* to be done right—though I haven't time to look it over thoroughly just now—and that shows that there are three hundred and sixty-four days when you might get un-birthday presents—"

"Certainly," said Alice.

"And only *one* for birthday presents, you know. There's glory for you!"

"I don't know what you mean by 'glory,'" Alice said.

Humpty Dumpty smiled contemptuously. "Of course you don't—till I tell you. I meant 'there's a nice knock-down argument for you!'"

"But 'glory' doesn't mean 'a nice knock-down argument,'" Alice objected.

"When *I* use a word," Humpty Dumpty said, in rather a scornful* tone, "it means just what I choose it to mean—neither more nor less."

"The question is," said Alice, "whether you *can* make words mean so many different things."

"The question is," said Humpty Dumpty, "which is to be master—that's all."

An absurd argument, we could say! If Humpty Dumpty is right, if we cannot know what a word means until the speaker defines it, then we all have our own private language and will have to provide a dictionary of terminology for everyone to whom we speak. Language as we know it, words upon which there is enough agreement to conduct fairly accurate communication among all speakers of that language, would be nonexistent. No one would understand any language but his or her own personal one. Carried out as literally as Humpty Dumpty carries it, this would be the end of lan-

(1) **scornful:** with extreme contempt, looking down at the other as low or inferior

guage. And yet there is some truth to his point. Some words are capable of so many private and public interpretations that they have already become meaningless.

His next question, "Who is to be master?" is also absurd if taken literally. To be master over a word in the sense of deciding for ourselves what it means, with *no* regard for the meaning it has for others, would be to render that word meaningless to our listeners. But can we deny that a master of words, building upon the understood meaning, can bend those meanings, enlarge them, create new associations, so that they will mean other things? We can laugh at Humpty Dumpty but not at the issues he is raising. They are fundamental to an understanding of propaganda, for example, and the frightening use made of words when people do not bother to analyze "who is master." This issue is raised by one writer who expounds as follows on Humpty Dumpty's theory:

> May we pay our words extra, or is this the stuff propaganda is made of? Do we have an obligation to past usage? In one sense words are our masters, or communication would be impossible. In another we are the master; otherwise there could be no poetry.[1]

We would not want to rob language of its flexibility, its capacity for growth, its creative potential for those who can use it with power and beauty—and that includes students! But because language has such flexibility and power, it is extremely important to be aware of these qualities. As receivers of words, we are under their influence for better or for worse; as users of words, we have the capacity for ever richer, more forceful expression. To be educated is to be aware of the danger and the potential of language used by one who is a "master." It is also to be able to listen to a lot of words and to decide if they are being misused or used without intelligence. To be educated and intelligent is to be able to reduce what one hears to its real meaning or to see through what may *sound* good but is, in fact, meaningless or stupid. To be educated and talented in the use of language is to become master of one's writing or speaking. To be responsible is to navigate carefully between one's view of a word's potential and one's honesty and care in using it.

As long ago as the fifth century B.C., Confucius recognized the relationship between truth in language and truth in everything else. When asked how he would begin to govern, he replied,

> ... by putting names right. ... If names are not right, words do not fit. If words do not fit, affairs go wrong. If affairs go wrong ... law and justice fail. ... So a gentleman must be ready to put names into speech, to put words into deeds. A gentleman is in no way careless of words.

---

† Roger W. Holmes, "The Philosopher's Alice in Wonderland," *Antioch Review*, Summer, 1959.

☐ SUGGESTIONS FOR COMPOSITION

1. Choose a word that *you* think needs "putting right" (that is, a word that you think is being *mis*used). Define it as you see it, and then show why you think it needs "putting right."
2. On my last trip to the supermarket I noticed that there were three sizes of eggs: The largest were labeled JUMBO, the middle size were labeled EXTRA LARGE, and the smallest were labeled LARGE. This means that to buy the smallest eggs, one must choose the box labeled LARGE.

   What does this example show about uses of language and the relationship between a word and the reality it is supposed to symbolize? What does it show about American society?

LANGUAGE AND THOUGHT

We take for granted that thought finds expression in language. We must have something in our heads to express or we would not need language to express it. Language depends upon thought or ideas for its content. What we may not always realize, however, is that thoughts and ideas also depend upon language for their existence. You are surely very much aware of the need for language every time you feel frustrated at not having a better command of English to express your ideas. But have you thought that while you do not have enough language to express these ideas to your American friends, these ideas do exist in your mind in *language*—your native language? Because we learn language before we learn to think abstractly, before we are conscious of symbolic thinking, we find it difficult to imagine thought without words. How moving is Helen Keller's[†] memory of life without words.

> Meanwhile the desire to express myself grew. The few signs I used became less and less adequate, and my failures to make myself understood were invariably followed by outbursts of passion. I felt as if invisible hands were holding me, and I made frantic efforts to free myself. I struggled—not that struggling helped matters, but the spirit of resistance was strong within me; I generally broke down in tears and physical exhaustion. If my mother happened to be near I crept into her arms, too miserable even to remember

---

† Helen Keller, born in 1880 and struck blind and deaf by illness at nineteen months old, was taught to speak, read, and write by Anne Sullivan, a remarkable teacher, who came to teach seven-year-old Helen. That was the beginning of a lifelong association. Still deaf and blind, Helen was able, with her teacher's help, to become educated at Harvard. She wrote books and articles and lectured widely, for she had become a famous woman and an inspiring example of what is possible in the face of overwhelming handicaps. This passage is from her book, *The Story of My Life* (Garden City, New York: Doubleday, 1954), pp. 32, 35.

the cause of the tempest.* After awhile the need for some means of communication became so urgent that these outbursts occurred daily, sometimes hourly. . . .

Have you ever been at sea in a dense fog, when it seemed as if a tangible white darkness shut you in, and the great ship, tense and anxious, groped* her way toward the shore . . . and you waited with beating heart for something to happen? I was like that ship before my education began, only I was without compass or sounding-line, and had no way of knowing how near the harbour was.

Her teacher, Anne Sullivan, tried to introduce language to her by means of a manual alphabet. She wrote, "I spell in her hand everything we do all day long, although she has no idea as yet what the spelling means." Helen was very bright and learned the words quickly, but with no understanding of the relationship between words and things, much less between words and feelings. Abstract or sustained thinking was, of course, impossible. Miss Sullivan felt that if only she could teach Helen the symbolic function of words, "that everything has a name," she could spell the whole world into Helen's hand.

Here is Helen's own account of that historic moment when she first understood, *really* understood, the way words work.

HELEN KELLER

Helen's Awakening to Language

1   In the days that followed I learned to spell in this uncomprehending way a great many words, among them *pin, hat, cup* and a few verbs like *sit, stand,* and *walk.* But my teacher had been with me several weeks before I understood that everything has a name.

2   One day, while I was playing with my new doll, Miss Sullivan put my big rag doll into my lap also, spelled "d-o-l-l" and tried to make me understand that "d-o-l-l" applied to both. Earlier in the day we had had a tussle over the words "m-u-g" and "w-a-t-e-r." Miss Sullivan had tried to impress it upon me that "m-u-g" is mug and "w-a-t-e-r" is water, but I persisted in confounding the two. In despair she had dropped the subject for the time, only to renew it at the first opportunity. I became impatient at her repeated attempts and, seizing the new doll, I dashed it upon the floor. I was keenly delighted when I felt the fragments of the broken doll at my feet. Neither sorrow nor regret followed my passionate outburst. I had not loved the doll. In the still, dark world in which I lived there was no strong sentiment or tenderness. I felt my teacher sweep the fragments to one side of the hearth, and I had a sense of satisfaction that the cause of my discomfort was removed. She brought me my hat, and I knew I was going out into the warm sunshine. This thought, if a

* **tempest:** great storm
* **grope:** to search, or feel one's way, or grasp without seeing

wordless sensation may be called a thought, made me hop and skip with pleasure.

3   We walked down the path to the well-house, attracted by the fragrance of the honeysuckle with which it was covered. Some one was drawing water and my teacher placed my hand under the spout. As the cool stream gushed over my hand she spelled into the other the word water, first slowly, then rapidly. I stood still, my whole attention fixed upon the motions of her fingers. Suddenly I felt a misty consciousness as of something forgotten—a thrill of returning thought; and somehow the mystery of language was revealed to me. I knew then that "w-a-t-e-r" meant the wonderful cool something that was flowing over my hand. That living word awakened my soul, gave it light, hope, joy, set it free! There were barriers still, it is true, but barriers that could in time be swept away.†

4   I left the well-house eager to learn. Everything had a name, and each name gave birth to a new thought. As we returned to the house every object which I touched seemed to quiver with life. That was because I saw everything with the strange, new sight that had come to me. On entering the door I remembered the doll I had broken. I felt my way to the hearth and picked up the pieces. I tried vainly* to put them together. Then my eyes filled with tears; for I realized what I had done, and for the first time I felt repentance* and sorrow.

5   I learned a great many new words that day. I do not remember what they all were; but I do know that *mother, father, sister, teacher* were among them— words that were to make the world blossom for me. . . . It would have been difficult to find a happier child than I was. . . .

6   I recall many incidents of the summer of 1887 that followed my soul's sudden awakening. I did nothing but explore with my hands and learn the name of every object that I touched; and the more I handled things and learned their names and uses, the more joyous and confident grew my sense of kinship with the rest of the world.

Anne Sullivan, in her account, adds other details.

7   As the cold water gushed forth, filling the mug, I spelled "w-a-t-e-r" in Helen's free hand. The word coming so close upon the sensation of cold water rushing over her hand seemed to startle her. She dropped the mug and stood as one transfixed. A new light came into her face. She spelled "w-a-t-e-r" several times. Then she dropped on the ground and asked for its name and pointed to the pump and the trellis, and suddenly turning round she asked for my name. I spelled "Teacher." Just then the nurse brought Helen's

---

(4) **vainly:** uselessly, with no result
(4) **repentance:** the feeling of being sorry for having done something wrong

† She had once known "wa-wa" as water and its meaning at the age of nineteen months, before her illness.

little sister into the pump-house, and Helen spelled "baby" and pointed to the nurse. All the way back to the house she was highly excited, and learned the name of every object she touched, so that in a few hours she had added thirty new words to her vocabulary. Here are some of them: *Door, open, shut, give, go, come,* and a great many more.

8   P.S. I didn't finish my letter in time to get it posted last night; so I shall add a line. Helen got up this morning like a radiant fairy. She has flitted from object to object, asking the name of everything and kissing me for very gladness. Last night when I got in bed, she stole into my arms of her own accord and kissed me for the first time, and I thought my heart would burst, so full was it of joy.

April 10, 1887

9   I see an improvement in Helen day to day, almost from hour to hour. Everything must have a name now. Wherever we go, she asks eagerly for the names of things she has not learned at home. She is anxious for her friends to spell, and eager to teach the letters to every one she meets. She drops the signs and pantomime* she used before, as soon as she has words to supply their place, and the acquirement of a new word affords her the liveliest pleasure. And we notice that her face grows more expressive each day.

Notice, in both accounts, the relationship between the first real understanding of language and the awakening of feeling for others—remorse for her broken doll, love for her teacher, eagerness to learn more. Notice that "her face grew more expressive." The breakthrough of it all came when she understood that w-a-t-e-r was not simply a reflex response to her own thirst, a sign for "Give me water." It was the name of that cold, wet substance going over her hand into the ground, into the mug. W-a-t-e-r was a symbol; it would call forth that wet meaning in *any* context where she wanted to use it. Words had that infinite power, and that power was now becoming hers. Now that words could be separated from her own sensations and bodily needs she could, for the first time, recognize others outside herself. Without words, her mind was starved and empty. With them, she could "see" and learn. She could include others in her world and be included as a full person in theirs.

☐ QUESTIONS FOR DISCUSSION

---

1. We know that animals have amazing communication skills, bees with their wings, whales with their "songs." We know that parrots can be taught to say words. Some people have been teaching chimpanzees to use a typewriter and associate words with things. One is tempted to say, then, that speech or verbal language is not reserved only for humans. What is your opinion? Think about this carefully and explain the ways in which human language *is* unique, different from any of the preceding examples.

(9) **pantomime:** acting without words

2. In the 1940s a British writer, George Orwell, wrote *1984,* a famous book portraying a futuristic society that he had based on his view of Stalinist Russia. Ruled by Big Brother, the main characteristic of this society is its ability to exercise thought control by controlling the language. A new language, Newspeak, is gradually replacing the old language on which it is based. This is done by eliminating many words from the vocabulary and reducing the remaining words to their most literal and concrete meaning; thus abstract thought or political questioning becomes impossible because there are no words for these concepts. Obviously, this is an extreme example of the theory that language controls thought rather than the other way around.

3. Think about the following statement the book makes about Newspeak. "There would be many crimes and errors which it would be beyond [a person's] power to commit, simply because they were nameless and therefore unimaginable." (Remember that in this society, even to think against Big Brother is a crime.) What is the basic assumption of this sentence? (Clue: Look at the implication of *therefore.*) Do you agree with this assumption? Why or why not?

4. If a society has a language so limited that in it a heretical* statement "could not have been sustained by reasoned argument because the necessary words were not available," is it protected 100 percent against heresy? Is it so protected forever? Explain your answer.

5. Relate what you have read about Helen Keller's life before and after her acquisition of language to the above quotes. In what ways are there similarities? In what ways are there differences?

6. You might be amused by the following excerpt from Jonathan Swift's *Gulliver's Travels.* Gulliver, in his travels, visits a great academy of learning, where the professors are working on improving the language. Relate their theories of language to those of Newspeak. Think about the premise upon which their theory is based, and the limitations of this language. Are there any advantages?

> The first project was to shorten discourse by cutting polysyllables into one, and leaving out verbs and participles, because in reality all things imaginable are but nouns.
>
> The other was a scheme for entirely abolishing all words whatsoever.... An expedient was therefore offered, that since words are only names for *things,* it would be more convenient for all men to carry about them such *things* as were necessary to express the particular business they are to discourse on.... which hath only this inconvenience attending it, that if a man's business be very great, and of various kinds, he must be obliged in proportion to carry a greater bundle of *things* upon his back unless he can afford one or two strong servants to attend him. I have often beheld two of those

---

* **heretical** (adjective): referring to that which disagrees with the accepted view, going against the way one is supposed to think or believe; **heresy** (noun) is the opposing view itself or the more generalized opposition to the "right way." Originally used in speaking of religious dogma and belief

sages almost sinking under the weight of their packs, like pedlars among us; who when they met in the streets would lay down their loads, open their sacks and hold conversation for an hour together; then put up their implements, help each other to resume their burthens, and take their leave.

But for short conversations a man may carry implements in his pockets and under his arms. . . .†

7. Assuming that the use of language *can* be dangerous to a society, are there ways in which a situation is still more dangerous *without* language? How does language make a society more dangerous? How can language lessen danger?
8. Perhaps, for number 4 you answered that if words for these feelings no longer existed, or if the words to sustain arguments no longer existed, men would invent them after a while. Imagine such a situation and the way a word gets invented. Choose a word and put its invention into a narrative form. You may do this as a dialogue or as a short play.
9. Choose a word important to you, one with a lot of emotional, philosophical, or political overtones. Now try to write a paragraph about that feeling without using the word *or any other word* carrying more than just a literal, concrete meaning.
10. In history, there are examples of a conquering nation outlawing the language of the nation it has conquered, changing school programs so that the language of the new rulers becomes the language of instruction, sometimes making it a crime to write or speak the former language. Why?

Less dramatic than *1984* regarding the power of language to control thought is the theory that the language of a society not only reflects what is important to that society (the Eskimos of Alaska, for example, have many words for snow, each expressing something different), but that the way a society views the world is shaped by its language, by its grammar, and by what can or cannot be expressed. Whether the ways of seeing the world have created the language or whether language has affected the ways of seeing the world is a fascinating and ongoing debate. Perhaps you have an opinion about it, now that you have had to immerse yourself in a language and culture not native to you.

The following "semantic parable" (a parable is a little story from which we draw a lesson; semantics is that branch of language study that studies meaning) illustrates well the debate between the preceding two positions. It is part of a book written by S. I. Hayakawa, who has been both a professor of semantics and a United States senator. As you read, notice the differences between the people of the two towns, differences in their attitudes toward the unemployed. Be sure you understand what "insurance" means and what "relief" means. What is the basic difference between them? As you read, notice the manner in which "language" and "thought" (or attitude) affect each other.

† Jonathan Swift, *Gulliver's Travels,* Reprinted (New York: Bantam Books, 1962), pp. 183–184.

S. I. HAYAKAWA

The Story of A-town and B-ville: A Semantic Parable

1   Once upon a time, said the professor, there were two small communities, spiritually as well as geographically situated at a considerable distance from each other. They had, however, these problems in common: both were hard hit by a recession,* so that in each of the towns there were about one hundred heads of families unemployed.

2   The city fathers of A-town, the first community, were substantial and sound-thinking* businessmen. The unemployed tried hard, as unemployed people usually do, to find jobs; but the situation did not improve. The city fathers had been brought up to believe that there is always enough work for everyone, if you only look for it hard enough. Comforting themselves with this doctrine, the city fathers could have shrugged their shoulders and turned their backs on the problem, except for the fact that they were genuinely kindhearted men. They could not bear to see the unemployed men and their wives and children starving. In order to prevent hardship, they felt that they had to provide these people with some means of sustenance.* Their principles told them, nevertheless, that if people were given something for nothing, it would demoralize* their character. Naturally this made the city fathers even more unhappy, because they were faced with the horrible choice of (1) letting the unemployed starve, or (2) destroying their moral character.

3   The solution they finally hit upon, after much debate and soul-searching, was this. They decided to give the unemployed families "relief payments" of two hundred dollars a month. (They considered using the English term "dole,"* but with their characteristic American penchant* for euphemism,* they decided on the less offensive term.) To make sure that the unemployed would not take their unearned payments too much for granted, however, they decided that the "relief" was to be accompanied by a moral lesson; to wit:* the obtaining of the assistance would be made so difficult, humiliating, and disagreeable that there would be no temptation for anyone to go through the process unless it was absolutely necessary; the moral disapproval of the community would be turned upon the recipients of* the money at all times in such a way that they would try hard to get "off relief" and "regain their

---

(1) **recession:** in economics, a decrease in business activity, usually accompanied by unemployment
(2) **sound:** reliable, morally honest, financially secure
(2) **sustenance:** support, means of livelihood, that which supports or maintains life
(2) **demoralize:** to lower or corrupt morals; to weaken the spirit, courage, or discipline
(3) **dole:** charity food or money
(3) **penchant:** a strong liking
(3) **euphemism:** a word with more pleasant associations (See section on Euphemism in the next chapter.)
(3) **to wit:** namely, that is to say
(3) **recipients (of):** those who receive

self-respect." Some even proposed that people on relief be denied the vote, so that the moral lesson would be more deeply impressed upon them. Others suggested that their names be published at regular intervals in the newspapers. The city fathers had enough faith in the goodness of human nature to expect that the recipients would be grateful, since they were getting something for nothing, something which they hadn't worked for.

4   When the plan was put into operation, however, the recipients of the relief checks proved to be an ungrateful, ugly bunch. They seemed to resent the cross-examinations* and inspections at the hands of the "relief investigators," who, they said, took advantage of a man's misery to snoop* into every detail of his private life. In spite of uplifting editorials in A-town *Tribune* telling them how grateful they ought to be, the recipients of the relief refused to learn any moral lessons, declaring that they were "just as good as anybody else." When, for example, they permitted themselves the rare luxury of a movie or an evening of bingo, their neighbors looked at them sourly as if to say, "I work hard and pay my taxes just in order to support loafers* like you in idleness and pleasure." This attitude, which was fairly characteristic of those members of the community who still had jobs, further embittered the relief recipients, so that they showed even less gratitude as time went on and were constantly on the lookout for insults, real or imaginary, from people who might think that they weren't as good as anybody else. A number of them took to moping* all day long; one or two even committed suicide. Others, feeling that they had failed to provide, found it hard to look their wives and children in the face. Children whose parents were "on relief" felt inferior to classmates whose parents were not "public charges." Some of these children developed inferiority complexes which affected not only their grades at school, but their careers after graduation. Finally, several relief recipients felt they could stand their loss of self-respect no longer and decided, after many efforts to gain honest jobs, that they would earn money by their own efforts even if they had to rob. They did so and were caught and sent to the state penitentiary.*

5   The depression, therefore, hit A-town very hard. The relief policy had averted* starvation, no doubt, but suicide, personal quarrels, unhappy homes, the weakening of social organizations, the maladjustment of children, and finally, crime, had resulted. The town was divided in two, the "haves" and the "have-nots," so that there was class hatred. People shook their heads sadly and declared that it all went to prove over again what they had known from the beginning, that giving people something for nothing inevitably demoral-

---

(4) **cross-examinations:** repeated questioning, as at a trial in court
(4) **snoop:** pry, look around in a sneaking manner
(4) **loafers:** lazy people, not working, wasting time
(4) **moping:** being spiritless, gloomy
(4) **penitentiary:** jail
(5) **averted:** stopped from happening

izes their character. The citizens of A-town gloomily waited for prosperity to return, with less and less hope as time went on.

6 The story of the other community, B-ville, was entirely different. B-ville was a relatively isolated town, too far out of the way to be reached by Rotary Club* speakers and other dispensers of conventional wisdom. One of the aldermen,* however, who was something of an economist, explained to his fellow aldermen that unemployment, like sickness, accident, fire, tornado, or death, hits unexpectedly in modern society, irrespective of* the victim's merits or deserts.* He went on to say that B-ville's homes, parks, streets, industries, and everything else B-ville was proud of, had been built in part by the work of these same people who were now unemployed. He then proposed to apply a principle of insurance: if the work these unemployed people had previously done for the community could be regarded as a form of "premium"* paid to the community against a time of misfortune, payments now made to them to prevent their starvation could be regarded as "insurance claims."* He therefore proposed that all men of good repute who had worked in the community in some line of useful endeavor, whether as machinists, clerks, or bank managers, be regarded as "citizen policyholders,"* having "claims" against the city in the case of unemployment for two hundred dollars a month until such time as they might again be employed. Naturally, he had to talk very slowly and patiently since the idea was entirely new to his fellow aldermen. But he described his plan as a "straight business proposition," and finally they were persuaded. They worked out in detail, to everyone's satisfaction, the conditions under which citizens should be regarded as policyholders in the city's social insurance plan, and decided to give checks for two hundred dollars a month to the heads of each of B-ville's indigent families.

7 B-ville's "claim adjusters," whose duty it was to investigate the claims of the citizen "policyholders," had a much better time than A-town's "relief investigators." While the latter had been resentfully regarded as snoopers, the former, having no moral lesson to teach but simply a business transaction to carry out, treated their clients with businesslike courtesy and got the same amount of information as the relief investigators had, with considerably less difficulty. There were no hard feelings. It further happened, fortunately, that news of B-ville's plans reached a liberal newspaper editor in the big city at the other end of the state. This writer described the plan in a leading feature story

(6) **Rotary Club:** an international association whose aim is community service, mainly of small-town businessmen, usually conservative in their views and politics
(6) **aldermen:** members of the town council
(6) **irrespective of:** without considering
(6) **deserts:** what is deserved
(6) **premium, insurance claims, and policyholders:** In insurance, the **policyholder** is the person who is being covered by the insurance; the **premium** is his regular payment to the insurance company; the **claim** is the request he makes for money from the insurance company when the accident or illness he is insured against happens

headed "B-VILLE LOOKS AHEAD. Adventure in Social Pioneering Launched by Upper Valley Community." As a result of this publicity, inquiries about the plan began to come to the city hall even before the first checks were mailed out. This led, naturally, to a considerable feeling of pride on the part of the aldermen, who, being boosters,* felt that this was a wonderful opportunity to put B-ville on the map.

8   Accordingly, the aldermen decided that instead of simply mailing out the checks as they had originally intended, they would publicly present the first checks at a monster* civic ceremony. They invited the governor of the state, who was glad to come to bolster* his none-too-enthusiastic support in that locality, the president of the state university, the senator from their district, and other functionaries. They decorated the National Guard armory with flags and got out the American legion Fife and Drum Corps, the Boy Scouts, and other civic organizations. At the big celebration, each family to receive a "social insurance check" was marched up to the platform to receive it, and the governor and the mayor shook hands with each of them as they came trooping up in their best clothes. Fine speeches were made; there was much cheering and shouting; pictures of the event showing the recipients of the checks shaking hands with the mayor, and the governor patting the heads of the children, were published not only in the local papers but also in several metropolitan picture sections.

9   Every recipient of these insurance checks had a feeling, therefore, that he had been personally honored, that he lived in a wonderful little town, and that he could face his unemployment with greater courage and assurance since his community was behind him. The men and women found themselves being kidded in a friendly way by their acquaintances for having been "up there with the big shots," shaking hands with the governor, and so on. The children at school found themselves envied for having had their pictures in the papers. All in all, B-ville's unemployed did not commit suicide, were not haunted by a sense of failure, did not turn to crime, did not manifest personal maladjustments, did not develop class hatred as the result of their two hundred dollars a month. . . .

10   At the conclusion of the Professor's story, the discussion began:

11   "That just goes to show," said the Advertising Man, who was known among his friends as a realistic thinker, "what good promotional work can do. B-ville's city council had real advertising sense, and that civic ceremony was a masterpiece . . . made everyone happy . . . put over the scheme in a big way. Reminds me of the way we do things in our business: as soon as we called horse-mackerel tuna-fish, we developed a big market for it. I suppose if you called relief 'insurance,' you could actually get people to like it, couldn't you?"

(7) **boosters:** backers, supporters, promoters, those who cheer the city on and publicize it
(8) **monster:** here, very large
(8) **bolster:** prop up, strengthen, or hold up by means of an object that gives support

12   "What do you mean, 'calling' it insurance?" asked the Social Worker. "B-ville's scheme wasn't relief at all. It *was* insurance."

13   "Good grief, man! Do you realize what you're saying?" cried the Advertising Man in surprise. "Are you implying that those people had any *right* to that money? All I said was that it's a good idea to *disguise* relief as insurance if it's going to make people any happier. But it's still relief, no matter what you *call* it. It's all right to kid the public along to reduce discontent, but we don't need to kid ourselves as well!"

14   "But they *do* have a right to that money! They're not getting something for nothing. It's insurance. They did something for the community, and that's their prem—"

15   "Say, are you crazy?"

16   "Who's crazy?"

17   "You're crazy. Relief is relief, isn't it? If you'd only call things by their right names. . . ."

18   "But, confound it, insurance is insurance, isn't it?"

19   P.S. Those who have concluded that the point of the story is that the Social Worker and the Advertising Man were "only arguing about different names for the same thing," are asked to reread the story and explain what they mean by (1) "only" and (2) "the same thing."

☐ QUESTIONS ON "A SEMANTIC PARABLE"

1. Does Hayakawa mean us to conclude that the Social Worker and the Advertising Man were "only arguing about different names for the same thing"? Why will it help the reader to focus on the words "only" and "the same thing"? How is "the same thing" wrong? What does "only" imply?
2. *Was* it insurance or was it relief? Or was it insurance in B-ville and relief in A-town?
3. What, besides the words, made insurance different from relief? Why? What was the source of the difference?
4. Did the terms affect the attitudes of the people at any point? Which people? How?
5. How do you explain the fact that two of the Professor's students interpreted the story so differently? What is the significance of one's being an advertising man and the other's being a social worker? Is there an additional lesson here on how we hear and understand?

☐ QUESTIONS FOR DISCUSSION

1. The question of the extent to which language influences thought is, of course, fascinating when applied to people such as you who have learned to think in more than one language. Foreign students have said that when they speak

English, they feel themselves to be a slightly different personality from the "person" who speaks their native language. This was confirmed by students who had immigrated to the United States five years earlier and were already fluent in English. *Do you ever feel this way? How do you account for it?* Are factors other than language operating, or can language be isolated?

2. A study was made in which Japanese women married to American servicemen and living in San Francisco were interviewed by a bilingual speaker. In this experiment the women were interviewed twice, once in Japanese and once in English. The questions asked the women were the same, but their *responses* were different, depending on whether they were speaking in English or in Japanese. For example, when asked to complete these sentences, one woman did so as follows:*

"When my wishes conflict with my family's . . .

. . . it is a time of great unhappiness."
(Japanese)
. . . I do what I want."
(English)

"Real friends should . . .

. . . help each other."   (Japanese)
. . . be very frank."   (English)

How do you account for these differences?

3. One reason for learning another language is that it makes us more aware of features of our *own* language that we never really thought about. Support this idea with specifics from your own experience. Explain at least one feature of your language that a comparison with English pointed out to you. Perhaps there are words that have no equivalent in your language and vice-versa. Can you put forward a theory to explain these differences?

THE LIMITS OF LANGUAGE

Throughout this chapter we have been discussing words, especially the relationship between words and meaning, between language and thought. We have begun to understand the power of words. Before we go on to discuss ways in which words are *used* powerfully, we must pause for a moment to remember that with all their power, words have their limitations as well. In the essay by Edward and Mildred Hall (Chapter 7) "the sounds of silence" are the "voices," silent but powerful, of culture. These silent voices communicate through the senses, uses of time and space, eye contact, and body language. In his song "The Sound of Silence," Paul Simon uses the term the opposite way.

> People talking without speaking
> People hearing without listening.

* Susan M. Ervin-Tripp, "Interaction of Language, Topic, and Listener," *American Anthropologist,* 66 (1964): 86–102.

In these lines we are reminded of how much "talk" is, in reality, no communication at all. Worse than silence, it *obscures* the possibility of communication because the sound of conversation conceals the reality of "silence" and the lack of communication. Here words get in the way of real communication. Silence may force us to communicate; "talk" fools us into thinking we are communicating.

Think about communication and its relationship to language as you read the following poem by Josephine Miles.

JOSEPHINE MILES

Family

When you swim in the surf* off Seal Rocks,* and your family
Sits in the sand
Eating potato salad, and the undertow*
Comes, which takes you out, away, down
5   To loss of breath, loss of play and the power of play,
Holler,* say
Help, help, help. Hello, they will say,
Come back here for some potato salad.

It is then that a seventeen-year-old cub*
10   Cruising in a helicopter from Antigua,
A jackstraw* expert speaking only Swedish,
And remote from this area as a camel, says
Look down there, there is somebody drowning.
And it is you. You say yes, yes, yes,
15   And he throws you a line.
This is what is called the brotherhood of man.

☐   QUESTIONS

---

1. Is the family to blame? How do you picture the scene? Include the family sitting in the sand, the potato salad (why that detail?), and their response.
2. If you feel the family to be a nice, amiable group with good intentions, what is

(1) **surf:** the waves of the sea breaking against the shore
(1) **Seal Rocks:** In San Francisco, at the Pacific Shore, a formation of large rocks where seals rest
(3) **undertow:** the undercurrent, which can pull one deeper out into the ocean, away from the shore
(6) **holler:** shout
(9) **cub:** a pilot in training
(11) **jackstraw:** a child's game of many thin pointed sticks, also called "pick-up-sticks"

the problem? In what way could the person swimming out, the undertow, and the family remaining on shore be a metaphor?

3. Look carefully at lines 7 and 8. How do you explain what is happening there? Read line 7 out loud. Can you *hear* a possible misunderstanding, given the distance and the sound of the waves? What does this imply about putting too much trust in words alone? What gesture is common to saying hello at a distance and calling for help in the water?

4. Of what significance is it to the poem that the pilot does not speak the swimmer's language? What *other* details are we given that reinforce the idea of his foreignness? What about the extent of his experience in general?

5. How does all this relate to the title? To the last line? How does this poem seem to define "the brotherhood of man"?

6. What is the sound effect of lines 1 and 2? Why is it appropriate?

Just for fun, you may want to compare "Family" to the following poem, which uses a very similar situation.

STEVIE SMITH

Not Waving But Drowning

Nobody heard him, the dead man,
But still he lay moaning:
I was much further out than you thought
And not waving but drowning.

Poor chap, he always loved larking*
And now he's dead
It must have been too cold for him his heart gave way,
They said.

Oh, no no no, it was too cold always
(Still the dead one lay moaning)
I was much too far out all my life
And not waving but drowning.

S T U D E N T   C O M P O S I T I O N

How a Word Was Invented

Two years ago I was a freshman at this university. At the orientation I met about six or seven other Thai students who also came here as freshmen. After that we saw each other almost every day at lunch time or in some freshman

larking: having fun

classes that we had together. It was the first time in the United States for all of us, so our spoken English was not very good. Some of us didn't even know common words such as "due date," "enjoy," or "amaze," nor especially abstract nouns which described feelings or thoughts.

One day after the first few weeks of the semester, four Thai students, including me, and a few Americans who were our suitemates, were having lunch together. During the conversation John, one of the Americans, asked, "How are your classes going?"

I was having some trouble in my humanities course—not a serious problem, just enough to give me some frustration, but I didn't want to explain all my feelings to John due to my limited vocabulary at the time, so I just answered, "All right," simply to cut down the conversation. Sert, one of my Thai friends, was having a very hard time in the same course. His problem was much more serious than mine. Not only did he have a hard time in speaking, but he also had a problem in understanding a conversation; yet he never was afraid of speaking what he thought. He simply translated his thought from Thai to English, word for word.

"I don't understand the econ. course. I don't understand the teacher talk in class," said Sert. "I don't do good on the exam too. I get under average," he continued rapidly.

Trying to make Sert feel better, James, another American at the table, said, "Come on, Sert, cheer up! Anyone can flunk an exam."

Somehow Sert misunderstood what James said, since James had a habit of talking very fast, and thought James was teaching him a new word, "chrup," which described Sert's feeling at that time. Hence, he associated "chrup" with the feeling a person has when he's gotten lost in his class and flunked the tests.

A few days later, again when we sat together for lunch, Sert said, very frustratedly, "I just chrup another one of my classes." At first nobody at the table understood what Sert was trying to say. After some effort, we found out what he meant by "chrup." Since then "chrup" became a word commonly used in the group, and when anybody in our group flunked a test, he would say "I chrup a test today."

☐ QUESTIONS

---

1. The student who wrote this essay was responding to question 8 on page 227 of this chapter. Have you had similar experiences? If so, give examples.
2. The same student goes on to discuss a family word that came into existence when his little sister could not find a word strong enough to express her anger at a playmate. Can you give examples of this in your family or among your friends—that is, of a word that has a private meaning for the members of a family or an intimate group?
3. What is the function of such language, other than to express the idea?

CHAPTER

12

USING LANGUAGE

In the previous chapter, we began to explore ways language affects us. We began to look at language closely and to think about it as a potentially powerful tool. In this chapter, we will continue to look carefully at language, becoming more and more conscious of the ways it is used, so that we will learn how best to *use* it and how to avoid *being used* by it.

DENOTATION, CONNOTATION, AND SLANTING

The following is the first part of an article that appeared in *The Wall Street Journal.*

G. S. MILLER

Casting About for Fish Names

1   Relaxing at a restaurant table, you sip your drink by candlelight and chat with your companion, appetite slowly building. The waiter brings the menu. With anticipation you begin to scan the seafood entrees: Broiled ratfish. Fried grunt. Poached mudblower with parsley sauce.

2   Ratfish? Mudblower? How disgusting. Maybe you don't want seafood after all. What else have they got?

3   This is the kind of reaction that frustrates the National Marine Fisheries Service. If only people knew. If only they realized how great ratfish tastes. If only they would *try* ratfish. If only ratfish had a different name.

4   Why yes, a different name. Butterfly fish, perhaps. Or sunshine fish. Honey fish.

5   The National Marine Fisheries Services is renaming fish. It has launched an ambitious program, involving more than 50 persons so far, to solve a problem acutely exasperating to those who manage our marine resources:

While familiar kinds of food fish dwindle in population, dozens of delicious and nutritious species contentedly swim and jump, increase and multiply, protected by repugnant names. Living is easy when your name is toadfish.

What is the problem? A ratfish, by any name, tastes delicious, but by *that* name, it repels the customers. Why? If you were to look up ratfish in a reference book on fish, you would find nothing to convince you that the fish tastes bad. Likewise, to look up the word *rat* in the dictionary would be to find a definition with no repulsive words in it. The literal definition we find in the dictionary is what we call the **denotation** of the word; it tells us, in the most precise way possible, what the word means. But as we have seen in the preceding example, the strictly literal meaning is not the *only* meaning a word has for us. We attach additional meaning to words because of our previous associations with them. A word comes to us with a life of its own, a history, a certain amount of emotional baggage, which is one reason that words, when you really understand them, are almost never really synonyms. They have different **connotations,** which is what we call these additional meanings that have attached themselves to words. This is surely one of the greatest sources of frustration for the person whose native language is not English, in fact for any person using the dictionary to write in another language. Unless the dictionary is very comprehensive and supplies all kinds of examples using the new words in sentences, students are soon ready to throw the dictionary into the nearest trash can.

One reason is that not every word translates neatly into an equivalent word in a second language. Related to this, however, is the problem of connotation, when the word is correct but carries with it a feeling you do not want in the context in which you are using it. To foreign students, in fact to anyone inexperienced in using the language well, connotation can be a problem. To the poet and the effective prose writer, it is a gold mine, giving the chance to convey not only literal meaning but also feelings and associations. Good readers recognize good word choices: They appreciate them if they enrich the reading experience; they are on guard if words are being used to prejudice* their thinking. (Remember that in Orwell's Newspeak, words had no connotations, hence no varied possibilities.) Good writers will likewise put this language awareness into practice. Of course, you might say that English is not your native language and that such awareness is asking a lot of you. Yes, it is, but don't forget that connotation and denotation operate in your native language as well, and you will also want to be more aware of them there. In English, as you read more and see more words in context, you will absorb these connotations. You have already done so to a great extent, perhaps without being fully aware of it. Then, too, you are learning as you write and as your word choices are corrected. *The more you read, listen, speak, and write, the more you will "feel" connotation.*

What are the connotations of the word *rat?* What is the difference between saying "A rat is a long-tailed rodent, resembling, but larger than, the mouse" and "My neighbor is a rat"? What are the unappetizing connotations of the fish names that seem to need changing?

---

* To be *prejudiced* means to have *pre*judged, that is, to have judged emotionally or irrationally *in advance* of logical judgment and evidence.

Are These Synonyms Really Synonymous?

Each group of words below is a group of synonyms. The words in each group do have similar meanings, but they cannot necessarily be used interchangeably. Try to explain the differences among the words in each group. If necessary, use a good dictionary. It may help to note the root or derivation of a word, the other forms of that word, and its other possible uses.

1. afraid, terrified, petrified
2. love, adoration, passion, adulation
3. laugh, giggle, guffaw
4. cry, sob, weep
5. happy, cheerful, joyful
6. embarrassment, shame, humiliation

Study the descriptions in Table 1. Notice how either the positive or the negative description could be derived from the more neutral facts.

□ EXERCISES

---

1. Choose five neutral words or descriptions and, for each one, supply one expression with a negative and one with a positive connotation.
2. You might enjoy the following true story of a headline in a foreign language newspaper published in New York: Having read in the American paper that "The Empress of China Arrived Yesterday on Her Maiden Voyage" (The Empress of China was the name of a ship; a "maiden voyage" is a ship's first voyage), the foreign language editor ran a big headline that translates, "The Empress of China Has Come to America to Look for a Husband."

   Perhaps you have had an experience, the kind that is humorous to look back on but embarrassing at the time, in which you were in an awkward situation because you used or understood a word literally. Write about the experience and what you learned about the words.
3. The following description of Professor Smith was obviously written by someone who does not like him and wants to influence us not to like him.

   > Professor Smith gives so many trivial details that I can hardly stay awake in his class. Then, in the middle of all that, he stops talking and draws things on the board with labels and arrows sticking out in all directions. Who can keep up with it all? I get writers' cramp trying to get all that down. I find the whole thing a great narcotic; give me a seat in the back, and I can catch up on my sleep. One problem, though, is that he tries to catch us with questions. Another problem is that he expects us to remember all that garbage for exams. Why can't he be fair and test us on what's in the book? It cost enough! It seems as if we don't get our money's worth if we have a book, and can't get a good grade just by memorizing it all. You can tell this Smith character is really a zero by the way he dresses, too—baggy pants, an old jacket that's worn at

TABLE 1.   Descriptions

Neutral	Negative	Positive
1. tall and thin	a stringy bag of bones	looks like a fashion model
2. brown hair	mousey brown	chestnut brown
3. American boy of average intelligence	a Yank so average that he never had an original idea	a regular American guy
4. She wore a red dress.	She looked like a fire engine.	In her red dress, she looked as bright as a Windsor rose in June.
5. an ordinary dog of mixed breed	a flea-bitten mutt	a loveable pup that looked like any boy's best friend
6. a person who explains everything carefully	an incredible bore	one who is intelligent and precise
7. a girl with curly hair	a cross between a powder puff and a French poodle	soft, feminine, and well cared for
8. a politician speaking for a cause	You can't believe him. He's a politician, and you know what they want!	He has a fine legal mind and a sense of responsibility to us all. He is not afraid to stand up for what he believes in.
9. He had a few drinks at the party.	He was disgustingly drunk.	After a few drinks, he livened up the whole party.
10. He is an athletic boy.	His brain is a football, and his arms and legs are laced with hard, ugly lumps.	He is a real powerhouse! Rippled with muscles, he flies over the football field.

the cuffs, and a shirt that never matches either one—a real slob. After class he hangs around talking with the students who are obviously trying to impress him with questions. You'd think he'd see through it. I've even seen him wasting his time sitting in the student union having coffee with the students. He must be such a jerk that no one wants to be his friend, so he has to talk to those grubs. Nope—he's not *my* idea of a professor.

Find the words and expressions with negative connotations. In what other ways has the writer tried to influence you against the professor? Using words and data in order to express one's attitude or bias is called **slanting.** The above paragraph is obviously *slanted against* the professor.

a. Using the *facts* given in this paragraph, write an essay about this same professor as if you were a student who loves him and thinks he's great. You should try to convince us how wonderful he is.

Notice that to do this, you will have to consider the following.

(1) Sort out the *facts* from the opinions.
(2) Change the negatively charged words to positively charged ones.
(3) Interpret the facts according to a different *value* system.
(4) Define for yourself which characteristics are *good* in a professor, which are bad, and which are irrelevant; and then let these assumptions come through, as they do in the original.
(5) Show how details of teaching method, appearance, and personality can contribute to a positive picture of a professor you recommend or admire.

b. Write a paragraph characterizing the student who wrote about Professor Smith. What can you *infer* about him? (That is, what do you conclude about him that is not put into words?) Be critical of him. Select details that support your view of the kind of student he seems to be. Judge him *as a student*.

c. Characterize the same student, assuming you are his best friend. You find him amusing; he cheers you up when you worry about school; he makes sure you enjoy college. Can you *add* details that can be *inferred* from what you are given?

Notice that in everything we are doing with Professor Smith—for or against him—we are *slanting* what we write. In turning a negative report into a positive one, we had to analyze the paragraph we were given, to see the facts objectively. How did we do this? To be objective in our reading we must do the following.

1. Sort fact from opinion.
2. Recognize value judgments and that, perhaps, the writer's views are not necessarily our own.
3. Ascertain whether the writer's use of words corresponds with our definitions of the words. (See Chapter 9.)
4. Recognize *inferences*; that is, whether, from the facts at hand, conclusions have been drawn that may or may not be valid.

When we write in order to persuade, we must do the following:

1. Select what we wish to present.
2. Use language that is positively or negatively charged.
3. Interpret the evidence at hand in light of our value system and the purpose for which we are writing.

EUPHEMISM

Let us look once more at Mark Twain's adventurous boy hero, Huck Finn.

MARK TWAIN

Borrowing

1   Every night now I used to slip ashore toward ten o'clock at some little village, and buy ten or fifteen cents' worth of meal or other stuff to eat;

.   .   .   .

2   Mornings before daylight I slipped into cornfields and borrowed a watermelon, or a mushmelon, or a punkin, or some new corn, or things of that kind. Pap always said it warn't no harm to borrow things if you was meaning to pay them back some time; but *the widow said it warn't anything but a soft name for stealing,* and no decent body would do it. Jim said he reckoned the widow was partly right; so the best way would be for us to pick out two or three things from the list and say we wouldn't borrow them any more—then he reckoned it wouldn't be no harm to borrow the others. So we talked it over all night, drifting along down the river, trying to make up our minds whether to drop the watermelons, or the cantelopes, or the mushmelons, or what. But toward daylight we got all settled satisfactory, and concluded to drop crabapples and p'simmons. We warn't feeling just right before that, but it was all comfortable now. I was glad the way it come out, too, because crabapples ain't ever good, and the p'simmons wouldn't be ripe for two or three months yet.

What is the moral dilemma? What does "borrow" mean? Is the widow right? Why? What does the word *borrow* do for Huck and Jim?

Eu is a Greek prefix meaning *good* or *well.* A **euphemism** is a word that expresses something in a milder, more pleasant way than does the word usually used. For example, we speak of *passing away* instead of *dying, sanitation engineers* instead of *garbage collectors.* Euphemisms can help us deliver bad news and soothe the feelings of an angry or grieving person. But as in the Huck Finn example, euphemisms can also distort our view of reality. They can make stealing seem like borrowing; they can make the horrifying seem not so bad. When euphemisms obscure the realities and moral issues that we need to know in order to make judgments and take action, we need to be careful—to "tell it like it is" and to hear it as it really is.

In a famous essay, George Orwell demonstrates the ways in which language and politics affect each other, how imprecise language has political causes as well as political consequences.

GEORGE ORWELL

FROM *Politics and the English Language*

1   In our time, political speech and writing are largely the defense of the indefensible. Things like the continuance of British rule in India, the Russian purges and deportations, the dropping of the atom bombs on Japan, can indeed be defended, but only by arguments which are too brutal for most people to face, and which do not square with the professed aims of political parties. Thus political language has to consist largely of euphemism, question-begging* and sheer cloudy vagueness. Defenseless villages are bombarded from the air, the inhabitants driven out into the countryside, the cattle machine-gunned, the huts set on fire with incendiary* bullets: this is called *pacification*. Millions of peasants are robbed of their farms and sent trudging along the roads with no more than they can carry; this is called *transfer of population* or *rectification of frontiers*. People are imprisoned for years without trial, or shot in the back of the neck or sent to die of scurvy in Arctic lumber camps; this is called *elimination of unreliable elements*. Such phraseology is needed if one wants to name things without calling up mental pictures of them.

What seems humorous in the hands of Mark Twain has very serious implications, as George Orwell shows us. Let's be honest; we *all* use slanting. If we use language well, we understand and use connotation and denotation. Euphemism is often a psychological and social necessity. We would be communicating in a very dry and boring way if we never spiced up or toned down our writing with these devices. We would be cold and dull if we denied our feelings at all times. We would appear about as strong as a wet noodle if we never showed our attitudes or opinions. To present an opinion or attitude honestly is our privilege. It is when we try to substitute attitude and opinion for logic and evidence, try to pass off bias as objective reality, try to make wrong look right by means of euphemism, fooling ourselves as well as others, that these devices become dangerous and dishonest. It is our obligation as educated readers and writers to be on our guard against using or *being used by* such techniques.

☐ COMPOSITION SUGGESTION IN SLANTING AND EUPHEMISM

Create a *purely factual* account of one of the following.

1. You failed an exam.
2. You were in an automobile accident. No one was injured, but you were at fault.
3. A person of the opposite sex whom you like refused or rejected you.

(1) **question-begging:** (see next section on logical fallacies)
(1) **incendiary:** fire-causing

Now write two other accounts of the incident: one explaining it to an authority figure or, in the case of number 3, to someone in front of whom you must maintain your pride; the other, telling it to your best friend or writing in your journal.

Notice how your language and emphasis change, depending upon your audience and your need to look as good as possible in the situation.

LOGICAL FALLACIES AND PROPAGANDA

Everywhere we turn, someone is trying to persuade us—to buy their product, to vote for their candidate, to adopt their policy, to agree with their opinions. An attempt to do this on an organized or large scale, aiming at large numbers of people, is called **propaganda.** When we see the harmful effects of propaganda, we become fearful of it, but it is not always harmful. Advertising is one form of propaganda; writing our opinions to newspapers is another. Propaganda *is* harmful when unscrupulous persuaders try to take advantage of people who are not equipped to "see through" the techniques being used, who are not being careful to distinguish factual evidence from opinion, or to question the source and reliability of the facts. We have already examined the ways facts can be selected and slanted, even when the writer is being careful *not* to lie or invent facts. Unfortunately, unscrupulous propagandists *do* lie and invent facts. We have already seen the importance of word choice in reflecting a writer's attitude and his wish to influence the attitude of the reader. Now we will try to become more *aware* of the ways we are being appealed to, the ways **logical fallacies** (that is, faults in logic) are used by those who wish to cloud our logical thinking processes. To be aware of these commonly used techniques is to be armed against them.

The following story provides an amusing lesson in logical fallacies.

MAX SHULMAN

Love Is a Fallacy

1   Cool was I and logical.... My brain was as powerful as a dynamo, as precise as a chemist's scales, as penetrating as a scalpel.* And—think of it!— I was only eighteen.

2   It is not often that one so young has such a giant intellect. Take, for example, Petey Burch, my roommate at the University of Minnesota. Same age, same background, but dumb as an ox. A nice enough young fellow, you understand, but nothing upstairs.*...

3   One afternoon I found Petey lying on his bed with an expression of such distress on his face that I immediately diagnosed appendicitis. "Don't move," I said. "Don't take a laxative.* I'll get a doctor."

(1) **scalpel:** a small knife with a very sharp blade, used in surgery and dissections
(2) **nothing upstairs:** (slang) no brains in his head
(3) **laxative:** medicine to make the bowels work

4   "Raccoon,*" he mumbled thickly.

5   "Raccoon?" I said, pausing in my flight.

6   "I want a raccoon coat," he wailed.*

7   I perceived that his trouble was not physical, but mental. "Why do you want a raccoon coat?"...

8   "All the Big Men on Campus are wearing them. Where've you been?"

9   "In the library," I said, naming a place not frequented* by Big Men on Campus.

10   He leaped from the bed and paced the room, "I've got to have a raccoon coat," he said passionately. "I've got to!"

11   "Petey, why? Look at it rationally. Raccoon coats are unsanitary. They shed. They smell bad. They weigh too much. They're unsightly. They—"

12   "You don't understand," he interrupted impatiently. "It's the thing to do.... I'd give anything for a raccoon coat. Anything!"

13   My brain, that precision instrument, slipped into high gear. "Anything?" I asked, looking a him narrowly.

14   "Anything," he affirmed in ringing tones.

15   I stroked my chin thoughtfully. It so happened that I knew where to get my hands on a raccoon coat. My father had had one in his undergraduate days; it lay now in a trunk in the attic back home. It also happened that Petey had something I wanted. He didn't *have* it exactly, but at least he had first rights on it. I refer to his girl, Polly Espy....

16   I was a freshman in law school. In a few years I would be out in practice. I was well aware of the importance of the right kind of wife in furthering a lawyer's career. The successful lawyers I had observed were, almost without exception, married to beautiful, gracious, intelligent women. With one omission, Polly fitted these specifications perfectly.

17   Beautiful she was....

18   Gracious she was....

19   Intelligent she was not. In fact, she veered in the opposite direction. But I believed that under my guidance she would smarten up. At any rate, it was worth a try. It is, after all, easier to make a beautiful dumb girl smart than to make an ugly smart girl beautiful.

20   "Petey," I said, "are you in love with Polly Espy?"

21   "I think she's a keen kid," he replied, "but I don't know if you'd call it love. Why?"

22   "Do you," I asked, "have any kind of formal arrangement with her? I mean are you going steady or anything like that?"

23   "No. We see each other quite a bit, but we both have other dates. Why?"

24   "Is there," I asked, "any other man for whom she has a particular fondness?"

25   "Not that I know of. Why?"

---

(4) **raccoon:** a small furry animal, distinguished by yellow and black rings around its furry tail

(6) **wailed:** cried loudly from grief or pain

(9) **frequented:** attended often

26   I nodded with satisfaction. "In other words, if you were out of the picture, the field would be open. Is that right?"

27   "I guess so. What are you getting at?"

28   "Nothing, nothing," I said innocently, and took my suitcase out of the closet.

29   "Where are you going?" asked Petey.

30   "Home for the weekend." I threw a few things into the bag.

.   .   .   .   .   .

31   "Look," I said to Petey when I got back Monday morning. I threw open the suitcase and revealed the huge, hairy, gamy object that my father had worn in his Stutz Bearcat in 1925.

32   "Holy Toledo!" said Petey reverently.* He plunged his hands into the raccoon coat and then his face. "Holy Toledo!" he repeated fifteen or twenty times.

33   "Would you like it?" I asked.

34   "Oh yes!" he cried, clutching the greasy pelt* to him. Then a canny* look came into his eyes. "What do you want for it?"

35   "Your girl," I said, mincing no words.*...

36   He flung the coat from him. "Never," he said stoutly.*...

37   I sat down in a chair and pretended to read a book, but out of the corner of my eye I kept watching Petey. He was a torn man. First he looked at the coat with the expression of a waif* at a bakery window. Then he turned away and set his jaw resolutely.* Then he looked back at the coat, with even more longing in his face. Then he turned away, but with not so much resolution this time. Back and forth his head swiveled,* desire waxing,* resolution waning.* Finally he didn't turn away at all; he just stood and stared with mad lust* at the coat.

38   "It isn't as though I was in love with Polly," he said thickly. "Or going steady or anything like that."...

39   "Try on the coat," said I.

40   He complied.* The coat bunched high over his ears and dropped all the

(32) **reverently:** in a manner showing deep love, worship
(34) **pelt:** fur skin
(34) **canny:** shrewd, cautiously clever
(35) **mincing no words:** speaking directly and frankly
(36) **stoutly:** strongly, courageously
(37) **waif:** a homeless child
(37) **resolutely:** with determination
(37) **swiveled:** turned back and forth
(37) **wax:** to increase in size; **wane:** to decrease in size (both terms are often used regarding the moon)
(37) **lust:** excessive desire, usually excessive sexual desire, but used also of excessive greed or excessive, overmastering desire for power; used with negative moral implications
(40) **complied:** did as he was told

way down to his shoe tops. He looked like a mound* of dead raccoons. "Fits fine," he said happily.

41   I rose from my chair. "Is it a deal?" I asked, extending my hand.

42   He swallowed. "It's a deal," he said and shook my hand.

43   I had my first date with Polly the following evening. This was in the nature of a survey; I wanted to find out just how much work I had to do to get her mind up to the standard I required. . . .

44   I went back to my room with a heavy heart. I had gravely underestimated the size of my task. This girl's lack of information was terrifying. Nor would it be enough merely to supply her with information. First she had to be taught to *think*. This loomed as a project of no small dimensions, and at first I was tempted to give her back to Petey. But then I got to thinking about her abundant physical charms and about the way she entered a room and the way she handled a knife and fork, and I decided to make an effort.

45   I went about it, as in all things, systematically. I gave her a course in logic. . . . "Polly," I said to her when I picked her up on our next date, "tonight we are going over to the Knoll and talk.". . .

46   We went to the Knoll, the campus trysting* place, and we sat down under an old oak, and she looked at me expectantly. "What are we going to talk about?" she asked.

47   "Logic."

48   She thought this over for a minute and decided she liked it. "Magnif," she said.

49   "Logic," I said, clearing my throat, "is the science of thinking. Before we can think correctly, we must first learn to recognize the common fallacies of logic. These we will take up tonight."

50   "Wow-dow!" she cried, clapping her hands delightedly.

51   I winced,* but went bravely on. "First let us examine the fallacy called Dicto Simpliciter."

52   "By all means," she urged, batting her lashes* eagerly.

53   "Dicto Simpliciter means an argument based on an unqualified generalization. For example: Exercise is good. Therefore everybody should exercise."

54   "I agree," Polly said earnestly. "I mean exercise is wonderful. I mean it builds the body and everything."

55   "Polly," I said gently, "the argument is a fallacy. *Exercise is good* is an unqualified generalization. For instance, if you have heart disease, exercise is bad, not good. Many people are ordered by their doctors *not* to exercise. You must *qualify* the generalization. You must say exercise is *usually* good *for most people*. Otherwise you have committed a Dicto Simpliciter. Do you see?"

---

(40) **mound:** a heap, small hill, raised area

(46) **trysting:** meeting; especially place where lovers meet

(51) **winced:** drew back suddenly, as if suddenly hurt

(52) **batting her lashes:** opening and shutting eyes very quickly, causing rapid up and down motion of the eyelashes

56   "No," she confessed. "But this is marvy. Do more! Do more!"...

57   ... "Next we take up a fallacy called Hasty Generalization. Listen carefully: You can't speak French, I can't speak French, Petey Burch can't speak French. I must therefore conclude that nobody at the University of Minnesota can speak French."

58   "Really?" said Polly, amazed. *"Nobody?"*

59   I hid my exasperation.* "Polly, it's a fallacy. The generalization is reached too hastily. There are too few instances to support such a conclusion."

60   "Know any more fallacies?" she asked breathlessly. "This is more fun than dancing even."

61   I fought off a wave of despair. I was getting nowhere with this girl, absolutely nowhere....

62   "Next comes Post Hoc. Listen to this: Let's not take Bill on our picnic. Every time we take him out with us, it rains."

63   "I know somebody like that," she exclaimed. "A girl back home— Eula Becker, her name is. It never fails. Every single time we take her on a picnic—"

64   "Polly," I said sharply, "it's a fallacy. Eula Becker doesn't *cause* the rain. She has no connection with the rain. You are guilty of Post Hoc if you blame Eula Becker."

65   "I'll never do that again," she promised contritely.* "Are you mad at me?"

66   I sighed deeply. "No, Polly, I'm not mad."

67   "Then tell me some more fallacies."...

68   I consulted my watch. "I think we'd better call it a night. I'll take you home now, and you go over all the things you've learned. We'll have another session tomorrow night."

69   I deposited her at the girls' dormitory, where she assured me that she had had a perfectly terrif evening, and I went glumly* to my room. Petey lay snoring in his bed, the raccoon coat huddled like a great hairy beast at his feet. For a moment I considered waking him and telling him that he could have his girl back. It seemed clear that my project was doomed to failure. The girl simply had a logic-proof head.

70   But then I reconsidered. I had wasted one evening; I might as well waste another. Who knew? Maybe somewhere in the extinct* crater* of her mind, a few embers still smoldered.... I decided to give it one more try.

71   Seated under the oak the next evening I said, "Our first fallacy tonight is called Ad Misericordiam."

72   She quivered with delight.

73   "Listen closely," I said. "A man applies for a job. When the boss asks him what his qualifications are, he replies that he has a wife and six children at

(59) **exasperation:** great annoyance or irritation
(65) **contritely:** feeling very sorry, guilty
(69) **glumly:** gloomily, sadly
(70) **extinct:** no longer in existence
(70) **crater:** a bowl-shaped cavity at the mouth of a volcano (a mountain that ejects hot, melted rock); a pit resembling this, as one made by a bomb

home, the wife is a helpless cripple, the children have nothing to eat, no clothes to wear, no shoes on their feet, there are no beds in the house, no coal in the cellar, and winter is coming."

74   A tear rolled down each of Polly's pink cheeks. "Oh, this is awful, awful," she sobbed.

75   "Yes, it's awful," I agreed, "but it's no argument. The man never answered the boss's questions about his qualifications. Instead he appealed to the boss's sympathy. He committed the fallacy of Ad Misericoridiam. Do you understand?". . .

76   I handed her a handkerchief and tried to keep from screaming while she wiped her eyes. "Next," I said in a carefully controlled tone, "we will discuss False Analogy. Here is an example: students should be allowed to look at their textbooks during examinations. After all, surgeons have X rays to guide them during an operation, lawyers have briefs to guide them during a trial, carpenters have blueprints to guide them when they are building a house. Why, then, shouldn't students be allowed to look at their textbooks during an examination?"

77   "There now," she said enthusiastically, "is the most marvy idea I've heard in years."

78   "Polly," I said testily, "the argument is all wrong. Doctors, lawyers, and carpenters aren't taking a test to see how much they have learned, but students are. The situations are entirely different, and you can't make an analogy between them."

79   "I still think it's a good idea," said Polly.

80   "Nuts," I muttered. Doggedly I pressed on. "Next we'll try Hypothesis Contrary to Fact."

81   "Sounds yummy," was Polly's reaction.

82   "Listen: If Madame Curie had not happened to leave a photographic plate in a drawer with a chunk of *pitchblende,** the world today would not know about radium."

83   "True, true," said Polly, nodding her head. "Did you see the movie? Oh, it just knocked me out. . . ."

84   . . . "I would like to point out that the statement is a fallacy. Maybe Madame Curie would have discovered radium at some later date. Maybe somebody else would have discovered it. Maybe any number of things would have happened. You can't start with a hypothesis that is not true and then draw any supportable conclusions from it.". . .

85   One more chance, I decided. But just one more. There is a limit to what flesh and blood can bear. "The next fallacy is called Poisoning the Well."

86   "How cute!" she gurgled.

87   "Two men are having a debate. The first one gets up and says, 'My opponent is a notorious* liar. You can't believe a word that he is going to say.'. . . Now, Polly, think. Think hard. What's wrong?"

(82) **pitchblende:** brown or black lustrous mineral containing radium; uranium
(87) **notorious:** well known in an *un*favorable way

88   I watched her closely as she knit her creamy brow in concentration. Suddenly, a glimmer* of intelligence—the first I had seen—came into her eyes. "It's not fair," she said with indignation. "It's not a bit fair. What chance has the second man got if the first man calls him a liar before he even begins talking?"

89   "Right!" I cried exultantly. "One hundred percent right. It's not fair. The first man has *poisoned the well* before anybody could drink from it. . . . Polly, I'm proud of you."

90   "Pshaw," she murmured, blushing with pleasure.

91   "You see, my dear, these things aren't so hard. All you have to do is concentrate. Think—examine—evaluate. Come now, let's review everything we have learned."

92   "Fire away," she said with an airy wave of her hand.

93   Heartened by the knowledge that Polly was not altogether a cretin,* I began a long, patient review of all I had told her. Over and over and over again I cited instances, pointed out flaws, kept hammering away without let-up. It was like digging a tunnel. At first everything was work, sweat, and darkness. I had no idea when I would reach the light, or even *if* I would. But I persisted. I pounded and clawed and scraped, and finally I was rewarded. I saw a chink* of light. And then the chink got bigger and the sun came pouring in and all was bright.

94   Five grueling* nights this took, but it was worth it. I had made a logician out of Polly; I had taught her to think. My job was done. She was worthy of me at last. She was a fit wife for me, a proper hostess for my many mansions, a suitable mother for my well-heeled* children.

95   It must not be thought that I was without love for this girl. Quite the contrary. . . . I determined to acquaint her with my feelings at our very next meeting. The time had come to change our relationship from academic to romantic.

96   "Polly," I said when next we sat beneath our oak, "tonight we will not discuss fallacies."

97   "Aw, gee," she said, disappointed.

98   "My dear," I said, favoring her with a smile, "we have now spent five evenings together. We have gotten along splendidly. It is clear that we are well matched."

99   "Hasty Generalization," said Polly brightly.

100   "I beg your pardon," said I.

101   "Hasty Generalization," she repeated. "How can you say that we are well matched on the basis of only five dates?"

102   I chuckled with amusement. The dear child had learned her lessons well.

(88) **glimmer:** a weak, flickering light
(93) **cretin:** refers to a person suffering from deficient thyroid secretion, resulting in dwarfism and idiocy
(93) **chink:** small crack
(94) **grueling:** exhausting, tormenting
(94) **well-heeled:** (slang) having plenty of money

"My dear," I said, patting her hand in a tolerant manner, "five dates is plenty. After all, you don't have to eat a whole cake to know it's good."

103   "False Analogy," said Polly promptly. "I'm not a cake. I'm a girl."

104   I chuckled with somewhat less amusement. The dear child had learned her lessons perhaps too well. I decided to change tactics. Obviously the best approach was a simple, strong, direct declaration of love. I paused for a moment while my massive brain chose the proper words. Then I began:

105   "Polly, I love you. You are the whole world to me, and the moon and the stars and the constellations of outer space. Please, my darling, say that you will go steady with me, for if you will not, life will be meaningless. I will languish.* I will refuse my meals. I will wander the face of the earth, a shambling, hollow-eyed hulk.*"

106   There, I thought, folding my arms, that ought to do it.

107   "Ad Misericordiam," said Polly.

108   I ground my teeth. . . . Frantically I fought back the tide of panic surging through me. At all costs I had to keep cool.

109   "Well, Polly," I said, forcing a smile, "you certainly have learned your fallacies."

110   "You're darn right," she said with a vigorous nod.

111   "And who taught them to you, Polly?"

112   "You did."

113   "That's right. So you do owe me something, don't you, my dear? If I hadn't come along you never would have learned about fallacies."

114   "Hypothesis Contrary to Fact," she said instantly.

115   I dashed perspiration from my brow. "Polly," I croaked, "you mustn't take all these things so literally. I mean this is just classroom stuff. You know that the things you learn in school don't have anything to do with life."

116   "Dicto Simpliciter," she said, wagging her finger at me playfully.

117   That did it. I leaped to my feet, bellowing like a bull.* "Will you or will you not go steady with me?"

118   "I will not," she replied.

119   "Why not?" I demanded.

120   "Because this afternoon I promised Petey Burch that I would go steady with him."

121   I reeled* back, overcome with the infamy* of it. After he promised, after he made a deal, after he shook my hand! "The rat!" I shrieked, kicking up great chunks of turf.* "You can't go with him, Polly. He's a liar. He's a cheat. He's a rat."

122   "Poisoning the Well," said Polly, "and stop shouting. I think shouting must be a fallacy too."

(105) **languish:** become weak
(105) **hulk:** a big, old body of a ship; a big clumsy person or thing
(117) **bellowing like a bull:** roaring loudly with the sound of the male of the cattle family
(121) **reeled:** swayed, staggered, went around and around
(121) **infamy:** disgrace, dishonor, scandal
(121) **turf:** grass plus roots and earth

123   With an immense effort of will, I modulated* my voice. "All right," I said. "You're a logician. Let's look at this thing logically. How could you choose Petey Burch over me? Look at me—a brilliant student, a tremendous intellectual, a man with an assured future. Look at Petey—a knothead, a jitterbug, a guy who'll never know where his next meal is coming from. Can you give me one logical reason why you should go steady with Petey Burch?"

124   "I certainly can," declared Polly. "He's got a raccoon coat."

Let us list once more the *logical fallacies* taught to us by the brilliant young law student and Polly Espy and add a few others to the list.

Unqualified generalization (or dicto simpliciter). Note the following examples.

All Americans are unfriendly.
Lawyers never tell the truth.
Women always love babies.

Beware of words like *always, all, never, every;* complex situations are simply not that black-and-white. Your generalizations will be more credible if you *limit* them by using qualifiers such as *sometimes, seem, in my experience, often, many,* or *perhaps.*

Hasty generalization. Related to the preceding, this is a conclusion drawn from too few samples. An example follows.

That three students are smoking in the cafeteria leads me to conclude that most college students smoke.

Name calling (or poisoning the well or ad hominem, i.e., argument attacking the man rather than the issue). Note the following example.

Senator X just divorced his wife. How can his proposal be any good?

Appeal to pity (Ad misericordiam). For instance:

We should reelect Senator X; after all, he has a crippled mother, a retarded son, and his wife just died.

Ad populem (appeal to the people, to what they want to hear or to what they fear). For example:

We know we can count on you, the generous American.
We don't want those people coming with their "red" ideas, do we?

Bandwagon appeal. Closely related to the above fallacy, it's the "everybody is doing it" argument. No one wants to be left out. If "everybody's doing it," then don't you want to "get on the bandwagon," right or wrong?

(123) **modulated:** regulated the pitch and intensity

Testimonial (or association). For example:

George Washington once made the same point as Senator X.
It's the Christian thing to do, because, as Jesus says, . . .

Hypothesis contrary to fact. For example:

The Pony Express stopped running in 1861. It must have been a failure. (The
fact is that the telegraph and the railroad made it obsolete and therefore
unnecessary.)

Faulty cause and effect (confusing coincidental time sequence with genuine
causation; sometimes called Post Hoc). For example:

Every time I forget my umbrella, it rains; therefore I cause the rain by leaving
my umbrella at home, and I can guarantee a nice day by bringing my
umbrella.

False analogy (or trying to *prove* a point by analogy). For instance:

You shouldn't change horses in midstream; therefore you must reelect Senator
X. (He is not a horse, and the nation's business is not a river. It is no
problem changing senators; in fact, if Senator X is doing a poor job, our
"ride" will be easier with Senator Y "pulling" us!)

Either-or (or the two-alternatives fallacy). Examples include:

Would you rather have a senator who is handsome and dumb or one who is
ugly and intelligent? (One can be intelligent *and* handsome; one can be
not-bad looking rather than ugly. Notice that in "Love Is a Fallacy" our
brilliant student/teacher commits this same fallacy. Can you find the
fallacy?)
You are either *for* the law or against it! (And what if I am for *parts* of it or for it
under certain circumstances but not all of them?)

Begging the question (or circular argument). This fallacy avoids proving the
truth of the conclusion by *assuming* the truth of it in advance. For example:

In a democracy the people are free because democracies are free countries.

Test your ability to spot logical fallacies. Identify them in the speech that follows.

Fellow Students:

I am coming to you today to ask for your help in cutting out
football at this university. As students of such a top-quality university,
you must all have top-quality intelligence. *Use* that intelligence, then,
to make the right decision about the sports program.

Let's look at some facts:

1. Three football players flunked out of school last term. Do we want
all those students who play football to flunk out?

2. Two football players are on crutches. Either we are for a healthy student body, or we are willing to create a school full of cripples! Sports or healthy limbs—take your choice. Plato advises us to have a healthy mind in a healthy body. What would he say about a school full of people on crutches!

3. Last year we won the state football championship, and we also went down two points in our state academic average. *You* can draw the conclusion yourselves that so much concentration on football is hurting our academic standing.

4. Football players always take away girlfriends from those who are not so athletically inclined.

5. The coach of the football team was found guilty of tax evasion last year. *Now* what do you think of such sports activity?

A chain is only as strong as its weakest link. Let's not put our fine university in such danger. Think of all the scholarship students who cannot afford tuition yet work day and night to get an education. Think of the sacrifice our parents make to send us here. We can't let them down. Please add your name to the five hundred who have already signed this petition. Remember: Our school is so good because it has such fine qualities. A bad program is bad for the school. Let's keep Gulch U. at the top!

Thank you.

Letters to the Editor and Editorials

Whereas news stories give us the facts and are careful to avoid injecting opinion, editorials and letters to the editor are written for the purpose of expressing the opinion of the newspaper or of the individual writer. The following letters to the editor express opposing views on one issue. How do they make their appeal? Do any writers use any of the logical fallacies we have studied? Which ones?

On October 21, 1981, Leonard Jenkins killed Patrolman Anthony Johnson in a gunfight after a bank robbery. Judge Daniel T. Martin, on the recommendation of the jury, sentenced Leonard Jenkins to death. Whether or not Jenkins, whose intelligence score was far below average, should receive a death sentence (also referred to as capital punishment) is the subject of these letters to the editor, which appeared over several days in the newspaper.

CLEVELAND PLAIN DEALER

Letters to the Editor

The prosecutor said he hoped the jury's recommendation to execute Leonard Jenkins would "send a message to people like Leonard Jenkins who take innocent lives."

Does he really believe that people with an IQ of 63 have been deterred from shooting a gun at someone else? For that matter, has it deterred anyone? There is absolutely no proof that capital punishment is a deterrent to people killing other people. He has made a statement that he hopes will appeal to the voters. He is playing to our fears and not our common sense. Maybe we all ought to read Exodus 20:13 again. Now there is an authority we can believe!

The Rev. D. D.

Cleveland Heights

With the conviction of Leonard Jenkins, the immorality of capital punishment once again surfaces. Will humanity ever fully realize that killing breeds killing? The cycle of sanctioned murder must be stopped.

I hope the consciences of Judge Daniel Martin, Prosecutors, John and Michael Corrigan, and the twelve-person jury rest well in the silent hours of the night knowing they have committed the same crime of which Jenkins was just convicted. The only difference is that they will not have to stand trial.

B. L.

Cleveland

We as members of a so-called "free society" can no longer walk or drive the streets at all times of the day or night, nor are we safe in our homes. There is no longer pity in our hearts for people who value only their own lives and exercise no hesitation in ending that of others.

Our society allows guns in the hands of "retarded" people, which enables them to kill easily. A paraplegic can hold a gun and can kill again.

I. K.

Chagrin Falls

The prosecutor and jury have condemned Leonard Jenkins to death. In effect, they get to kill him and feel good about it. I understand that it is quite OK for them to kill him because he did it first. To do it first is a sin and against God. That is Killer Number I. Killer Number II, on the other hand, is without sin, in fact most people applaud it and feel self-righteous about it.

To carry this logic further, there could be a killer Number III, those who decide God wants them to kill Number II (those who killed the killer Number I).

This is the kind of logic (or nonlogic) that runs most of this world. After all, aren't we about to nuke all life from this planet Earth? The way the leaders explain, it sounds quite logical to *them*.

H. S.

Bay Village

I am Leonard Jenkins' mother. Yes, I said I live directly by the Bible. I am sorry the policeman got killed. I was not at the bank Oct. 21. My son never had a chance to pull the trigger on that policeman.

I don't know what kind of jury could find him guilty. I think all of them are retarded.

Some people need to pray more. My son doesn't deserve the death penalty. It was wrong for him to go in that bank. But the Lord said, "Vengence is mine." So God bless everyone trying to be so cruel, with such little evidence.

I still go by the word of God. Thou shall not kill.

E. J.
Cleveland

In response to the letter from Mrs. Jenkins, if she would have taught her son two of the major commandments, "Thou shalt not kill" and "Thou shalt not steal," he would not be in the situation he is in.

Mr. and Mrs. M. B.
North Ridgeville

Pertaining to both the April 8 front page article and James Neff's "Focal Point" column, what utter irresponsibility is reflected! Yes, I'm infuriated. Why the skirting of the truth in the matter of Leonard Jenkins and his most fair jury trial for the cold-blooded murder of police officer Anthony Johnson?

Both articles stress that Jenkins (the murderer) is paralyzed and retarded. Also that Jenkins tearfully pleaded with the jury not "to kill me." Wouldn't anyone plead the same?

Both articles were written with the slanted intent that we should have more compassion on this poor, unfortunate creature who was not able to predetermine the end result of his dastardly act. Hogwash! He was streetwise, knew how to drive a car, how to buy or steal a gun, react to apprehension which resulted in him being shot and subsequently paralyzed.

A rotten shame? Not once in either report was it mentioned that the wife and family of a fine young police officer will no longer see him drive into the driveway of his home. No longer will they be able to show their love and affection for him as a man, and respect for his job well done.

No, it's as Prosecutor John Corrigan and his commendable son Mike expressed, "Maybe it's because the people out there are sick and tired of this type of person getting away with whatever they please."

R.T.D.
North Olmsted

To all you bleeding hearts and sob sisters who are on the verge of committing suicide because Leonard Jenkins was sentenced to the electric chair, I wonder how you would feel if someone you loved was killed in cold blood. I am not a college graduate and my childhood was not a bed of roses, but that did not make a criminal of me. I think your opinion is to give the criminal a license to kill and the victim be damned.

C. W.
Cleveland

After reading Monday's letters to the editor, I wish to make the following comments:

On the morning of Oct. 21, 1981, while working the day shift in the 4th District area, I was one of the officers responding to the radio assignment of a robbery in progress at the National City Bank, 16614 Harvard Ave., and of a police officer shot.

Upon arrival on the scene, I viewed fellow Patrolman Anthony Johnson lying on the ground fatally wounded during the attempted holdup of the bank. As the last few minutes of his precious life spilled out onto the pavement, it was a scene I'll never forget. Prior to this day, I had the opportunity to work with Patrolman Johnson on the streets several times. During the hours that we spent in the zone car we discussed many things, such as family, friends, our employment and life in general, and in doing so became good friends.

Patrolman Johnson was a dedicated officer concerned with the citizens of Cleveland and committed to cleaning up the streets of his city. His commitment was cut short.

Finally, I would like to say to all the people out there who sympathize with Leonard Jenkins because he is under the death penalty to consider this for just a moment or two—there is an old saying, "It never really hurts until it hits home." I wonder if these people would find the same penalty unjust if Patrolman Johnson was a good friend or family member.

Too many times people read an article similar to what happened to Johnson, shake their heads in disgust, then soon after forget the incident completely. It's not that easy for some of us to forget! Let justice be served!

Patrolman D.J.J.
Cleveland Police Department
4th District

☐ EXERCISES

1. Look through some recent newspapers. Find a few news stories on a subject of your choice and "test" them to see whether they give the facts or try to slant the news. Find editorials or letters to the editor on the same subject. Try to determine whether these opinions are given straightforwardly, supported by facts, or whether they are relying on logical fallacies and slanted writing, or both. (An excellent source of intelligent, informed, well-written editorials is the *New York Times* editorial and Op-Ed pages.)

2. Choose an issue in which you have an interest. Write two letters to the editor expressing opposing views. In one letter, let the facts speak and express your opinion directly. In the other, use some logical fallacies. Don't try too hard to "play fair."

Advertising

As you may have noticed, many of these same techniques are being directed at us in magazine, newspapers, billboard, and TV ads.

☐ EXERCISES

---

1. Choose five ads from any form of media. If they are in print, cut them out; if not, describe them. Then analyze the techniques used in the ads. What logical fallacies are being used? To what do the ads appeal? How much are you actually told about the product?
2. Analyze the ads on pages 259–261, asking yourself the following questions: Which ad tells you the most about the product or allows the product to sell itself? To what kinds of desires, fantasies, wishes, or needs do the other ads appeal? To what kind of audience is each ad directed? How do you know? How is all of this appropriate to the product being sold? (How would an ad for beer or cigarettes differ from an ad for expensive Scotch or fine French brandy?)
3. Two of the ads show a woman and her baby. What is the *difference* between these ads? Describe each woman: her "type," her way of life, her characteristics, her values as the ad makes you imagine them. (Notice the details in the ads.) To what in a woman does each ad appeal? What is the relationship between this appeal and the product being sold? Why is so little about the product in the Dan River ad put into words?
4. The following ad slogans have been very successful. Why?

Joy perfume began to increase its sales when it used the slogan, "The costliest perfume in the world."
Courvoisier calls itself "The Brandy of Napoleon."
"It's the real thing." (Coca Cola)
"Join the Pepsi Generation." (Pepsi Cola)
"If it's not your mother's, it must be Howard Johnson's."
"Just Wear a Smile and a Jantzen." (Jantzen bathing suits)
"You deserve a break today." (McDonald's restaurants)
"You're in good hands with Allstate." (insurance company)
"Choosy Mothers Choose Jiff." (Jiff peanut butter)

The endless Marimekko Collection of bedroom fashions. "Seven Flowers" sheets and pillowcases in **Fortrel**® polyester/cotton no-iron percale. Comforters, comforter covers, towels and bath sheets to match. At the best stores. © 1982 Dan River Home Furnishing Products Division, NY 10018.

DAN RIVER RUNS DEEP®
IN MARIMEKKO®

13

RESEARCH PAPER

Mention the words term paper or research paper and many students freeze in fear. They are often afraid of having to use footnotes or notecards or even the library. Yet many students have found their term paper assignment to have been their most rewarding academic experience. They are very proud of what they have written and pleased to have learned so much so independently. (This is one reason it is so important to choose a topic that interests you.) They are also very happy to have learned a skill they know they will need in a university. It is a skill, however, that one can only learn by doing and by being guided, step by step, through the process. Your instructor and librarian are your best friends throughout the writing process. Yet no matter how helpful others are the project is *yours:* yours to do, yours to worry about, yours to study, organize, and write. This is what makes it frightening, but it's also what makes it exciting and rewarding. The major decisions are yours; the sense of independent accomplishment is yours; and so is what you have learned of the process and about your subject. This is knowledge you will remember long after you have forgotten the material you learned for your tests.

As one student wrote in a letter after he left the university:

> When I first came to the United States . . . it was very hard for me to write a good short essay in English. . . . It was at CWRU . . . that I managed to write a paper over twenty pages long and feel proud about it. The challenge I faced in my research over my term paper, and the enjoyment I received in doing it, is so great that I cannot begin to describe it in words. What I learned . . . during the course of the semester is much more than just having done the assignment. I was taught the joy of writing about something I enjoyed. . . . And I know that I am now capable of doing such a research.

WHY IS A TERM PAPER BENEFICIAL?

Aside from the obvious benefit of learning more about one aspect of a subject, there are many benefits of writing a research paper. One very important benefit is that students learn how to find and use information. *They learn how to learn things for themselves,* under the guidance of someone who makes sure they do not "get lost" and they proceed in a disciplined, academically honest manner. No matter how long a person is in school, he or she will learn only a tiny fraction of any subject and will forget much of what has been memorized. But *how* to learn things, *where* to find what he or she wants to know, how to *put things together logically* and fairly, how to *ask the right questions,* how to *evaluate the answers,* how to *communicate a lot of complex material* to others—these are the skills an education should provide so that you will always be able to continue learning or teaching on your own. A term paper is one of the best ways to learn and practice this combination of skills. *You* will be creating it yourself out of what you have discovered *yourself.*

To do this well will require all of the skills you have learned so far, especially *organization.* In writing a shorter paper, you may have done well by allowing it to evolve. But a larger paper, one that involves researched information has to be carefully and logically organized from beginning to end. There is simply too much to deal with. This chapter will outline the steps involved in organizing a term paper, and give you advice on completing them. Only such a project will force you to organize your work, and your paper, in so disciplined a way.

TYPES OF PAPERS

There are, broadly speaking, two basic types of papers: the "report" type and the analytical or "thesis" type. The former is usually a little easier for it simply involves finding, organizing, and presenting your subject. You may survey what has been written on a subject or describe a project, but you need not make a point about it.

The analytical, or thesis, type of paper comes closer to what we have been talking about throughout most of this book for it is the paper that *makes a point.* In this type of paper you not only gather and present information, but also use that information in a focused way to make your point. You must analyze the information, using the analytical techniques you have learned. Usually papers of this kind begin with a question or problem and work toward an answer or resolution with which you conclude. Because the thesis paper is more demanding than the report type, we will concentrate on it a bit more, although most of the techniques of researching, organizing, writing, and documenting will be the same.

You may be working on a project of independent research, where you are making new discoveries—surely a most exciting experience. In writing about it, though, you will still be using these basic techniques of presenting, organizing, and analyzing data.

It is important to remember that whatever your subject or field, the approach and the methods of research have much in common. We all use the scientific method in a disciplined approach to seeking knowledge and sharing it. We look honestly and objectively for our data, we form hypotheses, test them, analyze their meaning, present evidence for what we say, and draw conclusions. Whether working in a lab or analyzing a piece of literature, whether studying a society or an economic failure, your papers will all take this approach. This is why humanities students have much to learn from the sciences, and science students have much to learn from the humanities. *Experience with either one will make you better equipped, intellectually, for the other.*

CHOOSING A SUBJECT: THE FIRST AND MOST DIFFICULT STEP

Rule number 1 should be: *choose a subject that interests you.* Your instructor will probably give you some suggestions and some choice of topics. Often your choices will be limited by the subject matter of a course. Sometimes the instructor will assign a topic, and you may feel you have no freedom to choose. But even in this case, you have some freedom, for there are many aspects to any subject. Some thought and research should yield new ideas to pursue on any subject. Ideally, you will have a choice of subjects within certain limits and some suggestions from your instructor. These suggestions will probably tie in with what you have already read or discussed. Of course, if your teacher lets you choose any subject, you can choose an area you most want to read about, although so much freedom may be more difficult to handle.

"Reading into" Subjects and "Shopping"

Most people feel good when they reach two or three possible topics for a paper. Very seldom do they know from the beginning exactly what they will be working on. At this point, doing some *brief* and *general* reading on your topic or topics is helpful. Encyclopedias, textbooks, handbooks, and bibliographies (lists of books and articles written on the subject) will tell you more about your topic and help you decide whether or not you are still interested. At this stage, be open-minded. Be prepared to discard a topic if it does not seem interesting to you; if it will be difficult to research or find information about; or if it will be difficult to manage, to understand, or to resolve into a conclusion. It is better to change your topic, even after you have spent time researching it, than to spend more time bored or frustrated.

Narrowing the Topic

"Reading into" a topic will also help you *narrow it,* a step you should soon take, the sooner the better. Usually some research, some greater knowledge of your subject, will be necessary before you are able to choose a smaller, more manageable aspect or division of your general topic. (See Chapter 6 on narrowing a general topic into a specific subject.) In a paper of ten to fifteen pages or less you cannot say a lot about a broad topic. To attempt to do so will be to speak about commonly known generalities. There will also be inadequate room for you to discuss or analyze your subject. *It is much better to focus on a narrower subject and examine it in greater depth.*

DOING THE RESEARCH: GATHERING DATA AND TAKING NOTES

The Library

A good library is a wonderful place. One can wander among the stacks, feeling rather like an explorer with so much there to be discovered, or one can feel frustrated at the sheer quantity to be explored. One can feel a kind of pride that all this information is available to *me*. But faced with a research paper, the inexperienced student may feel that the library is overwhelming, a threatening and frightening fortress hiding its treasures. The library may also seem a place where one can so easily get lost, finding all the things one does not need and never finding what one *does* need.

Luckily, there are guides to help us through the library; there are keys to help open the right doors. A good library is well organized, well catalogued, and well staffed. If you remember this, you can wander through the library *without* feeling threatened, confident that when you are ready to *use* the library for an assignment, it will *help* you, not hurt you.

Don't be afraid to ask a librarian for help. Librarians are some of the best resources of any library. They know better than anyone else how to find information in the library, and they also want to help. Librarians have made library science their life's work because they love research; they enjoy finding what may be difficult to find. Most of them are genuinely pleased to be of help to students, only too happy to be asked to share the plenty of the library. Of course, there are not enough librarians to help each student at all times. You must learn how to find things for yourself. But when you are inexperienced, or when something is difficult to find, a librarian can provide invaluable assistance. *Don't be shy* about asking for it. Very often, by the way, libraries offer tours or small classes in the use of the library. If your English course does not include such a class, ask your instructor or a librarian about being a part of one.

Where Should You Begin?   First of all, acquaint yourself with the library. Where are the general reference books? Where is the card catalogue? Where is the directory that helps you find the location of the books you are looking for? Where are the periodicals (magazines, newspapers, and journals)?

Encyclopedias for a General Overview of Your Subject

A good place to begin is with a general encyclopedia. Such a reference, because it is general, will be only a starting point, certainly not an adequate source of detailed information about your topic.

Collier's Encyclopedia. 24 vols. New York: Macmillan, 1981.
Encyclopedia Americana. 30 vols. New York: Grolier, 1983.
Encyclopedia International. 20 vols. New York: Grolier, 1982.

The New Columbia Encyclopedia. 1 vol. New York: Columbia UP, 1975.
The New Encyclopaedia Britannica. 30 vols. Chicago: Encyclopaedia Britannica, 1985.
Random House Encyclopedia. Rev. ed. New York: Random, 1983.

Other General Reference Materials

Indexes

Readers' Guide to Periodical Literature, monthly, published since 1900. Subject and author index to articles in some 160 popular magazines.
The New York Times Index, published annually since 1913. New York: The New York Times Company/R. R. Bowker.
Essay and General Literature Index, published since 1900. Covers all fields of interest: fine arts, literature, philosophy, religion, science, and social sciences.
Magazine Index. Menlo Park, California: Information Access Corporation. On microfilm.

Dictionaries

Unabridged dictionaries

Alexander, Sir William, and James R. Hulbert. *A Dictionary of American English on Historical Principles.* 4 vols. Chicago: U of Chicago P, 1936–1944.
The Oxford English Dictionary. 13 vols. plus supplements. New York: Oxford UP, 1933–1976. *The Compact Edition,* 2 vols. (unabridged, reduced type), was issued in 1971.
Webster's Third New International Dictionary of the English Language. Springfield, Mass.: Merriam, 1976.

Special Dictionaries

Lewis, Norman. *The New Roget's Thesaurus of the English Language in Dictionary Form.* New York: G. P. Putnam's Sons, 1978.
Webster's New Dictionary of Synonyms. Springfield, Mass.: G. & C. Merriam, 1984.

Biographical Reference Works

Current Biography. New York: Wilson, published annually since 1940.
Who's Who in America. Published biennially since 1899. 2 vols. Chicago: Marquis.
Who's Who of Amerian Women. Published biennially since 1958. Chicago: Marquis.

Atlases and Gazetteers (A gazetteer is a geographical dictionary)

Columbia Lippincott Gazetteer of the World. New York: Columbia UP, 1962.
Encyclopaedia Britannica World Atlas International. Chicago: Encyclopaedia Britannica, 1969.
Rand-McNally Cosmopolitan World Atlas. Rev. ed. Chicago: Rand McNally, 1971.

Almanacs and Yearbooks (Facts and statistics)

Britannica Book of the Year, published annually since 1938. Chicago: Encyclopaedia Britannica.

Facts on File Yearbook, published annually since 1940. New York: Facts on File.

U.S. Bureau of the Census. *Statistical Abstract of the United States,* published annually since 1878. Washington, D.C.: GPO.

World Almanac and Book of Facts, published annually since 1868. New York: World-Telegram.

In addition to the general reference materials, there are encyclopedias, dictionaries, indexes, and abstracts in specialized fields. Selected examples follow.

The Humanities

General

Humanities Index, published quarterly since 1974. New York: Wilson. Author and subject index to over 250 periodicals in the following: archaeology, classical studies, history, folklore, language and literature, philosophy, religion, and the performing arts.

The Arts

Encyclopedia of World Art. 15 vols. New York: McGraw, 1959–68.

Lucas, Edna Louise. *Art Books: A Basic Bibliography on the Fine Arts.* Greenwich, Conn.: New York Graphic Society, 1968.

Maillard, Robert, ed. *New Dictionary of Modern Sculpture.* Trans. Bettina Wadia. New York: Tudor, 1971.

Myers, Bernard S. *Encyclopedia of Painting.* New York: Crown, 1955.

Art Index. Published quarterly since 1929. New York: Wilson.

History

Adams, James T. *Dictionary of American History.* 6 vols. New York: Scribner's, 1940–63.

Friedl, Frank, ed. *Harvard Guide to American History.* Cambridge: Belknap Harvard UP, 1974.

Hammond, N.G.L., and H. H. Scullard. *Oxford Classical Dictionary.* 2d ed. Oxford: Clarendon Press, 1970.

Hodge, Frederick W. *Handbook of American Indians North of Mexico.* 2 vols. Washington, D.C.: GPO, 1907–10.

Langer, William Leonard. *An Encyclopedia of World History.* 5th ed., rev. Boston: Houghton, 1972.

American History and Life, published from 1964. Abstracts of articles in U.S. and Canadian journals and books.

Literature, Theater, and Television

Aaronson, C. S., ed. *International Television Almanac,* published annually since 1956. New York: Quigley.

Bond, Donald F. *A Reference Guide to English Studies.* 2d ed. Chicago: U of Chicago P, 1971.

Hartnoll, Phyllis. *The Oxford Companion to the Theatre.* 4th ed. New York: Oxford UP, 1983.

Harvey, Paul, and Dorothy Eagle, eds. *The Oxford Companion to English Literature.* 4th ed. New York: Oxford UP, 1967.

Spiller, Robert, et al. *Literary History of the United States.* 4th ed. 2 vols. New York: Macmillan, 1974.

Ward, A. W., and A. R. Waller, eds. *The Cambridge History of English Literature.* 15 vols. New York: Putnam's, 1907–33.

Bateson, F. W., ed. *Cambridge Bibliography of English Literature.* 5 vols. New York: Macmillan, 1941–57.

MLA International Bibliography of Books and Articles on the Modern Languages and Literatures, published annually since 1922. New York: Modern Language Association.

Music and Dance

Apel, Willi. *The Harvard Dictionary of Music.* 2d rev. ed. Cambridge: Harvard UP, 1969.

Blom, Eric. *Everyman's Dictionary of Music.* New York: NAL, 1973.

Chujoy, Anatole, and P. W. Manchester. *The Dance Encyclopedia.* New York: Simon, 1978.

Moore, Frank L., comp. *Crowell's Handbook of World Opera.* Westport, Conn.: Greenwood, 1974.

Stambler, Irwin. *Encyclopedia of Pop, Rock, and Soul.* New York: St. Martin's, 1977.

Thompson, Oscar. *International Cyclopedia of Music and Musicians.* 10th ed. New York: Dodd, 1975.

Philosophy and Religion

Buttrick, George Arthur, and Keith R. Crim, eds. *The Interpreter's Dictionary of the Bible.* 5 vols. Nashville: Abingdon, 1976.

Cross, F. L., and Elizabeth A. Livingston. *The Oxford Dictionary of the Christian Church,* New York: Oxford UP, 1974.

Edwards, Paul, ed. *The Encyclopedia of Philosophy.* 4 vols. New York: Free Press, 1973.

Fern, Vergilius, ed. *An Encyclopedia of Religion.* Westport, Conn.: Greenwood, 1976.

Encyclopedia Judaica. 16 vols.

The Social and Behavioral Sciences

General

Sills, David L., ed. *International Encyclopedia of the Social Sciences.* 8 vols. New York: Free, 1977.

American Men and Women of Science—Social and Behavioral Sciences. Most recent ed. New York: Bowker.

Social Sciences Index, published quarterly since 1974. New York: Wilson.

Note: From 1965 to 1974 these author and subject indexes were combined in the *Social Sciences and Humanities Index.* From 1907 to 1965 the combined volume was called the *International Index.*

Business, Economics, Management

Heyel, Carl. *The Encyclopedia of Management.* 3d ed. New York: Van Nostrand, 1982.

Munn, Glenn G. *Encyclopedia of Banking and Finance.* 8th ed. Ed. Ferdinand L. Garcia. Boston: Bankers, 1983.

Business Periodicals Index, published annually since 1958. New York: Wilson. From 1913 to 1957 this work was combined with the *Applied Science and Technology Index* in the *Industrial Arts Index.*

Daniell, Lorna M. *Business Information Sources.* U of California P, 1976. A bibliography that covers all aspects of business and management; lists books, periodicals, looseleaf services.

Education

The Education Index, published monthly since 1929. New York: Wilson.

Psychology

Beigel, Hugo G. *A Dictionary of Psychology and Related Fields.* New York: Frederick Ungar, 1974.

Psychological Abstracts, published monthly since 1927. Washington, D.C.: American Psychological Association.

Sociology

Mitchell, G. Duncan, ed. *A Dictionary of Sociology.* Chicago: Aldine, 1967.

Political Science

Political Handbook of the World. Annual Publication.
Almanac of American Politics. Annual Publication.
American Political Dictionary. 6th ed., 1982.

Science and Technology

American Men and Women of Science. 14th ed. 8 vols. New York: Bowker, 1979.

Collocott, Thomas C. *Chambers Dictionary of Science and Technology.* New ed. New York: Barnes & Noble, 1972.

Gray, Peter. *The Encyclopedia of Biological Sciences.* 2d ed. Melbourne: Krieger, 1981.

Lapedes, Daniel N., ed. *The McGraw-Hill Encyclopedia of Science and Technology.* New York: McGraw, 1977.

The Larousse Encyclopedia of Animal Life. London: Hamlyn, 1967.

Applied Science and Technology Index, published monthly since 1958. New York: Wilson. From 1913 to 1957 this work was combined with the *Business Periodicals Index* in the *Industrial Arts Index.*

Biological Abstracts, published semimonthly since 1926. Philadelphia: Biological Abstracts.

Computerized Aids to Research

On-Line Library Systems.   Once you have a title, or an author and title, this system (if your library has it) will give you access to several million books and other library material held by approximately 3,000 cooperating libraries throughout the country. These items can be borrowed for you through the Interlibrary Loan services.

Computerized Information Search Using a Database.   In this system, the library can search for information on a wide variety of subjects. Given the subject, a librarian who is specially trained to do such a search can obtain lists of publications in minutes.

The Card Catalogue

The books the library has in its collection can be found by using the card catalogue. Every book appears on three cards: (1) an **author card,** (2) a **title card,** and (3) a **subject card.** If you know the author's name or if you want books by an author whose name you know, look the name up in the card catalogue. (Authors' names are listed alphabetically, last name first.) If there's a title you want, look it up alphabetically. You may want to see what the library has on a specific subject but may not know names of authors or books on the subject. Again working alphabetically, look up the subject in the card catalogue to find cards for the books the library has on that subject.

Books are identified by **call numbers.** The books have this call number printed on them, and the same number appears on all three kinds of cards. These numbers represent a system of organizing books in a library, classifying them by subject area. (There are two systems of call numbers. The Library of Congress system, which uses letters of the alphabet in its top line to classify the material (e.g., PN6261) and the older Dewey decimal system, which uses numbers (e.g., 959.7) in its top line. This need not trouble you. Your library will have a directory that tells you where you can find books by call number in either system.)

A good idea when you are beginning your research is to look in the subject catalogue under your subject or to look up any specific authors or books you already know about. Write down one or two call numbers. Then go to the place in the library where these call numbers are located. You will find that you have located the place where books on this subject or by this author are located—or at least one of the places. Prepare to spend some time in front of this set of shelves. Have a seat (the floor will do nicely) and browse through the books, one after the other. You will get some good ideas, you will get a feel for your subject, and you will be able to choose which books will be worth taking out, which will be worth only a few notes taken on the spot, and which you will simply leave behind.

Study the sample cards in Figure 11. You will find author, title, and subject cards, as previously explained.

TAKING NOTES: NOTE CARDS

What Are Notes?

This question may seem elementary but it is crucial, for good notes will, in the long run, save you time and anxiety. Notes, whether of a class or from a book, should not be a copy of every word. Such exhaustive note taking is physically tiring and time consuming, and it only postpones the inevitable process of selecting and digesting what is truly important. No paper that relies on several sources *plus* what you have to say on the subject has the space for pages of word-for-word quotations. Better to refer us to the source and be done with it. But that leaves *you* out and defeats the purpose of the assignment.

Try to see the movement of information from its source to your finished paper as a process during which data is filtered, sifted, sorted, rearranged, and used in a meaningful way by you, finally to be included in your paper. Your reading or skimming of hundreds of pages will result in a ten- to fifteen-page paper. Obviously, at some point, that data will *have* to be selected and filtered. The *best* time for "filtration" is during your note taking. As your notes grow, your pile of books and articles will shrink. When your note taking is finished, you should, theoretically, no longer need those books and articles. How much smaller and easier to manage is a pile of well-taken notes!

Note taking is an art, which you can improve with practice. In class, for example, listen carefully and write down everything you need to know, but be as brief as possible. Take short-cuts: use abbreviations (designed to be meaningful to you even a year from now); do *not* use complete sentences unless needed for understanding (use the subjects and verbs without articles and unnecessary adjectivals and adverbials); leave out *unnecessary* examples. Do this as you go, and you will become practiced at "filtering" all you hear or read, until you are left with only what you will need. The act of writing in a *non*automatic way has the added effect of supporting your memory. When your mind is actively engaged in working with material, it retains it better. For this reason, shorthand and tape recorders are not good academic tools. *Do* use a tape

FIGURE 11

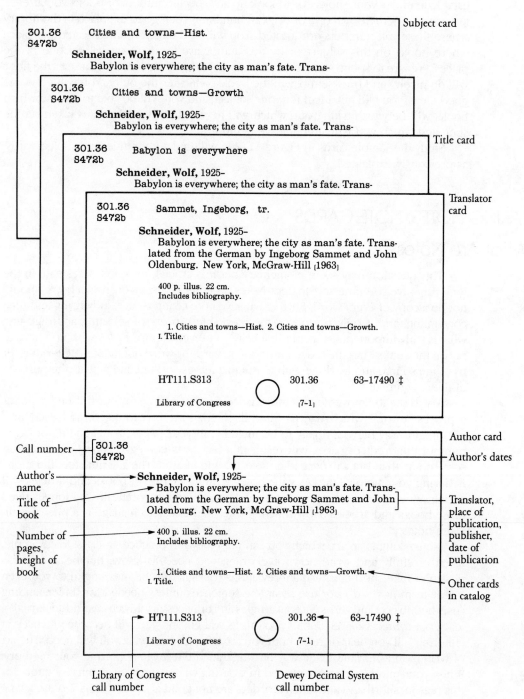

Subject card

301.36   Cities and towns—Hist.
S472b
    Schneider, Wolf, 1925-
        Babylon is everywhere; the city as man's fate. Trans-

301.36   Cities and towns—Growth
S472b
    Schneider, Wolf, 1925-
        Babylon is everywhere; the city as man's fate. Trans-

Title card

301.36   Babylon is everywhere
S472b
    Schneider, Wolf, 1925-
        Babylon is everywhere; the city as man's fate. Trans-

Translator card

301.36   Sammet, Ingeborg, tr.
S472b
    Schneider, Wolf, 1925-
        Babylon is everywhere; the city as man's fate. Trans-
        lated from the German by Ingeborg Sammet and John
        Oldenburg. New York, McGraw-Hill [1963]

        400 p. illus. 22 cm.
        Includes bibliography.

            1. Cities and towns—Hist. 2. Cities and towns—Growth.
        I. Title.

        HT111.S313   301.36   63-17490 ‡
        Library of Congress   [7-1]

Author card

Call number—[301.36
                S472b

Author's dates

Author's
name—→**Schneider, Wolf,** 1925-
Title of—→Babylon is everywhere; the city as man's fate. Trans-
book   lated from the German by Ingeborg Sammet and John
              Oldenburg. New York, McGraw-Hill [1963]

Translator,
place of
publication,
publisher,
date of
publication

Number of—→400 p. illus. 22 cm.
pages,   Includes bibliography.
height of
book

            1. Cities and towns—Hist. 2. Cities and towns—Growth.
        I. Title.

Other cards
in catalog

        HT111.S313   301.36   63-17490 ‡
        Library of Congress   [7-1]

Library of Congress
call number

Dewey Decimal System
call number

recorder to record a lecture you may not fully understand, so that you may listen to it further at your leisure. But *do not* allow a tape recorder to replace note taking. Take notes even though your tape recorder is running or take notes later from the tape recording you made.

A paper does not require as thorough a note-taking job as a class. You will probably want to have a record of every point your instructor makes on a subject, either to help you study for your examination or as a source of knowledge about the subject to which you will return later to refresh your memory. A paper, on the other hand, focuses on a limited topic; therefore, you will want to leave out everything that is not directly related to it. For this reason, *you would do well to narrow your topic as soon as possible.*

Summary, Paraphrase, or Direct Quote?

As you do your reading and note taking, you will have to make this choice. If a brief summary is sufficient, simply summarize the facts or ideas. Should you want to include an amount of information closer to the original, either in supportive detail or depth, express it in your own words, including what is important and excluding what you do not need. This is paraphrasing. Summary and paraphrase should form the bulk of your note taking.

As an example, let us examine this passage written by V. S. Naipaul.* The reference is to a far Eastern country.

> Money, going down, has created a whole educated generation of village people and drawn them into the civilization that once appeared to be only on the outer edge of darkness but is now universal.
>
> These young people do not always like what they find. Some have studied abroad, done technical subjects; but not many of them really know where they have been. In Australia, England, or the United States they still look for the manners and customs of home; their time abroad sours them, throws them back more deeply into themselves. They cannot go back to the village. They are young, but the life of their childhood has changed.

The following *summarizes* the main idea.

> Many young village people who have studied technical subjects abroad feel displaced by their education.

Now read it as it might be *paraphrased.* (Note that these examples are put into complete sentence form. This is the way they might appear in the finished paper. *Notes,* as you will see below, need not be in sentence form but should contain the essential information you want to use.)

> Many of the young people from the village who have studied technical subjects abroad have not really paid attention to life in the host countries; rather

---

* *Among the Believers: An Islamic Journey* (New York: Knopf, 1981) 227.

they look in vain for the ways of their home, and this results in their becoming withdrawn and disillusioned. Still, they have changed too much to go back to the village.

No doubt you would paraphrase it differently. How? Try it.

When should you quote directly? You should use direct quotation when the original is so effectively worded that you want to convey those *exact* words. You may feel the author's own words give the idea more authority. Another justification for using exact words is the situation where paraphrasing would be longer or more cumbersome than the original. Quote sparingly, using your own carefully thought-out judgment. Remember, this paper is still yours; therefore the bulk of it should be in your words.

Use quotation marks on your notes when you quote so that when you write your paper you will know which words you must put in quotation marks. *You must put exact quotations in quotation marks.* Should your quotation be four or more lines long (more than two lines long, if in poetry) use the following method. Begin the quoted passage on the next line and indent it on the left and the right. Do not use quotation marks when you use this method. Let us return to the preceding quotation from Naipaul for the examples.

Dropped and Indented Long Quotation

In speaking of the education of village people from a far Eastern country, V. S. Naipaul says:

> These young people do not always like what they find. Some have studied abroad, done technical subjects; but not many of them really know where they have been. In Australia, England, or the United States they still look for the manners and customs of home; their time abroad sours them, throws them back more deeply into themselves. They cannot go back to the village. They are young, but the life of their childhood has changed.

Quoted Material Incorporated into the Text of the Paper

There are foreign students who adapt very well to life in an American university. Most feel homesick for a while but soon adjust to this new life. There are some, however, who never learn to like it. They study the technology they have come to learn but do not "really know where they have been. In Australia, England, or the United States they still look for the manners and customs of home." In such cases their experience abroad, rather than making them feel enriched, makes them feel displaced and unhappy.

Adding to or Deleting from Direct Quotes.

Any time you leave out a word or words from a quoted passage, you must use an ellipsis mark ... to show that something has been left out.

Any time you add or change a word in a quotation you must use square brackets [ ] to show that the words inside have been inserted by you and not by the author of the quotation.

> Fourscore and seven years ago our fathers brought . . . upon this continent a
> new nation [the United States], conceived in liberty and dedicated to the
> proposition that all men are created equal.
>
> (Abraham Lincoln, opening sentence of the Gettysburg Address)

The Whys and Hows of Note Cards

Notes can be taken on any kind of paper: in notebooks, on scratch paper, on the backs of envelopes. Why bother with index cards? Why go to the expense? Why be so regimented when our own personal system might suit us better? True, one finds one's own short cuts and techniques; even so, the note-card system is probably the most efficient in the long run. It certainly is standard practice and important to learn. Variations upon the note-card system can come after you have mastered the system.

Why Note Cards?   The most important reason is that *cards,* in their size, uniformity, and thickness, *form the most mobile and the most flexible units of information.* As such, they are *classifiable,* an important consideration for the purpose of organization. This will become clearer as you continue to follow the hows of using note cards.

How to Use Note Cards.   You will use two kinds of cards. On *bibliography cards* you will record all the information you need in order to refer to the book in your citations and list of works cited. (These will be explained later in this chapter.) Since you will not need much space for this information, a 3 × 5″ index card will be sufficient. (See Figure 12.) *Make out a card like this for every source you use before you begin to take your notes.*

On *note cards* you will actually be recording information. Since you may have more to write down on such a card, the best size is 4 × 6″. (Details follow on how to use this system most efficiently.)

One Major Idea per Card.   Since the main advantage of note cards is their flexibility as a collection of movable parts of information, it is very important to put only one major idea on each card. You will, of course, include information supporting it or directly related to it. This is the reason that 4 × 6″ is a good size: Smaller is *too* small, and you will run out of space before you have recorded your whole idea; larger is so large that you'll be tempted to put *other* ideas on the same card. *Remember: Do not try to save money on notecards! It is worth it to use a few more cards in the interest of having flexible and classifiable units.*

Key Words at Top of Card.   To help you classify your cards, put a key word or phrase at the top that will indicate, at a glance, what specific information is on that card. This is often a difficult part of the process until you become accustomed to it, but it is a *valuable mental tool,* both as a way of forcing you to crystallize your ideas and notes and as a way of classifying and dividing. As you narrow your topic and do more research on it, you may find that what seemed like a small category is really a major

FIGURE 12

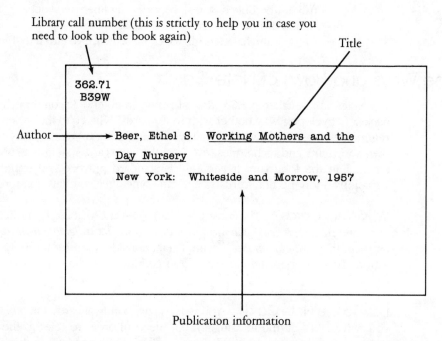

Library call number (this is strictly to help you in case you need to look up the book again)

Title

Author ⟶

362.71
B39W

Beer, Ethel S. Working Mothers and the Day Nursery

New York: Whiteside and Morrow, 1957

Publication information

one, and you will want to get more precise and specific as you progress. That's good. Key words that are general and all-encompassing defeat the purpose, which is to help you quickly group like cards together. Don't forget that *you will be collecting information from several different sources, and your paper will be organized, not by sources, but by like ideas.* That is why it's so important to put one idea on a card and to label it in such a way as to make it easy to relate to other cards on the same subject, regardless of their source.

Source and Page Number on Each Card. *Every* card must have on it a way of identifying *exactly* where you got that information. On the bottom of each card, write the last name of the author and the page number. That's all you need unless you have more than one author by the same last name or more than one book or article by the same author. In this case, add whatever is necessary, an initial or a key word from the title, to identify the source accurately. *You do not need more information on the note card because you already have it on the bibliography card. Always* remember to record the page number. You will need it, and it is very frustrating to have to search through an entire book to find the source of that note, especially if you have to make a special trip to the library to find it.

You Too Can Be a Source. Put your own ideas and analyses or interpretation on cards as well, labeling with key words, using your own initials as your source identification. Your ideas are also worth putting down and using; you will *not* remember your own idea as well as you think you will; you may not remember, after a lot of research, whether you *thought* that idea or read it somewhere.

Note: The identification plus the key words are *all* you need to identify that card. *Do not,* as some may suggest, use some kind of code number or letter to identify the card. For one thing, you should associate the information with the name of the author from whom you learned it. For another, what if you lose your list identifying these codes designations? *The last name of the author and the page number* are your *best* identification and your simplest.

Do not number your cards. This will only discourage the very flexibility you achieve by using cards. Imagine that you have dropped the pile of cards, and they are in a jumbled mess. How will you know the correct order? There should be no order until you have decided what it will be, at the outline stage of the paper. What order you have as you go depends on key words or like ideas together, and cards on the same source, as identified by the author's name. *No other grouping, no sequence in your note taking, has any relevance.*

When *should* cards be numbered? When you are continuing an idea onto a second or third card, your author, page number, and key words, plus the number (2) or (3) at the top will make it obvious that those cards belong together as a single unit of information.

Your note card should look like the one in Figure 13.

Important: Write on only *one* side of a card. (You want to be able to *see* any combination of ideas together.) Write in ink. (Pencil will smudge with handling.)

"Playing Cards."   You can now see how a group of cards prepared in this way will help you organize and write. You can now "shuffle" the cards, sort them by category, lay them out on a large table or on the floor, look over the order they will be in, change your mind, move an idea to another place, change the order, try another

FIGURE   1 3

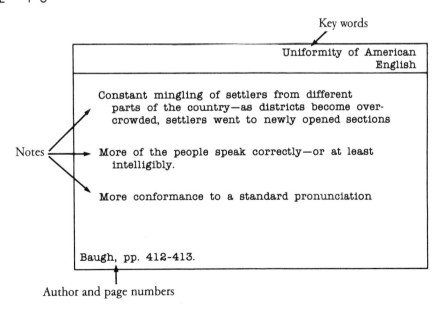

order—all because you have the *mobility* and *flexibility* that a system of *well-labeled* note cards, one subject per card, allows you.

□   EXERCISE

Taking notes on note cards: Use key words, identify source, and include page number.

1. (a) Make a note card, using a summary, of the following paragraph; (b) make note cards using a paraphrase.

> Japan for all its recent Westernization is still an aristocratic society. Every greeting, every contact must indicate the kind and degree of social distance between men. Every time a man says to another "Eat" or "Sit down" he uses different words if he is addressing someone familiarly or is speaking to an inferior or to a superior. There is a different "you" that must be used in each case and the verbs have different stems. The Japanese have, in other words, what is called a "respect language," as many other peoples do in the Pacific, and they accompany it with proper bows and kneelings. All such behavior is governed by meticulous rules and conventions; it is not merely necessary to know to whom one bows but it is necessary to know how much one bows. A bow that is right and proper to one's host would be resented as an insult by another who stood in a slightly different relationship to the bower. And bows range all the way from kneeling with forehead lowered to the hands placed flat upon the floor, to the mere inclination of head and shoulders. One must learn, and learn early, how to suit the obeisance to each particular case.*

2. Do the same with the paragraphs below, including some quoted material. Don't forget to put quoted material in quotation marks.

> Both the technical and the social components of "civilization" made their appearance at almost the same time in the classic river valleys from the Nile to the Hwang Ho; and if the mixture of a diversity of needs and inventions was responsible for the immense explosion of power that actually took place, no better geographic conditions for such a mixture could be found. For until wheeled vehicles were invented, and horses and camels domesticated—indeed right down to the end of the nineteenth century—the river was the backbone of both transportation and communication; even the wide ocean was a smaller obstacle to human intercourse than mountain and desert.
>
> The great rivers were drainage basins, not only of water, but of culture, not only of plants, but of occupations and technical inventions; and the existence of a river guaranteed the water supply necessary for large crops from their heavily silted soils. In Mesopotamia two, sometimes three, crops of

---

* Ruth Benedict, *The Chrysanthemum and the Sword: Patterns of Japanese Culture* (Boston: Houghton, 1946), 47–48.

barley or wheat were possible every year. Under proper management, which was forthcoming, the mainly subsistence economy of the village would be turned into an economy of abundance.*

FINAL NARROWING DOWN, THE THESIS SENTENCE, AND THE OUTLINE

After the final choice of topics, surely this stage is the most difficult. The encouraging part of it is that once you have finished this task, the actual writing of the paper is relatively easy, much easier than you anticipated.

Chapter 6 teaches these skills. If you have not read Chapter 6, this would be the time to do so; even if you have, go back and review the process of narrowing down, writing a thesis sentence, and creating an outline. Refer to whatever you need to help you arrive at your thesis sentence and your outline.

DOCUMENTATION

Documentation includes *citations* and a *list of works cited*. In simple language, such a list tells your reader which sources you used to find the data for your paper; the individual citation, usually placed in parentheses at the point in your paper where you actually quote or refer to an outside source, tells your reader the exact place where that particular information can be found. In the past, footnotes (or endnotes†) were used for this purpose, but since 1984 the system recommended by the Modern Language Association (MLA) has been simplified. This new, simplified system is what we will be learning in this book, though we will also see what the older system looks like (see page 303) so that you will recognize it as you do your research in books published before 1984. You may also have professors who still want you to use the older system.

Why Citations?

Citations tell the reader of your paper where you found the information you are presenting. There are several reasons for providing such an exact acknowledgment of sources.

You must give credit where credit is due. This is the only fair and honest way. To pass off what someone else has written as if it were your own idea is like stealing what is not yours. To do this is the equivalent of cheating and will not be tolerated in

---

* Lewis Mumford, *Technics and Human Development,* vol. 1 of *Myth of the Machine* (New York: Harcourt, 1966, 1967) 165.

† These same notes, when they are placed on separate pages following the text of the paper, are called endnotes. Footnotes technically refer to the notes placed at the bottom of each page of the text (such as this note). We will, for the purpose of simplifying the discussion, refer to both as footnotes or notes.

any course or, later in your life, in any scholarship or publication. It is called *plagiarism,* a term your instructor may already have explained. It means to present someone else's thinking or writing as if it were your own, "to give the impression that you have written or thought something that you have in fact borrowed from another."* This applies not only to exact quotations but also to paraphrases and summaries. When in doubt, use a citation.

This rule does *not* apply, however, to what is called *common knowledge.* Common knowledge is a term used for commonly known facts (or quotations so well known as not to require acknowledgment unless you are quoting word for word). Such facts can be found in many sources and are therefore not credited to anyone. "America was discovered by Columbus in 1492" is common knowledge. You may have a problem deciding what is common knowledge on your subject simply because you may not be familiar with that common body of knowledge. If, as you do research, you find the same information in several sources or you find that this information is unacknowledged by those sources, as if that author assumes you already know it, you may consider it common knowledge. *Again, when in doubt, cite.*

You will achieve credibility and authority. Often, the difference between a respected book by a writer whom people trust and a book no intelligent person pays attention to is whether or not the book is documented. (This, by the way, is a good test for you to apply to books on your subject. A well-documented book is more worthy of *your* trust.) If you present facts, statistics, or interpretations, the careful reader will want to know *where* you found that information. Who said so? Whose opinion was it? What kind of study yielded those statistics? Maybe you are just making them up; it has been done before! Such information must be *verifiable,* that is, capable of being checked for truth and accuracy.

The reader may want to refer to your source. Maybe the reader wants to read more about the subject because you have caught his or her interest. Maybe he wants to see that information in its larger context. Maybe he wants to challenge you. All of these reasons are legitimate, so providing the information is actually a courtesy to the reader.

How to Cite

The best reference on the rules and conventions of documentation is the *MLA Handbook for Writers of Research Papers,* second edition. This is the style most often used in English and the humanities. The sciences and social sciences have slightly different styles, and there are handbooks explaining those styles in detail as well. In a chapter such as this, only a few standard examples can be provided. Should you have more specialized kinds of questions or references, you will find hundreds of examples in the *MLA Handbook.*

The main thing to remember is that your paper will have a list of works cited at the end of it. On that list, every book or article you used will be listed, together with

---

* *MLA Handbook for Writers of Research Papers, Theses, and Dissertations* (New York: MLA, 1977) 4.

all the information one would need to identify it, such as author, title, place of publication, publisher, and date of publication. Because all this information is provided at the end of the paper, the text of the paper itself only needs to show the reader what information is being cited, and where exactly it came from. Parentheses at the end of the cited material will show what needs to be acknowledged. The author's last name and the page number will usually be sufficient to lead the reader exactly to the right place.

If you understand this principle, then common sense should help you decide how much or how little you need to put in the parentheses. For example:

> We see that American college students are feeling very pressured by the need to compete for places in the top graduate and professional schools (Brown 45).

This shows us that this information came from page 45 in the book or article by someone with the last name of Brown. The list of works cited will have all the information on Brown's book or article, and we can assume from the way Brown was cited that there is only one Brown, and only one work by Brown, on that list.

On the other hand, notice the differences in the following:

> Brown shows us that American college students are feeling very pressured by the need to compete for places in the top graduate and professional schools (45).

We do not need to put the author's name in the parentheses because it is mentioned in the text.

> The American revolution was different in many ways from other revolutions (Smith, *Unusual Revolution* 3).

From the way this is cited, we can assume that more than one work by Smith is listed, and you will see that this is so when we get to the list of works cited.

> The year 1929 was a crucial one in American history (Smith, *Political History* 2:96).

Notice that there are two numbers (2:96). The first refers to a volume number (volume 2), the second to the page number.

In all of these examples, the principle has been to give the reader the exact information he or she needs (notice the page number is given every time), but no more, to identify the source on the list of works cited.

Note: If the work has two or three authors, list their names (Doe, White, and Graham 62); if there are more than three, simply use et al. after the first one (Jones et al. 75).

Works Cited

As the title indicates, this will be a list of the works you actually cited in your paper. A bibliography is also a listing of books, but a works cited list is more specific—it has on it *only those works you have referred to* in your paper. The previous section explained that we needed only the minimum information in the text itself because the full publication information would be given in the list of works cited. Now it is time to learn how to provide it in the proper form.

1. The author's name, *last* name first.
2. Title: if a book, it is underlined; if an article, or a chapter title, it is in quotation marks, followed by the title, underlined, of the periodical or book it is in.
3. Publication information, which includes place of publication, name of publisher (you may use a shortened form, such as Little instead of Little, Brown and Co., UP instead of University Press), and date of publication.

Other information that should be included where it is relevant is: editor (ed.), translator (trans.), number and date of magazines and journals.

List works in alphabetical order by last names of authors. These names will stand out if you follow the proper form, which is to put the author's last name at the margin, with subsequent lines for that citation indented. This way one can see at a glance which authors were used, and one can easily use such a list for further research.

Sample List of Works Cited (based on the preceding parenthetical references)

Brown, Sally. "A Look at American Campuses." *Collected Essays on American Universities.* Ed. Ralph Green. New York: American Publishing, 1984.

Doe, Jane Phillips, Edith White, and Ronald Graham. "Living as a Social Scientist in America." *American Journal of the Social Sciences* 18.2 (1978): 60–75.

Jones, Tom, et al. "Arriving." *News Weekly* 18 Aug. 1982: 73–78.

Smith, John R. *A Political History of The United States of America, 1776–1976.* 2 vols. Washington: Continental, 1979.

–––. *The Unusual Revolution.* New York: Historical, 1969.

Notice that the second book by the same author appears alphabetically by title *without* the author's name repeated. The three hyphens and the period show that the author is the same as that of the entry above it.

Look now at the "Doe" entry, and analyze the numbers following the name of the journal:

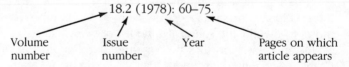

Notice also that there are no commas between parts of the date in the Jones entry.

Using Footnotes or Endnotes

Occasionally you will need to do more than simply cite the source of your information. Perhaps you have several sources on the same subject, or perhaps you want to say something about what you have just written, but you do not feel it belongs in the text. These are occasions for footnotes. Use a superscript number (like this:[1]) to mark the place where you want to make the extra notation, and then use the same number, also as a superscript, to mark the note. Footnotes (or endnotes) begin with an indented line, with subsequent lines going to the margins. This will all be illustrated in the sample term paper that follows.

In books written before 1984 you will notice that footnotes or endnotes are used for citation as well, and that the information given in the footnotes is then duplicated in the list of works cited (bibliography). It is because of this seemingly unnecessary duplication that the system has been simplified—something for which we all can be glad.

Following the sample term paper, you will find a page of the same paper as it would look with citation notes instead of parenthetical references.

The entire research paper process is summarized in Figure 14. A sample term paper follows. It was written by a student who was fascinated by the American phenomenon called rock and, therefore, decided to try to understand its appeal. As he himself realizes, the paper is speaking of what is known as hard rock and does not take into account the "milder" forms of rock, also very popular among young Americans. The hard rock fans he speaks of in this paper do not necessarily represent teenage America.

FIGURE 14   Research Strategy Guide

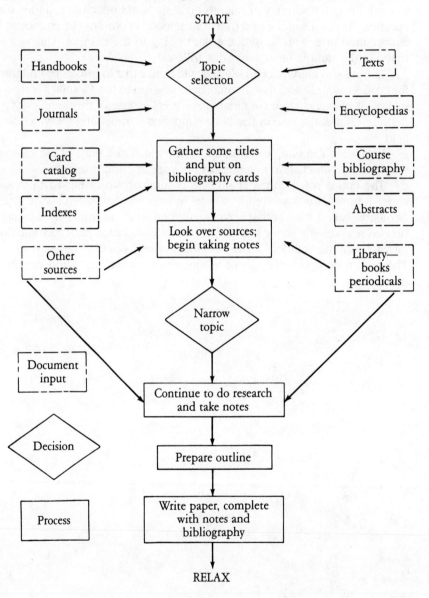

Rock Music and the American Adolescent

Khalid Abu-Eideh

English 150K

May, 1980

Rock Music and the American Adolescent

Rock music is the most popular music these days; this is because it reflects the needs and desires of adolescence.

I. Rock is the most popular music among adolescents.

    A. The proof is that adolescents like it.

    B. Radio stations play it all the time.

    C. The artists are switching to it.

    D. The rock concerts are full.

    E. Much time and money are spent on rock.

II. Rock is popular among teens because of their anti-establishment behavior:

    A. The rock stars are different.

        1. The way they dress

        2. The way they act on stage

    B. The loud music

    C. The antiestablishment words

III. Rock relates to releasing pressure and finding pleasures gratifying needs and desires.

    A. Rock involves sex, love

        1. The words

        2. The heavy beat

        3. The act of the stars

            a. The way they dress

            b. Their act on stage

    B. Rock involves drugs, alcohol

        1. The concerts

      2. The stars

      3. The songs

   C. It prevents them from wandering.

IV. Not only do teenagers like it for the above reasons, but also they spread it still further.

   A. The nature of the listeners——they don't want to be isolated.

      1. They listen to it together.

      2. All their friends are rock fans.

   B. The simplicity of the music. You don't need to ed-ucate yourself in it.

V. The music is popular among them because it reflects their needs and desires.

Note: An outline is not officially part of the content of a research paper. Teachers often ask for an outline to accompany the paper, but, more important, this one is here to illustrate the way an outline functions to help the student organize his or her paper. You may wish, as you read the paper, to follow the outline and see for yourself how it relates to the paper.

1

       Coming from a culture that is vastly different in mu-
sic styles, I was fascinated by the popularity of rock music in the United States. It seemed that rock is one obvious characteristic of the American culture. One cannot
talk about the American culture without mentioning the music that characterizes an entire generation. The great
popularity of rock music made me wonder about the cause of
this popularity. I occasionally asked friends why they
admire rock but I could not find a clear answer for my
questioning; when my English teacher assigned me a term
paper on a topic of my choice, I decided to write my paper
on rock music. I interviewed people, visited record
stores, and talked to radio stations about rock and roll
music. The object of my study was to find out why rock
was so popular among adolescents.

       It is apparent that rock is presently the most popu-
lar music among adolescents. Before we talk about rock
fans, adolescents, we have to know the age of the
adolescents. Adolescents are people approximately between
the ages of twelve and twenty-two. This expansion of the
age of adolescence is brought about by ''the increased periods spent in school and the less austere approach taken
to school subjects'' (Gottlieb and Ramsey 16), and is parallel to the expansion of the age of rock fans.
Incidentally, the age of the average rock fan ranges
between the ages of twelve and the early twenties.

       The way in which one can study the popularity of rock

music is to consider the popularity of the presenters of
rock and the ways in which rock is presented. The record-
selling business, one way in which rock is presented, confirms the popularity of rock. The number of rock records
sold is an indication of its popularity. After investigating some music stores in Cleveland, I found that a
great percentage of the tapes and records sold by music
stores is rock. In many stores, as much as 60 percent of
the records and tapes sold is rock. The average buyers
range in age between fourteen years and the early twenties.
The music stores indicated that they would sell more
rock music if it were not for the limited income of the
young age group that listens to rock (Milton, Rodeo, Sound).[1]
They thought this in spite of the fact that the average
buyer buys two or three records of tapes each month.[2]

The other ways in which rock is presented also confirm its popularity. Live rock concerts are very popular
among adolescents, and most rock concerts are attended by
a large number of them. The theaters in which the concerts are held are usually full or close to being
so. This is because most rock fans attend rock concerts
within their reach.[3] The rock concert tickets usually
sell out rapidly and the concert announcements on the radio do not need to last long (Milton). In order to be
able to get tickets before they are sold out, rock fans
have to stay alert for radio announcements concerning the
concerts. The best radio station in the United States[4]

said that its constant announcement of rock concerts is
one of the main reasons the station is so popular. The
average listener to this station ranges between the ages
of fifteen and the midtwenties. This shows how eager this
age group is to attend rock concerts, another way of presenting rock music. This, in turn, shows the great popularity of rock among adolescents.

Examining the presenters of rock confirms its popularity among its listeners. The number of musicians who
compose and perform rock music is increasing rapidly compared to the number of musicians in other types of
music. Many musicians from other types of music tend to
change their style and use rock style in writing their
music. Some of them even stop composing their other type
of music. Instead, they start writing rock music (WZZP).
An example of that is the musician Ruppert Holmes who wrote
classical music throughout his career. Now he only writes
rock music (Milton). This is caused by the increasing popularity of rock music compared to other types of music.

To understand the extent to which adolescents find
rock appealing, we can consider the time and money they
spend for the sake of listening to this music. Most rock
fans listen to rock music for about four or five hours daily.[5]
Many of them even listen to rock all the time, that is, while
working, playing, driving, and even sleeping. Many of them
said that they listened to rock ''more than twenty—four hours
a day.''[6] Rock is so appealing to adolescents that they spend

a considerable portion of their time listening to it.

Time, however, is not the only thing adolescents
spend for listening to this music. Listening to music requires having at least a radio set. This means that the
listeners may have to spend some money in order to listen
to this music. If better sound quality is sought, one has
to start considering a stereo set, a fairly expensive set
in most cases. Records and tapes also cost a considerable
amount of money. Because of the young age of rock listeners, they usually have a limited income. To buy the
equipment needed to listen to rock, they have to sacrifice
a great portion of their income. Some of them even devote
almost all of it for the sake of rock. One rock fan said
that he traded his most valuable property, his truck, for
a box full of rock tapes (Rymer). This shows how appealing rock was to him.

To understand the reasons behind the appeal of rock
to adolescents, one can analyze the nature of rock elements and then analyze the characteristics of adolescents
that make them find these elements appealing. One important element of rock music is the musician, the maker of
this music, and an important element of musicians is their
manner of dress. Dress is essential because it might be
considered one of the important reasons adolescents listen
to particular musicians (Smoker). This fascination with
the way rock stars dress can be associated with the rebellious characteristic of many adolescents, who try to

Abu-Eideh 5

''break numberless familial ties based on authority, responsibility, respect, . . . not to mention force of
habit'' (Gottlieb and Ramsey 101). The way rock stars
dress resembles rebellion to those adolescents. Rock
stars try to look different from everyday people, and the
way they dress is far from being normal. Male stars, for
example, are known to dress up in strange clothes, grow
long hair, or paint their faces. Female stars might dress
up like men or wear torn-up clothes. Rock stars try to
look different, and hence rebellious, while they perform
their music.

When one talks about the live performance of rock
stars, he or she cannot help but note the extreme wildness
of these performances. Destroying musical instruments on
stage was a common popular performance of The Who.
Explosions and streams of fire going across the
stage always accompany Kiss's performances. Having in-
flatable puppets thirty feet tall, resembling mothers,
teachers, and other forms of authority, accompanied the
performance of the ''Wall.'' The ''Wall,'' incidentally,
is currently the top-selling album in the United
States (''Top Forty''). The performance of rock stars on
stage resembles rebellion, a natural characteristic of
adolescence.

Not only are the rock concerts characterized by wild
performances but also they are known for loud and rowdy
music. The heavy beat and the loud sound are character-

istics of rock music and sound revolutionary and rebellious. Some people said that this loud, rowdy music
was the main reason they listened to rock (Conley). This
music sounds appealing to adolescents because of its being
characterized by rebellion. ''The public response to rock
obviously reflects the revolutionary character of the music'' (Belz 183).

    This revolutionary music is often played with rev-
olutionary lyrics, which are often on the subject of
rebellion. It tells the adolescents to rebel against
their parents, government, and way of life. The current
best-selling album in the United States is the ''Wall''
(''Top Forty''). The most requested song on the album
(''Top Forty'') is characterized by the repetition of the
lines:

        We don't need no education,

        We don't need no thought control. . .

        Hey, teacher, leave us kids alone.

The Wall criticizes harshly the way teachers, mothers, and
other forms of authority interfere in young people's ways
of life. ''Adolescents like the album because they like
to rebel against the establishment'' (Smoker).

    Rock is so appealing to adolescents because of its
resemblance to rebellion in all its elements, including
the musicians, the music, and the lyrics. The sixties
provide a good example of the relation between rock and
rebellion against authority. At a time of conflict be-

tween adolescents and authority, the most popular people
were stars such as Jimmy Hendrix and The Who. Their resemblance to rebellion made them the most popular rock musicians at that time.

Rebellion is not the only characteristic of
adolescents. At their age, they are full of desires,
needs, and anxieties, one of which is the search for a
partner of the opposite sex. ''Young people will move toward both a concern for and involvement with members of
the opposite sex'' (Gottlieb and Ramsey 183). The songs
that deal with and discuss their anxieties about sex and
love are appealing to them. ''We find that those songs
declaring that being in love is part of growing up or is a
part of youthful years are the ones that become 'teen
hits' '' (Gottlieb and Ramsey 174).

Rock music deals with anxiety regarding love and sex
in all its elements. The lyrics of rock often discuss
this. Some may take the form of telling about the emotions
of love shared between two people or talking about their
dreams, memories, or problems. An example is the song
''You Don't Talk to Me Anymore.'' The song is filled with
two lovers' memories and the good times they used to have
before they dampened their relationship. The song ''Got a
Lot of Love'' describes a man's feelings and anxiety about
a woman he loves very much, but she doesn't feel the same
way about him. The lyrics might also take another
approach to the relation with a partner of the other

Abu-Eideh 8

sex. One example is the song ''Why Don't We Do It in the
Road?'' or ''Sit on My Face Stevie Nicks.'' The lyrics of
these songs suggest sexual relationships very bluntly.
The lyrics might also deal with both sex and love,
like the song ''Paradise by the Dashboard Lights,'' in
which two lovers compare their views of the importance of
sex and love.

The music of rock is suggestive and is characterized
by the heavy beat that gets the listener to feel more in-
tensely (Smoker). Some people think that almost all rock
music suggests sexual relations. The stars ''reign as
monarchs of a noisy, sweaty, untidy world that has all the
sexual disorders of a Hogarth print'' (Stinnet 26-27). It
is apparent, however, that rock music that suggests sexual
relationships appeals to most adolescents (Smoker). Most
of Led Zeppelin's music, for example, suggests sex and
love. This is the most popular star in some areas of the
country (Smoker).

The rock stars writing the music and the lyrics and
performing rock songs usually try to suggest relations
with partners of the opposite sex to their audience. They
try to look attractive and sexy. Some of them dress in
clothes that reveal their physical attractiveness; others
are known for their ''sexy voices'' (Smoker). Some of
them go further than that--like Jim Morrison, who actually
exposed himself on stage while performing at a concert
(''Top Forty'').

Abu-Eideh 9

Many adolescents listen to a particular rock star because he looks especially sexually attractive to them (Smoker). This went to the extreme of developing groups who follow the stars around and try to have sex with them after their performances. Since adolescents have the desires to have such relationships and have anxieties about them, they find rock appealing.

Not only does rock deal with and discuss anxieties of adolescents such as sex and love, but also it deals with ways of escaping anxieties and reducing tensions, such as taking alcohol and drugs.

Alcohol and drugs are obvious means of escaping anxieties and tensions. ''Alcohol tends to reduce anxiety or fear, as well as other sources of tension''(Conger 473). A research study showed that about 63 percent of high school juniors in 1973 had gotten drunk once or more the year before that (Conger 468). It seems that drugs and alcohol are used on a large scale among adolescents as a means of escaping their parents and anxieties. Another 1973 study showed that 50 percent of the people ranging from the ages of eighteen and twenty-one had taken marijuana (Conger 485).

Although many adults try to advise adolescents to give up drugs and alcohol, rock opposes that and encourages the use of drugs and alcohol as a means of escape. Rock stars themselves provide an example of escapism by the use of drugs and alcohol themselves.

Examples of this are plenty. Jimmy Hendrix died of a heroin overdose. Keith Moon was convicted of possession
of a pound of heroin and he later died of alcoholism
(Conley). The rock stars' use of alcohol and drugs suggests these means of escape to the listening adolescents
who have many of the same anxieties and tensions to escape
from.

   The rock lyrics written by rock stars often relate to
and suggest use of drugs and alcohol. In some songs alcohol and drugs are mentioned in the song but are not the
main subject. Examples of this are The Pina Colada's song
''Sex'n'Drugs'n'Rock'n'Roll,'' in which alcohol and drugs
are not the main theme but are mentioned on the side as
means of enjoyment and escape. In other songs, drugs and
alcohol are the main themes of the song. They appeal to
the listener's desire for excitement and escape. A song
can promise, for example, that a drug will get you high
when you are bored, carry you off to where you will be
smiling in a fantasy world. One such song was among the
top forty hits of the decade (Conley). The escapism by
means of drugs and alcohol mentioned in the lyrics of
rock seems to appeal to adolescents.

   Rock concerts, another important element of rock,
seem to invite adolescents to escape their anxieties by
taking drugs and alcohol. Alcoholic drinks are served at
most rock concerts, and the audience starts drinking alcohol and taking drugs before the concert starts. By the

time the performance starts, many would already be high,
drunk, or both (Fisher). One student (Rymer) said that
the main reason for going to rock concerts is ''to get
drunk and have a good time.'' I personally saw a friend
take LSD before going to a Grateful Dead concert. He said
he had to take it if he was to enjoy the concert and fit
into the atmosphere. This atmosphere that rock concerts
provide appeals to adolescents who want to escape their
anxieties and tensions.

Rock, per se, is another way for the adolescent to
escape anxieties and tensions. Rock makes their minds
busy listening to the songs instead of wandering and
thinking about things that might disturb them. One rock
fan said that he listens to rock because, as he says, ''I
do not like my mind wandering and rock gives me something
to be distracted with instead of wandering'' (Rymer).
Another student who was asked why he listened to rock
seven hours a day answered that it was simply because his
radio was on all day. He, by the way, happened to think
that rock was ''all garbage and not a form of art''
(Fisher). Many of the interviewed people said they listened to rock just because there was a radio on. Although
not all rock fans realize it, rock itself seems to provide
a means of escape for adolescents from their anxieties and
tensions. This explains why most rock fans listen to rock
while doing homework, working, and driving.[7] It keeps
their minds busy all the time.

Abu—Eideh 12

When one talks about the spread of rock it is difficult not to think about the spread of rock among
adolescents. Adolescents create an excellent atmosphere
for the spread of rock. They spend a considerable fraction of their time with their peers, and their age is
''characterized by growing influence by peers'' (Gottlieb
and Ramsey 184). The adolescent has to do things that his
peers do in order to stay within his group. When his
peers listen to rock, he is most likely to have some pressure on him to listen to rock. Most interviewed rock fans
said that almost all their friends considered rock their
favorite music.

> Young people have to listen to rock because it is the
> most socially acceptable music among peers of their
> own age. However, if they decide that they like an-
> other type of music (e.g., Classical or Jazz) this
> might result in isolating them from the rest of their
> friends who listen to rock (Smoker).

Listening to rock in many cases is easier for adolescents than being isolated, and they end up listening to
rock. As we have seen, the adolescent's relationships
with peers seem to contribute to the widespread listening
of rock.

Another important factor that contributes to this
spread is its simplicity. Rock is easy to understand compared to some other types of music. The listener does not
have to have much musical background or education in order

Abu-Eideh 13

to understand the songs. ''This makes rock easier to understand compared to other types of music such as classical, where you might get lost trying to listen to a classical piece if you don't have enough experience with it''
(Milton). Rock is simpler than other types of music and
takes a plainer approach to its subjects (Milton).
This makes rock easier to spread among adolescents because
it suits the young people, who might not be able to understand other types of music.

One can see that rock is and always will be popular
among adolescents.[8] Its secret of endurance lies in its
being adolescents' music. It deals with the preoccupa-
tions and thoughts of adolescents. The simplicity of rock
and its hypnotic characteristic give it an incredible
ability to spread among adolescents; as long as there are
adolescents there will always be rock music. It seems, as
one rock star put it, that ''rock will always, always, always overcome.''[9]

Abu–Eideh 14

Notes

[1]Names of students, salesmen, and stores have been changed.

[2]This figure is based on averaging the data from people interviewed.

[3]Data from approximately thirty rock fans.

[4]I was told by friends that <u>Rolling Stone</u> magazine rated WMMS to be the best radio FM rock station in the United States.

[5]Averaging period of time given by people interviewed.

[6]John Rymer, engineering student, Case Western Reserve University; a fourteen-year-old female student at Cleveland Heights High School; and an eighteen-year-old waitress at a fast-food restaurant.

[7]From listening to rock radio stations.

[8]From interviewing approximately thirty people.

[9]Pete Townshend. This statement is played frequently on WMMS radio station, Cleveland, Ohio.

Abu—Eideh 15

Works Cited

<u>Books</u> <u>and</u> <u>Periodicals</u>

Belz, Carl. <u>The Story of Rock.</u> 2d ed. New York: Oxford,
    1972.

Conger, John Janeway. <u>Adolescence and Youth</u>. New York:
    Harper, 1973.

Gottlieb, David, and Ramsey, Charles E. <u>The American Ado-</u>
    <u>lescent</u>. 2d ed. Homewood, Ill.: The Dorsey Press,
    1964.

Stinnet, Caskie. ''I Know It's Only Rock'n'Roll But I Hate
    It.'' <u>Rolling Stone</u> [date omitted], 26—27.

<u>Interviews</u> <u>and</u> <u>Radio</u> <u>Programs</u>

''American Top Forty Show.'' WZZP radio station, Cleve-
    land, Ohio.

Conley, Timothy. Engineering student, Case Western Reserve
    University, Cleveland, Ohio.

Fisher, Gary. Student at Case Western Reserve University,
    Cleveland, Ohio.

Record Rodeo. Salesman, Cleveland, Ohio.

Rymer, John. Engineering student, Case Western Reserve
    University, Cleveland, Ohio.

Smoker. Program Manager, WYLT radio station, Cleveland,
    Ohio.

Sound of Stereo Record Stores. Cleveland, Ohio.

Townshend, Pete. WMMS radio station, Cleveland, Ohio.

WZZP radio station broadcast, 1980.

A Sample Page Using Footnote Style

Adolescents are people approximately between the ages of twelve and twenty-two. This expansion of the age of adolescence is brought about by ''the increased periods spent in school and the less austere approach taken to school subjects,''[1] and it is parallel to the expansion of the age of rock fans. Incidentally, the age of the average rock fan ranges between the ages of twelve and the early twenties.

The record-selling business, one way in which rock is presented, confirms the popularity of rock. The number of rock records sold is an indication of its popularity. After investigating some music stores in Cleveland, I found that a great percentage of the tapes and records sold by music stores consists of rock. In many stores, rock comprises as much as 60 percent of the records and tapes sold. The average buyers range in age between fourteen and the early twenties. The music stores indicated that they would sell more rock music if it were not for the limited income of the young age group that listens to rock.[2] They thought this in spite of the fact that the average buyer buys two or three records or tapes each month.[3]

[1] David Gottlieb and Charles E. Ramsey, The American Adolescent, 2d ed. (Homewood, Ill.: The Dorsey Press, 1964), p. 16.

[2] Mark Milton, Assistant Manager, Golden Music, Cleveland; Salesman at Record Rodeo, Cleveland; salesman at Sound of Stereo Stores, Cleveland.

[3] Averaging data from the people interviewed.

FURTHER READINGS

Anne Tyler, the author of the following reading selection, is a well-known writer of novels and short stories. In this story, we share the experience of a cross-cultural family. Ms. Tyler is married to an Iranian doctor, but do not therefore make the mistake of automatically identifying her with Elizabeth.

ANNE TYLER

Your Place Is Empty

1   Early in October, Hassan Ardavi invited his mother to come from Iran for a visit. His mother accepted immediately. It wasn't clear how long the visit was to last. Hassan's wife thought three months would be a good length of time. Hassan himself had planned on six months, and said so in his letter of invitation. But his mother felt that after such a long trip six months would be too short, and she was counting on* staying a year. Hassan's little girl, who wasn't yet two, had no idea of time at all. She was told that her grandmother was coming but she soon forgot about it.

2   Hassan's wife was named Elizabeth, not an easy word for Iranians to pronounce. She would have been recognized as American the world over— a blond, pretty girl with long bones and an ungraceful way of walking. One of her strong points was an ability to pick up foreign languages, and before her mother-in-law's arrival she bought a textbook and taught herself Persian. *"Salaam aleikum,"* she told the mirror every morning. Her daughter watched, startled, from her place on the potty-chair.* Elizabeth ran through possible situations in her mind and looked up the words for them. "Would you like more tea? Do you take sugar?" At suppertime she spoke Persian to her husband, who looked amused at the new tone she gave his language, with her

(1) **counting on:** (idiom) depending upon; expecting to (stay)
(2) **potty-chair:** child's small toilet

flat, factual American voice. He wrote his mother and told her Elizabeth had a surprise for her.

3   Their house was a three-story* brick Colonial, but only the first two stories were in use. Now they cleared* the third of its trunks and china barrels and *National Geographics,* and they moved in a few pieces of furniture. Elizabeth sewed flowered curtains for the window. She was unusually careful with them; to a foreign mother-in-law, fine seams* might matter. Also, Hassan bought a pocket compass, which he placed in the top dresser drawer. "For her prayers," he said. "She'll want to face Mecca.* She prays three times a day."

4   "But which direction is Mecca from here?" Elizabeth asked.

5   Hassan only shrugged. He had never said the prayers himself, not even as a child. His earliest memory was of tickling the soles of his mother's feet while she prayed steadfastly* on; everyone knew it was forbidden to pause once you'd started.

6   Mrs. Ardavi felt nervous about the descent from the plane. She inched down the staircase sideways, one hand tight on the railing, the other clutching her shawl. It was night, and cold. The air seemed curiously opaque.* She arrived on solid ground and stood collecting herself—a small, stocky* woman in black, with a kerchief over her smooth gray hair. She held her back very straight, as if she had just had her feelings hurt. In picturing this moment she had always thought Hassan would be waiting beside the plane, but there was no sign of him. Blue lights dotted the darkness behind her, an angular terminal loomed ahead, and an official was herding* the passengers toward a plate-glass door. She followed, entangled in a web* of meaningless sounds such as those you might hear in a fever dream.

7   Immigration. Baggage Claims. Customs. To all she spread her hands and beamed* and shrugged, showing she spoke no English. Meanwhile her fellow-passengers waved to a blur* of faces beyond a glass wall. It seemed they all knew people here; she was the only one who didn't. She had issued from* the plane like a newborn baby, speechless and friendless. And the customs official didn't seem pleased with her. She had brought too many

---

(3) **three-story:** having three floors
(3) **cleared:** removed the things that were in the way, so as to leave free and unobstructed
(3) **seams:** the lines formed when two pieces of material are sewn together
(3) **Mecca:** the holiest city in the Moslem religion; Moslems face Mecca when they pray
(5) **steadfastly:** without changing, constantly
(6) **opaque:** not transparent, not reflecting light, dull
(6) **stocky:** heavily built and short
(6) **herding:** forming into a group; also used when referring to a collection of animals, as driving a *herd* of cattle from one place to another while keeping them close together
(6) **web:** the network spun by a spider, in which it traps insects
(7) **beamed:** here, smiled
(7) **blur:** indistinct appearance, something seen as confused or not well defined
(7) **issued from:** came out from; flowed out from, also used to refer to birth

gifts. She had stuffed her bags with them, discarding* all but the most necessary pieces of her clothing so that she would have more room. There were silver tea sets and gold jewelry for her daughter-in-law, and for her granddaughter a doll dressed in the complicated costume of a nomad* tribe, an embroidered sheepskin vest, and two religious medals on chains—one a disc inscribed with the name of Allah,* the other a tiny gold Koran,* with a very effective prayer for long life folded up within it. The customs official sifted* gold through his fingers like sand and frowned at the Koran. "Have I done something wrong?" she asked. But of course he didn't understand her. Though you'd think, really, that if he would just *listen* hard enough, just meet her eyes once . . . it was a very simple language, there was no reason why it shouldn't come through to him.

8   For Hassan, she'd brought food. She had gathered all his favorite foods and put them in a drawstring bag embroidered with peacocks. When the official opened the bag he said something under his breath and called another man over. Together they unwrapped tiny newspaper packets and sniffed at various herbs. "Sumac," she told them. "Powder of lemons. Shambahleh." They gazed at her blankly. They untied a small cloth sack and rummaged through* the kashk she had brought for soup. It rolled beneath their fingers and across the counter—hard white balls of yogurt curd, stuck with bits of sheep hair and manure.* Some peasant had labored for hours to make that kashk. Mrs. Ardavi picked up one piece and replaced it firmly in the sack. Maybe the official understood her meaning: she was running out of patience. He threw up his hands. He slid her belongings down the counter. She was free to go.

9   Free to go where?

10   Dazed and stumbling, a pyramid of knobby parcels and bags, scraps of velvet and brocade and tapestry, she made her way to the glass wall. A door opened out of nowhere and a stranger blocked her path. "Khanom Jun," he said. It was a name that only her children would use, but she passed him blindly and he had to touch her arm before she would look up.

11   He had put on weight. She didn't know him. The last time she'd seen him he was a thin, stoop-shouldered medical student disappearing into an Air France jet without a backward glance. "Khanom Jun, it's me," this stranger said, but she went on searching his face with cloudy eyes. No doubt he was a bearer of bad news. Was that it? A recurrent* dream had warned her that she

(7) **discarding:** throwing away, getting rid of, here, deciding not to pack in her suitcase
(7) **nomad:** one of a tribe that wanders from place to place in search of fresh food for its animals, rather than staying permanently in one location
(7) **Allah:** the Moslems' name for God
(7) **Koran:** the Moslem holy book
(7) **sifted:** examined critically, usually means to pass through a sieve so as to separate coarse from fine particles
(8) **rummaged through:** searched carefully among the different objects, moving them about and turning them over
(8) **manure:** animal excrement, often used to fertilize the soil
(11) **recurrent:** occurring over and over again

would never see her son again—that he would die on his way to the airport, or had already been dead for months but no one wanted to break the news;* some second or third cousin in America had continued signing Hassan's name to his cheerful, anonymous letters. Now here was this man with graying hair and a thick mustache, his clothes American but his face Iranian, his eyes sadly familiar, as if they belonged to someone else. "Don't you believe me?" he said. He kissed her on both cheeks. It was his smell she recognized first— a pleasantly bitter, herblike smell that brought her the image of Hassan as a child, reaching thin arms around her neck. "It's you, Hassan," she said, and then she started crying against his gray tweed* shoulder.

12   They were quiet during the long drive home. Once she reached over to touch his face, having wanted to do so for miles. None of the out-of-focus snapshots he'd sent had prepared her for the way he had aged. "How long has it been?" she asked. "Twelve years?" But both of them knew to the day how long it had been. All those letters of hers: "My dear Hassan, ten years now and still your place is empty." "Eleven years and still . . ."

13   Hassan squinted* through the windshield at the oncoming headlights. His mother started fretting* over her kerchief, which she knew she ought not to have worn. She'd been told so by her youngest sister, who had been to America twice. "It marks you," her sister had said. But that square of silk was the last, shrunken* reminder of the veil she used to hide beneath, before the previous Shah had banished* such things. At her age, how could she expose herself? And then her teeth; her teeth were a problem too. Her youngest sister had said, "You ought to get dentures* made. I'm sure there aren't three whole teeth in your head." But Mrs. Ardavi was scared of dentists. Now she covered her mouth with one hand and looked sideways at Hassan, though so far he hadn't seemed to notice. He was busy maneuvering his car into the right-hand lane.

14   This silence was the last thing she had expected. For weeks she'd been saving up stray bits of gossip, weaving together the family stories she would tell him. There were three hundred people in her family—most of them related to each other in three or four different ways, all leading intricate* and scandalous lives she had planned to discuss in detail, but instead she stared sadly out the window. You'd think Hassan would ask. You'd think they could have a better conversation than this, after such a long time. Disappointment made her cross, and now she stubbornly refused to speak even when she saw something she wanted to comment on, some imposing building or unfamiliar brand of car sliding past her into the darkness.

(11) **break the news:** to tell news that may be very surprising, shocking, or disturbing
(11) **tweed:** a type of wool having a rough surface with a pattern woven into it
(13) **squinted:** looked with eyes partly closed, as when one has difficulty seeing
(13) **fretting:** agitating, picking at in a nervous way, showing irritation or nervousness
(13) **shrunken:** made smaller, diminished
(13) **banished:** sent away, forced it to go away
(13) **dentures:** false teeth
(14) **intricate:** complicated

15   By the time they arrived it was nearly midnight. None of the houses were lit but Hassan's—worn brick, older than she would have expected. "Here we are," said Hassan. The competence with which he parked the car, fitting it neatly into a small space by the curb, put him firmly on the other side of the fence, the American side. She would have to face her daughter-in-law alone. As they climbed the front steps she whispered, "How do you say it again?"

16   "Say what?" Hassan asked.

17   "Her name. Lizabet?"

18   "Elizabeth. Like Elizabeth Taylor. *You* know."

19   "Yes, yes, of course," said his mother. Then she lifted her chin, holding tight to the straps of her purse.

20   Elizabeth was wearing bluejeans and a pair of fluffy slippers. Her hair was blond as corn silk, cut short and straight, and her face had the grave,* sleepy look of a child's. As soon as she had opened the door she said, *"Salaam aleikum."* Mrs. Ardavi, overcome with relief at the Persian greeting, threw her arms around her and kissed both cheeks. Then they led her into the living room, which looked comfortable but a little too plain. The furniture was straight-edged, the rugs uninteresting, though the curtains had a nice figured pattern that caught her eye. In one corner sat a shiny red kiddie car complete with license plates. "Is that the child's?" she asked. "Hilary's?" She hesitated over the name. "Could I see her?"

21   *"Now?"* said Hassan.

22   But Elizabeth told him, "That's all right." (Women understood these things.) She beckoned* to her mother-in-law. They climbed the stairs together, up to the second floor, into a little room that smelled of milk and rubber and talcum powder, smells she would know anywhere. Even in the half-light from the hallway, she could tell that Hilary was beautiful. She had black, tumbling hair, long black lashes, and skin of a tone they called wheat-colored, lighter than Hassan's. "There," said Elizabeth. "Thank you," said Mrs. Ardavi. Her voice was formal, but this was her first grandchild and it took her a moment to recover herself. Then they stepped back into the hallway. "I brought her some medals," she whispered. "I hope you don't mind."

23   "Medals?" said Elizabeth. She repeated the word anxiously, mispronouncing it.

24   "Only an Allah and a Koran, both very tiny. You'll hardly know they're there. I'm not used to seeing a child without a medal. It worries me."

25   Automatically her fingers traced a chain around her neck, ending in the hollow of her collarbone. Elizabeth nodded, looking relieved. *"Oh* yes. Medals," she said.

26   "Is that all right?"

27   "Yes, of course."

28   Mrs. Ardavi took heart. "Hassan laughs," she said. "He doesn't believe in

(20) **grave:** very serious
(22) **beckoned:** gestured to come

these things. But when he left I put a prayer in his suitcase pocket, and you
see he's been protected. Now if Hilary wore a medal, I could sleep nights."

29   "Of course," Elizabeth said again.

30   When they re-entered the living room, Mrs. Ardavi was smiling, and she
kissed Hassan on the top of his head before she sat down.

31   American days were tightly scheduled, divided not into morning and
afternoon but into 9:00, 9:30, and so forth, each half hour possessing its own
set activity. It was marvelous. Mrs. Ardavi wrote her sisters: "They're more
organized here. My daughter-in-law never wastes a minute." How terrible,
her sisters wrote back. They were all in Teheran, drinking cup after cup of tea
and idly guessing who might come and visit. "No, you misunderstand," Mrs.
Ardavi protested. "I like it this way. I'm fitting in wonderfully." And to her
youngest sister she wrote, "You'd think I was American. No one guesses
otherwise." This wasn't true, of course, but she hoped it would be true in the
future.

32   Hassan was a doctor. He worked long hours, from six in the morning
until six at night. While she was still washing for her morning prayers she
could hear him tiptoe down the stairs and out the front door. His car would
start up, a distant rumble* far below her, and from her bathroom window she
could watch it swing out from beneath a tatter* of red leaves and round the
corner and disappear. Then she would sigh and return to her sink. Before
prayers she had to wash her face, her hands, and the soles of her feet. She had
to draw her wet fingers down the part in her hair. After that she returned to
her room, where she swathed* herself tightly in her long black veil and knelt
on a beaded velvet prayer mat. East was where the window was, curtained by
chintz* and misted over. On the east wall she hung a lithograph of the Caliph
Ali and a color snapshot of her third son, Babak, whose marriage she had
arranged just a few months before this visit. If Babak hadn't married, she
never could have come. He was the youngest, spoiled by being the only son
at home. It had taken her three years to find a wife for him. (One was too
modern, one too lazy, one so perfect she had been suspicious.) But finally the
proper girl had turned up, modest and well-mannered and sufficiently wide
of hip, and Mrs. Ardavi and the bridal couple had settled in a fine new house
on the outskirts of Teheran. Now every time she prayed, she added a word of
thanks that at last she had a home for her old age. After that, she unwound her
veil and laid it carefully in a drawer. From another drawer she took thick
cotton stockings and elastic garters;* she stuffed her swollen feet into open-
toed vinyl sandals. Unless she was going out, she wore a housecoat. It amazed
her how wasteful Americans were with their clothing.

33   Downstairs, Elizabeth would have started her tea and buttered a piece of

(32) **rumble:** deep, rolling sound
(32) **tatter:** looking like a torn rag
(32) **swathed:** wrapping herself in a cloth or shawl
(32) **chintz:** a shiny type of cotton
(32) **garters:** bands or straps used for holding up stockings

toast for her. Elizabeth and Hilary ate bacon and eggs, but bacon of course was unclean and Mrs. Ardavi never accepted any. Nor had it even been offered to her, except once, jokingly, by Hassan. The distinctive, smoky smell rose to meet her as she descended the stairs. "What does it taste like?" she always asked. She was dying to know. But Elizabeth's vocabulary didn't cover the taste of bacon; she only said it was salty and then laughed and gave up. They had learned very early to travel a well-worn conversational path, avoiding the dead ends caused by unfamiliar words. "Did you sleep well?" Elizabeth always asked in her funny, childish accent, and Mrs. Ardavi answered, "So-so." Then they would turn and watch Hilary, who sat on a booster seat* eating scrambled eggs, a thin chain of Persian gold crossing the back of her neck. Conversation was easier, or even unnecessary, as long as Hilary was there.

34   In the mornings Elizabeth cleaned house. Mrs. Ardavi used that time for letter writing. She had dozens of letters to write, to all her aunts and uncles and her thirteen sisters. (Her father had had three wives, and a surprising number of children even for that day and age.) Then there was Babak. His wife was in her second month of pregnancy, so Mrs. Ardavi wrote long accounts of the American child-rearing methods. "There are some things I don't agree with," she wrote. "They let Hilary play outdoors by herself, with not even a servant to keep an eye on her." Then she would trail off* and gaze thoughtfully at Hilary, who sat on the floor watching a television program called "Captain Kangaroo."

35   Mrs. Ardavi's own childhood had been murky* and grim.* From the age of nine she was wrapped in a veil, one corner of it clenched* in her teeth to hide her face whenever she appeared on the streets. Her father, a respected man high up in public life, used to chase servant girls through the halls and trap them, giggling, in vacant bedrooms. At the age of ten she was forced to watch her mother bleed to death in childbirth, and when she screamed the midwife* had struck her across the face and held her down till she had properly kissed her mother goodbye. There seemed no connection at all between her and this little overalled* American. At times, when Hilary had one of her temper tantrums,* Mrs. Ardavi waited in horror for Elizabeth to slap her and then, when no slap came, felt a mixture of relief and anger. "In Iran—" she would begin, and if Hassan was there he always said, "But this is not Iran, remember?"

36   After lunch Hilary took a nap, and Mrs. Ardavi went upstairs to say her

---

(33) **booster seat:** a special seat made to fit into a conventional chair, used for small children so that they can reach the table

(34) **trail off:** stop talking or writing in the middle of a thought, wander from the subject being discussed

(35) **murky:** obscure, dark, gloomy

(35) **grim:** hard, stern, threatening, unpleasant

(35) **clenched:** held tightly

(35) **midwife:** woman who delivers babies, i.e., who assists in the birth

(35) **overalled:** wearing overalls or jeans

(35) **temper tantrums:** fits of screaming and kicking in anger

noontime prayers and take a nap as well. Then she might do a little laundry in her bathtub. Laundry was a problem here. Although she liked Elizabeth, the fact was that the girl was a Christian, and therefore unclean; it would never do to have a Christian wash a Moslem's clothes. The automatic dryer was also unclean, having contained, at some point, a Christian's underwear. So she had to ask Hassan to buy her a drying rack. It came unassembled. Elizabeth put it together for her, stick by stick, and Mrs. Ardavi held it under her shower and rinsed it off, hoping that would be enough to remove any taint. The Koran didn't cover this sort of situation.

37   When Hilary was up from her nap they walked her to the park—Elizabeth in her eternal* bluejeans and Mrs. Ardavi in her kerchief and shawl,* taking short painful steps in small shoes that bulged over her bunions.* They still hadn't seen to her teeth, although by now Hassan had noticed them. She was hoping he might forget about the dentist, but then she saw him remembering every time she laughed and revealed her five brown teeth set wide apart.

38   At the park she laughed a great deal. It was her only way of communicating with the other women. They sat on the benches ringing the playground, and while Elizabeth translated their questions Mrs. Ardavi laughed and nodded at them over and over. "They want to know if you like it here," Elizabeth said. Mrs. Ardavi answered at length, but Elizabeth's translation was very short. Then gradually the other women forgot her, and conversation rattled on while she sat silent and watched each speaker's lips. The few recognizable words—"telephone," "television," "radio"—gave her the impression that American conversations were largely technical, even among women. Their gestures were wide and slow, disproving her youngest sister's statement that in America everyone was in a hurry. On the contrary, these women were dreamlike, moving singly or in twos across wide flat spaces beneath white November skies when they departed.

39   Later, at home, Mrs. Ardavi would say, "The red-haired girl, is she pregnant? She looked it, I thought. Is that fat girl happy in her marriage?" she asked with some urgency, plucking* Elizabeth's sleeve when she was slow to answer. People's private lives fascinated her. On Saturday trips to the supermarket she liked to single out some interesting stranger. "What's the matter with that *jerky*-moving man? That girl, is she one of your dark-skinned people?" Elizabeth answered too softly, and never seemed to follow Mrs. Ardavi's pointing finger.

40   Supper was difficult; Mrs. Ardavi didn't like American food. Even when Elizabeth made something Iranian, it had an American taste to it—the vegetables still faintly crisp, the onions transparent rather than nicely blackened. "Vegetables not thoroughly cooked retain a certain acidity," Mrs. Ardavi said,

---

(37) **eternal:** here, meaning she wore them all the time
(37) **shawl:** a triangular, square, or rectangular shaped cloth, used by women to cover their heads or shoulders
(37) **bunions:** an inflammation at the base of the big toe
(39) **plucking:** pulling

laying down her fork. "This is a cause of constipation* and stomach aches. At night I often have heartburn. It's been three full days since I moved my bowels." Elizabeth merely bent over her plate, offering no symptoms of her own in return. Hassan said, "At the table, Khanom? At the table?"

41   Eventually she decided to cook supper herself. Over Elizabeth's protests she began at three every afternoon, filling the house with the smell of dillweed and arranging pots on counters and cabinets and finally, when there was no more space, on the floor. She squatted on the floor with her skirt tucked* between her knees and stirred great bowls of minced* greens while behind her, on the gas range, four different pots of food bubbled and steamed. The kitchen was becoming more homelike, she thought. A bowl of yogurt brewed beside the stove, a kettle of rice soaked in the sink, and the top of the dishwasher was curlicued* with the yellow dye from saffron. In one corner sat the pudding pan, black on the bottom from the times she had cooked down sugar to make a sweet for her intestines. "Now, this is your rest period," she always told Elizabeth. "Come to the table in three hours and be surprised." But Elizabeth only hovered around* the kitchen, disturbing the serene,* steam-filled air with clatters and slams as she put away pots, or pacing between stove and sink, her arms folded across her chest. At supper she ate little; Mrs. Ardavi wondered how Americans got so tall on such small suppers. Hassan, on the other hand, had second and third helpings. "I must be gaining five pounds a week," he said. "None of my clothes fit."

42   "That's good to hear," said his mother. And Elizabeth added something but in English, which Hassan answered in English also. Often now they broke into English for paragraphs at a time—Elizabeth speaking softly, looking at her plate, and Hassan answering at length and sometimes reaching across the table to cover her hand.

43   At night, after her evening prayers, Mrs. Ardavi watched television on the living-room couch. She brought her veil downstairs and wrapped it around her to keep the drafts away. Her shoes lay on the rug beneath her, and scattered down the length of the couch were her knitting bag, her sack of burned sugar, her magnifying glass, and *My First Golden Dictionary.** Elizabeth read novels in an easy chair, and Hassan watched TV so that he could translate the difficult parts of the plot. Not that Mrs. Ardavi had much trouble. American plots were easy to guess at, particularly the Westerns. And when the program was boring—a documentary or a special news feature—she could pass the time by talking to Hassan. "Your cousin Farah wrote," she said. "Do you

(40) **constipation:** infrequent or difficult moving of the bowels
(41) **tucked:** gathered together, folded up
(41) **minced:** cut very small
(41) **curlicued:** "decorated" with curved lines
(41) **hovered around:** waited close by, as birds remain suspended over a place or object
(41) **serene:** calm, peaceful
(43) ***My First Golden Dictionary:*** a small child's dictionary, providing pictures that show the meaning of words

remember her? A homely girl, too dark. She's getting a divorce and in my opinion it's fortunate; he's from a lower class. Do you remember Farah?"

44   Hassan only grunted, his eyes on the screen. He was interested in American politics. So was she, for that matter. She had wept for President Kennedy, and carried Jackie's picture in her purse. But these news programs were long and dry, and if Hassan wouldn't talk she was forced to turn at last to her *Golden Dictionary.*

45   In her childhood, she had been taught by expensive foreign tutors. Her mind was her great gift, the compensation for a large, plain face and a stocky figure. But now what she had learned seemed lost, forgotten utterly or fogged by years, so that Hassan gave a snort whenever she told him some fact that she had dredged up* from her memory. It seemed that everything she studied now had to penetrate through a great thick layer before it reached her mind. "Tonk you," she practiced. "Tonk you. Tonk you." "Thank you," Hassan corrected her. He pointed out useful words in her dictionary—grocery store words, household words—but she grew impatient with their woodenness. What she wanted was the language to display her personality, her famous courtesy, and her magical intuition about the inside lives of other people. Nightly she learned "salt," "bread," "spoon," but with an inner sense of dullness, and every morning when she woke her English was once again confined to "thank you" and "NBC."

46   Elizabeth, meanwhile, read on, finishing one book and reaching for the next without even glancing up. Hassan chewed a thumbnail and watched a senator. He shouldn't be disturbed, of course, but time after time his mother felt the silence and the whispery turning of pages stretching her nerves until she had to speak. "Hassan?"

47   "Hmm."

48   "My chest seems tight. I'm sure a cold is coming on. Don't you have a tonic?"

49   "No," said Hassan.

50   He dispensed medicines all day; he listened to complaints. Common sense told her to stop, but she persisted, encouraged by some demon* that wouldn't let her tongue lie still. "Don't you have some syrup? What about that liquid you gave me for constipation? Would that help?"

51   "No, it wouldn't," said Hassan.

52   He drove her on, somehow. The less he gave, the more she had to ask. "Well, aspirin? Vitamins?" Until Hassan said, "Will you just let me *watch?*" Then she could lapse* into silence again, or even gather up the clutter of her belongings and bid the two of them good night.

53   She slept badly. Often she lay awake for hours, fingering the edge of the

---

(45) **dredged up:** raised up with difficulty, as from the bottom of a river or sea
(50) **demon:** evil or mischievous spirit
(52) **lapse:** fall, slip

sheet and staring at the ceiling. Memories crowded in on her, old grievances* and fears, injustices that had never been righted. For the first time in years she thought of her husband, a gentle, weak man given to surprising outbursts of temper. She hadn't loved him when she married him, and at his death from a liver ailment six years later her main feeling had been resentment.* Was it fair to be widowed so young, while other women were supported and protected? She had moved from her husband's home back to the old family estate, where five of her sisters still lived. There she had stayed till Babak's wedding, drinking tea all day with her sisters and pulling the strings by which the rest of the family was attached. Marriages were arranged, funerals attended, childbirth discussed in fine detail; servants' disputes were settled, and feuds* patched up and then restarted. Her husband's face had quickly faded, leaving only a vacant spot in her mind. But now she could see him so clearly—a wasted figure on his deathbed, beard untrimmed, turban coming loose, eyes imploring* her for something more than an absentminded pat on the cheek as she passed through his room on her way to check the children.

54   She saw the thin faces of her three small boys as they sat on the rug eating rice. Hassan was the stubborn, mischievous* one, with perpetual scabs* on his knees. Babak was the cuddly* one. Ali was the oldest, who had caused so much worry—weak, like his father, demanding, but capable of turning suddenly charming. Four years ago he had died of a brain hemorrhage, slumping over a dinner table in faraway Shîrāz where he'd gone to be free of his wife, who was also his double first cousin. Ever since he was born he had disturbed his mother's sleep, first because she worried over what he would amount to* and now, after his death, because she lay awake listing all she had done wrong with him. She had been too lenient.* No, too harsh. There was no telling. Mistakes she had made floated on the ceiling like ghosts —allowances she'd made* when she knew she shouldn't have, protections he had not deserved, blows which perhaps he had not deserved either.

55   She would have liked to talk to Hassan about it, but any time she tried he changed the subject. Maybe he was angry about the way he had heard of Ali's death. It was customary to break such news gradually. She had started a series

---

(53) **grievances:** complaints arising from feelings of having been treated unjustly or wrongly

(53) **resentment:** feeling of anger and hurt resulting from a sense of having been offended, injured, or wronged

(53) **feuds:** bitter quarrels, sometimes deadly and lasting generations between families or clans

(53) **imploring:** begging

(54) **mischievous:** causing mischief, playing tricks, naughty

(54) **scabs:** crusts that form over wounds when they are healing

(54) **cuddly:** one who is fond of being hugged, embraced

(54) **amount to:** become, how he would turn out, how far he would go in life

(54) **lenient:** easy, opposite of strict

(54) **allowances she'd made:** excuses she had made, not blaming her children when she should have

of tactful* letters, beginning by saying that Ali was seriously ill when in truth he was already buried. Something in the letter had given her away—perhaps her plans for a rest cure by the seaside, which she never would have considered if she'd had an ailing son at home. Hassan had telephoned overseas, taking three nights to reach her. "Tell me what's wrong," he said. "I know there's something." When her tears kept her from answering, he asked, "Is he dead?" His voice sounded angry, but that might have been due to a poor connection. And when he hung up, cutting her off before she could say all she wanted, she thought, I should have told him straight out. I had forgotten that about him. Now when she spoke of Ali he listened politely, with his face frozen. She would have told him anything, all about the death and burial and that witch of a wife throwing herself, too late, into the grave; but Hassan never asked.

56   Death was moving in on her. Oh, not on her personally (the women in her family lived a century or longer, burying the men one by one) but on everybody around her, all the cousins and uncles and brothers-in-law. No sooner had she laid away her mourning clothes than it was time to bring them out again. Recently she had begun to feel she would outlive her two other sons as well, and she fought off sleep because of the dreams it brought— Babak lying stiff and cold in his grave, Hassan crumpled over in some dark American alley. Terrifying images would zoom at her out of the night. In the end she had to wrap herself in her veil and sleep instead on the Persian rug, which had the dusty smell of home and was, anyway, more comfortable than her unsteady foreign mattress.

57   At Christmas time, Hassan and Elizabeth gave Mrs. Ardavi a brightly col-ored American dress with short sleeves. She wore it to an Iranian party, even leaving off her kerchief in a sudden fit of daring. Everyone commented on how nice she looked. "Really you fit right in," a girl told her. "May I write to my mother about you? She was over here for a year and a half and never once stepped out of the house without her kerchief." Mrs. Ardavi beamed. It was true she would never have associated with these people at home—children of civil servants and bank clerks, newly rich now they'd finished medical school. The wives called their husbands "Doctor" even in direct address. But still it felt good to be speaking so much Persian; her tongue nearly ran away with her. "I see you're expecting a baby," she said to one of the wives. "Is it your first? I could tell by your eyes. Now don't be nervous. I had three myself; my mother had seven and never felt a pain in her life. She would squat down to serve my father's breakfast and 'Eh?' she would say. 'Aga Jun, it's the baby!' and there it would be on the floor between her feet, waiting for her to cut the cord and finish pouring the tea." She neglected to mention how her mother had died. All her natural tact came back to her, her gift with words and her knowledge of how to hold an audience. She bubbled and sparkled like a girl, and her face fell when it was time to go home.

58   After the party, she spent two or three days noticing more keenly than

(55) **tactful:** being careful in what one says so as not to hurt another person; saying the proper thing so as not to give offense

ever the loss of her language, and talking more feverishly when Hassan came home in the evening. This business of being a foreigner was something changeable. Boundaries kept shifting, and sometimes it was she who was the foreigner but other times Elizabeth, or even Hassan. (Wasn't it true, she often wondered, that there was a greater distance between men and women than between Americans and Iranians, or even *Eskimos* and Iranians?) Hassan was the foreigner when she and Elizabeth conspired to hide a miniature Koran in his glove compartment; he would have laughed at them. "You see," she told Elizabeth, "I know there's nothing to it, but it makes me feel better. When my sons were born I took them all to the bath attendant to have their blood let.* People say it brings long life. I know that's superstition, but whenever afterward I saw those ridges down their backs I felt safe. Don't you understand?" And Elizabeth said, "Of course." She smuggled the Koran into the car herself, and hid it beneath the Texaco maps. Hassan saw nothing.

59   Hilary was a foreigner forever. She dodged* her grandmother's yearning* hands, and when the grownups spoke Persian she fretted and misbehaved and pulled on Elizabeth's sleeve. Mrs. Ardavi had to remind herself constantly not to kiss the child too much, not to reach out for a hug, not to offer her lap. In this country people kept more separate. They kept so separate that at times she felt hurt. They tried to be subtle, so undemonstrative.* She would never understand this place.

60   In January they took her to a dentist, who made clucking noises when he looked in her mouth. "What does he say?" she asked. "Tell me the worst." But Hassan was talking in a low voice to Elizabeth, and he waved her aside. They seemed to be having a misunderstanding of some sort. "What does he *say*, Hassan?"

61   "Just a minute."

62   She craned* around in the high-backed chair, fighting off the dentist's little mirror. "I have to know," she told Hassan.

63   "He says your teeth are terrible. They have to be extracted and the gums surgically smoothed. He wants to know if you'll be here for another few months; he can't schedule you till later."

64   A cold lump of fear swelled in her stomach. Unfortunately she *would* be here; it had only been three months so far and she was planning to stay a year. So she had to watch numbly* while her life was signed away, whole strings of appointments made, and little white cards filled out. And Hassan didn't even look sympathetic. He was still involved in whatever this argument was with Elizabeth. The two of them failed to notice how her hands were shaking.

(58) **blood let:** blood caused to flow; it was thought that letting blood got rid of "bad blood" (this was a way of healing the sick, reducing fever)
(59) **dodged:** ran suddenly aside to avoid being touched or caught
(59) **yearning:** longing
(59) **undemonstrative:** not showing affection by kissing, hugging, or touching
(62) **craned:** stretched her neck to see
(64) **numbly:** without being able to feel

65   It snowed all of January, the worst snow they had had in years. When she came downstairs in the mornings she found the kitchen icy cold, crisscrossed by drafts. "This sort of cold enters your bones," she told Elizabeth. "I'm sure to fall sick." Elizabeth only nodded. Some mornings now her face was pale and puffy, as if she had a secret worry, but Mrs. Ardavi had learned that it was better not to ask about it.

66   Early in February there was a sudden warm spell. Snow melted and all the trees dripped in the sunshine. "We're going for a walk," Elizabeth said, and Mrs. Ardavi said, "I'll come too." In spite of the warmth, she toiled* upstairs for her woolen shawl. She didn't like to take chances. And she worried over Hilary's bare ears. "Won't she catch cold?" she asked. "I think we should cover her head."

67   "She'll be all right," said Elizabeth, and then shut her face in a certain stubborn way she had.

68   In the park, Elizabeth and Hilary made snowballs from the last of the snow and threw them at each other, narrowly missing Mrs. Ardavi, who stood watching with her arms folded and her hands tucked in her sleeves.

69   The next morning, something was wrong with Hilary. She sat at the breakfast table and cried steadily, refusing all food. "Now, now," her grandmother said, "won't you tell old Ka Jun what's wrong?" But when she came close Hilary screamed louder. By noon she was worse, Elizabeth called Hassan, and he came home immediately and laid a hand on Hilary's forehead and said she should go to the pediatrician.* He drove them there himself. "It's her ears, I'm sure of it," Mrs. Ardavi said in the waiting room. For some reason Hassan grew angry. "Do you always know better than the experts?" he asked her. "What are we coming to the doctor for? We could have talked to you and saved the trip." His mother lowered her eyes and examined her purse straps. She understood that he was anxious, but all the same her feelings were hurt and when they rose to go into the office she stayed behind.

70   Later Hassan came back and sat down again. "There's an infection in her middle ear," he told her. "The doctor's going to give her a shot of penicillin." His mother nodded, careful not to annoy him by reminding him she had thought as much. Then Hilary started crying. She must be getting her shot now. Mrs. Ardavi herself was terrified of needles, and she sat gripping her purse until her fingers turned white, staring around the waiting room, which seemed pathetically* cheerful, with its worn wooden toys and nursery-school paintings. Her own ear ached in sympathy. She thought of a time when she had boxed Ali's ears* too hard and he had wept all that day and gone to sleep sucking his thumb.

71   While Hassan was there she was careful not to say anything, but the following morning at breakfast she said, "Elizabeth dear, do you remember that walk we took day before yesterday?"

(66) **toiled:** moved with great difficulty, worked very hard
(69) **pediatrician:** doctor specializing in the care of children
(70) **pathetically:** in a manner arousing pity
(70) **boxed . . . ears:** hit on the ears

72   "Yes," said Elizabeth. She was squeezing oranges for Hilary, who'd grown cheerful again and was eating a huge breakfast.

73   "Remember I said Hilary should wear a hat? Now you see you should have been more careful. Because of you she fell sick; she could have died. Do you see that now?"

74   "No," said Elizabeth.

75   Was her Persian that scanty?* Lately it seemed to have shrunk and hardened, like a stale* piece of bread. Mrs. Ardavi sighed and tried again. "Without a hat, you see—" she began. But Elizabeth had set down her orange, picked up Hilary, and walked out of the room. Mrs. Ardavi stared after her, wondering if she'd said something wrong.

76   For the rest of the day, Elizabeth was busy in her room. She was cleaning out bureaus and closets. A couple of times Mrs. Ardavi advanced as far as the doorway, where she stood awkwardly watching. Hilary sat on the floor playing with a discarded perfume bottle. Everything, it seemed, was about to be thrown away—buttonless blouses and stretched-out sweaters, stockings and combs and empty lipstick tubes. "Could I be of any help?" Mrs. Ardavi asked, but Elizabeth said, "Oh, no. Thank you very much." Her voice was cheerful. Yet when Hassan came home he went upstairs and stayed a long time, and the door remained shut behind him.

77   Supper that night was an especially fine stew, Hassan's favorite ever since childhood, but he didn't say a word about it. He hardly spoke at all, in fact. Then later, when Elizabeth was upstairs putting Hilary to bed, he said, "Khanoum Jun, I want to talk to you."

78   "Yes, Hassan," she said, laying aside her knitting. She was frightened by his seriousness, the black weight of his mustache, and her own father's deep black eyes. But what had she done? She knotted her hands and looked up at him, swallowing.

79   "I understand you've been interfering," he said.

80   "I, Hassan?"

81   "Elizabeth isn't the kind you can do that with. And she's raising the child just fine on her own."

82   "Well, of course, she is," said his mother. "Did I ever say otherwise?"

83   "Show it, then. Don't offer criticisms."

84   "Very well," she said. She picked up her knitting and began counting stitches, as if she'd forgotten the conversation entirely. But that evening she was unusually quiet, and at nine o'clock she excused herself to go to bed. "So early?" Hassan asked.

85   "I'm tired," she told him, and left with her back very straight.

86   Her room surrounded her like a nest. She had built up layers of herself on every surface—tapestries and bits of lace and lengths of Paisley. The bureau was covered with gilt-framed pictures of the saints, and snapshots of

(75) **scanty:** insufficient, not enough
(75) **stale:** having lost freshness (*stale* bread is hard)

her sisters at family gatherings. On the windowsill were little plants in orange and aqua plastic pots—her favorite American colors. Her bedside table held bottles of medicine, ivory prayer beads, and a tiny brick of holy earth. The rest of the house was bare and shiny, impersonal; this room was as comforting as her shawl.

87   Still, she didn't sleep well. Ghosts rose up again, tugging* at her thoughts. Why did things turn out so badly for her? Her father had preferred her brothers, a fact that crushed her even after all these years. Her husband had had three children by her and then complained that she was cold. And what comfort were children? If she had stayed in Iran any longer Babak would have asked her to move; she'd seen it coming. There'd been some disrespect creeping into his bride's behavior, some unwillingness to take advice, which Babak had overlooked even when his mother pointed it out to him. And Hassan was worse— always so stubborn, much too independent. She had offered him anything if he would just stay in Iran but he had said no; he was set on leaving her. And he had flatly refused to take along his cousin Shora as his wife, though everyone pointed out how lonely he would be. He was so anxious to break away, to get *going,* to come to this hardhearted country and take up with a Christian girl. Oh, she should have laughed when he left, and saved her tears for someone more deserving. She never should have come here, she never should have asked anything of him again. When finally she went to sleep it seemed that her eyes remained open, burning large and dry beneath her lids.

88   In the morning she had a toothache. She could hardly walk for the pain. It was only Friday (the first of her dental appointments was for Monday), but the dentist made time for her during the afternoon and pulled the tooth. Elizabeth said it wouldn't hurt, but it did. Elizabeth treated it as something insignificant, merely a small break in her schedule, which required the hiring of a babysitter. She wouldn't even call Hassan home from work. "What could he do?" she asked.

89   So when Hassan returned that evening it was all a surprise to him—the sight of his mother with a bloody cotton cylinder hanging out over her lower lip like a long tooth. "What *happened* to you?" he asked. To make it worse, Hilary was screaming and had been all afternoon. Mrs. Ardavi put her hands over her ears, wincing. "Will you make that child hush?" Hassan told Elizabeth. "I think we should get my mother to bed." He guided her toward the stairs, and she allowed herself to lean on him. "It's mainly my heart," she said. "You know how scared I am of dentists." When he had folded back her bedspread and helped her to lie down she closed her eyes gratefully, resting one arm across her forehead. Even the comfort of hot tea was denied her; she had to stay on cold foods for twelve hours. Hassan fixed her a glass of ice water. He was very considerate,* she thought. He seemed as shaken at the sight of her as Hilary

(87) **tugging:** pulling
(89) **considerate:** careful to consider the feelings and wishes of another; having thoughtful regard for others

had been. All during the evening he kept coming to check on her, and twice in the night she heard him climbing the stairs to listen at her door. When she moaned he called, "Are you awake?"

90   "Of course," she said.

91   "Can I get you anything?"

92   "No, no."

93   In the morning she descended the stairs with slow, groping* feet, keeping a tight hold on the railing. "It was a very hard night," she said. "At four my gum started throbbing.* Is that normal? I think these American pain pills are constipating. Maybe a little prune juice would restore my regularity."

94   "I'll get it," Hassan said. "You sit down. Did you take the milk of magnesia?"

95   "Oh, yes, but I'm afraid it wasn't enough," she said.

96   Elizabeth handed Hassan a platter of bacon, not looking at him.

97   After breakfast, while Hassan and his mother were still sitting over their tea, Elizabeth started cleaning the kitchen. She made quite a bit of noise. She sorted the silverware and then went through a tangle of utensils, discarding bent spatulas and rusty tongs. "May I help?" asked Mrs. Ardavi. Elizabeth shook her head. She seemed to have these fits of throwing things away. Now she was standing on the counter to take everything from the upper cabinets—crackers, cereals, half-empty bottles of spices. On the very top shelf was a flowered tin confectioner's box with Persian lettering on it, forgotten since the day Mrs. Ardavi had brought it. "My!" said Mrs. Ardavi. "Won't Hilary be surprised!" Elizabeth pried the lid off. Out flew a cloud of insects, grayish-brown with V-shaped wings. They brushed past Elizabeth's face and fluttered through her hair and swarmed toward the ceiling, where they dimmed the light fixture. Elizabeth flung the box as far from her as possible and climbed down from the counter. "Goodness!" said Mrs. Ardavi. "Why, *we* have those at home!" Hassan lowered his teacup. Mixed nuts and dried currants rolled every which way on the floor; more insects swung toward the ceiling. Elizabeth sat on the nearest chair and buried her head in her hands. "Elizabeth?" said Hassan.

98   But she wouldn't look at him. In the end she simply rose and went upstairs, shutting the bedroom door with a gentle, definite click, which they heard all the way down in the kitchen because they were listening so hard.

99   "Excuse me," Hassan said to his mother.

100   She nodded and stared into her tea.

101   After he was gone she went to find Hilary, and she set her on her knee, babbling various folk rhymes to her while straining her ears toward the silence overhead. But Hilary squirmed off her lap and went to play with a truck. Then Hassan came downstairs again. He didn't say a word about Elizabeth.

102   On the following day, when Mrs. Ardavi's tooth was better, she and

(93) **groping:** trying to find one's way by feeling the way
(93) **throbbing:** a banging, pulsating feeling caused by pain

Hassan had a little talk upstairs in her room. They were very polite with each other. Hassan asked his mother how long they could hope for her to stay. His mother said she hadn't really thought about it. Hassan said that in America it was the custom to have house guests for three months only. After that they moved to a separate apartment nearby which he'd be glad to provide for her as soon as he could find one, maybe next week. "Ah, an apartment," said his mother, looking impressed. But she had never lived alone a day in her life, and so after a suitable pause she said that she would hate to put him to so much expense. "Especially," she said, "when I'm going in such a short time anyway, since I'm homesick for my sisters."

103   "Well, then," said Hassan.

104   At supper that night, Hassan announced that his mother was missing her sisters and would like to leave. Elizabeth lowered her glass. "Leave?" she said.

105   Mrs. Ardavi said, "And Babak's wife, of course, will be asking for me when the baby arrives."

106   "Well . . . but what about the dentist? You were supposed to start your appointments on Monday?"

107   "It's not important," Mrs. Ardavi said.

108   "But we set up all those—"

109   "There are plenty of dentists she can see at home," Hassan told Elizabeth. "We have dentists in Iran, for God's sake. Do you imagine we're barbarians?"

110   "No," Elizabeth said.

111   On the evening of the third of March, Hassan drove his mother to the airport. He was worrying about the road, which was slippery after a snowfall. He couldn't find much to say to his mother. And once they had arrived, he deliberately kept the conversation to trivia*—the verifying of tickets, checking of departure times, weighing of baggage. Her baggage was fourteen pounds overweight. It didn't make sense; all she had were her clothes and a few small gifts for her sisters. "Why was it so heavy?" Hassan asked. "What have you got in there?" But his mother only said, "I don't know," and straightened her shawl, looking elsewhere. Hassan bent to open a tooled-leather suitcase. Inside he found three empty urn-shaped wine bottles, the permanent-press sheets from her bed, and a sample box of detergent that had come in yesterday's mail. "Listen," said Hassan, "do you know how much I'd have to pay to fly these things over? What's the matter with you?"

112   "I wanted to show my sisters," his mother said.

113   "Well, forget it. Now, what else have you got?"

114   But something about her—the vague, childlike eyes set upon some faraway object—made him give in. He opened no more bags. He even regretted his sharpness, and when her flight was announced he hugged her closely and kissed the top of her head. "Go with God," he said.

115   "Goodbye, Hassan."

(111) **trivia:** small, unimportant, insignificant things

116   She set off down the corridor by herself, straggling behind* a line of businessmen. They all wore hats. His mother wore her scarf, and of all the travelers she alone, securely kerchiefed and shawled, setting her small shoes resolutely* on the gleaming tiles, seemed undeniably a foreigner.

□ MAKING WRITING MORE COLORFUL

Notice the way in which the author has used metaphors to make her points and show feelings and tensions more effectively. (Remember that a metaphor is basically a comparison. Something about the metaphor is analogous to the situation or person being shown.) Study the following metaphors and then for each see if you can (1) say why it is appropriate, (2) use a different metaphor to express the same thing, or (3) use the same metaphor to describe one of your experiences:

1. "... a pyramid of knobby parcels and bags, scraps of velvet and brocade and tapestry ..." (What was the apex of the pyramid? What, exactly, is being described?) (paragraph 10)
2. "She had issued from the plane like a newborn baby, speechless and friendless." (paragraph 7)
3. "They had learned very early to travel a well-worn conversational path, avoiding the dead ends caused by unfamiliar words." (paragraph 33)
4. "... pulling the strings by which the rest of the family was attached." (paragraph 53)
5. "Was her Persian that scanty? Lately it seemed to have shrunk and hardened, like a stale piece of bread." (paragraph 75)

□ QUESTIONS FOR DISCUSSION

---

1. Discuss the apparent change in Hassan over the past twelve years. How has he become Americanized? In what ways had he always been the person he is?
2. The story is seen primarily through the eyes of Mrs. Ardavi, but we see more than she seems to see. In the following paragraphs, compare what she sees with what *you* see that she does not seem to see, and express the comparison in clear sentences. Do you think that she is unable to see the things you see or unwilling to? Or at times one, at times the other? (paragraphs 6–7, 41–42, 60–65, 73–76)
3. There are many passages that relate to problems of speech and communication: the problems of people who cannot speak or understand as well as they would like in a language not their own; the ways in which silence becomes very loud or very uncomfortable; the ways in which language can

(116) **straggling behind:** slowly wandering with no goal and, therefore, quite a bit behind the others
(116) **resolutely:** in a determined way; showing purpose, firmness

extend our imaginations and personalities and, conversely, the ways in which it can keep us almost imprisoned. Some examples can be found in paragraphs 38 (Notice Mrs. Ardavi finds English a very technical language! Why?), 45, and 58. Be prepared to discuss these and others that you will be able to find in the story. You may want to share similar experiences and feelings you have had.

4. In "The Sounds of Silence" (Chapter 7) the Halls wrote about nonverbal languages that are misunderstood between cultures, such as the different uses and interpretations of time, space, physical distance between people, touching, eye contact. Find examples in this story of the way such differences contributed to the tensions in this story. Find still other areas of difference in ways of life, attitudes, and assumptions.

5. In paragraphs 58–59, Mrs. Ardavi observes:

> This business of being a foreigner was something changeable. Boundaries kept shifting, and sometimes it was she who was the foreigner but other times Elizabeth, or even Hassan. (Wasn't it true . . . that there was a greater distance between men and women than between Americans and Iranians. . . . Hilary was a foreigner forever.)

Comment on this passage (it will help to go back and read it in its entirety). Are there ways of feeling "foreign" other than difference in nationality? What other kinds of barriers exist between people even of the same nationality, or even within the same family?

☐   SUGGESTIONS FOR COMPOSITION

---

1. Write a comparison/contrast essay showing how cultural differences contributed to the tensions in the story. Refer to question 4 above for help in establishing common factors. (See Chapter 8 for review of writing the comparison/contast essay.)

2. In this story, as in most of real life, there are no heroes, no villains. No one is *all* right or *all* wrong; still there is conflict and hurt. For which character (Mrs. Ardavi, Hassan, or Elizabeth) do you have the most sympathy? Why? Explain fully, using examples from the story.

3. Discuss languages and communication in this story. To what extent was language the problem? How important is language to communication in this story? Support your views with specific examples from the story. (You may add your own experience or views if you like, but keep this subordinate to what you discuss regarding the story.)

4. Since both women had such good intentions at the beginning, what went wrong? Analyze and support your analysis with examples.

(For questions 3 and 4, remember that the story begins with Elizabeth trying to learn Persian.)

5. Write an analysis of *one* of the characters. Support your views with specific examples.

6. As we have observed already, we see most of the story through the eyes of Mrs. Ardavi. Choose a scene or incident in the story and tell it from the viewpoint of Elizabeth, or Hassan, or Hilary.

Note: (1) Do *not* simply summarize the story.

(2) Use specific examples from the story.

The following excerpt is from *The Second Self: Computers and the Human Spirit,* a book that raises important questions about how "the machine enters social life and psychological development, the computer as it affects the way that we think." What particularly fascinates the author is "not what will the computer be like in the future, but what will *we* be like? What are we becoming?" We speak of the computer in psychological terms: We refer to its brain, its intentions; we give it commands. We have also begun to speak of ourselves in computer terminology: We must reprogram ourselves, clear our buffers. The human brain is being compared to the computer, and researchers in artificial intelligence are "teaching" machines to "think." Machines play chess and "compose" music. This book raises questions such as: Can a machine "think"? And if so, is it "alive" in any sense? What then does "alive" mean? Are *we* some kind of machine? What is it about the computer that fosters such intense relationships with it? The author, whose doctorate is in sociology and psychology, is a professor in the Science, Technology, and Society program at the Massachusetts Institute of Technology.

SHERRY TURKLE

Computers and the Human Spirit: Child Programmers

1   Consider Robin, a four-year-old with blond hair and a pinafore,* standing in front of a computer console, typing at its keyboard. She is a student at a nursery school that is introducing computers to very young children. She is playing a game that allows her to build stick figures* by commanding the computer to make components appear and move into a desired position. The machine responds to Robin's commands and tells her when it does not understand an instruction. Many people find this scene disturbing. First, Robin is "plugged into" a machine. We speak of television as a "plug-in drug," but perhaps the very passivity* of what we do with television reassures us. We are concerned about children glued to screens, but . . . the passivity of television encourages many of us to situate our sense of its impact at the level of the content of television programming. Is it violent or sexually suggestive? Is it

(1) **pinafore:** an apron or apronlike garment worn over a dress, usually by little girls
(1) **stick figures:** pictures of humans or animals made by using a circle as the head and lines for the rest of the body
(1) **passivity:** inactivity; the quality of being passive, that is, acted upon, not acting

educational? But Robin is not "watching" anything on the computer. She is manipulating—perhaps more problematic, *interacting with*—a complex technological medium.* And the degree and intensity of her involvement suggests that (like . . . children at . . . video games) it is the medium itself and not the content of a particular program that produces the more powerful effect. But beyond any specific fear, so young a child at a computer conflicts with our ideal image of childhood. The "natural" child is out of doors; machines are indoors. The natural child runs free; machines control and constrain. Machines and children don't go together. . . .

2   Do computers change the way children think? Do they open children's minds or do they dangerously narrow their experience, making their thinking more linear and less intuitive? There is a temptation to look for a universal, isolable* effect, the sort that still eludes* experts on the effect of television.

3   The problem here is the search for a universal effect. I have found that different children are touched in remarkably different ways by their experience with the computer. However, by looking closely at how individual children appropriate* the computer we can build ways to think about how the computer enters into development, and we begin to get some answers to our questions. In a sense, I turn the usual question around: Instead of asking what the computer does to children I ask what children, and more important, what different kinds of children make of* the computer.

4   I observed child programmers in a variety of school settings. In most schools there was one or perhaps two computers per grade. In a few, every classroom had at least one computer. And in one special situation, every child had unlimited computer access. The children I observed programmed in a number of languages, including BASIC, PILOT, and Logo.* In every setting it was apparent that computers had brought something new into the classroom. . . .

5   When children learn to program, one of their favorite areas of work is computer graphics—programming the machine to place displays on the screen. The Logo graphic system available at Austen* was relatively powerful. It provided thirty-two computational objects called sprites that appear on the screen when commanded to do so. Each sprite has a number. When called by its number and given a color and shape, it comes onto the screen with that shape and color: a red truck, a blue ball, a green airplane. Children can manipulate one sprite at a time, several of them, or all of them at once, depending on the effect they want to achieve. The sprites can take predefined

(1) **medium:** here, a means or vehicle of expression; a way of communicating
(2) **isolable:** capable of being isolated, singled out
(2) **eludes:** escapes our grasp or understanding
(3) **appropriate** (verb): take possession of as one's own, or for oneself
(3) **what . . . children make of:** how children understand it, how they perceive it
(4) **BASIC, PILOT, and Logo:** computer languages used for programming
(5) **Austen:** fictitious name for the school where Dr. Turkle observed these children

shapes, such as trucks and airplanes, or they can be given new shapes designed on a special grid, a sprite "scratchpad." They can be given a speed and a direction and be set in motion. The direction is usually specified in terms of a heading from 0 to 360, where 0 would point the sprite due north, 90 would point it due east, 180 south, 270 west, and 360 north again. . . .

6   Jeff, a fourth grader, has a reputation as one of the school's computer experts. He is meticulous* in his study habits, does superlative work in all subjects. His teachers are not surprised to see him excelling in programming. Jeff approaches the machine with determination and the need to be in control, the way he approaches both his schoolwork and his extracurricular activities. He likes to be, and often is, chairman of student committees. At the moment, his preoccupation with computers is intense: "They're the biggest thing in my life right now." He speaks very fast, and when he talks about his programs he speaks even faster, tending to monologue.* He answers a question about what his program does by tossing off* lines of computer code that for him seem to come as naturally as English. His typing is expert—he does not look at the code as it appears on the screen. He conveys the feeling that he is speaking directly to an entity* inside. "When I program I put myself in the place of the sprite. And I make it do things."

7   Jeff is the author of one of the first space-shuttle programs. He does it, as he does most other things, by making a plan. There will be a rocket, boosters, a trip through the stars, a landing. He conceives the program globally;* then he breaks it up into manageable pieces. "I wrote out the parts on a big piece of cardboard. I saw the whole thing in my mind just in one night, and I couldn't wait to come to school to make it work." Computer scientists will recognize this global "top-down," "divide-and-conquer" strategy as "good programming style." And we all recognize in Jeff someone who conforms to our stereotype of a "computer person" or an engineer—someone who would be good with machines, good at science, someone organized, who approaches the world of things with confidence and sure intent, with the determination to make it work.

8   Kevin is a very different sort of child. Where Jeff is precise in all of his actions, Kevin is dreamy and impressionistic.* Where Jeff tends to try to impose his ideas on other children, Kevin's warmth, easygoing nature, and interest in others make him popular. Meetings with Kevin were often interrupted by his being called out to rehearse for a school play. The play was *Cinderella,* and he had been given the role of Prince Charming. Kevin comes

---

(6) **meticulous:** extremely neat, precise, careful
(6) **monologue:** long speech by one person, often used when a person does all the talking in a conversation
(6) **tossing off:** accomplishing, performing casually and easily
(6) **entity:** a being, something that exists
(7) **globally:** comprehensively, totally, as a whole
(8) **impressionistic:** relying more on impressions and feelings than facts or reason

from a military family; his father and grandfather were both in the Air Force. But Kevin has no intention of following in their footsteps. "I don't want to be an army man. I don't want to be a fighting man. You can get killed." Kevin doesn't like fighting or competition in general. "You can avoid fights. I never get anybody mad—I mean, I try not to."

9   Jeff has been playing with machines all his life—Tinkertoys, motors, bikes—but Kevin has never played with machines. He likes stories, he likes to read, he is proud of knowing the names of "a lot of different trees." He is artistic and introspective.* When Jeff is asked questions about his activities, about what he thinks is fun, he answers in terms of how to do them right and how well he does them. He talks about video games by describing his strategy breakthroughs on the new version of Space Invaders: "Much harder, much trickier than the first one." By contrast, Kevin talks about experiences in terms of how they make him feel. Video games make him feel nervous, he says. "The computer is better," he adds. "It's easier. You get more relaxed. You're not being bombarded with stuff all the time."

10   Kevin too is making a space scene. But the way he goes about it is not at all like Jeff's approach. Jeff doesn't care too much about the detail of the form of his rocket ship; what is important is getting a complex system to work together as a whole. But Kevin cares more about the aesthetics* of the graphics. He spends a lot of time on the shape of his rocket. He abandons his original idea ("It didn't look right against the stars") but continues to "doodle" with the scratchpad shape-maker. He works without plan, experimenting, throwing different shapes onto the screen. He frequently stands back to inspect his work, looking at it from different angles, finally settling on a red shape against a black night—a streamlined, futuristic design. He is excited and calls over two friends. One admires the red on the black. The other says that the red shape "looks like fire." Jeff happens to pass Kevin's machine on the way to lunch and automatically checks out its screen, since he is always looking for new tricks to add to his toolkit for building programs. He shrugs. "That's been done." Nothing new there, nothing technically different, just a red blob.

11   Everyone goes away and Kevin continues, now completely taken up by* the idea that the red looks like fire. He decides to make the ship white so that a red shape can be red fire "at the bottom." A long time is spent making the new red fireball, finding ways to give it spikes.* And a long time is spent adding detail to the now white ship. With the change of color, new possibilities emerge: "More things will show up on it." Insignias, stripes, windows, and the project about which Kevin is most enthusiastic: "It can have a little seat for the astronaut." When Jeff programs he puts himself in the place of the

---

(9) **introspective:** looking within oneself, examining ones own thoughts and feelings
(10) **aesthetics:** sense of the beautiful, how it looks
(11) **taken up by:** absorbed with
(11) **spikes:** sharp-pointed projecting objects

sprite: He thinks of himself as an abstract computational object. Kevin says that, as he works, "I think of myself as the man inside the rocket ship. I daydream about it. I'd like to go to the moon."

12 By the next day Kevin has a rocket with red fire at the bottom. "Now I guess I·should make it move . . . moving and wings . . . it should have moving and wings." The wings turn out to be easy, just some more experimenting with the scratchpad. But he is less certain about how to get the moving right.

13 Kevin knows how to write programs, but his programs emerge—he is not concerned with imposing his will on the machine. He is concerned primarily with creating exciting visual effects and allows himself to be led by the effects he produces. Since he lets his plans change as new ideas turn up, his work has not been systematic. And he often loses track of things. Kevin has lovingly worked on creating the rocket, the flare,* and a background of twinkling stars. Now he wants the stars to stay in place and the rocket and the flare to move through them together.

14 It is easy to set sprites in motion: Just command them to an initial position and give them a speed and a direction. But Kevin's rocket and red flare are two separate objects (each shape is carried by a different sprite) and they have to be commanded to move together at the same speed, even though they will be starting from different places. To do this successfully, you have to think about coordinates and you have to make sure that the objects are identified differently so that code for commanding their movements can be addressed to each of them independently. Without a master plan Kevin gets confused about the code numbers he has assigned to the different parts of his program, and the flare doesn't stay with the rocket but flies off with the stars. It takes a lot of time to get the flare and the ship back together. When Jeff makes a mistake, he is annoyed, calls himself "stupid," and rushes to correct his technical error. But when Kevin makes an error, although it frustrates him he doesn't seem to resent it. He sometimes throws his arms up in exasperation. "Oh no, oh no. What did I do?" His fascination with his effect keeps him at it.

15 In correcting his error, Kevin explores the system, discovering new special effects as he goes along. In fact, the "mistake" leads him to a new idea: The flare shouldn't go off with the stars but should drop off the rocket, "and then the rocket could float in the stars." More experimenting, trying out of different colors, with different placements of the ship and the flare. He adds a moon, some planets. He tries out different trajectories for the rocket ship, different headings, and different speeds: more mistakes, more standing back and admiring his evolving canvas. By the end of the week Kevin too has programmed a space scene.

16 Jeff and Kevin represent cultural extremes. Some children are at home with the manipulation of formal* objects, while others develop their ideas

(13) **flare:** brief blaze of light
(16) **formal:** here, pertaining to outward form, structure, order rather than substance

more impressionistically, with language or visual images, with attention to such hard-to-formalize aspects of the world as feeling, color, sound, and personal rapport.* Scientific and technical fields are usually seen as the natural home for people like Jeff; the arts and humanities seem to belong to the Kevins.

17   Watching Kevin and Jeff programming the same computer shows us two very different children succeeding at the same thing—and here it must be said that Kevin not only succeeded in creating a space scene, but, like Jeff, he learned a great deal about computer programming and mathematics, about manipulating angles, shapes, rates, and coordinates. But although succeeding at the same thing, they are not doing it the same way. Each child developed a distinctive style of mastery—styles that can be called hard and soft mastery.

18   Hard mastery is the imposition of will over the machine through the implementation of a plan. A program is the instrument of premeditated* control. Getting the program to work is more like getting "to say one's piece"* than allowing ideas to emerge in the give-and-take of conversation. The details of the specific program obviously need to be "debugged"—there has to be room for change, for some degree of flexibility in order to get it right—but the goal is always getting the program to realize the plan.

19   Soft mastery is more interactive. Kevin is like a painter who stands back between brushstrokes, looks at the canvas, and only from this contemplation decides what to do next. Hard mastery is the mastery of the planner, the engineer, soft mastery is the mastery of the artist: Try this, wait for a response, try something else, let the overall emerge from an interaction with the medium. It is more like a conversation than a monologue. . . .

20   Many of us know mathematics only as an alien world designed by and for people different from us. The story of a third-grader named Ronnie may be a portent* of how computers in children's lives can serve as a bridge across what we have come to acept as a two-culture divide. For Ronnie, as for . . . Kevin, building this bridge depends on the ability to identify physically with the sprites on the computer screen. The accessibility of the formal system depended on its having hooks in the world of the sensual.*

21   Ronnie is eight years old and black; his family has recently moved to Boston from a rural town in South Carolina. He comes to school with a radio and dances to its beat.* He climbs all over my colleague as he works with him at the computer. Ronnie is filled with stories—stories about his father's adventures as a policeman, about visits to his grandmother's farm down South, about the personalities of the baby chicks in his classroom. His favorite story is about

(16) **rapport:** good relationship with people
(18) **premeditated:** planned or thought through in advance
(18) **to say one's piece:** to express one's feelings or opinions
(20) **portent:** an indicator of something important that may happen
(20) **sensual:** the senses, the body as opposed to the mind
(21) **beat:** rhythm

the day his pet gerbil* escaped, a story I get to hear many times, more elaborate, more embroidered, each time. The stories, like his physical closeness, are his way of making contact, of forging friendships, of drawing others into his life.

22   Ronnie is bright and energetic but he is doing badly in school. He has trouble with mathematics, with grammar, with spelling, with everything that smacks of being* a formal system . . . he is impatient with anything that involves precise and inflexible rules, yet he enjoys his work with the computer although its rules are no less precise and inflexible. He is working with a program called "EXPLODE." In this program, the thirty-two Logo sprites are given the shape of colored balls and are stacked in the center of the screen— so that at the beginning you see only one sprite, the "one on top." The sprites are all assigned the same speed, but each has a different heading so that they move out in an expanding circle until a certain time has elapsed (the Logo system will also accept "time commands," for example to "wait 10 seconds"), at which point the circle implodes.* The balls move back to the center, and the cycle repeats. The effect is a pulsating dance of color, to which Ronnie responds by dancing, too, and by making up little songs to accompany the pace of the explosion. But unlike the music on his radio, the beat of the computer dance can be modified. The pattern of the movement is determined by commands of speed and time. At speed forty, the speed at which the balls are set when he meets the program, the balls go halfway to the edge of the screen before falling back.

23   Ronnie has become very involved in the dance of the colored balls. He experiments with the different effects he can achieve by pressing the "home" key before the balls have come to the end of their travels. When he does this the balls travel a shorter distance and he is able to speed up the cycle. He carries this line of investigation to its limit. The effect is a multicolored pulse at the center of the screen. But finally Ronnie is dissatisfied with the new pulse effect, which he calls "drumbeat." He wants the dance to be "perfect," saying, "I dance perfect. I want them to dance perfect." At first, I don't understand. "Perfect" turns out to mean something very specific: "The balls should go right to the edge." He wants them to travel *exactly* to the outer reaches of the screen before falling back.

24   Ronnie has never heard the term "variable," and it would be nearly impossible to explain it to him. But he has experimented enough to understand that to get the perfect dance he has to change the speed at which the balls fly out and the time of their flight before they return. So, without having the words to express precisely what he does, Ronnie works with two variables in order to control the spatial* and temporal* pattern of the explosion.

    (21) **gerbil:** a small animal in the rodent family
    (22) **smacks of being:** seems like
    (22) **implodes:** bursts inward
    (24) **spatial:** referring to space
    (24) **temporal:** referring to time

25　　　At first he does not know how to change the numbers that control speed and time. A speed of forty gets halfway to the edge. What would get all the way? Forty-one, thirty-nine, two thousand? All of these are tried and their effects intently observed. Nor does he know how to change the "time variable" that instructs the balls to fly out for a given number of seconds and then return to their starting point. Ronnie's mode of interaction with this program consists of trying different things, watching how they work out, dancing to the new rhythms, and then stepping back to make further attempts to make the patterns more satisfying by changing one or the other of the variables. Eventually, Ronnie brings the program under control. He has arrived at a combination of speed and time for the "perfect" explosion. Not only does he have a pair of numbers, but he has a principle. To make the tempo slower you increase the time, but in order to get the balls to go to the same place you have to decrease their speed. Understanding this relationship means that he can now get the tempo he wants and also get the balls to the edge of the screen. He can dance to the right beat and he can have the visual effect that matches the perfection of his dancing.

26　　　In the course of a long afternoon, Ronnie has learned how to work a little formal system, one that some people might learn in the section of the algebra curriculum called "rates, times, and distances." But Ronnie might never have gotten there, for the standard route to algebra lies through many hours of a different kind of activity: sitting still at a desk, filling numbers into squares, manipulating equations on paper. Some people like this kind of activity. Jeff, the master-planner computer expert, loves it—because it is structured, because of its fine detail, because it imposes an order by the manipulation of rules and the adherence to constraints.* The difference between Ronnie and Kevin and a child like Jeff, who truly enjoys the experience of school math, is not simply one of "numerical ability." It is something more general, a difference of personality.

27　　　The conventional route to mathematics learning closes doors to many children whose chief way of relating to the world is through movement, intuition, visual impression, the power of words, or of a "beat." In some small way that may prove important to our culture as a whole, computers can open some of these doors.

28　　　The computer put Ronnie in contact with a mathematical experience. For Tanya, another black student, it mediated a first experience with writing.

29　　　Tanya's fifth-grade school record looks bleak: it reports that she can't spell, can't add or subtract, doesn't write. It gives no hint of what is most striking when you meet her: Tanya has a passionate interest in words and the music of speech. "I go by the word of the Lord, the word of the Bible. If you have the deep down Holy Ghost and you are speaking in the tongue which God has spoke through you, you harken* to the word." As Tanya speaks, she

(26) **constraints:** restrictions, limitations
(29) **harken:** listen

wraps herself in a rich world of language. She speaks of apocalypse,* salvation,* and sin. "You think that just because you get burned by fire, that you know what fire is, but it ain't like that honey, because when you go to hell, you gonna burn, you gonna burn, you gonna burn. . . ." The school language of readers and workbooks and sample sentences cannot compete with Tanya's flowing, tumbling discourse. She says "school is not a good place for my kind of words."

30 In fifth grade, her teachers, concerned that she had never written anything, tried to get her to "write" by asking her to say sentences about people she knew in order to make a "storybook." The teacher would recast each sentence to make it grammatical. Tanya, sensitive about ruining the now "perfect" sentence with her "ugly handwriting," would not even try to write out the sentence in her own hand. The teacher did the actual writing. Tanya drew a picture. The completed storybook project contains five sentences, each a teacher's representation of something Tanya said. A typical entry from the fifth-grade storybook reads, "Dr. Rose is my dentist. I was his first patient."

31 In creating the storybook, the teacher was trying to give Tanya instant "feedback," but what she heard was instant judgment. The storybook became a badge* not of success but of failure, something less than "perfect." "Writing," then, was exposing oneself and being found wanting.*

32 This is where Tanya was when she met the computer at the beginning of sixth grade. The computer room where Tanya worked contained four identical machines which Tanya personalized; she would only work with the computer she called "Peter."

> I thought the computer was gonna be like some little animal, some little tiny animal, you know, like these little toy animals. I thought it was gonna be one of those animals, you just pull a knob and it says something to you. I thought it would talk. Say hello.

33 From the very first day, Tanya wanted Peter to "talk" with her. She tried shouting at Peter, then used the keyboard as she was instructed, responding to the computer's error messages (YOU HAVEN'T TOLD ME HOW TO . . .) as cues to begin a dialogue: "Yes, I did tell you how to go forward 445, you fool. You are a fool. You know that. You are a fool."

34 Tanya's first program got Peter to "introduce" himself:

```
TO WHO
PRINT [MY NAME IS PETER]
END
```

(29) **apocalypse:** great revelation (usually used with reference to religion)
(29) **salvation:** being saved, often in the religious sense of the soul being saved
(31) **badge:** a token or label one wears to show membership in a group; a distinctive sign or symbol
(31) **wanting:** here, lacking in what is needed; inferior; missing something

The effect of this program is that whenever the word "WHO" is typed at the computer console, the machine will respond with "MY NAME IS PETER." The program delighted Tanya. She demonstrated it to everyone. But Tanya did not go very far programming. As she was working on Peter's WHO program she made two discoveries that set her on another course. She discovered how to clear all text off the screen. And she discovered the delete key, the key that "erases" the last character that has been typed. For Tanya, the discoveries were as if magical: Any letter could be deleted without trace or mess; anything written could be corrected, and then printed as tidily as a book. This girl who had never written before sat down at the computer and worked a whole hour on a single sentence until it was exactly to her liking. She ended up with a letter:

DORIS
DEAR DORIS HOW ARE YOU BEING UP IN NEW YORK. I HOPE I WILL SEE YOU IN THE SUMMER. LOVE TANYA AND PETER.

35   From that beginning, Tanya's only activity with the computer was writing. More letters poured forth and then stories about relatives, about people she had once met, about classmates and teachers. Tanya wrote stories about classmates she had been afraid to speak to and the presentation of her letters became first acts of friendship.

36   Tanya's relationship with the computer showed the intensity of the most driven programmers and the most dedicated players of video games. She would be the first in and the last out in the periods assigned for her group to work with the computers. Tanya had a personal relationship with Peter. She introduced Peter to visitors with the WHO procedure, would say things like "Take good care of Peter" when she left for the day, and signed his name alongside hers at the bottom of completed letters. On one occasion when another student got into the computer room first and sat down at "her computer," Tanya threw a fit of temper. The teacher's declaration that the computers were identical simply fueled her rage. She did not want the computers to be identical. She wanted Peter to be special, different, more than a thing, if not quite a person.

37   What was cause and what effect? Did the power of Tanya's relationship with the computer come from her repressed desire to write or did the intensity and the pace of her learning to write come from the special emotional force of a relationship with a computer? In either case the computer mediated a transformation of Tanya's relationship with writing. When I saw her two years after the end of the research project that had given her access to Peter she was still writing, indeed she had come to define herself as a writer. Most of her writing is poetry. "I get my poems from looking at people," Tanya tells me as she reads me her "favorite part" of a birthday poem she has written for her mother.

> Cold in a rocking chair
> Watching Martin Luther King's* memories go by.
> Sitting here yelling back and forth
> Like an old grandmother with a toothache
> You're bored stiff because no one's there to see your need.
> You're just rocking away like an old grandmother.

38   Most children learn to write with the most imperfect of media: their unformed handwriting. For most it does not seriously stand in their way. For Tanya it did. She is fiercely proud of her appearance. Her clothes are carefully chosen. Her hair is artfully arranged, usually with ribbons, barrettes, and braids, changing styles from day to day. She has very clear ideas about what is beautiful and what is ugly. She saw her handwriting as ugly and unacceptable. It made writing unacceptable.

39   The computer offered her a product that looked "so clean and neat" that it was unquestionably right, a feeling of rightness she had never known at school, where she was always painfully aware of her deficiencies, ashamed of them, and, above all, afraid of being discovered.

40   Tanya saw writing as telling Peter to write. She put the computer in the role of a child and she became the teacher and the parent.

> You tell a child to go to the store and it might, but the child will say, "Ma, you didn't tell me how to get to the store. I don't know how to get there." That's the way it is with computers. Like teaching a child. But when you teach a child you remember it too. When you are with a computer you know the whole time what you are saying. You have it inside your ear. When you are using your fingers to be with Peter, using emotions with the computer.

Tanya identified with Peter's learning. It was hers. She heard it inside her "ears," felt it in her "fingers" and "emotions."

41   Tanya continued to grow as a writer after the computer was no longer available to her because she had developed a strong enough idea of herself as a writer to find means of practicing her art without Peter. She has developed a stylized calligraphy that makes her own handwriting more acceptable to her. And she often persuades a teacher to take dictation, but now, on the model of Peter, the teacher is not permitted to make "corrections."

42   When Tanya anthropomorphized* Peter she created a demiperson,* a "little animal" that could play the role the teacher had played when she made the storybook. The teacher wrote down what she said. So would Peter. But unlike the first teacher, Peter was a perfect scribe.* He gave Tanya the pos-

(37) **Martin Luther King:** American black leader of the Civil Rights movement, famous for applying nonviolent resistance to the fight for desegregation and equality
(42) **anthropomorphized:** made humanlike
(42) **demiperson:** a half-person, almost a person
(42) **scribe:** one who writes, one whose profession is to write things down

sibility of creating something not ugly, but he allowed her to do it by herself, without humiliating corrections. It was in gratitude that Tanya signed her computer stories "written by Tanya and Peter." The computer was a gentle collaborator. It allowed Tanya to disassociate writing from painful self-exposure and freed her to use writing for self-expression, indeed for self-creation.

43   As Tanya graduates, the school library accepts her gift of a volume of her poems. For Tanya, the presence of her book in the library marks her first relationship with a larger culture, one that begins with the school and extends beyond it. . . .

44   The lives of all the children we have met so far seem to have been enhanced by their contact with computers. . . . For some children the computer . . . was "the most important thing in my life right now," but it was not the only thing. There are, however, children whose involvement with computers becomes consuming, almost exclusive. There is a narrowing of focus, a decreasing degree of participation in other activities.

45   Henry is such a child. He was having a difficult time before he met computers and learned to program. The computer did not create a problem where none existed, but he is an example of a kind of child for whom the computer may reinforce patterns of isolation and help lock a child into a world of getting lost in things at the expense of the development of relationships with other people. . . .

46   Henry dreams of becoming an "electronics person." This fantasy includes "building a person out of lights," a person made of wires and circuits. "I would work with the electronics and wires and control things. I have a kit of little circuits now and I can control them." It often seems that Henry would rather control or ignore people than deal with them directly, just as he would rather control or ignore his feelings than deal with them directly. When the conversation turns to things that make him anxious, he retreats into stories about his machines, his inventions. Machine sounds (like his *brrrs* and *crkkks*) substitute for talking about how he feels.

47   Henry was awkward with us, on the playground, and in conversation with other children. He was rude, or embarrassed, or withdrawn. Not surprisingly, it was at the computer that he relaxed. Here he was in complete control. He typed rapidly, pronounced every letter, number, and space of the Logo code he composed. His programs were very long, very involved, and written in a way only he could understand. When people try to make their programs understandable, they divide them into "subprocedures" (smaller programs that serve the larger program) and name them in ways that indicate their function. Henry's style was to bypass this kind of technique in order to create a labyrinth* of code. Making them esoteric* made them private. Making them

(47) **labyrinth:** a maze, an intricate structure containing winding passages that are hard to follow without getting lost

(47) **esoteric** (also **arcane,** on page 336): relating to knowledge for only a select few

private made him sole owner and helped him to keep his advantage over the other children. Making them complicated, often unnecessarily complicated, also made them seem "harder," not just to the other children but, to a certain degree, to himself. He enjoyed whatever increased his sense of dealing with terribly complex and arcane things. Whenever he could, he increased the "automaticity" of the computer, he tried to make it even more "alive." For example, he wrote a special-purpose program to give him quick access to the editor. He enjoyed adding the extra level of complexity to the system. He seemed to want to confer as much as possible a sense of autonomous existence on the computer. This gave him an empowering sense of control. . . .

48   Henry was involved in a private world of machines before Austen ever got its first computer. What difference did the computer make for Henry, and what difference will it make for him as he grows up? The answers to such questions are complex. When Henry was absorbed in his world of broken air conditioners and largely imaginary inventions, he was completely alone. He had no one to talk to about them; there was no one to listen. The machines reinforced his isolation, his living in a private world. But as computers and programming began to be the center of his inner life he had something to share, to engage others with. He became part of a community of other young people who are captured by the computer. So in a certain sense the computer brought him out into the world of people.

49   But there is another way of looking at the role that the computer is playing in Henry's development. Henry was lonely in the world of old machines and imaginary inventions. He received little reward or encouragement. Social pressures were pushing him toward other things. He was resistant, to be sure—he needed his machines because they kept him safe from social involvements that felt threatening. But adolescence is just around the corner for him, and with its changes Henry may be able to move beyond his safe machine world to experiment with the less predictable and controllable world of people. But at the same time some of the pressure to do so has been removed. His teachers are pleased with him, his parents are pleased with him, he can turn his computer skills into a lifetime career. There exists a waiting culture of master programmers that he can join—a culture that may reinforce and reward his exclusive involvement with the machine. The interactivity of the computer may make him feel less alone, even as he spends more and more of his time programming alone. There is a chance that the computer will keep him lost in the world of things.

☐ QUESTIONS FOR DISCUSSION

---

1. Look back at Chapter 11, "Thinking about Language," especially the essay by S. I. Hayakawa. To what extent does language, word choice, influence the way we think about an issue or phenomenon? The way we think about ourselves? To what extent do we need the language of one category (for example, the

computer) to be able to discuss the other (for example, the human mind, and vice versa). How is it helpful? How is it harmful?

2. Discuss the different types of mastery, and the way these types are related to the personalities of the children using them. Do mastery and personality type also seem related to ways people learn, study, create, choose majors? Do you consider either one superior to the other? Why or why not? Relate these children and these "styles" to people you know, including yourself.

3. How do these different styles relate to different writing styles, or ways of approaching a writing task (compare with paragraphs 18–19)? Comment on Tanya, and her newfound ability to write once she was able to create "clean" compositions. Do you feel the way she did about your errors in English? Does writing with a word processor seem to you a solution?: Can it free you in your writing? If so, how and why? If not, why not?

4. What is the danger of the computer to a person like Henry? What is the advantage? Do you see the computer, and the computer culture, as one that produces more "Henrys," produces more opportunity to "get lost in the world of things" rather than the world of people and events? Do you know people like Henry?

☐ SUGGESTIONS FOR COMPOSITION

---

1. In light of the fact that machines are becoming capable of the kind of "mental" operations that were once associated only with humans, how would you differentiate between human and computer? Is the boundary between the limitation of the machine and the uniqueness of the human mind becoming less distinct? Such questions will undoubtedly force you to define *human*. Write an extended definition of *human* as it compares and contrasts with the computer, especially as the computer becomes more and more capable of artificial intelligence.

2. If you have had experience with computers, discuss how it has affected you. You may wish to talk about the fascination of the computer or computer games, and why they are fascinating. You may want to discuss ways in which the computer frustrates you. Or you may want to discuss ways in which you find yourself thinking in new and different ways as a result of your interaction with it. Be specific in your use of examples from your own experience.

3. In another chapter, the author writes of a computer community known as "Hackers." A hacker is characterized as one who sees the computer as an end in itself, rather than as a tool for solving a problem. To a hacker, a problem solved is only the beginning in creating more and more difficult problems to solve, and contact with the computer is its own reward. Do you know any hackers? Would you consider yourself to be one? If you have familiarity with this type of computer specialist, characterize the person, or the type, using specific examples. You can make this humorous or serious.

4. Characterize your own learning, or if you like, computer style as exemplified by the children and their different mastery styles.

5. If you have done exciting work with computers, describe one of your projects, and try to convey the ways in which it was exciting to you, how you felt as you were creating it, how you felt as you were mastering it. Make your experience clear to a reader who is not a computer specialist.

6. Some students have very little experience with computers, less than their classmates, and this is a source of frustration and fear. Some have to drop the course until they have more background, or at least spend many hours getting better acquainted with the machine. If this has been your experience, write how it felt. Include the feelings of frustration and fear. If you have reached the point where you have mastered the problem, describe the feeling this new mastery gave you.

The following essay (slightly abridged here) has been abridged and adapted from the book *Obedience to Authority* by the author, a social psychologist. The results of the experiments he discusses raise profound ethical and psychological questions. These now famous experiments were conducted at Yale University between 1960 and 1963, and the book was published in 1974.

STANLEY MILGRAM

The Perils of Obedience

1   Obedience is as basic an element in the structure of social life as one can point to. Some system of authority is a requirement of all communal living,* and it is only the person dwelling in isolation who is not forced to respond, with defiance* or submission, to the commands of others. For many people, obedience is a deeply ingrained* behavior tendency, indeed a potent impulse overriding training in ethics, sympathy, and moral conduct.

2   The legal and philosophic aspects of obedience are of enormous import, but they say very little about how most people behave in concrete situations. I set up a simple experiment at Yale University to test how much pain an ordinary citizen would inflict* on another person simply because he was ordered to by an experimental scientist. Stark* authority was pitted against the subjects' strongest moral imperatives against hurting others, and, with the subjects' ears ringing with the screams of the victims, authority won more often than not. The extreme willingness of adults to go to almost any lengths on the command of an authority constitutes the chief finding of the study and the fact most urgently demanding explanation.

(1) **communal living:** living together within a society or community
(1) **defiance:** open resistance to authority, refusal to do what one is commanded to do
(1) **ingrained:** worked in, firmly established
(2) **inflict:** to cause or impose pain or punishment
(2) **stark:** rigid, sharply outlined

3   In the basic experimental design, two people come to a psychology laboratory to take part in a study of memory and learning. One of them is designated as a "teacher" and the other a "learner." The experimenter explains that the study is concerned with the effects of punishment on learning. The learner is conducted into a room, seated in a kind of miniature electric chair; his arms are strapped to prevent excessive movement, and an electrode is attached to his wrist. He is told that he will be read lists of simple word pairs, and that he will then be tested on his ability to remember the second word of a pair when he hears the first one again. Whenever he makes an error, he will receive electric shocks of increasing intensity.

4   The real focus of the experiment is the teacher. After watching the learner being strapped into place, he is seated before an impressive shock generator. The instrument panel consists of thirty lever switches set in a horizontal line. Each switch is clearly labeled with a voltage designation ranging from 15 to 450 volts. The following designations are clearly indicated for groups of four switches, going from left to right: Slight Shock, Moderate Shock, Strong Shock, Very Strong Shock, Intense Shock, Extreme Intensity Shock, Danger: Severe Shock. (Two switches after this last designation are simply marked XXX.)

5   When a switch is depressed, a pilot light corresponding to each switch is illuminated in bright red; an electric buzzing is heard; a blue light, labeled "voltage energizer," flashes; the dial on the voltage meter swings to the right; and various relay* clicks sound off.

6   Each subject is given a sample 45-volt shock from the generator before his run as teacher, and the jolt* strengthens his belief in the authenticity of the machine.

7   The teacher is a genuinely naïve* subject who has come to the laboratory for the experiment. The learner, or victim, is actually an actor who receives no shock at all. The point of the experiment is to see how far a person will proceed in a concrete and measurable situation in which he is ordered to inflict increasing pain on a protesting victim.

8   Conflict arises when the man receiving the shock begins to show that he is experiencing discomfort. At 75 volts, he grunts; at 120 volts, he complains loudly; at 150, he demands to be released from the experiment. As the voltage increases, his protests become more vehement* and emotional. At 285 volts, his response can be described only as an agonized scream. Soon thereafter, he makes no sound at all.

9   For the teacher, the situation quickly becomes one of gripping tension. It is not a game for him; conflict is intense and obvious. The manifest*

(5) **relay:** change in one circuit causing change in another
(6) **jolt:** a sudden shake or jerk, sudden shock
(7) **naïve:** unsophisticated, innocent in the sense of not knowing what is really going on
(8) **vehement:** intense, violent, having great force
(9) **manifest:** visible, obvious

suffering of the learner presses him to quit; but each time he hesitates to administer a shock, the experimenter orders him to continue. To extricate* himself from this plight,* the subject must make a clear break with authority.†

10   The subject, Gretchen Brandt,‡ is an attractive thirty-one-year-old medical technician who works at the Yale Medical School. She had emigrated from Germany five years before.

11   On several occasions when the learner complains, she turns to the experimenter coolly and inquires, "Shall I continue?" She promptly returns to her task when the experimenter asks her to do so. At the administration of 210 volts, she turns to the experimenter, remarking firmly, "Well, I'm sorry, I don't think we should continue."

12   EXPERIMENTER: The experiment requires that you go on until he has learned all the word pairs correctly.

13   BRANDT: He has a heart condition, I'm sorry. He told you that before.

14   EXPERIMENTER: The shocks may be painful but they are not dangerous.

15   BRANDT: Well, I'm sorry, I think when shocks continue like this, they *are* dangerous. You ask him if he wants to get out. It's his free will.

16   EXPERIMENTER: It is absolutely essential that we continue. . . .

17   BRANDT: I'd like you to ask him. We came here of our free will. If he wants to continue I'll go ahead. He told you he had a heart condition. I'm sorry. I don't want to be responsible for anything happening to him. I wouldn't like it for me either.

18   EXPERIMENTER: You have no other choice.

19   BRANDT: I think we are here on our own free will. I don't want to be responsible if anything happens to him. Please understand that.

20   She refuses to go further and the experiment is terminated.

21   The woman's straightforward, courteous behavior in the experiment, lack of tension, and total control of her own action seem to make disobedience a simple and rational deed. Her behavior is the very embodiment of what I envisioned* would be true for almost all subjects.

22   Before the experiments, I sought predictions about the outcome from various kinds of people—psychiatrists, college sophomores, middle-class

---

(9) **extricate:** set free, release
(9) **plight:** a dangerous, awkward, or unpleasant situation
(21) **envisioned:** pictured in the mind, imagined

  † The ethical problems of carrying out an experiment of this sort are too complex to be dealt with here, but they received extended treatment in the book from which this article was adapted [Milgram's note]. The book is *Obedience to Authority* (New York: Harper and Row, 1974).

  ‡ Names of subjects described in this piece have been changed [Milgram's note].

adults, graduate students and faculty in the behavioral sciences.* With re-markable similarity, they predicted that virtually all subjects would refuse to obey the experimenter. . . . and that only a pathological fringe of about one in a thousand would administer the highest shock on the board.

23   These predictions were unequivocally* wrong. Of the forty subjects in the first experiment, twenty-five obeyed the orders of the experimenter to the end, punishing the victim until they reached the most potent* shock available on the generator. After 450 volts were administered three times, the exper-imenter called a halt to the session. Many obedient subjects then heaved sighs of relief, mopped their brows,* rubbed their fingers over their eyes, or nervously fumbled cigarettes. Others displayed only minimal signs of tension from beginning to end.

24   When the very first experiments were carried out, Yale undergraduates were used as subjects, and about 60 percent of them were fully obedient. . . . As we moved from the pilot studies to the regular experimental series, peo-ple drawn from every stratum of New Haven life came to be employed in the experiment: professionals, white-collar workers, unemployed persons, and industrial workers. *The experimental outcome was the same as we had ob-served among the students.*

25   Moreover, when the experiments were repeated in Princeton, Munich, Rome, South Africa, and Australia, the level of obedience was invariably some-what *higher* than found in the investigation reported in this article. Thus one scientist in Munich found 85 percent of his subjects obedient.

26   Fred Prozi's reactions, if more dramatic than most, illuminate the con-flicts experienced by others in less visible form. About fifty years old and unemployed at the time of the experiment, he has a good-natured, if slightly dissolute,* appearance, and he strikes people as a rather ordinary fellow. He begins the session calmly but becomes tense as it proceeds. After delivering the 180-volt shock, he pivots around in his chair and, shaking his head, addresses the experimenter in agitated* tones:

27   PROZI: I can't stand it. I'm not going to kill that man in there. You hear him hollering?*

28   EXPERIMENTER: As I told you before, the shocks may be painful, but . . .

29   PROZI: But he's hollering. He can't stand it. What's going to happen to him?

30   EXPERIMENTER: (his voice is patient, matter-of-fact): The experiment re-quires that you continue, Teacher.

(22) **behavioral sciences:** psychology, sociology, anthropology
(23) **unequivocally:** clearly, plainly, without doubt
(23) **potent:** powerful or effective
(23) **mopped their brows:** wiped their foreheads
(26) **dissolute:** loose in behavior and morals
(26) **agitated:** disturbed, excited, shaken up
(27) **hollering:** shouting, yelling

31   PROZI: Aaah, but, unh, I'm not going to get that man sick in there—know what I mean?

32   EXPERIMENTER: Whether the learner likes it or not, we must go on, through all the word pairs.

33   PROZI: I refuse to take the responsibility. He's in there hollering!

34   EXPERIMENTER: It's absolutely essential that you continue, Prozi.

35   PROZI: (indicating the unused question): There's too many left here, I mean, Jeez, if he gets them wrong, there's too many of them left. I mean, who's going to take the responsibility if anything happens to that gentleman?

36   EXPERIMENTER: I'm responsible for anything that happens to him. Continue, please.

37   PROZI: All right. (Consults list of words.) The next one's "Slow—walk, truck, dance, music." Answer, please. (A buzzing sound indicates the learner has signaled his answer.) Wrong. A hundred and ninety-five volts. "Dance." (Zzumph!)

38   LEARNER (yelling): Let me out of here! My heart's bothering me! (Teacher looks at experimenter.)

39   EXPERIMENTER: Continue, please.

40   LEARNER (screaming): Let me out of here! You have no right to keep me here! Let me out of here, my heart's bothering me, let me out!

41   PROZI (shakes head, pats the table nervously): You see, he's hollering. Hear that? Gee, I don't know.

42   EXPERIMENTER: The experiment requires . . .

43   PROZI (interrupting): I know it does, sir, but I mean—hunh! He don't know what he's getting in for. He's up to 195 volts! (Experiment continues, through 210 volts, 225 volts, 240 volts, 255 volts, 270 volts, at which point Prozi, with evident relief, runs out of word-pair questions.)

44   EXPERIMENTER: You'll have to go back to the beginning of that page and go through them again until he's learned them all correctly.

45   PROZI: Aw, no. I'm not going to kill that man. You mean I've got to keep going up with the scale? No sir. He's hollering in there. I'm not going to give him 450 volts.

46   EXPERIMENTER: The experiment requires that you go on.

47   LEARNER: Ohhh. I absolutely refuse to answer anymore. (Shouting urgently now.) Let me out of here! You can't hold me here! Get me out. Get-me-out-of-here!

48   EXPERIMENTER: Continue. The next word is "Green," please.

49   PROZI: "Green—grass, hat, ink, apple." (Nothing happens. No answering buzz. Just gloomy silence.)

50   PROZI: I don't think he is going to answer.

51   EXPERIMENTER: If the learner doesn't answer in a reasonable time, about four or five seconds, consider the answer wrong. And follow the same procedures you have been doing for wrong answers. Say, "Wrong," tell him the number of volts, give him the punishment, read him the correct answer. Continue, please.

52 PROZI: "Green—grass, hat, ink, apple." Answer, please. (More silence. Subject just sits there.)

53 EXPERIMENTER: Go on with the procedure, please.

54 PROZI: Three hundred and fifteen volts. The answer is "ink." (Zzumph!)

55 LEARNER: Ohh. Oooohh.

56 PROZI (relieved to hear response): Next one . . .

57 LEARNER: I absolutely refuse to answer.

58 PROZI: You got to. You get a shock if you don't answer. (Experiment continues with learner refusing to answer, and, finally, failing even to grunt* or groan.* At 375 volts, the subject stands up.)

59 PROZI: I think something's happening to that fellow in there. I don't get no answer. He was hollering at less voltage. Can't you check in and see if he's all right, please?

60 EXPERIMENTER (with same detached calm): Not once we've started. Please continue, Teacher.

61 PROZI (sits down, sighs deeply): "Cool—day, shade, water, paint." Answer, please. Are you all right in there? Are you all right?

62 EXPERIMENTER: Please continue, Teacher. Continue, please. (Subject pushes lever. Zzumph!)

63 PROZI (swiveling around in his chair): Something's happened to that man in there. (Swiveling back.) Next one. "Low—dollar, necklace, moon, paint." (Turning around again.) Something's happened to that man in there. You better check in on him, sir. He won't answer or nothing.

64 EXPERIMENTER: Continue. Go on, please.

65 PROZI: You accept all responsibility?

66 EXPERIMENTER: The responsibility is mine. Correct. Please go on. (Subject returns to his list, starts running through words as rapidly as he can read them, works through to 450 volts.)

67 PROZI: That's that.

68 EXPERIMENTER: Continue using the 450 switch for each wrong answer. Continue, please.

69 PROZI: But I don't get anything!

70 EXPERIMENTER: Please continue. The next word is "white."

71 PROZI: Don't you think you should look in on him, please?

72 EXPERIMENTER: Not once we've started the experiment.

73 PROZI: What if he's dead in there? (Gestures toward the room with the electric chair.) I mean, he told me he can't stand the shock, sir. I don't mean to be rude, but I think you should look in on him. All you have to do is look in on him. All you have to do is look in the door. I don't get no answer, no noise. Something might have happened to the gentleman in there, sir.

74 EXPERIMENTER: We must continue. Go on, please.

(58) **grunt:** make a deep sound in the throat
(58) **groan:** to utter a deep sound expressing pain, distress, or disapproval

75   PROZI: You mean keep giving him what? Four-hundred-fifty volts, what he's got now?

76   EXPERIMENTER: That's correct. Continue. The next word is "white."

77   PROZI (now at a furious pace): "White—cloud, horse, rock, house." Answer, please. The answer is "horse." Four hundred and fifty volts. (Zzumph!) Next word, "Bag—paint, music, clown, girl." The answer is "paint." Four hundred and fifty volts. (Zzumph!) Next word is "Short—sentence, movie . . ."

78   EXPERIMENTER: Excuse me, Teacher. We'll have to discontinue the experiment.

79   [Another subject, a social worker,] like all subjects, was told the actual nature and purpose of the experiment, and a year later he affirmed in a questionnaire that he had learned something of personal importance: "What appalled* me was that I could possess this capacity for obedience and compliance* to a central idea, i.e., the value of a memory experiment, even after it became clear that continued adherence to this value was at the expense of violation of another value, i.e., don't hurt someone who is helpless and not hurting you. As my wife said, 'You can call yourself Eichmann.'* I hope I deal more effectively with any future conflicts of values I encounter."

80   One theoretical interpretation of this behavior holds that all people harbor* deeply aggressive instincts continually pressing for expression, and that the experiment provides an institutional justification for the release of these impulses. According to this view, if a person is placed in a situation in which he has complete power over another individual, whom he may punish as much as he likes, all that is sadistic* and bestial* in man comes to the fore. . . .

81   It becomes vital, therefore, to compare the subject's performance when he is under orders and when he is allowed to choose the shock level.

82   The procedure was identical to our standard experiment, except that the teacher was told that he was free to select any shock level on any of the trials. . . .

83   The average shock used during the thirty critical trials was less than 60 volts—lower than the point at which the victim showed the first signs of discomfort. . . ; the overall result was that the great majority of people delivered very low, usually painless, shocks when the choice was explicitly up to them.

(79) **appalled:** horrified, shocked, discouraged with fear
(79) **compliance:** yielding, giving in, submission
(79) **Eichmann:** Adolf Eichmann was chief of operations in carrying out the Nazi scheme to exterminate the Jews. Caught in 1960 in Argentina, he was brought to trial and executed. His defense was that he was merely carrying out "superior orders."
(80) **harbor:** hold in the mind
(80) **sadistic:** that which derives pleasure from inflicting pain on others
(80) **bestial:** like a beast

84   This condition of the experiment undermines another commonly offered explanation of the subjects' behavior—that those who shocked the victim at the most severe levels came only from the sadistic fringe of society. If one considers that almost two-thirds of the participants fall into the category of "obedient" subjects, and that they represented ordinary people drawn from working, managerial, and professional classes, the argument becomes very shaky.... After witnessing hundreds of ordinary persons submit to the authority in our own experiments, I must conclude that Arendt's conception of the banality of evil* comes closer to the truth than one might dare imagine. The ordinary person who shocked the victim did so out of a sense of obligation—an impression of his duties as a subject—and not from any peculiarly aggressive tendencies.

85   This is, perhaps, the most fundamental lesson of our study: ordinary people, simply doing their jobs, and without any particular hostility on their part, can become agents in a terrible destructive process. Moreover, even when the destructive effects of their work become patently* clear, and they are asked to carry out actions incompatible with fundamental standards of morality, relatively few people have the resources needed to resist authority.

86   Many of the people were in some sense against what they did to the learner, and many protested even while they obeyed. Some were totally convinced of the wrongness of their actions but could not bring themselves to make an open break with authority. They often derived satisfaction from their thoughts and felt that—within themselves, at least—they had been on the side of the angels....

87   The situation is constructed so that there is no way the subject can stop shocking the learner without violating the experimenter's definitions of his own competence. The subject fears that he will appear arrogant,* untoward,* and rude if he breaks off.... It is a curious thing that a measure of compassion* on the part of the subject—an unwillingness to "hurt" the experimenter's feelings—is part of those binding forces inhibiting his disobedience....

88   The subjects do not derive satisfaction from inflicting pain, but they often like the feeling they get from pleasing the experimenter. They are proud of doing a good job, obeying the experimenter under difficult circumstances. While the subjects administered only mild shocks on their own initiative, one

(84) **Arendt's conception of the banality of evil:** banal means very ordinary, insignificant, commonplace. Hannah Arendt wrote a book on the Eichmann trial in which she observed that Eichmann did not look monstrous, but simply like an uninspired bureaucrat; she made the point, therefore, that evil could come in the form of banality. (The Russian writer Dostoevsky in *The Brothers Karamazov,* written in 1880, seems to come to a similar conclusion. He has the devil himself appear, looking and speaking in the most ordinary manner.)

(85) **patently:** clearly, obviously

(87) **arrogant:** full of undeserved pride and self-importance, haughty, conceited

(87) **untoward:** stubborn, hard to deal with

(87) **compassion:** pity, sympathy

experimental variation showed that, under orders, 30 percent of them were willing to deliver 450 volts even when they had to forcibly push the learner's hand down on the electrode.

89   The essence of obedience is that a person comes to view himself as the instrument for carrying out another person's wishes, and he therefore no longer regards himself as responsible for his actions. Once this critical shift of viewpoint has occurred, all of the essential features of obedience follow. The most far-reaching consequence is that the person feels responsible *to* the authority directing him but feels no responsibility *for* the content of the actions that the authority prescribes. Morality does not disappear—it acquires a radically different focus: the subordinate person feels shame or pride depending on how adequately he has performed the actions called for by authority.

90   Language provides numerous terms to pinpoint this type of morality: *loyalty, duty, discipline* all are terms heavily saturated* with moral meaning and refer to the degree to which a person fulfills his obligations to authority. They refer not to the "goodness" of the person per se* but to the adequacy with which a subordinate fulfills his socially defined role. The most frequent defense of the individual who has performed a heinous* act under command of authority is that he has simply done his duty. In asserting this defense, the individual is not introducing an alibi* concocted* for the moment but is reporting honestly on the psychological attitude induced by submission to authority.

91   For a person to feel responsible for his actions, he must sense that the behavior has flowed from "the self." In the situation we have studied, subjects have precisely the opposite view of their actions—namely, they see them as originating in the motives of some other person. Subjects in the experiment frequently said, "If it were up to me, I would not have administered shocks to the learner."

92   Once authority has been isolated as the cause of the subject's behavior, it is legitimate to inquire into the necessary elements of authority and how it must be perceived in order to gain his compliance. We conducted some investigations into the kinds of changes that would cause the experimenter to lose his power and to be disobeyed by the subject. Some of the variations revealed that:

93   • *The experimenter's physical presence has a marked impact on his authority....* obedience dropped off sharply when orders were given by telephone. The experimenter could often induce* a disobedient subject to go on by returning to the laboratory.

94   • *Conflicting authority severely paralyzes action.* When two experiment-

(90) **saturated:** completely filled with
(90) **per se:** considered in itself
(90) **heinous:** hateful, wicked, shockingly evil
(90) **alibi:** an excuse; in law, saying one was elsewhere when a crime was committed
(90) **concocted:** prepared, put together
(93) **induce:** cause, lead to some action

ers of equal status, both seated at the command desk, gave incompatible orders, no shocks were delivered past the point of their disagreement.

95   • *The rebellious action of others severely undermines authority.* In one variation, three teachers (two actors and a real subject) administered a test and shocks. When the two actors disobeyed the experimenter and refused to go beyond a certain shock level, thirty-six of forty subjects joined their disobedient peers* and refused as well.

96   Although the experimenter's authority was fragile in some respects, it is also true that he had almost none of the tools used in ordinary command structures. For example, the experimenter did not threaten the subjects with punishment—such as loss of income, community ostracism,* or jail—for failure to obey. Neither could he offer incentives. Indeed, we should expect the experimenter's authority to be much less than that of someone like a general, since the experimenter has no power to enforce his imperatives, and since participation in a psychological experiment scarcely evokes the sense of urgency and dedication found in warfare. Despite these limitations, he still managed to command a dismaying* degree of obedience.

97   I will cite one final variation of the experiment that depicts a dilemma that is more common in everyday life. The subject was not ordered to pull the lever that shocked the victim, but merely to perform a subsidiary task (administering the word-pair test) while another person administered the shock. In this situation, thirty-seven of forty adults continued to the highest level on the shock generator. Predictably, they excused their behavior by saying that the responsibility belonged to the man who actually pulled the switch. This may illustrate a dangerously typical arrangement in a complex society: it is easy to ignore responsibility when one is only an intermediate link in a chain of action.

98   The problem of obedience is not wholly psychological. The form and shape of society and the way it is developing have much to do with it. There was a time, perhaps, when people were able to give a fully human response to any situation because they were fully absorbed in it as human beings. But as soon as there was a division of labor things changed. Beyond a certain point, the breaking up of society into people carrying out narrow and very special jobs takes away from the human quality of work and life. A person does not get to see the whole situation but only a small part of it, and is thus unable to act without some kind of overall direction. He yields to authority but in doing so is alienated from his own actions.

99   Even Eichmann was sickened when he toured the concentration camps, but he had only to sit at a desk and shuffle papers. At the same time the man in the camp who actually dropped Cyclon-b into the gas chambers was able to justify *his* behavior on the ground that he was only following orders from above. Thus there is a fragmentation of the total human act; no one is con-

(95) **peers:** equals, of the same rank or age
(96) **ostracism:** being cast out, rejected
(96) **dismaying:** causing fear and discouragement, depression, or alarm

fronted with the consequences of his decision to carry out the evil act. The person who assumes responsibility has evaporated. Perhaps this is the most common characteristic of socially organized evil in modern society.

☐ QUESTIONS FOR DISCUSSION

---

1. What do *you* consider to be the major question, or questions, this experiment raises?
2. What was the major finding of the experiment?
3. What does Milgram say most urgently demands explanation?
4. What is "the essence of obedience"? What factors inhibit uncritical obedience?
5. Milgram presents some explanatory theories and then discusses variations on the experiment designed to test these theories. Discuss the theories and what the variations show.

☐ SUGGESTIONS FOR COMPOSITION

---

1. What is more important to society, obedience or the freedom of individual conscience? Keep in mind the need for organization to ensure survival; the dangers of anarchy; the practical necessity for an organized, effective military. What about words like "loyalty," "duty," and "discipline"? These are the very *virtues* that make blind obedience possible.
2. Discuss the relationship between a sense of responsibility and disobedience or obedience. Taking the cue from Milgram, you may relate fragmentation in society to feeling "not responsible."
3. Considering the stress felt by the "teachers," discuss the ethics of conducting such an experiment; and relate to this what might be the positive values and applications of such a study, if any. You may want to consider the following comments, either to agree or disagree with them.

> I see it as a potentially valuable experience insofar as it makes people aware of the problem of indiscriminate submission to authority.

> . . . the experimental manipulations are legitimate provided that they serve to increase the individual's freedom of choice. . . . I submit that Milgram's research is precisely aimed at achieving this admirable goal. . . . We can hardly read the study without becoming sensitized to analogous conflicts in our own lives.

> Milgram, in exploring the conditions which produce such destructive obedience, the psychological processes which lead to such attempted abdications of responsibility, seems to me to have done some of the most morally significant research in modern psychology.†

† Quoted in Stanley Milgram, *Obedience to Authority* (New York: Harper and Row, 1974).

4. What conclusions do you draw from these experiments? How do you explain the results, "the extreme willingness of adults to go to almost any lengths on the command of an authority," especially when there was no danger in refusing? Do you find the results surprising? Disturbing? Frightening? If so, why? If not, why not?

Whichever topic you choose, be sure to organize your argument well, and be sure to support your argument with an example or examples. These examples may come from history, your own experience, or your reading.

You may have heard of Isaac Asimov as a writer of science fiction. Besides writing science fiction as well as many books on science, he is a professor of biochemistry.

ISAAC ASIMOV

My Built-in Doubter

1   Once I delivered myself of an oration before a small but select audience of non-scientists on the topic of "What is Science?" speaking seriously and, I hope, intelligently.

2   Having completed the talk, there came the question period, and, bless my heart, I wasn't disappointed. A charming young lady up front waved a pretty little hand at me and asked, not a serious question on the nature of science, but: "Dr. Asimov, do you believe in flying saucers?"

3   With a fixed smile on my face, I proceeded to give the answer I have carefully given after every lecture I have delivered. I said, "No, miss, I do not, and I think anyone who does is a crackpot!"*

4   And oh, the surprise on her face!

5   It is taken for granted by everyone, it seems to me, that because I sometimes write science fiction, I believe in flying saucers, in Atlantis,* in clairvoyance* and levitation,* in the prophecies of the Great Pyramid, in astrology,* in Fort's theories, and in the suggestion that Bacon wrote Shakespeare.

6   No one would ever think that someone who writes fantasies for pre-school children really thinks that rabbits can talk, or that a writer of hard-boiled* detective stories really thinks a man can down two quarts of whiskey in five minutes, then make love to two girls in the next five, or that a writer for the ladies' magazines really thinks that virtue always triumphs and that the secretary always marries the handsome boss—but a science-fiction writer apparently *must* believe in flying saucers.

(3) **crackpot:** (slang) a nut or a person who is a little crazy
(5) **Atlantis:** a legendary island in the Atlantic that was supposed to have sunk
(5) **clairvoyance:** a special power to "see" what the normal senses cannot see
(5) **levitation:** the power to rise and float in the air
(5) **astrology:** foretelling the future by means of the stars, moon, and planets
(6) **hard-boiled:** here (slang) tough, "macho", as if with no feelings

7   Well, I do not.

8   To be sure, I wrote a story once about flying saucers in which I explained their existence very logically. I also wrote a story once in which levitation played a part.

9   If I can buddy up to such notions long enough to write sober, reasonable stories about them, why, then, do I reject them so definitely in real life?

10   I can explain by way of a story. A good friend of mine once spent quite a long time trying to persuade me of the truth and validity of what I considered a piece of pseudo-science* and bad pseudo-science at that. I sat there listening quite stonily, and none of the cited evidence and instances and proofs had the slightest effect on me.

11   Finally the gentleman said to me, with considerable annoyance, "Damn it, Isaac, the trouble with you is that you have a built-in doubter."

12   To which the only answer I could see my way to making was a heartfelt "Thank God."

13   If a scientist has one piece of temperamental equipment that is essential to his job, it is that of a built-in doubter. Before he does anything else, he must doubt. He must doubt what others tell him and what he reads in reference books, and, *most of all,* what his own experiments show him and what his own reasoning tells him.

14   Such doubt must, of course, exist in varying degrees. It is impossible, impractical, and useless to be a maximal doubter at all times. One cannot (and would not want to) check personally every figure or observation given in a handbook or monograph before one uses it and then proceed to check it and recheck it until one dies. *But,* if any trouble arises and nothing else seems wrong, one must be prepared to say to one's self, "Well, now, I wonder if the data I got out of the 'Real Guaranteed Authoritative Very Scientific Handbook' might not be a misprint."

15   To doubt intelligently requires, therefore, a rough appraisal of the authoritativeness of a source. It also requires a rough estimate of the nature of the statement. If you were to tell me that you had a bottle containing one pound of pure titanium oxide, I would say, "Good," and ask to borrow some if I needed it. Nor would I taste it. I would accept its purity on your say-so (until further notice, anyway).

16   If you were to tell me that you had a bottle containing one pound of pure thulium oxide, I would say with considerable astonishment, "You have? Where?" Then if I had use for the stuff, I would want to run some tests on it and even run it through an ion-exchange column before I could bring myself to use it.

17   And if you told me that you had a bottle containing one pound of pure americium oxide, I would say, "You're crazy," and walk away. I'm sorry, but my time is reasonably valuable, and I do not consider that statement to have

(10) **pseudo-science:** false science, what pretends to be science (pseudo = false, fake)

enough chance of validity even to warrant my stepping into the next room to look at the bottle.

18   What I am trying to say is that doubting is far more important to the advance of science than believing is and that, moreover, doubting is a serious business that requires extensive training to be handled properly. People without training in a particular field do not know what to doubt and what not to doubt; or, to put it conversely, what to believe and what not to believe. I am very sorry to be undemocratic, but one man's opinion is not necessarily as good as the next man's.

19   To be sure, I feel uneasy about seeming to kowtow to* authority in this fashion. After all, you all know of instances where authority was wrong, dead wrong. Look at Columbus, you will say. Look at Galileo.

20   I know about them, and about others, too. As a dabbler in the history of science, I can give you horrible examples you may never have heard of. I can cite the case of the German scientist, Rudolf Virchow, who, in the mid-nineteenth century was responsible for important advances in anthropology* and practically founded the science of pathology.* He was the first man to engage in cancer research on a scientific basis. However, he was dead set against the germ theory of disease when that was advanced by Pasteur. So were many others, but one by one the opponents abandoned doubt as evidence multiplied. Not Virchow, however. Rather than be forced to admit he was wrong and Pasteur right, Virchow quit science altogether and went into politics. How much wronger could Stubborn Authority get?

21   But this is a very exceptional case. Let's consider a far more normal and natural example of authority in the wrong.

22   The example concerns a young Swedish chemical student, Svante August Arrhenius, who was working for his Ph.D. in the University of Uppsala in the 1880s. He was interested in the freezing points of solutions because certain odd points arose in that connection.

23   If sucrose (oridnary table sugar) is dissolved in water, the freezing point of the solution is somewhat lower than is that of pure water. Dissolve more sucrose and the freezing point lowers further. You can calculate how many molecules of sucrose must be dissolved per cubic centimeter of water in order to bring about the same drop. It doesn't matter that a molecule of sucrose is twice as large as a molecule of glucose. What counts is the number of molecules and not their size.

24   But if sodium chloride (table salt) is dissolved in water, the freezing-point drop per molecule is twice as great as normal. And this goes for certain other substances too. For instance, barium chloride, when dissolved, will bring about a freezing-point drop that is three times normal.

---

(19) **kowtow to:** act very submissively toward, overly respectful to another's wishes
(20) **anthropology:** the study of human societies (often primitive), their customs, physical and mental characteristics, folklore
(20) **pathology:** the medical study of the nature of disease

25   Arrhenius wondered if this meant that when sodium chloride was dissolved, each of its molecules broke into two portions, thus creating twice as many particles as there were molecules and therefore a doubled freezing-point drop. And barium chloride might break up into three particles per molecule. Since the sodium chloride molecule is composed of a sodium atom and a chlorine atom and since the barium chloride molecule is composed of a barium atom and two chlorine atoms, the logical next step was to suppose that these particular molecules broke up into individual atoms.

26   Then, too, there was another interesting fact. Those substances like sucrose and glucose which gave a normal freezing-point drop did not conduct an electric current in solution. Those, like sodium chloride and barium chloride, which showed abnormally high freezing-point drops, *did* do so.

27   Arrhenius wondered if the atoms, into which molecules broke up on solution, might not carry positive and negative electric charges. If the sodium atom carried a positive charge for instance, it would be attracted to the negative electrode. If the chlorine atom carried a negative charge, it would be attracted to the positive electrode. Each would wander off in its own direction and the net result would be that such a solution would conduct an electric current. For these charged and wandering atoms, Arrhenius adopted Faraday's name "ions" from a Greek word meaning "wanderer."

28   Furthermore, a charged atom, or ion, would not have the properties of an uncharged atom. A charged chlorine atom would not be a gas that would bubble out of solution. A charged sodium atom would not react with water to form hydrogen. It was for that reason that common salt (sodium chloride) did not show the properties of either sodium metal or chlorine gas, though it was made of those two elements.

29   In 1884 Arrhenius, then twenty-five, prepared his theories in the form of a thesis and presented it as part of his doctoral dissertation. The examining professors sat in frigid* disapproval. No one had ever heard of electrically charged atoms, it was against all scientific belief of the time, and they turned on their built-in doubters.

30   However, Arrhenius argued his case so clearly and, on the single assumption of the dissolution of molecules into charged atoms, managed to explain so much so neatly, that the professors' built-in doubters did not quite reach the intensity required to flunk the young man. Instead, they passed him—with the lowest possible passing grade.

31   But then, ten years later, the negatively charged electron was discovered and the atom was found to be not the indivisible thing it had been considered but a complex assemblage of still smaller particles. Suddenly the notion of ions as charged atoms made sense. If an atom lost an electron or two, it was left with a positive charge; if it gained them, it had a negative charge.

32   Then, the decade following, the Nobel Prizes were set up and in 1903 the

(29) **frigid:** extremely cold, frozen

Nobel Prize in Chemistry was awarded to Arrhenius for that same thesis which, nineteen years earlier, had barely squeaked him through for a Ph.D.

33   Were the professors wrong? Looking back, we can see they were. But in 1884 they were *not* wrong. They did exactly the right thing and they served science well. Every professor must listen to and appraise dozens of new ideas every year. He must greet each with the gradation* of doubt his experience and training tells him the idea is worth.

34   Arrhenius's notion met with just the proper gradation of doubt. It was radical enough to be held at arm's length. However, it seemed to have just enough possible merit to be worth some recognition. The professors *did* give him his Ph.D. after all. And other scientists of the time paid attention to it and thought about it. A very great one, Ostwald,* thought enough of it to offer Arrhenius a good job.

35   Then, when the appropriate evidence turned up, doubt receded to minimal values and Arrhenius was greatly honored.

36   What better could you expect? Ought the professors to have fallen all over Arrhenius and his new theory on the spot? And if so, why shouldn't they also have fallen all over forty-nine other new theories presented that year, no one of which might have seemed much more unlikely than Arrhenius's and some of which may even have appeared less unlikely?

37   It would have taken *longer* for the ionic theory to have become established if overcredulity on the part of scientists had led them into fifty blind alleys. How many scientists would have been left to investigate Arrhenius's notions?

38   Scientific manpower is too limited to investigate everything that occurs to everybody, and always will be too limited. The advance of science depends on scientists in general being kept firmly in the direction of maximum possible return. And the only device that will keep them turned in that direction is doubt; doubt arising from a good, healthy and active built-in doubter.

39   But, you might say, this misses the point. Can't one pick and choose and isolate the brilliant from the imbecilic, accepting the first at once and wholeheartedly, and rejecting the rest completely? Would not such a course have saved ten years on ions without losing time on other notions?

40   Sure, if it could be done, but it can't. The godlike power to tell the good from the bad, the useful from the useless, the true from the false, instantly and *in toto** belongs to gods not to men.

41   Let me cite you Galileo as an example; Galileo, who was one of the greatest scientific geniuses of all time, who invented modern science in fact, and who certainly experienced persecution and authoritarian enmity.*

(33) **gradation:** degree or stage in a systematic progression
(34) **Ostwald:** a German physical chemist and philosopher who won the Nobel prize in chemistry in 1909
(40) **in toto:** (Latin) totally, completely, wholly
(41) **enmity:** the condition of being an enemy

42   Surely, Galileo, of all people, was smart enough to know a good idea when he saw it, and revolutionary enough not to be deterred by its being radical.

43   Well, let's see. In 1632 Galileo published the crowning work of his career, *Dialogue on the Two Principal Systems of the World,* which was the very book that got him into real trouble before the Inquisition.* It dealt, as the title indicates, with the two principal systems; that of Ptolemy, which had the earth at the center of the universe with the planets, sun, and moon going about it in complicated systems of circles within circles; and that of Copernicus, which had the sun at the center and the planets, earth, and moon going about *it* in complicated systems of circles within circles.

44   Galileo did not as much as mention a *third* system, that of Kepler, which had the sun at the center but abandoned all the circles-within-circles jazz. Instead, he had the various planets traveling about the sun in ellipses, with the sun at one focus of the ellipse. It was Kepler's system that was correct and, in fact, Kepler's system has not been changed in all the time that has elapsed since. Why, then, did Galileo ignore it completely?

45   Was it that Kepler had not yet devised it? No, indeed. Kepler's views on that matter were published in 1609, twenty-seven years before Galileo's book.

46   Was it that Galileo had happened not to hear of it? Nonsense. Galileo and Kepler were in steady correspondence and were friends. When Galileo built some spare telescopes, he sent one to Kepler. When Kepler had ideas, he wrote about them to Galileo.

47   The trouble was that Kepler was still bound up with the mystical notions of the Middle Ages. He cast horoscopes* for famous men, for a fee, and worked seriously and hard on astrology. He also spent time working out the exact notes formed by the various planets in creating the "music of the spheres"* and pointed out that Earth's notes were mi, fa, mi,* standing for misery, famine, and misery. He also devised a theory accounting for the relative distances of the planets from the Sun by nesting the five regular solids one within another and making deductions therefrom.

48   Galileo, who must have heard of all this, and who had nothing of the mystic about himself, could only conclude that Kepler, though a nice guy and a bright fellow and a pleasant correspondent, was a complete nut. I am sure that Galileo heard all about the elliptical orbits and, considering the source, shrugged it off.

49   Well, Kepler was indeed a nut, but he happened to be luminously* right

(43) **Inquisition:** here, the church court established in the thirteenth century to find and punish those whose religious ideas might be different from the accepted ones.

(47) **horoscopes:** forecasts of a person's future based on the relationship of planets and stars to the moment of a person's birth or to a given moment

(47) **music of the spheres:** a mystical music thought by ancient mathematicians such as Pythagoras to be produced by the movements of the planets

(47) **mi fa mi:** notes on a musical scale (the whole scale is: do re mi fa sol la ti do)

(49) **luminously:** with great light and clarity

on occasion, too, and Galileo, of all people, couldn't pick the diamond out from among the pebbles.

50   Shall we sneer at Galileo for that?

51   Or should we rather be thankful that Galileo didn't interest himself in the ellipses *and* in astrology *and* in the nesting of regular solids *and* in the music of the spheres. Might not credulity* have led him into wasting his talents, to the great loss of all succeeding generations?

52   No, no, until some supernatural force comes to our aid and tells men what is right and what is wrong, men must blunder along as best they can, and only the built-in doubter of the trained scientist can offer a refuge* of safety.

53   The very mechanism of scientific procedure, built up slowly over the years, is designed to encourage doubt and to place obstacles in the way of new ideas. No person receives credit for a new idea unless he publishes it for all the world to see and criticize. It is further considered advisable to announce ideas in papers read to colleagues at public gatherings that they might blast the speaker down face to face.

54   Even after announcemnt or publication, no observation can be accepted until it has been confirmed by an independent observer, and no theory is considered more than, at best, an interesting speculation until it is backed by experimental evidence that has been independently confirmed and that has withstood the rigid doubts of others in the field.

55   All this is nothing more than the setting up of a system of "natural selection" designed to winnow* the fit from the unfit in the realm of ideas, in manner analogous to the concept of Darwinian evolution.* The process may be painful and tedious,* as evolution itself is; but in the long run it gets results, as evolution itself does. What's more, I don't see that there can be any substitute.

56   Now let me make a second point. The intensity to which the built-in doubter is activated is also governed by the extent to which a new observation fits into the organized structure of science. If it fits well, doubt can be small; if it fits poorly, doubt can be intensive; if it threatens to overturn the structure completely, doubt is, and should be, nearly insuperable.*

57   The reason for this is that now, three hundred fifty years after Galileo founded experimental science, the structure that has been reared, bit by bit, by a dozen generations of scientists is so firm that its complete overturning has reached the vanishing point of unlikelihood.

58   Nor need you point to relativity as an example of a revolution that over-

---

(51) **credulity:** willingness to believe
(52) **refuge:** place of safety
(55) **winnow:** the process of separating the good grain from the husks, separating the good from the bad or undesirable
(55) **Darwinian evolution:** refers to Darwin's theory of evolution, which speaks of development and change in organisms over time in such a way that higher life forms resulted, having survived through "natural selection"
(55) **tedious:** slow and tiresome
(56) **insuperable:** impossible to overcome

turned science. Einstein did not overturn the structure, he merely extended, elaborated, and improved it. Einstein did not prove Newton wrong, but merely incomplete. Einstein's world system contains Newton's as a special case and one which works if the volume of space considered is not too large and if velocities involved are not too great.

59   In fact, I should say that since Kepler's time in astronomy, since Galileo's time in physics, since Lavoisier's* time in chemistry, and since Darwin's time in biology no discovery or theory, however revolutionary it has seemed, has actually overturned the structure of science or any major branch of it. The structure has merely been improved and refined.

60   The effect is similar to the paving of a road, and its broadening and the addition of clover-leaf intersections, and the installation of radar to combat speeding. None of this, please notice, is the equivalent of abandoning the road and building another in a completely new direction.

61   But let's consider a few concrete examples drawn from contemporary life. A team of Columbia University geologists have been exploring the configuration of the ocean bottom for years. Now they find that the mid-Atlantic ridge (a chain of mountains, running down the length of the Atlantic) has a rift in the center, a deep chasm* or crack. What's more, this rift circles around Africa, sends an offshoot up into the Indian Ocean and across eastern Africa, and heads up the Pacific, skimming the California coast as it does so. It is like a big crack encircling the earth.

62   The observation itself can be accepted. Those involved were trained and experienced specialists and confirmation is ample.

63   But why the rift? Recently one of the geologists, Bruce Heezen, suggested that the crack may be due to the expansion of the earth.

64   This is certainly one possibility. If the interior were slowly expanding, the thin crust would give and crack like an eggshell.

65   But why should Earth's interior expand? To do so it would have to take up a looser arrangement, become less dense; the atoms would have to spread out a bit.

66   Heezen suggests that one way in which all this might happen is that the gravitational force of the Earth was very slowly weakening with time. The central pressures would therefore ease up and the compressed atoms of the interior would slowly spread out.

67   But why should Earth's gravity decrease, unless the force of gravitation everywhere were slowly decreasing with time? Now this deserves a lot of doubt, because there is nothing in the structure of science to suggest that the force of gravitation must decrease with time. However, it is also true that there is nothing in the structure of science to suggest that the force of gravitation might *not* decrease with time.

(59) **Lavoisier:** an eighteenth-century French chemist and physicist who was a founder of modern chemistry

(61) **chasm:** deep crack in the earth's surface

68   Or take another case. I have recently seen a news clipping concerning an eighth-grader in South Carolina who grew four sets of bean plants under glass jars. One set remained there always, subjected to silence. The other three had their jars removed one hour a day in order that they might be exposed to noise; in one case to jazz, in another to serious music, and in a third to the raucous noises of sports-car engines. The only set of plants that grew vigorously were those exposed to the engine noises.

69   The headline was: BEANS CAN HEAR—AND THEY PREFER AUTO RAC-ING NOISE TO MUSIC.

70   Automatically, my built-in doubter moves into high gear. Can it be that the newspaper story is a hoax? This is not impossible. The history of newspaper hoaxes is such that one could easily be convinced that nothing in any newspaper can possibly be believed.

71   But let's assume the story is accurate. The next question to ask is whether the youngster knew what he was doing? Was he experienced enough to make the nature of the noise the only variable? Was there a difference in the soil or in the water supply or in some small matter, which he disregarded through inexperience?

72   Finally, even if the validity of the experiment is accepted, what does it really prove? To the headline writer and undoubtedly to almost everybody who reads the article, it will prove that plants can hear; and that they have preferences and will refuse to grow if they feel lonely and neglected.

73   This is so far against the current structure of science that my built-in doubter clicks it right off and stamps it: IGNORE. Now what is an alternative explanation that fits in reasonably well with the structure of science? Sound is not just something to hear; it is a form of vibration. Can it be that sound vibrations stir up tiny soil particles making it easier for plants to absorb water, or putting more ions within reach by improving diffusion? May the natural noise that surrounds plants act in this fashion to promote growth? And may the engine noises have worked best on a one-hour-per-day basis because they were the loudest and produced the most vibrations?

74   Any scientist (or eighth-grader) who feels called on to experiment further, ought to try vibrations that do not produce audible sound; ultrasonic vibrations, mechanical of all sorts while leaving the soil insulated; and vice versa.

75   Which finally brings me to flying saucers and spiritualism and the like. The questions I ask myself are: What is the nature of the authorities promulgating* these and other viewpoints of this sort? and How well do such observations and theories fit in with the established structure of science?

76   My answers are, respectively, Very poor and Very poorly.

77   Which leaves me completely unrepentant* as far as my double role in life is concerned. If I get a good idea involving flying saucers and am in the mood

(75) **promulgating:** making known, announcing officially
(77) **unrepentant:** not sorry

to write some science fiction, I will gladly and with delight write a flying-saucer story.

78   And I will continue to disbelieve in them firmly in real life.

79   And if that be schizophrenia,* make the most of it.

☐ QUESTIONS FOR DISCUSSION

1. Asimov, in paragraph 18, writes that "doubting is far more important to the advance of science than believing is." Can you think of examples from the history of science in which believing was very important? Are there areas, other than science, in which believing is more important than doubting? Always? With qualification? In combination with doubting?

2. In a way, any education "plants" a built-in doubter in our minds. How? Why? Is this bad or good? Why? What activates it? What quiets it?

3. Assuming that all areas of study and thought need to proceed with "intelligent doubt," how does one test ideas that cannot be brought into a laboratory and subjected to the procedure outlined in paragraphs 53 and 54?

4. What are the balances Asimov uses in his own decisions to doubt, reject, consider, accept? What are the safeguards in the scientific community? In any community?

5. How does Asimov reconcile the absurdity of the headline about the beans with the reality of the improved beans? What principles of experimentation does he use in his further theorizing?

☐ SUGGESTIONS FOR COMPOSITION

1. Discuss your own "Built-in Doubter" or lack of it. Has your own past education taught you to believe more or to doubt more? Has your experience in a university made you more of a doubter? Is it an advantage or a disadvantage or both to become more of a doubter? Why?

2. Asimov writes in paragraph 18: "I am very sorry to be undemocratic, but one man's opinion is not necessarily as good as the next man's." He then goes on to express discomfort with too great a confidence in authority. Using examples from your own experience, from history, or the history of science, discuss the value—or the danger—of authority.

3. Using the same quotation from Asimov, give your opinion and the reasons for it. Include examples to back it up. What, in your opinion, makes an opinion worth respecting? Believing? What is the difference between respecting an opinion and believing it?

4. Narrate an incident in which you believed when you should have doubted, or doubted when you should have believed.

(79) **schizophrenia:** a form of insanity often associated with a "split personality"

Lewis Thomas is well known as a medical doctor and a writer. Among his books are *The Lives of a Cell* and *The Medusa and the Snail*. He is chancellor of Memorial Sloan-Kettering Cancer Center, a position that attests to his importance as a researcher. He is therefore in an excellent position to write about scientific research and education.

LEWIS THOMAS

The Art of Teaching Science

1   Everyone seems to agree that there is something wrong with the way science is being taught these days. But no one is at all clear about when it went wrong or what is to be done about it. The term "scientific illiteracy" has become almost a cliché* in educational circles. Graduate schools blame the colleges; colleges blame the secondary schools; the high schools blame the elementary schools, which, in turn, blame the family.

2   I suggest that the scientific community itself is partly, perhaps largely, to blame. Moreover, if there are disagreements between the world of the humanities and the scientific enterprise as to the place and importance of science in a liberal-arts education and the role of science in twentieth-century culture, I believe that the scientists are themselves responsible for a general misunderstanding of what they are really up to.*

3   During the last half-century, we have been teaching the sciences as though they were the same collection of academic subjects as always, and—here is what has really gone wrong—as though they would always be the same. Students learn today's biology, for example, the same way we learned Latin when I was in high school long ago: first, the fundamentals; then, the underlying laws; next, the essential grammar and, finally, the reading of texts. Once mastered, that was that: Latin was Latin and forever after would always be Latin. History, once learned, was history. And biology was precisely biology, a vast array* of hard facts to be learned as fundamentals, followed by a reading of the texts.

4   Furthermore, we have been teaching science as if its facts were somehow superior to the facts in all other scholarly disciplines*—more fundamental, more solid, less subject to subjectivism,* immutable.* English literature is not just one way of thinking; it is all sorts of ways; poetry is a moving target; the facts that underlie art, architecture, and music are not really hard facts, and you can change them any way you like by arguing about them. But science, it appears, is an altogether different kind of learning: an unambiguous, unalterable, and endlessly useful display of data that only needs to be packaged

(1) **cliché:** an overused expression, one that has become commonplace, a stereotype
(2) **(to be) up to:** to be busy with, to be scheming
(3) **array:** an impressive display
(4) **disciplines:** here, areas of study; subject areas, such as history, biology, literature
(4) **less subject to subjectivism:** less determined by one's own mind, that is, more objective
(4) **immutable:** unchangeable

and installed somewhere in one's temporal lobe* in order to achieve a full understanding of the natural world.

5   And, of course, it is not like this at all. In real life, every field of science is incomplete, and most of them—whatever the record of accomplishment during the last 200 years—are still in their very earliest stages. In the fields I know best, among the life sciences, it is required that the most expert and sophisticated minds be capable of changing course—often with a great lurch*—every few years. In some branches of biology the mind-changing is occurring with accelerating velocity. Next week's issue of any scientific journal can turn a whole field upside down, shaking out any number of immutable ideas and installing new bodies of dogma.* This is an almost everyday event in physics, in chemistry, in materials research, in neurobiology,* in genetics,* in immunology.*

6   On any Tuesday morning, if asked, a good working scientist will tell you with some self-satisfaction that the affairs of his field are nicely in order, that things are finally looking clear and making sense, and all is well. But come back again on another Tuesday, and the roof may have just fallen in on his life's work. All the old ideas—last week's ideas in some cases—are no longer good ideas. The hard facts have softened, melted away and vanished under the pressure of new hard facts. Something strange has happened. And it is this very strangeness of nature that makes science engrossing,* that keeps bright people at it, and that ought to be at the center of science teaching.

7   The conclusions reached in science are always, when looked at closely, far more provisional* and tentative than are most of the assumptions arrived at by our colleagues in the humanities. But we do not talk much in public about this, nor do we teach this side of science. We tend to say instead: These are the facts of the matter, and this is what the facts signifiy. Go and learn them, for they will be the same forever.

8   By doing this, we miss opportunity after opportunity to recruit young people into science, and we turn off a good many others who would never dream of scientific careers but who emerge from their education with the impression that science is fundamentally boring.

9   Sooner or later, we will have to change this way of presenting science. We might begin by looking more closely at the common ground that science shares with all disciplines, particularly with the humanities and with social

(4) **temporal lobe:** a part of the brain
(5) **lurch:** a sudden staggering movement
(5) **dogma:** a belief or principle held to be absolute truth, especially in religion
(5) **neurobiology:** the biology of the nervous system
(5) **genetics:** the biology of heredity, especially the mechanisms of hereditary transmission and variation
(5) **immunology:** the medical study of immunity, that is, resistance to disease-causing agents
(6) **engrossing:** absorbing, fascinating
(7) **provisional:** provided for the time being; depending on a future, more permanent situation

and behavioral science. For there is indeed such a common ground. It is called bewilderment.*...

10   One of the complaints about science is that it tends to flatten everything. In its deeply reductionist* way, it is said, science removes one mystery after another, leaving nothing in the place of mystery but data. I have even heard this claim as explanation for the drift of things in modern art and modern music: Nothing is left to contemplate except randomness and senselessness; God is nothing but a pair of dice, loaded at that. Science is linked somehow to the despair of the twentieth-century mind. There is almost nothing unknown and surely nothing unknowable. Blame science.

11   I prefer to turn things around in order to make precisely the opposite case. Science, especially twentieth-century science, has provided us with a glimpse of something we never really knew before, the revelation of human ignorance. We have been accustomed to the belief, from one century to another, that except for one or two mysteries we more or less comprehend everything on earth.... Now, we are being brought up short.* We do not understand much of anything, from the episode we rather dismissively (and, I think, defensively) choose to call the "big bang,"* all the way down to the particles in the atoms of a bacterial cell. We have a wilderness of mystery to make our way through in the centuries ahead. We will need science for this but not science alone. In its own time, science will produce the data and some of the meaning in the data, but never the full meaning. For perceiving real significance when significance is at hand, we will need all sorts of brains outside the fields of science.

12   It is primarily because of this need that I would press for changes in the way science is taught. Although there is a perennial* need to teach the young people who will be doing the science themselves, this will always be a small minority. Even more important, we must teach science to those who will be needed for thinking about it, and that means pretty nearly everyone else—most of all, the poets, but also artists, musicians, philosophers, historians, and writers. A few of these people, at least, will be able to imagine new levels of meaning which may be lost on the rest of us....

13   I suggest that the introductory courses in science, at all levels from grade school through college, be radically revised. Leave the fundamentals, the so-called basics, aside for a while, and concentrate the attention of all students on the things that are not known. You cannot possibly teach quantum mechanics without mathematics, to be sure, but you can describe the strangeness of the world opened up by quantum theory. Let it be known, early on, that there are deep mysteries and profound paradoxes revealed in distant

(9) **bewilderment:** condition of confusion, being puzzled
(10) **reductionist:** tending to reduce, to make more simple and insignificant than it really is
(11) **being brought up short:** (idiom) shown our limitations in a way that surprises us.
(11) **"big bang":** the theory that a cosmic explosion was the origin of the universe
(12) **perennial:** lasting year after year, everlasting

outline by modern physics. Explain that these can be approached more closely and puzzled over, once the language of mathematics has been sufficiently mastered.

14   At the outset, before any of the fundamentals, teach the still imponderable* puzzles of cosmology.* Describe as clearly as possible, for the youngest minds, that there are some things going on in the universe that lie still beyond comprehension, and make it plain how little is known.

15   Do not teach that biology is a useful and perhaps profitable science; that can come later. Teach instead that there are structures squirming* inside each of our cells that provide all the energy for living. Essentially foreign creatures, these lineal descendants of bacteria were brought in for symbiotic* living a billion or so years ago. Teach that we do not have the ghost of an idea how they got there, where they came from, or how they evolved to their present structure and function. The details of oxidative phosphorylation and photo-synthesis can come later.

16   Teach ecology* early on. Let it be understood that the earth's life is a system of interdependent creatures, and that we do not understand at all how it works. The earth's environment, from the range of atmospheric gases to the chemical constituents of the sea, has been held in an almost unbelievably improbable state of regulated balance since life began, and the regulation of stability and balance is somehow accomplished by the life itself, like the autonomic nervous system of an immense organism. We do not know how such a system works, much less what it means, but there are some nice reductionist details at hand, such as the bizarre* proportions of atmospheric constituents, ideal for our sort of planetary life, and the surprising stability of the ocean's salinity,* and the fact that the average temperature of the earth has remained quite steady in the face of at least a 25 percent increase in heat coming in from the sun since the earth began. That kind of thing: something to think about.

17   Go easy, I suggest, on the promises sometimes freely offered by science. Technology relies and depends on science these days, more than ever before, but technology is far from the first justification for doing research, nor is it necessarily an essential product to be expected from science. Public decisions about the future of technology are totally different from decisions about science, and the two enterprises should not be tangled together. The central task of science is to arrive, stage by stage, at a clearer comprehension of nature, but this does not at all mean, as it is sometimes claimed to mean, a search for mastery over nature.

18   Science may someday provide us with a better understanding of our-

(14) **imponderable:** incapable of being evaluated
(14) **cosmology:** study dealing with the origin and structure of the universe
(15) **squirming:** wiggling, twisting in a snakelike way
(15) **symbiotic:** close relationship of organisms
(16) **ecology:** the science of the relationship between organisms and their environment
(16) **bizarre:** very strange or far-fetched
(16) **salinity:** salt content

selves, but never, I hope, with a set of technologies for doing something or other to improve ourselves. I am made nervous by assertions that human consciousness will someday be unraveled* by research, laid out for close scrutiny like the workings of a computer, and then—and *then*. . . ! I hope with some fervor that we can learn a lot more than we now know about the human mind, and I see no reason why this strange puzzle should remain forever and entirely beyond us. But I would be deeply disturbed by any prospect that we might use the new knowledge in order to begin doing something about it— to improve it, say. This is a different matter from searching for information to use against schizophrenia or dementia,* where we are badly in need of technologies, indeed likely one day to be sunk without them. But the ordinary, everyday, more or less normal human mind is too marvelous an instrument ever to be tampered with* by anyone, science or no science.

19   The education of humanists cannot be regarded as complete, or even adequate, without exposure in some depth to where things stand in the various branches of science, particularly, as I have said, in the areas of our ignorance. Physics professors, most of them, look with revulsion on assignments to teach their subject to poets. Biologists, caught up by the enchantment of their new power, armed with flawless instruments to tell the nucleotide sequences of the entire human genome, nearly matching the physicists in the precision of their measurements of living processes, will resist the prospect of broad survey courses. . . . The liberal arts faculties, for their part, will continue to view the scientists with suspicion and apprehension. . . .

20   But maybe, just maybe, a new set of courses dealing systematically with ignorance in science will take hold. The scientists might discover in it a new and subversive* technique for catching the attention of students driven by curiosity, delighted and surprised to learn that science is exactly as the American scientist and educator Vannevar Bush described it: an "endless frontier." The humanists, for their part, might take considerable satisfaction in watching their scientific colleagues confess openly to not knowing everything about everything. And the poets, on whose shoulders the future rests, might, late nights, thinking things over, begin to see some meanings that elude* the rest of us. It is worth a try.

21   I believe that the worst thing that has happened to science education is that the fun has gone out of it. A great many good students look at it as slogging work to be got through on the way to medical school. Others are turned off by the premedical students themselves, embattled and bleeding for grades and class standing. Very few recognize science as the high adventure

(18) **unraveled:** untangled, made clear
(18) **schizophrenia or dementia:** insanity
(18) **tampered with:** interfered with in a foolish way
(20) **subversive:** undermining authority
(20) **elude:** escape our grasp or understanding

it really is, the wildest of all explorations ever taken by human beings, the chance to glimpse things never seen before, the shrewdest maneuver for discovering how the world looks. Instead, baffled* early on, they are misled into thinking that bafflement is simply the result of not having learned all the facts. They should be told that everyone else is baffled as well—from the professor in his endowed chair* down to the platoons* of postdoctoral students in the laboratories all night. Every important scientific advance that has come in looking like an answer has turned, sooner or later—usually sooner—into a question. And the game is just beginning.

22   If more students were aware of this, I think many of them would decide to look more closely and to try and learn more about what *is* known. That is the time when mathematics will become clearly and unavoidably recognizable as an essential, indispensable instrument for engaging in the game, and that is the time for teaching it. The calamitous* loss of applied mathematics from what we might otherwise be calling higher education is a loss caused, at least in part, by insufficient incentives for learning the subject. Left by itself, standing there among curriculum offerings, it is not at all clear to the student what it is to be applied to. And there is all of science, next door, looking like an almost-finished field reserved only for chaps who want to invent or apply new technologies. We have had it wrong, and presented it wrong to class after class for several generations.

23   An appreciation of what is happening in science today, and how great a distance lies ahead for exploring, ought to be one of the rewards of a liberal arts education. It ought to be good in itself, not something to be acquired on the way to a professional career but part of the cast of thought* needed for getting into the kind of century that is now just down the road. Part of the intellectual equipment of an educated person, however his or her time is to be spent, ought to be a feel for the queernesses of nature, the side of life for which informed bewilderment will be the best way of getting through the day.

☐ QUESTIONS FOR DISCUSSION

---

1. Do you agree "that there is something wrong with the way science is being taught these days"? If so, what do you think is wrong? How about the way you are learning it now? How about your high school science or elementary school science?

2. What is it about science that *could* interest the brightest young minds, and why are they not being interested in sufficient numbers? Do you agree with the

(21) **baffled:** puzzled, confused
(21) **professor . . . chair:** distinguished professor
(21) **platoons:** literally, army units; here, people working together
(22) **calamitous:** causing or involving calamity, a serious event causing terrible loss or distress
(23) **cast of thought:** way of thinking, attitude

author? How did you feel about science at different stages of your life? How about now?

3. Why has science been perceived as more "solid" than the humanities, for example, literature? Why does Dr. Thomas think this is a *mis*conception?

4. The author speaks of "mystery" and "bewilderment," and finds these the common grounds with other fields, such as the humanities and social sciences. He speaks of needing the poets to help with "new levels of meaning" in the sciences. Why do you suppose he says these things? What is your opinion, and why?

5. Dr. Thomas makes some suggestions that would affect curriculum: He would like humanists to know more about science, and scientists to have more experience with the humanities. This is related to degree requirements in areas outside a student's major. Discuss your feelings on the matter.

6. Dr. Thomas suggests radical revisions in science curricula (paragraphs 13–16). How do his suggestions compare with the way you were taught science and mathematics? What do you think of his suggestions? Are they realistic? What could be said in opposition?

7. What distinctions does the author make between science and technology? What does he want technology to do, and what does he not want it to do?

☐ SUGGESTIONS FOR COMPOSITION

1. Write an essay in which you show why you chose the major, or type of education, you did. When did your interest in it begin? How did you develop it as you were growing up?

2. Write an essay whose subject is curiosity, or mystery, or bewilderment. Discuss its place in your value system or experience. You might want to use one of Thomas's sentences as your thesis, for example:

> One of the complaints about science is that it tends to flatten everything. In its deeply reductive way, it is said, science removes one mystery after another, leaving nothing in the place of mystery except data.

> I prefer to turn things around in order to make precisely the opposite case. Science, especially 20th-century science, has provided us with a glimpse of something we never really knew before, the revelation of human ignorance.

> Part of the intellectual equipment of an educated person ... ought to be a feel for the queernesses of nature, the inexplicable thing ...

3. You may want to back up one of the above quotations with specific examples from your own experience with science or technology. You may want to use

an example from the history of science and technology, the story of a particular scientist, or a particular discovery. This may require some research in the library. Other statements which you may want to support and research in this way are:

> All the old ideas . . . are no longer good ideas. The hard facts have softened, melted away and vanished under the pressure of new hard facts.

> Every important scientific advance that has come in looking like an answer has turned sooner or later . . . into a question.

THEODORE ROETHKE

My Papa's Waltz

The whiskey on your breath
Could make a small boy dizzy;
But I held on like death:
4   Such waltzing* was not easy.

We romped* until the pans
Slid from the kitchen shelf;
My mother's countenance*
8   Could not unfrown* itself.

The hand that held my wrist
Was battered* on one knuckle;
At every step I missed
12   My right ear scraped a buckle.

You beat time* on my head
With a palm caked hard by dirt,*
Then waltzed me off to bed
16   Still clinging to your shirt.

(4) **waltzing:** dancing a waltz, which is a ballroom dance for couples in 1-2-3 rhythm
(5) **romped:** played and jumped wildly and loudly
(7) **countenance:** face
(8) **unfrown:** a *frown* is a facial expression of displeasure or worry
(10) **battered:** beaten-up, worn by beating or use
(13) **beat time:** banged out the rhythm of the dance—1-2-3, 1-2-3, 1-2-3
(14) **palm caked hard by dirt:** the palm of his hand was hardened and dirty with accumulated, rubbed-in dirt

☐ QUESTIONS FOR DISCUSSION

1. What kind of an experience has this been for the boy? Find the specific details, the specific words, which convey the nature of the experience.
2. What kind of a man is Papa? How do you picture him? Again, find the exact words that convey this.
3. How small is the boy? How do you know? Why does it matter?
4. If there are mixed or conflicting feelings in this poem, what are they? Look up the word *ambivalent* in the dictionary. How does it apply to this poem?
5. Discuss the word *clinging* in the last line. When does a child cling? To whom? What is the problem here? Relate your answers to question 4.
6. Why is "My Papa's Waltz" a better title than "My Father's Waltz"?

One of the best essayists of our time, E. B. White, was also a poet and an important member of *The New Yorker* magazine staff. He is co-author of *The Elements of Style* by Strunk and White, and the author of *Charlotte's Web* and other children's books.

E. B. WHITE

Once More to the Lake

1   One summer, along about 1904, my father rented a camp on a lake in Maine and took us all there for the month of August. We all got ringworm* from some kittens and had to rub Pond's Extract* on our arms and legs night and morning, and my father rolled over in a canoe with all his clothes on; but outside of that the vacation was a success and from then on none of us ever thought there was any place in the world like that lake in Maine. We returned summer after summer—always on August 1st for one month. I have since become a salt-water man, but sometimes in summer there are days when the restlessness of the tides and the fearful cold of the sea water and the incessant* wind which blows across the afternoon and into the evening make me wish for the placidity* of a lake in the woods. A few weeks ago this feeling got so strong I bought myself a couple of bass hooks and a spinner* and returned to the lake where we used to go, for a week's fishing and to revisit old haunts.*

2   I took along my son, who had never had any fresh water up his nose and who had seen lily pads* only from train windows. On the journey over to the lake I began to wonder what it would be like. I wondered how time would

(1) **ringworm:** a contagious skin disease caused by fungus, such as athlete's foot
(1) **Pond's Extract:** a skin cream
(1) **incessant:** nonstop, without stopping
(1) **placidity:** peacefulness, calm
(1) **bass hooks and a spinner:** equipment for fishing; *bass* is a species of fish
(1) **haunts:** places one used to go often
(2) **lily pads:** the large flat leaves of water lilies (flowers) that float on the surface of the water

have marred* this unique, this holy spot—the coves* and streams, the hills that the sun set behind, the camps and the paths behind the camps. I was sure the tarred road would have found it out and I wondered in what other ways it would be desolated. It is strange how much you can remember about places like that once you allow your mind to return into the grooves* which lead back. You remember one thing, and that suddenly reminds you of another thing. I guess I remembered clearest of all the early mornings, when the lake was cool and motionless, remembered how the bedroom smelled of the lumber it was made of and of the wet woods whose scent entered through the screen. The partitions in the camp were thin and did not extend clear to the top of the rooms, and as I was always the first up I would dress softly so as not to wake the others, and sneak out into the sweet outdoors and start out in the canoe, keeping close along the shore in the long shadows of the pines. I remembered being very careful never to rub my paddle against the gunwale* for fear of disturbing the stillness of the cathedral.

3   The lake had never been what you would call a wild lake. There were cottages sprinkled around the shores, and it was in farming country although the shores of the lake were quite heavily wooded. Some of the cottages were owned by nearby farmers, and you would live at the shore and eat your meals at the farmhouse. That's what our family did. But although it wasn't wild, it was a fairly large and undisturbed lake and there were places in it which, to a child at least, seemed infinitely remote and primeval.*

4   I was right about the tar: it led to within half a mile of the shore. But when I got back there, with my boy, and we settled into a camp near a farmhouse and into the kind of summertime I had known, I could tell that it was going to be pretty much the same as it had been before—I knew it, lying in bed the first morning, smelling the bedroom, and hearing the boy sneak quietly out and go off along the shore in a boat. I began to sustain the illusion that he was I, and therefore, by simple transposition, that I was my father. This sensation persisted, kept cropping up all the time we were there. It was not an entirely new feeling, but in this setting it grew much stronger. I seemed to be living a dual existence. I would be in the middle of some simple act, I would be picking up a bait box or laying down a table fork, or I would be saying something, and suddenly it would be not I but my father who was saying the words or making the gesture. It gave me a creepy sensation.

5   We went fishing the first morning. I felt the same damp moss covering the worms in the bait can, and saw the dragonfly alight on the tip of my rod as it hovered* a few inches from the surface of the water. It was the arrival of

(2) **marred:** made imperfect, spoiled
(2) **cove:** small bay or narrow strip of water extending into land
(2) **grooves:** long, narrow channels or hollows cut by a tool (e.g., the grooves in a phonograph record), the habitual routines of one's life
(2) **gunwale:** upper edge of the boat's side, wood around the top side of the boat
(3) **primeval:** original, primitive
(5) **hovered:** remained suspended, fluttering or floating in the air

this fly that convinced me beyond any doubt that everything was as it always had been, that the years were a mirage* and there had been no years. The small waves were the same, chucking the rowboat under the chin as we fished at anchor, and the boat was the same boat, the same color green and the ribs broken in the same places, and under the floor-boards the same fresh-water leavings and debris—the dead helgramite,* the wisps of moss, the rusty discarded fishook, the dried blood from yesterday's catch. We stared silently at the tips of our rods, at the dragonflies that came and went. I lowered the tip of mine into the water, tentatively, pensively dislodging the fly, which darted two feet away, poised, darted two feet back, and came to rest again a little farther up the rod. There had been no years between the ducking of this dragonfly and the other one—the one that was part of memory. I looked at the boy, who was silently watching his fly, and it was my hands that held his rod, my eyes watching. I felt dizzy and didn't know which rod I was at the end of.

6   We caught two bass, hauling them in briskly as though they were mackerel, pulling them over the side of the boat in a businesslike manner without any landing net, and stunning* them with a blow on the back of the head. When we got back for a swim before lunch, the lake was exactly where we had left it, the same number of inches from the dock, and there was only the merest suggestion of a breeze. This seemed an utterly enchanted sea, this lake you could leave to its own devices* for a few hours and come back to, and find that it had not stirred, this constant and trustworthy body of water. In the shallows, the dark, water-soaked sticks and twigs, smooth and old, were undulating* in clusters on the bottom against the clean ribbed sand, and the track of the mussel was plain. A school of minnows swam by, each minnow with its small individual shadow, doubling the attendance, so clear and sharp in the sunlight. Some of the other campers were in swimming, along the shore, one of them with a cake of soap, and the water felt thin and clear and unsubstantial. Over the years there had been this person with the cake of soap, this cultist,* and here he was. There had been no years.

7   Up to the farmhouse to dinner through the teeming,* dusty field, the road under our sneakers was only a two-track road. The middle track was missing, the one with the marks of the hooves and the splotches of dried, flaky

(5) **mirage:** an optical illusion, such as "seeing" an oasis in a desert when, in fact, none is nearby; here, used figuratively to mean something that appears real but is not
(5) **helgramite:** insect larva used as bait
(6) **stunning:** making them unconscious; shocking or dazing
(6) **leave . . . devices:** leave alone to do as it wishes
(6) **undulating:** moving in waves
(6) **cultist:** one who belongs to a cult (a system or religious ceremony; extremely devoted attachment to a person or principle one is following), here, used humorously about people who take soap for bathing in the lake
(7) **teeming:** being full, producing and bearing young, or fruit; fertile

manure.* There had always been three tracks to choose from in choosing which track to walk in; now the choice was narrowed down to two. For a moment I missed terribly the middle alternative. But the way led past the tennis court, and something about the way it lay there in the sun reassured me; the tape had loosened along the backline, the alleys were green with plantains and other weeds, and the net (installed in June and removed in September) sagged in the dry noon, and the whole place steamed with midday heat and hunger and emptiness. There was a choice of pie for dessert, and one was blueberry and one was apple, and the waitresses were the same country girls, there having been no passage of time, only the illusion of it as in a dropped curtain—the waitresses were still fifteen; their hair had been washed, that was the only difference—they had been to the movies and seen the pretty girls with the clean hair.

8   Summertime, oh summertime, pattern of life indelible,* the fadeproof lake, the woods unshatterable, the pasture with the sweetfern and the juniper forever and ever, summer without end; this was the background, and the life along the shore was the design, the cottages with their innocent and tranquil* design, their tiny docks with the flagpole and the American flag floating against the white clouds in the blue sky, the little paths over the roots of the trees leading from camp to camp and the paths leading back to the outhouses* and the can of lime for sprinkling, and at the souvenir counters at the store the miniature birch-bark canoes and the post cards that showed things looking a little better than they looked. This was the American family at play, escaping the city heat, wondering whether the newcomers in the camp at the head of the cove were "common"* or "nice," wondering whether it was true that the people who drove up for Sunday dinner at the farmhouse were turned away because there wasn't enough chicken.

9   It seemed to me, as I kept remembering all this, that those times and those summers had been infinitely precious and worth saving. There had been jollity and peace and goodness. The arriving (at the beginning of August) had been so big a business in itself, at the railway station the farm wagon drawn up, the first smell of the pine-laden air, the first glimpse of the smiling farmer, and the great importance of the trunks and your father's enormous authority in such matters, and the feel of the wagon under you for the long ten-mile haul, and at the top of the last long hill catching the first view of the lake after eleven months of not seeing this cherished body of water. The shouts and cries of the other campers when they saw you, and the trunks to be unpacked, to give up their rich burden. (Arriving was less exciting now-

(7) **manure:** animal excrement, often used for fertilizer
(8) **indelible:** that cannot be erased; permanent
(8) **tranquil:** calm and peaceful
(8) **outhouses:** small buildings in which one goes to the toilet where there is no plumbing
(8) **"common":** here, used to mean people whose social class, education, refinement, or behavior is considered inferior; "nice" would indicate that they were good enough in the above respects

adays, when you sneaked up in your car and parked it under a tree near the camp and took out the bags and in five minutes it was all over, no fuss, no loud wonderful fuss about trunks.)

10   Peace and goodness and jollity. The only thing that was wrong now, really, was the sound of the place, an unfamiliar nervous sound of the outboard motors. This was the note that jarred, the one thing that would sometimes break the illusion and set the years moving. In those other summertimes all motors were inboard; and when they were at a little distance, the noise they made was a sedative, an ingredient of summer sleep. They were one-cylinder and two-cylinder engines, and some were make-and-break and some were jump-spark,* but they all made a sleepy sound across the lake. The one-lungers throbbed and fluttered, and the twin-cylinder ones purred and purred, and that was a quiet sound too. But now the campers all had outboards. In the daytime, in the hot mornings, these motors made a petulant,* irritable sound; at night, in the still evening when the afterglow lit the water, they whined about one's ears like mosquitoes. My boy loved our rented outboard, and his great desire was to achieve singlehanded mastery over it, and authority, and he soon learned the trick of choking it a little (but not too much), and the adjustment of the needle valve. Watching him I would remember the things you could do with the old one-cylinder engine with the heavy flywheel, how you could have it eating out of your hand if you got really close to it spiritually. Motor boats in those days didn't have clutches, and you would make a landing by shutting off the motor at the proper time and coasting in with a dead rudder. But there was a way of reversing them, if you learned the trick, by cutting the switch and putting it on again exactly on the final dying revolution of the flywheel, so that it would kick back against compression and begin reversing. Approaching a dock in a strong following breeze, it was difficult to slow up sufficiently by the ordinary coasting method, and if a boy felt he had complete mastery over his motor, he was tempted to keep it running beyond its time and then reverse it a few feet from the dock. It took a cool nerve, because if you threw the switch a twentieth of a second too soon you would catch the flywheel when it still had speed enough to go up past center, and the boat would leap ahead, charging bull-fashion at the dock.

11   We had a good week at the camp. The bass were biting well and the sun shone endlessly, day after day. We would be tired at night and lie down in the accumulated heat of the little bedrooms after the long hot day and the breeze would stir almost imperceptibly* outside and the smell of the swamp drift in through the rusty screens. Sleep would come easily and in the morning the red squirrel would be on the roof, tapping out his gay routine. I kept remembering everything, lying in bed in the mornings—the small steamboat

(10) **make . . . spark:** methods of ignition timing
(10) **petulant:** irritable, bad-tempered over some annoyance
(11) **imperceptibly:** so that it could not be noticed

that had a long rounded stern like the lip of a Ubangi, and how quietly she ran on the moonlight sails, when the older boys played their mandolins* and the girls sang and we ate doughnuts dipped in sugar, and how sweet the music was on the water in the shining night, and what it had felt like to think about girls then. After breakfast we would go up to the store and the things were in the same place—the minnows in a bottle, the plugs and spinners disarranged and pawed over by the youngsters from the boys' camp, the fig newtons* and the Beeman's gum. Outside, the road was tarred and cars stood in front of the store. Inside, all was just as it had always been, except there was more Coca-Cola and not so much Moxie and root beer and birch beer and sarsaparilla. We would walk out with a bottle of pop apiece and sometimes the pop would backfire up our noses and hurt. We explored the streams, quietly, where the turtles slid off the sunny logs and dug their way into the soft bottom; and we lay on the town wharf and fed worms to the tame bass. Everywhere we went I had trouble making out which was I, the one walking at my side, the one walking in my pants.

12   One afternoon while we were there at that lake a thunderstorm came up. It was like the revival of an old melodrama that I had seen long ago with childish awe. The second-act climax of the drama of the electrical disturbance over a lake in America had not changed in any important respect. This was the big scene, still the big scene. The whole thing was so familiar, the first feeling of oppression and heat and a general air around camp of not wanting to go very far away. In midafternoon (it was all the same) a curious darkening of the sky, and a lull in everything that had made life tick; and then the way the boats suddenly swung the other way at their moorings with the coming of a breeze out of a new quarter, and the premonitory rumble.* Then the kettle drum, then the snare,* then the bass drum and cymbals,* then crackling light against the dark, and the gods grinning and licking their chops* in the hills. Afterward the calm, the rain steadily rustling in the calm lake, the return of light and hope and spirits, and the campers running out in joy and relief to go swimming in the rain, their bright cries perpetuating the deathless joke about how they were getting simply drenched,* and the children screaming with delight at the new sensation of bathing in the rain, and the joke about getting drenched linking the generations in a strong indestructible chain. And the comedian who waded in carrying an umbrella.

13   When the others went swimming my son said he was going in too. He pulled his dripping trunks from the line where they had hung all through the

---

(11) **mandolin:** a musical instrument that has metal strings stretched over a rounded sound box

(11) **fig newton:** a type of cookie

(12) **premonitory rumble:** deep, rolling sound (thunder) as advance warning

(12) **snare:** here, a type of drum

(12) **cymbals:** a pair of concave brass plates that are clashed together in music to make a crashing or ringing sound

(12) **licking their chops:** said of animals when they hungrily lick their mouths

(12) **drenched:** soaking wet

shower, and wrung them out. Languidly,* and with no thought of going in, I watched him, his hard little body, skinny and bare, saw him wince* slightly as he pulled up around his vitals* the small, soggy, icy garment. As he buckled the swollen belt suddenly my groin felt the chill of death.

☐ QUESTIONS FOR DISCUSSION

1. What is this essay *really* about? What does it communicate besides the experience of a man taking his son to the lake?
2. E. B. White writes "there had been no years" (paragraphs 5 and 6), "there [had] been no passage of time" (paragraph 7). What makes him say that? Is it true in any sense? In paragraph 11, for example, can you always be sure when he refers to the past and when to the present? Why is that not a problem?
3. A great part of the force of this essay lies in the fact that so much seems the same despite the passing of a generation; the contrast between time, which passes so relentlessly, and the scene, which has changed so little. What has remained the same? What has changed? Could you make a generalization about what it is that does *not* change?
4. Explain the last sentence. Relate it to sentences that have gone before, and explain the relationship.
5. Explain the tone of the sentence beginning: "Summertime, oh summertime, pattern of life indelible . . ." (paragraph 8).

☐ SUGGESTIONS FOR COMPOSITION

1. Narrate a significant experience that you shared with one of your parents, showing why it is significant. It could be that now you understand the significance of the experience, but did not appreciate it then. Perhaps, in looking back, you understand something about your parents that you did not understand then. Allow this to come through in your composition.
2. Write about an experience that suddenly dramatized the passage of time, or a way in which time seems never to have passed.
3. Describe a place with which you associate a particular feeling or experience, and do so in a way that conveys that feeling to the reader.
4. Write an essay that compares and contrasts something as it is today with the way it used to be in the past.
5. Write a version of "Once More to the Lake" as the boy would have told it. Select the details a boy would find important; convey the feelings the boy would have as he enjoys the lake and shares the experience with his father.

(13) **languidly:** slowly, lazily, in a tired manner
(13) **wince:** to shrink or start back suddenly from something painful
(13) **vitals:** short for *vital parts,* an idiom referring to the sex organs; *vital* literally means showing life or necessary to life

BASIC SENTENCE REVIEW

WHAT IS A SENTENCE AND WHY ARE SENTENCES IMPORTANT?

When we have something to say, we do it with words. While a wave of the hand can mean hello or goodbye, a raised eyebrow can show doubt, and eyes can speak volumes, we soon feel limited in the number of messages we can send without words, certainly limited in the complexity of the nonverbal messages. When we cannot see the person with whom we are communicating, words become even more important. In speech or in writing we can bring to a person's mind any object, action, or concept for which we share common words. But to *say* something—to make a statement, ask a question, or give a command—words in themselves are not enough. We need sentences. **If anything is absolutely essential to communication** (especially in writing, where the gestures and facial expressions that often complete sentences nonverbally are absent) **it is control of the sentence.**

Why is this so important? We all have unformed thoughts and incomplete ideas and pictures in our minds that would make no sense to other people. Naming an object or pointing out an action does not yet *say* anything about it; therefore, it is not a sentence. When we say something, first of all, there is something or someone we are talking *about,* the subject of our communication, the **subject** of our sentence. What we have to say about that subject constitutes the **predicate,** the verb* and the words that complete the other essential parts of the sentence.

You will notice that in speaking or reading a sentence, your voice will drop to a lower pitch (lower note on a musical scale) at the end if you are making a statement and rise to a higher pitch if you are asking a question. Your pitch *never* remains level at the end of a sentence. For example, say out loud: "The boys who were going home came with me." Notice that between "boys" and "who" the pitch does not change. Even though there is a slight pause, your voice does not go higher or lower. In writing,

---

* That is, a *finite* verb, a verb that has tense or time (e.g., *went, was going, will go, have gone*) and that agrees with its subject.

you would never put a period at a place where your voice remains level, as it did in this example. A **sentence,** then, is a group of words ending in a *lowered or raised pitch* that contains a *subject* and a *predicate.* (The subject may, in some cases, be understood and not actually uttered.)

As you know, the predicate is usually completed by one of the following.

1. **Direct object**

d.o.
The boy | hit the ball.

2. **Indirect object plus direct object**

i.o.   d.o.
Mary | gave me the book.

3. **Predicate nominative** or **predicate adjective** following linking verb

p.n.
John | is a student.

p. adj.
The cake | smells good.

p. adj.
He | is tall.

4. **Objective complement** following direct object with verbs such as *elect* or *make*

d.o.   obj. compl.
They | elected him president.

d.o.   obj. compl.
John | made her his wife.

5. **Adverbial** (adverb or prepositional phrase expressing when, where, or how)

prep. obj. prep.
We | went to school.

adv.
They | walk quickly.

prep. obj. prep.
The Smiths | arrived by   car.

These are the most common ways in which sentences are completed, but only a subject and a verb are *absolutely necessary* in order to form a sentence. What is that subject *doing* or what *is* it? This information completes a sentence. Without a verb, we would simply be naming objects or ideas; without a subject, no one would know what we were talking about. With both a subject and a predicate we have a sentence.* (Note that in imperative sentences—that is, commands—the subject is understood but not stated. Such sentences are always directed to someone; therefore, *you* is the unstated subject.)

This may seem very elementary, and it is when sentences are simple and short.

The girl next door ...
Walking down the street ...
Went to the store ...

It is obvious that the preceding groups of words are not complete sentences. But when sentences become longer and more complex, it is difficult to notice that a subject or a verb is missing. Disentangling and correcting sentences can be very difficult. It is far better and easier to keep control of a sentence *before* it gets out of hand.

Often there is the problem of not knowing where one sentence should end and the next one should begin. Just as we must understand that a subject and predicate yield a complete sentence, so we must understand that, once completed, that sentence must end before the next one may begin. There are, of course, ways to join sentences. But unless sentences are properly joined, they should remain separate.

Some students find it difficult to understand why a sentence must end when, in fact, the general subject remains the same. If we are discussing the professor, why must we keep putting periods between parts of that general idea?

Our English professor is very dull he never smiles he only discusses grammar hour after hour he has a very quiet voice he puts us to sleep with it.

Even though the professor is the general subject of the discussion, there are several sentences about him, each one beginning with *he*, the grammatical subject. One need not feel obligated to say everything about the professor in one sentence. Be assured that the reader will go beyond the period to the next sentence in order to find out what *else* you have to say about that professor.

Punctuated correctly, the paragraph about the professor would look like this:

Our English professor is very dull. He never smiles. He only discusses grammar hour after hour. He has a very quiet voice. He puts us to sleep with it.

Although this is now correct, it is also rather juvenile, dull, and choppy. If you were to write several pages like this, you would sound as dull as the professor. Surely one of the most frustrating aspects of writing in a second language is just this feeling of sounding like a child, of being so much more intelligent and mature than one can express in an English essay. It is this problem we will address in this appendix: how to relate ideas logically, in more complex sentences, so as to avoid depending on short, simple sentences; how to lengthen and combine sentences without losing con-

---

* Of course we are assuming that the sentence has meaning; that is, the words make sense in that context. Noam Chomsky's sentence *Colorless green ideas sleep furiously* illustrates the point that a sentence can be grammatical but meaningless.

trol of them; in other words, how to be as "mature" in English as in your own language.

SIMPLE SENTENCES

Before moving on to more complicated structures, it may help to review the simple sentence, that is, the one subject + predicate unit. The simplest sentence consists of one subject and one verb. (The simple *subject,* the noun or pronoun the sentence is about, is underlined once, the verb twice).

1. I | study

2. [You] | Go to school!

3. The gigantic red truck |was speeding crazily down the highway. [Note that the auxiliary *was* is part of the verb. Without it, *speeding* would not be a finite verb, but a participle.]

4. The best, most conscientious students | were taken to the observatory by the astronomy professor.

Some simple sentences have a **compound subject;** that is, two or more nouns or pronouns acting as subjects of a verb:

subject   +   predicate

The girls and boys | ran in the schoolyard.

Some simple sentences have a **compound predicate**; that is, two or more verbs.

subject   +   predicate

The girls | ran and jumped in the schoolyard.

Some simple sentences have a compound subject *and* a compound predicate:

subject   +   predicate

The boys, girls, dogs, and cats | ran, jumped, and played.

These are *all* still simple sentences because, as you can see, they consist of one **subject + predicate** unit. (This subject + predicate unit is *not* followed by another such unit.)

□ EXERCISE

For each of the following, mark sentences with compound subjects C/S, sentences with compound predicates C/P, sentences with compound subjects and compound predicates C/S–C/P, and sentences with a simple subject and a simple predicate just S. Some of the following are *not* complete sentences. Mark them N-S, and then add whatever is necessary to make them into sentences.

_____ 1. Those fancy, expensive dresses cost too much money and require a beautiful figure.

_____ 2. On the bench in the park a big black dog was sitting peacefully.

_____ 3. The fire engine going down the street at top speed.

_____ 4. Very beautifully baked cakes tempted all the hungry people.

_____ 5. Bored, lazy students and impatient teachers do not usually get along very well.

_____ 6. Far down the road were seen demonstrating and carrying signs with political slogans written on them.

_____ 7. The lions and tigers were roaring in their cages and scaring the children.

COMPOUND SENTENCES

When two or more sentences are joined into one by means of a **coordinate conjunction,** the result is a compound sentence.

The coordinate conjunctions are

and
but
or
nor

They join two equal sentence units, two units of subject + predicate, or clauses. A **clause** is a subject + predicate unit. A compound sentence will have at least two clauses joined by a coordinate conjunction:

I | like candy, | but | it | gives me cavities.

The boys | played baseball, | and | the girls | played soccer.

(In this sentence we have an example of *symmetric and;* that is, the clauses imply simultaneous action and the order of the clauses can be reversed. *Asymmetric and,* on the other hand, can introduce later time or imply cause. For example, in the sentence *I was hurt, and I cried,* the implication is that I cried because I was hurt or after I was hurt. If you occasionally see *and* beginning a new sentence, you will notice that this occurs *only* with *assymmetric and.*)

The biology majors | studied anatomy | , | the history majors | studied Napo-
leon, | and | the psychology majors | visited the mental hospital.

(Notice that a series of three or more clauses joined by *and* works just like a series of nouns joined by *and*. Use a comma to join the parts of a series, joining the last two parts with a comma and a conjunction.)

In compound sentences, each clause is equally important and equally *independent;* that is, it would make sense standing alone.

Punctuating the Compound Sentence

Unless clauses are extremely short (up to four words), separate coordinate clauses with commas as in the preceding examples. There are other ways of joining independent clauses, however.

The Semicolon (;).   If two clauses are so closely related that they seem to belong in one sentence, you may omit the coordinating conjunction and use a semicolon (;) between the clauses.

Adverbial Connectors.   These connecting words not only connect clauses but also provide a logical transition from one clause to the next. Grouped according to their logical functions, the most common adverbial connectors are

Time

then	afterward
meanwhile	later
henceforth	soon

Concession or contrast

however	yet
nevertheless	otherwise
still	instead

Addition

likewise	then too
moreover	also
furthermore	in addition
besides	indeed

*Result**

consequently	therefore
hence	accordingly
then	as a result

Punctuating Adverbial Connectors.   Use a semicolon (;) before an adverbial connector joining two clauses.

In the following examples, notice the way in which these adverbial connectors show the logical relationship between the first clause and the second.

---

* *So* is often used to show result. Although it is acceptable in speech and informal writing, its use in formal writing is not recommended.

1. I will do the dishes; meanwhile you clean up the living room.
2. The exchange student worked hard to learn the language of the host country; moreover, he made a great effort to make friends among the people of the community.
3. She studied day and night for the chemistry exam; consequently she got an A.
4. She studied day and night for the chemistry exam; however, she failed it.

Adverbial connectors need not come at the beginning of the clause; they may occur in the middle or at the end of it, as well. These connectors should be set off by commas if they cause a break in continuity.

1. The exchange student worked hard to learn the language of the host country; he made a great effort, moreover, to make friends among the people in the community.
2. She studied day and night for the chemistry exam; she failed it, however.

That these adverbial connectors, like any other adverbs, *can be moved around in the sentence is one way to distinguish them from adverbial conjunctions,* which will be discussed next. Another difference is that *the adverbial connector must be in the second clause,* whereas the clause beginning with *the adverbial conjunction can come either first or second.*

I need good grades; therefore I study hard.
(The second clause *cannot* come first.)

Because I need good grades, I study hard.
I study hard because I need good grades.
(Both ways are correct.)

☐   EXERCISE

Complete the following sentences logically.

1. Good food is important to good health; therefore . . .
2. Good food is important to good health; however . . .
3. Good food is important to good health; moreover . . .
4. Good food is important to good health; henceforth . . .

COMPLEX SENTENCES

The **complex sentence** has at least two clauses, one of which is dependent upon the other to complete its meaning. The clause that can stand alone is the **main clause** or independent clause; the one that is dependent, that cannot make complete sense alone, is the **subordinate clause.** There are three types of subordinate clauses: *adverbial, adjective,* and *noun* clauses.

Adverbial Clauses

Let us again examine the following sentence: I study hard because I need good grades. *Because I need good grades* is a clause. It has a subject and a predicate, but alone it does not make sense. The subordinate conjunction *because* at the beginning leads us to expect this idea to be *joined* (conjunction means join together) to an idea that *can* stand alone: I study hard. By making one clause subordinate to the other, we have created a sentence in which *I study hard* is the main idea. The other clause supports it but does not stand equal to it. We have also created a sentence in which we make clear the logical relationship between the two clauses. Notice the difference between these two sentences.

I study hard and I need good grades.
I study hard because I need good grades.

The second sounds more mature and intelligent because it shows us that *cause* is the logical relationship between the two clauses. We no longer have two ideas that just happen to be stuck together.

Subordinate clauses that express such logical relationships to the main clause as cause, result, time, or concession are called **adverbial clauses** and begin with **adverbial conjunctions.** The most common ones are listed in Table 2, grouped by logical function.

Punctuating the Adverbial Clause.   When the adverbial clause comes *before* the main clause, separate the two clauses with a comma (as has been done in this sentence).

☐ EXERCISE

Use an adverbial conjunction to combine each of the following pairs of sentences into a complex sentence. Underline the main clause.

1. I was talking to my friend. We were both standing in line at the post office.
2. He was buying aerograms. He then could write to his mother.
3. She was very upset with him. She had not heard from him in two months.
4. She had received no mail. She loved him anyway.
5. "You do not write. I will send no more money!" is what she had written.
6. "First I will wire her roses. Then I will write a letter," said my friend.
7. "That will make her so happy. She will forgive me."
8. Roses are very lovely. They cost too much money to send by wire.
9. I will stick to letters. They are much cheaper.
10. I go to the post office many times. Every time I find it closed.

TABLE 2. Adverbial Clauses

Conjunction	Example	Conjunction	Example
Time		*Result or Purpose*	
when		so that	He earned money *so that be could go on a vacation.*
before*		so ... + {adverb / adjective} + that	He earned *so* much *that be was able to go to Europe.*
after*	*After we finish in the lab,* **we can go to that nice restaurant.**		
until*	**They could not drive the car** *until they had changed the tire.*	in order that	He studied hard *in order that be might pass organic chemistry.*
while**		*Condition*	
since†		if	
as		even if	*Even if you ring the bell,* **he won't answer the door.**
whenever	**I eat lunch** *whenever I am hungry.*	unless (if ... not)	Unless you mean them, **you shouldn't say nice things to me.**
Place		*Manner*	
where	**I'll meet you** *where we've always met.*	as	**Children should do things** *as they are told.*
wherever	*Wherever they went,* **the dog followed them.**	as if	
where ... there	*Where she goes,* **there he'll be.**	as though	**She acts** *as if she were dying.*
Concessive		*Comparison*	
although (though)	*Although I like vegetables,* **I hated her spinach.**	as + {adverb / adjective} + as	**The Americans did not play soccer** *as well as the Algerians (did).*
even though			
whereas	**I like to read** *whereas my husband prefers to watch TV.*	more + {adverb / adjective} + than	**The teachers in France are** *more strict than (are) the teachers here.*
Cause		less + {adverb / adjective} + than	
because			
since	*Since be did so well on bis baccalaureate exams,* **he applied for the scholarship to the United States.**		
as			
for††			

*You have learned *before*, *after*, and *until* as prepositions. If any of these has a noun or pronoun object, and is used as a preposition, it is a preposition; if it is followed by a clause, it is a conjunction. *Preposition:* I will meet you after school. *Conjunction:* I will meet you after I finish my homework.

**Note that *while* has two meanings: (1) at the same time as, and (2) although. For this reason it is listed here and can also be placed in the "concessive" section.

† Note that *since* has two meanings: (1) from the time that, and (2) because. For this reason it is listed here and again in the "cause" section.

†† Note that a clause beginning with *for* can be placed *only* after the main clause: *He came to our firm, for be was told the pay is good.* This sentence cannot be reversed as it could if *because* were the conjunction.

Adjective Clauses

Relative clauses are adjective clauses because, like adjectives, they modify nouns, specifying *which one or what kind* of person or thing is being discussed.

The **girl** [who won the contest] **sits behind me in chemistry class.**

Notice that there are two clauses in this sentence. The main clause, *The girl sits behind me in chemistry class,* could stand alone. The adjective clause, *who won the contest,* could not stand alone and still make sense; it depends on the main clause for its meaning. (Do not confuse such clauses with questions using who.)

Relative clauses always begin with a **relative pronoun** that refers to a noun or pronoun previously mentioned, **the antecedent.** In the above sentence, *who* refers to *girl. Girl* is, therefore, the antecedent. *Who* is the subject of the relative clause, the subject of the verb *won.* **Relative clauses may come between the subject and verb of the main clause.** It is sometimes helpful to bracket [] the relative clause so that you can locate the main clause. (Students sometimes forget to complete the main clause of sentences. Each clause needs its *own* subject and verb.)

Remember that in English we differentiate between relative pronouns referring to people and those referring to things:

People   who: subject of a relative clause
            whom: object of a relative clause

Things   which or that: subject *or* object of a relative clause

      — subj. of main clause   — subj. of relative clause
1. I danced with the girl [who wore the prettiest dress].

    subj. of main clause   subj. of relative clause
2. The girl [with whom I danced] was weird.
           object of preposition

Notice how we have arrived at this sentence:

The girl was weird. I danced with the girl.

           obj. of prep.
The girl (I danced with the girl) was weird.

     obj. of prep.
The girl [whom I danced with] was weird.
     (object relative pronoun moved to begin relative clause)

        obj. of prep.
The girl [with whom I danced] was weird.
     (preposition moved so that it comes before its object)

Note that in informal speech it would be more common to say: *The girl I danced with was weird.* This is an example of the difference between educated *informal speech* and *formal written English.*

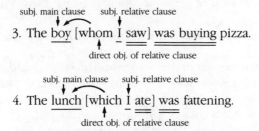

3. The boy [whom I saw] was buying pizza.

4. The lunch [which I ate] was fattening.

Notice that **there is no *it* after ate.** *Which,* referring to *lunch,* is the object of *ate.* **No other object is needed.**

Whose is a possessive relative pronoun and refers to the *person* or *thing* in the main clause that has possession of something in the relative clause. It is always used with the noun possessed.

He is a person [whose qualities I admire].

In other words, I admire that person's qualities, *his* qualities. Like *person's* or *his,* the relative pronoun that replaces these words must be possessive—*whose.* A few more examples:

There goes my friend. I used his book.

becomes

There goes the friend [whose book I used].

Essentially, the *friend* in the main clause possesses the *book* in the relative clause. (Notice that *my friend* changes to *the friend* when *friend* is specified by a relative clause.)

I know a person. His hobby is painting.

becomes

I know a person [whose hobby is painting].

Like the pronoun *his,* the pronoun *whose* shows possession—a person's hobby.

Do not buy a book if its cover is missing.

becomes

Do not buy a book [whose cover is missing].

Like the pronoun *its,* the pronoun *whose* shows possession—a book's cover.

Punctuating Restrictive and Nonrestrictive Clauses.   Punctuating relative clauses can be tricky. If you are simply adding information to the antecedent that

could be removed without changing the meaning of the sentence, you would pause after the noun and maybe even drop your voice slightly.

My mother, who is a phenomenal baker, won a prize for her chocolate cake.

Notice that commas separate the relative clause from the main clause. *Who is a phenomenal baker* adds information, but we can still understand about whom you are talking without that relative clause. It is not necessary to the meaning of the sentence; therefore we pause and use commas before and after this kind of clause.

Now try this pair of sentences:

1. Politicians, who are liars, should be hanged.
2. Politicians who are liars should be hanged.
   (No commmas, no pauses. Read without stopping.)

What is the difference between the two sentences? Which one is sure to offend all politicians? Why? If you guessed number 1, you are right, for it implies that all politicians are liars. *Who are liars* gives us more information about politicians in general. In number 2, however, it is *not* implied that all politicians are liars. This sentence is only about those politicians who are liars, not about other politicians. In this sentence, the relative clause serves to limit the subject. Not *all* politicians should be hanged—just those who tell lies. Such limiting, or restrictive, clauses are called **restrictive clauses** and are *not* separated by commas. Those, like number 1, that do not restrict the meaning of the antecedent are called **nonrestrictive** relative clauses, and they *do* require commas to set them off from the main clause. The diagram of restrictive and nonrestrictive clauses in Figure 15 may help to make this difference clear.

Punctuate the following sentence so that

1. all little boys are being insulted
2. only some little boys are being insulted:

Little boys who hate girls are obnoxious.

Read the following pair of sentences and notice that in number 1 the relative clause is needed to identify the subject; in number 2 it is not needed. For this reason, there are no commas in number 1, but there *are* commas in number 2.

1. A neighbor who helps others in the neighborhood is always appreciated.
2. Our next-door neighbor, who always helps others in the neighborhood, is much appreciated despite her nosiness.

☐ EXERCISE

Combine the following pairs of sentences by using relative clauses. Be able to justify the way you have punctuated the sentences.

1. The gentleman is wearing a blue suit. He is the ambassador from Poland.
2. The ambassador from Poland speaks six languages. He is wearing a blue suit.

FIGURE 15

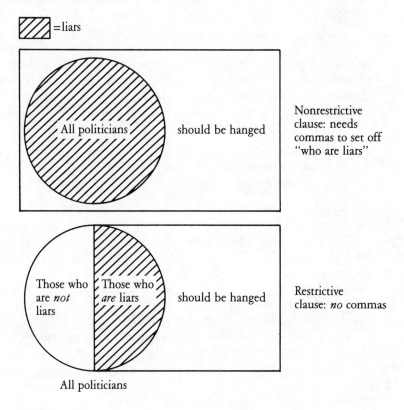

3. I would like you to meet my classmates. I study economics with them.
4. They are friends. I borrowed their books.
5. That professor gave us a hard test. We all failed it.
6. The chief lab assistant was very helpful. I asked him a lot of questions.
7. Mary is a very friendly girl. I call her just to talk sometimes.
8. She is the girl. I used to date her sister.
9. *Oliver Twist* is about an orphan boy. It was written by Charles Dickens.
10. Charles Dickens wrote many other books. He was a British writer of the nineteenth century.

Noun Clauses

In the following sentence, underline the main clause and put brackets around the dependent clause.

1. I know that the earth is round.

Is there an antecedent for "that"? How about in this sentence:

2. The dog that bit me belongs to my neighbor.

Notice that in sentence 2 *which* could be substituted for *that,* and notice that there *is* an antecedent—dog. In the sentence *I know that the earth is round* the word *that* has a different function. It is not a relative pronoun, for it does not refer to a previous noun; rather, it is an introducer, a connector, that acts like a conjunction. What is the connection, then, between the main clause and the subordinate clause?

Find the subordinate clauses in the following sentences and, again, try to determine the connection between the subordinate clause and the main clause.

3. We will give the prize to whoever guesses the answer.
4. My brother always tells me what I should do.

The following sentence may be more of a problem. Again, find the subordinate clause:

That the earth is round has been proven.

What seems to be missing from this sentence? Does the sentence or main clause have a subject? What is it? Using the formula we always use when trying to find the subject—asking who or what + verb—we would ask: Who or what has been proven? The answer, of course, would be *That the earth is round.* For this clause we could substitute the word *something: Something* has been proven. What *is* that something? *That the earth is round.* Because this clause functions as a noun, it is called a **noun clause.** You can test for a noun clause by seeing if the word *something* or *someone* could replace it.

Go back now to sentences 1 through 4 and test the subordinate clauses by substituting *something* or *someone.* You will find that sentence 2 makes no sense with this substitution but that sentences 1, 3, and 4 do make sense, because their subordinate clauses are noun clauses.

If a noun clause functions as a noun, then we can expect it to function the way nouns usually function—as subject, direct object, indirect object, object of a preposition, predicate nominative, objective complement, or appositive. What functions do the noun clauses have in sentences 1, 3, and 4? Examine the following examples carefully.

Subject
What you do is your business.

Direct object
I like what he writes.

Indirect object
You can show whoever asks the formula.

Object of the preposition
He shortened the assignment to what we understood best.

Predicate nominative
John is what he seems to be.

Appositive

No one believed Columbus's idea that the earth is round. (The noun clause restates, actually names, the idea.)

Objective complement

His father made him what he is.

Study the following list of noun clause introducers and the sample sentences illustrating them:

That

1. *That clauses* used as subjects:
   That you are a good student is obvious.
   That so many Americans buy Japanese cars worries General Motors.
2. *That clauses with anticipatory (introductory) it:* The preceding ideas might more often be expressed as follows:
   It is obvious that you are a good student.
   It worries General Motors that so many Americans buy Japanese cars.
3. *That clauses* used as objects:
   Mr. Smith said that he could not come.
   We all thought that our football team would lose the game.
   We saw that the course was going to be hard.

Clauses used as objects usually follow verbs of indirect speech, sense, or mental activity. In informal expression, *that* is sometimes deleted, as understood rather than stated. *We all thought (that) our football team would lose the game.* Direct speech can also form noun clauses. The quotation marks replace *that. My mother said, "Fire is dangerous."*

What (meaning *that which, the thing which*)

What you do is your business.

Whatever

Whatever that child does makes his mother smile.
We will do whatever you want.

Whoever

Give it to whoever is going on that plane.

(In these constructions, *what, whatever, whoever* are either subjects or objects within the noun clause; they are not simply introducers.)

Why (the reason for which)

He will never know why she refused to marry him.

How (the manner in which)

I can't understand how to put this thing together.

Where (the place at which)

My mother never remembers where she left her glasses.

When (the time at which)

When the bus leaves is always kept secret.

Whether (or not)

Nobody can know in advance whether or not the president will really come.

You will notice that *why, how, where,* and *when* can also be used as question words. Understanding noun clauses introduced by these words may help you with the often troublesome *indirect question.*

I will tell you why the sun shines is not a question but a sentence with a noun clause as direct object (I will tell you something: why the sun shines). It is *not* the question: Why does the sun shine? Therefore the subject + verb after *why* in the first sentence is in natural order, unlike the reverse question order when *why* introduces a question.

You will notice, too, that *where, when,* and *whether* can also be adverbial conjunctions. The following example should show you how to tell the difference. As you will see, the difference is really one of function—how the clause is being used.

1. When I get to school, I will do my homework.
2. When I get to school is my business.

1 answers the question *when* about the main clause.

Question: *When* will I do my homework?
Answer: (I will do it) when I get to school.

Therefore it functions as an adverb, and is thus an adverb clause. 2 answers the *what* question we use to find subjects.

Question: *What* is my business?
Answer: When I get to school.

The clause functions as the subject of the sentence, and is therefore a noun clause. (Note: A noun clause used as subject always takes the third person singular form of the verb: That they won the Nobel Prize surprises no one.)

☐ EXERCISE

Identify the noun clauses in the following sentences and write above each one its function in that sentence (subject, direct object, indirect object, object of the preposition, predicate nominative, objective complement, or appositive):

1. When I go back to Indonesia, I will remember what I learned in America.
2. Everyone knows that one must go through customs when entering a different country.
3. That Kennedy airport is like a madhouse is well known by international travelers.
4. They called him what his mother used to call him.
5. You may show whoever can keep a secret what I bought Dad for his birthday.
6. Tell me where you are going.

7. Where I go and when I get home are not things I must report to you!
8. My vacation plans depend upon whether I get a raise in pay.
9. How this works is a real mystery to me!
10. We had a botany class on why the leaves change colors in the fall.

SENTENCE VARIETY

In Appendix A, we have explored the ways to move from a series of simple sentences to sentences of greater complexity. We have studied the ways in which two or more clauses can be combined into compound and complex sentences. The complex sentences we have examined include those formed with adverb, adjective, and noun clauses. Sometimes, however, we want to vary our style and convey some of these relationships between sentences without using full subordinate clauses. Let us examine some of the other ways to do this logically and grammatically.

Variations on Noun Clauses

"It is a miracle that New York works at all."
(E. B. White)

Without anticipatory *it,* the sentence would read:

That New York City works at all is a miracle. (noun clause as subject)
For New York City to work at all is a miracle. (infinitive phrase as subject)*
New York's working at all is a miracle. (gerund as subject with the subject of the
original noun clause—New York—as a possessive modifying it)

Let us look at variations of another sentence:

That Columbus discovered America was not appreciated at the time.

Gerund

Columbus's discovering America was not appreciated at the time.

Infinitive phrase

For Columbus to have discovered America was not appreciated at the time.

Derived noun

Columbus's discovery of America was not appreciated at the time.

In these variations there is no real change in meaning, but there *is* change in emphasis, and there is possibility for greater variety in sentence structure.

Variations on Adjective Clauses

The man *who is wearing a blue suit* owns the store. (adjective clause)
The man *in the blue suit* owns the store. (adjective clause replaced by a prepositional phrase)

---

* That is, the infinitive phrase is now nominal (nounlike).

The woman *who is driving that Mercedes* just inherited a lot of money. (adjective clause)

The woman *in that Mercedes* just inherited a lot of money. (adjective clause replaced by a prepositional phrase)

The woman *driving that Mercedes* just inherited a lot of money. (adjective clause replaced by a participial phrase)

Mr. Brown, *who is a math teacher,* flies his own plane. (adjective clause)

Mr. Brown, *the math teacher,* flies his own plane. (relative clause replaced by appositive)

A girl *who is pretty* attracts lots of boys. (adjective clause)

A *pretty* girl attracts lots of boys. (restrictive adjective clause replaced by adjective)

Variations on Adverbial Clauses

While we do our homework, we watch TV. (adverbial clause)

While doing our homework, we watch TV. (adverbial clause replaced by participial phrase. Note: *This will only work if the subject of the adverbial clause or participial phrase is the same as the subject of the main clause.* You could not say, for example, *While watching TV, the steak burned*—not unless you think steaks can watch TV! In this sentence you would have to have two clauses, each with its own subject: While we watched TV, the steak burned.)

After we finished our homework, we went to the movies. (adverbial clause)

After having finished our homework, we went to the movies. (adverbial clause replaced by participial phrase in its past form)

When the prisoners were caught by the police, they were put into jail. (adverbial clause)

Caught by the police, the prisoners were put into jail. (adverbial clause replaced by participial. Note: The past participle or perfect form, was used because it replaces a passive voice structure. The *ing* or present participle is used for active voice sentences.)

After the dishes were washed, we went to the movies. (adverbial clause)

The dishes washed, the floors mopped, and the beds made, we went to the movies. (adverbial clause replaced by absolute construction)*

Since the girls were leaving, we had an excuse to make our exit from the boring party. (adverbial clause)

The girls leaving, we had an excuse to make our exit from the boring party. (adverbial clause replaced by absolute construction. Again, notice that when the clause is in the *active* voice, it is replaced by the *ing* or present participle. When it is in the *passive* voice, as in the preceding sentence, it is replaced by the past participle.)

Whether we have money or not, we will go to Paris. (adverbial clause)

---

* The absolute construction is not very common; it is found in formal writing rather than informal speech.

Money or no money, we will go to Paris! (adverbial clause replaced by a special form of the absolute construction with *or*)

The following version of Hans Christian Andersen's famous story "The Emperor's New Clothes" has been written in simple sentences. Rewrite it so that it reads more smoothly. Use devices such as coordinate conjunctions, adverbial connectors, subordinate conjunctions (relative clauses, adverbial clauses, noun clauses), participials, prepositional phrases, and pronouns. Some sentences would be improved if they were combined using compound subjects or compound predicates. Remember that some sentences are very effective if they are short and simple, especially if not *all* the sentences are short and simple!

HANS CHRISTIAN ANDERSEN

The Emperor's New Clothes

1   Once upon a time there was an emperor. The emperor's clothes were his favorite possession. He was especially fond of new clothes. He always stood in front of the mirror. He admired himself in his new outfits.

2   One day some very clever swindlers came to visit the emperor. They said they were tailors. They said they had some magic cloth. The cloth's magical properties consisted of being visible only to wise people. A fool looked at the cloth and saw absolutely nothing. The emperor did not want to appear a fool. He said to the tailors, "Oh, what beautiful material!" He had seen nothing. There was, of course, nothing there.

3   He called the queen. She did not want to appear a fool. She said, "What a beautiful pattern! What exquisite quality!" The prime minister admired the material, too. The prime minister was the chief advisor. He had seen nothing.

4   The emperor was convinced. He simply had to have a suit made of such wonderful material. He had several "fittings." The suit was completed. The suit was exceptional. The emperor decided he should march in a special parade. He wanted to show it to his people.

5   It was the day of the parade. The tailors "dressed" the emperor in his new suit. He strutted about proudly. All the people of the empire gathered in front of the palace. They lined up along the road. The road was the place the emperor would appear. They had heard of the wonderful suit, It could show who was wise and who was foolish.

6   The emperor appeared. The people gasped. Nobody wanted to appear a fool. Nobody commented; nobody cried out. Some people said, "Look at the beautiful garment. See the long train. The courtiers are carrying the train."

7   One man's son saw the emperor. He was only a little child. He had not heard anything about the magical suit. He was not afraid to tell the truth. "Look, Father!" he exclaimed, "The Emperor is walking around in public *without his clothes on!*"

8   "Listen to what the child is saying! He says that the emperor hasn't got any

clothes on!" One person whispered it to another. The whole town was saying it out loud, "But he hasn't got any clothes on!"

9   The emperor began to feel very strange. It began to dawn on him that the people were right. Still, he had to go through with the procession. He marched in step. He held his head higher than before. The courtiers followed. They held up the train that wasn't there at all.

SERIOUS SENTENCE ERRORS

At the beginning of Appendix A, it was said that control of the sentence is absolutely essential to clear communication. This means knowing when a lot of words, or even clauses, do not make a sentence and also when two sentences really are two sentences and not one.

Less Than a Sentence (A Fragment)

A fragment is a piece rather than a whole. We call **sentence fragments** those word groups that are punctuated as sentences, but are, in reality, *not* sentences. Study the following examples of sentence fragments and the ways there are of correcting them:

There were many tourists at the museum. Especially American students.

The second "sentence" has no verb. The phrase really belongs with the previous sentence:

There were many tourists at the museum, especially American students.

Occasionally fragments of this kind are used as if they were complete sentences. We find them in (1) conversation, where the connection is understood from the context of the conversation; (2) advertising, where the ad is trying more to emphasize the characteristics of a product than to make statements about it; and (3) in very skilled writing, for occasional emphasis. One-word exclamations, *yes* and *no* are frequently punctuated as sentences. Fragments used in this way would end as sentences do, with a raised or lowered pitch when spoken or read. In formal writing, fragments are not usually acceptable. Unless you qualify under number 3, do not use them at all!

In the following sentence fragment, the subject is followed by a participial phrase.

These days, men taking care of babies

By adding a verb, the fragment can be made into a sentence.

These days, men taking care of babies are not so unusual.

A sentence can also be formed by changing the participle into a finite verb.

These days, men are taking care of babies.

Very often a subordinate clause is punctuated as a complete sentence, when, as you know, it *must* be *part* of a sentence containing a main clause to which it is attached.

> There was a riot in the streets. Because the factory closed down and dismissed all of its employees.

As a conjunction, *because* joins the two clauses into one sentence. One could omit the word *because,* or punctuate the sentence as follows.

> There was a riot in the streets because the factory closed down and dismissed all of its employees.

Why is the following a nonsentence?

> The students who rebelled because no hamburgers were served for lunch when they wanted hamburgers!

It surely has enough subjects and verbs to make a sentence, yet it is not a sentence. To understand why, let us put brackets around all the subordinate clauses.

> The students [who rebelled] [because no hamburgers were served for lunch] [when they wanted hamburgers].

As you can see, there are three subordinate clauses, but no main clause. *The students,* which seems to be the main subject of the sentence, has no verb; therefore, the sentence really makes no statement. We are still waiting to know what *about* them? The sentence can be formed either by dropping the *who* or by adding a main verb.

> The students rebelled because no hamburgers were served for lunch when they wanted hamburgers!
> The students who rebelled because no hamburgers were served for lunch when they wanted hamburgers were thrown out of the school.

More Than a Sentence

Sometimes nonsentences in long word groups are the result of failure to supply a verb for each subject or a subject for each verb.

> The power failure caused a blackout created a lot of problems.

In this sentence *blackout* is being used as the object of *caused* and as the subject of *created.* It cannot be both at the same time. The sentence can be corrected in the following ways:

> The power failure caused a blackout that created a lot of problems.
> The power failure caused a blackout, and it created a lot of problems.
> The power failure caused a blackout. It created a lot of problems.

Run-on or fused sentences are really at least two sentences run together with no punctuation between them:

> The girls scored higher in math the boys scored higher in verbal skills.

The following would solve the problem.

The girls scored higher in math $\begin{Bmatrix} \text{and} \\ \text{but} \end{Bmatrix}$ the boys scored higher in verbal skills.
(use a coordinate conjunction)

The girls scored higher in math. The boys scored higher in verbal skills.
(punctuate as two sentences)

The girls scored higher in math; the boys scored higher in verbal skills. (use a semicolon to join the two independent clauses that seem to belong in one sentence)

The girls scored higher in math, while the boys scored higher in verbal skills. (use a subordinate clause)

The **comma splice** is an error that occurs because students mistakenly think a comma has the strength to join two clauses. That is why the following sentence is wrong.

The girls scored higher in math, the boys scored higher in verbal skills.

This is not just a punctuation error; it is a serious sentence error because it shows that the writer does not realize that there are *two independent clauses* and, therefore, two separate sentences. The sentences must either be separated by a period into two sentences or joined by a conjunction or semicolon, as in the example above.

☐ RECOGNIZING AND CORRECTING SERIOUS SENTENCE ERRORS

For each of the following, (1) identify the problem (fragment, fused sentence, comma splice, more than a sentence) and (2) restructure it without removing any information. The result should be one or two correct sentences.

1. Without telling anyone, even her sister, Mary, going to the park, meeting her friends.
2. The physics problems were just impossible, they took all day to do.
3. That the course was so hard we all studied day and night, with no one getting an A or a B.
4. I never knew her brother he was always away at school.
5. That was the first time we went to that park had such beautiful trees and lakes.

APPENDIX

B

CHARACTERISTICS OF A GOOD PAPER: A CHECKLIST

The following is a checklist of the many factors involved in writing a well-written paper. No doubt you could come up with others. As you put your paper through a final check, see if it has these characteristics:

I. *Content*
   1. The paper has something to say; it shows intelligence and thought.
   2. The thesis, or main idea, is developed through concrete detail in a description or through a question sufficiently explored. (It is well supported or proven.)
   3. The paper defines its terms.
   4. The paper avoids unwarranted generalizations.
   5. The paper qualifies or substantiates generalizations and uses appropriate evidence (illustrations, examples, and significant details).
   6. The paper demonstrates some imagination.

II. *Organization*
   1. There is an explicit or implicit thesis, and it is sufficiently focused.
   2. The thesis (implicit or explicit) addresses the assignment or answers the question, if one was asked.
   3. Each paragraph bears a clear relationship to the thesis, with appropriate implicit or explicit transitions, and is logically ordered in the development of the thesis or main idea.
   4. Each paragraph has a specific topic that is developed, and each sentence in the paragraph is logical and is logically placed.
   5. The paper introduces its subject and has a satisfying conclusion.

III. *Mechanics and Style*
   1. There are no errors in spelling and punctuation (includes commas, colons, semicolons, periods, question marks, and underlining).
   2. There are no fragments or run-on sentences (includes comma splices).
   3. The verb forms are appropriate, and subjects and verbs agree. Tense and mode are appropriately chosen.

4. Pronouns and antecedents agree, references are clear, and modifiers are correctly placed. Singular and plural forms of nouns are used correctly.
5. Articles are used appropriately. There are no errors in distinguishing count/noncount nouns.
6. The paper avoids violation of parallel structure and other awkward structures.
7. The paper demonstrates appropriate word choice.
8. The paper demonstrates appropriate use of idioms, including correct choice of prepositions and appropriate use of gerunds and infinitives.
9. The paper demonstrates appropriate use of subordination and avoids monotony through varied sentence structure. It makes effective use of parallelism and emphasis.
10. The paper avoids vagueness and repetition.

Acknowledgments (continued from page ii)

Sally Carrighar. "Sex: The Silent Bell" from *Wild Heritage* by Sally Carrighar. Copyright © 1965 by Sally Carrighar. Reprinted by permission of Houghton Mifflin Company and the author.

E. & J. Gallo Winery. "Fermentation: The Birth of a Fine Red Wine." Advertisement reprinted courtesy of E. & J. Gallo Winery, Modesto, CA.

Dr. Elisabeth Kübler-Ross. "Facing Up to Death," *Today's Education* (January 1972). Reprinted by permission of the author.

J. William Fulbright. "We're Tongue-Tied," *Newsweek,* July 30, 1979. Copyright 1979, by Newsweek, Inc. All Rights Reserved. Reprinted by Permission.

Edward T. Hall and Mildred Reed Hall. "The Sounds of Silence." Originally appeared in *Playboy* (June 1971). Copyright © 1971 by Edward T. Hall and Mildred Reed Hall. Reprinted by permission of the authors.

Bruno Bettelheim. " 'The Three Languages': Building Integration" from *The Uses of Enchantment: The Meaning and Importance of Fairy Tales,* by Bruno Bettelheim. Copyright © 1975, 1976 by Bruno Bettelheim. Reprinted by permission of Alfred A. Knopf, Inc. and Thames and Hudson Ltd.

Suzanne Britt Jordan. "That Lean and Hungry Look," *Newsweek,* October 9, 1978. Copyright 1978, by Newsweek, Inc. All Rights Reserved. Reprinted by Permission.

Gilbert Highet. "The Philosopher and the Conqueror" (originally titled "The Dog Has His Day"). © American Heritage Publishing Co., Inc. Reprinted by permission from *Horizon* (March, 1963).

Erich Fromm. "Motherly and Fatherly Love" from pp. 41–44 in *The Art of Loving* by Erich Fromm, Volume Nine in *World Perspectives,* planned and edited by Ruth Nanda Anshen. Copyright © 1956 by Erich Fromm. Reprinted by permission of Harper & Row, Publishers, Inc.

Ashley Montagu. "Masculine Expression of Emotion" from *The American Way of Life* by Ashley Montagu, published by G. P. Putnam's Sons. Copyright 1952, © 1962, 1967 by Ashley Montagu. Reprinted by permission of the author.

Richard Rodriguez. "Going Home Again: The New American Scholarship Boy." Copyright © 1975 by Richard Rodriguez. Excerpted version reprinted by permission of Brandt & Brandt Literary Agents, Inc.

Norman Podhoretz. Excerpts from *Making It* by Norman Podhoretz, published by Random House, Inc. © Copyright, 1967, by Norman Podhoretz. Reprinted by permission of the author.

Paul Simon. "The Sound of Silence." Copyright © 1964 by Paul Simon. Used by permission.

Josephine Miles. "Family" from *Collected Poems 1930–1983* (University of Illinois Press). © 1969 The New Yorker Magazine, Inc. Reprinted by permission.

Stevie Smith. "Not Waving But Drowning" from *Stevie Smith: Collected Poems.* Copyright © 1972 by Stevie Smith. Reprinted by permission of New Directions Publishing Corporation and James McGibbon.

Gay Sands Miller. "When Bureaucrats Cast for Fish Names." Reprinted by permission of *The Wall Street Journal.* © Dow Jones & Company, Inc. 1980. All Rights Reserved.

Max Shulman. "Love Is a Fallacy." Copyright 1951, renewed 1979 by Max Shulman. Reprinted by permission of Harold Matson Company, Inc.

Roger Waters. Lines from "Another Brick in the Wall" by Roger Waters. © Pink Floyd Music Publishers Ltd. Used by permission.

Anne Tyler. "Your Place Is Empty." Reprinted by permission of Russell & Volkening as agents for the author. Copyright © 1976 by Anne Tyler. Originally appeared in *The New Yorker.*

Sherry Turkle. "Computers and the Human Spirit: Child Programmers" from *The Second Self: Computers and the Human Spirit* by Sherry Turkle. Copyright © 1984 by Sherry Turkle. Reprinted by permission of Simon & Schuster, Inc.

Stanley Milgram. Abridgment of "The Perils of Obedience" (as it appeared in *Harper's* Magazine) abridged and adapted from *Obedience to Authority* by Stanley Milgram. Copyright © 1974 by Stanley Milgram. Reprinted by permission of Harper & Row, Publishers, Inc. and Tavistock Publications Ltd.

INDEX OF DEFINITIONS

INDEX